CIMA's Official
Learning System

Managerial Level

Organisational Management and Information Systems

Bob Perry

ELSEVIER

AMSTERDAM   BOSTON   HEIDELBERG   LONDON   NEW YORK   OXFORD
PARIS   SAN DIEGO   SAN FRANCISCO   SINGAPORE   SYDNEY   TOKYO

CIMA Publishing is an imprint of Elsevier
Linacre House, Jordan Hill, Oxford OX2 8DP, UK
30 Corporate Drive, Suite 400, Burlington, MA 01803, USA

First edition 2007

British Library Cataloguing in Publication Data
A catalogue record for this book is available from the British Library

978 0 7506 8428 6

For information on all CIMA publications
visit our web site at books.elsevier.com

Typeset by Integra Software Services Pvt. Ltd, Pondicherry, India
www.integra-india.com
Printed and bound in the Netherlands
07 08 09 10 11   10 9 8 7 6 5 4 3 2 1

Working together to grow
libraries in developing countries

www.elsevier.com | www.bookaid.org | www.sabre.org

ELSEVIER   BOOK AID International   Sabre Foundation

Contents

3 People Issues: Motivation, Rewards and Ethical Considerations

The CIMA
Learning System

Acknowledgements

Every effort has been made to contact the holders of copyright material, but if any here have been inadvertently overlooked the publishers will be pleased to make the necessary arrangements at the first opportunity.

How to use your CIMA *Learning System*

This *Organisational Management and Information Systems Learning System* has been devised as a resource for students attempting to pass their CIMA exams, and provides:

- a detailed explanation of all syllabus areas;
- extensive 'practical' materials, including readings from relevant journals;
- generous question practice, together with full solutions;
- an exam preparation section, complete with exam standard questions and solutions.

This Learning System has been designed with the needs of home-study and distance-learning candidates in mind. Such students require full coverage of the syllabus topics, and also the facility to undertake extensive question practice. However, the Learning System is also ideal for fully taught courses.

The main body of the text is divided into a number of chapters, each of which is organised on the following pattern:

- *Detailed learning outcomes* expected after your studies of the chapter are complete. You should assimilate these before beginning detailed work on the chapter, so that you can appreciate where your studies are leading.
- *Step-by-step topic coverage.* This is the heart of each chapter, containing detailed explanatory text supported where appropriate by worked examples and exercises. You should work carefully through this section, ensuring that you understand the material being explained and can tackle the examples and exercises successfully. Remember that in many cases knowledge is cumulative: if you fail to digest earlier material thoroughly, you may struggle to understand later chapters.
- *Readings and activities.* Most chapters are illustrated by more practical elements, such as relevant journal articles or other readings, together with comments and questions designed to stimulate discussion.

- *Question practice.* The test of how well you have learned the material is your ability to tackle exam-standard questions. Make a serious attempt at producing your own answers, but at this stage do not be too concerned about attempting the questions in exam conditions. In particular, it is more important to absorb the material thoroughly by completing a full solution than to observe the time limits that would apply in the actual exam.
- *Solutions.* Avoid the temptation merely to 'audit' the solutions provided. It is an illusion to think that this provides the same benefits as you would gain from a serious attempt of your own. However, if you are struggling to get started on a question you should read the introductory guidance provided at the beginning of the solution, and then make your own attempt before referring back to the full solution.

Having worked through the chapters you are ready to begin your final preparations for the examination. The final section of the CIMA *Learning System* provides you with the guidance you need. It includes the following features:

- A brief guide to revision technique.
- A note on the format of the examination. You should know what to expect when you tackle the real exam, and in particular the number of questions to attempt, which questions are compulsory and which optional, and so on.
- Guidance on how to tackle the examination itself.
- A table mapping revision questions to the syllabus learning outcomes allowing you to quickly identify questions by subject area.
- Revision questions. These are of exam standard and should be tackled in exam conditions, especially as regards the time allocation.
- Solutions to the revision questions. As before, these indicate the length and the quality of solution that would be expected of a well-prepared candidate.

If you work conscientiously through this CIMA *Learning System* according to the guidelines above you will be giving yourself an excellent chance of exam success. Good luck with your studies!

Guide to the icons used within this text

Key term or definition

Equation to learn

Exam tip to topic likely to appear in the exam

Exercise

Question

Solution

Comment or Note

Study technique

Passing exams is partly a matter of intellectual ability, but however accomplished you are in that respect you can improve your chances significantly by the use of appropriate study and revision techniques. In this section we briefly outline some tips for effective study during the earlier stages of your approach to the exam. Later in the text we mention some techniques that you will find useful at the revision stage.

Planning

To begin with, formal planning is essential to get the best return from the time you spend studying. Estimate how much time in total you are going to need for each subject that you face. Remember that you need to allow time for revision as well as for initial study of the material. The amount of notional study time for any subject is the minimum estimated time that students will need to achieve the specified learning outcomes set out earlier in this chapter. This time includes all appropriate learning activities, for example, face-to-face tuition, private study, directed home study, learning in the workplace, revision time, etc. You may find it helpful to read *Better exam results* by Sam Malone, CIMA Publishing, ISBN: 075066357X. This book will provide you with proven study techniques. Chapter by chapter it covers the building blocks of successful learning and examination techniques.

The notional study time for Managerial Level *Organisational Management and Information Systems* is 200 hours. Note that the standard amount of notional learning hours attributed to one full-time academic year of approximately 30 weeks is 1,200 hours.

By way of example, the notional study time might be made up as follows:

	Hours
Face-to-face study: up to	60
Personal study: up to	100
'Other' study – e.g. learning in the workplace, revision, etc.: up to	40
	200

Note that all study and learning-time recommendations should be used only as a guideline and are intended as minimum amounts. The amount of time recommended for face-to-face tuition, personal study and/or additional learning will vary according to the type of course undertaken, prior learning of the student, and the pace at which different students learn.

Now split your total time requirement over the weeks between now and the examination. This will give you an idea of how much time you need to devote to study each week. Remember to allow for holidays or other periods during which you will not be able to study (e.g. because of seasonal workloads).

With your study material before you, decide which chapters you are going to study in each week, and which weeks you will devote to revision and final question practice.

Prepare a written schedule summarising the above – and stick to it!

The amount of space allocated to a topic in the study material is not always a very good guide as to how long it will take you.

It is essential to know your syllabus. As your course progresses you will become more familiar with how long it takes to cover topics in sufficient depth. Your timetable may need to be adapted to allocate enough time for the whole syllabus.

Tips for effective studying

1. Aim to find a quiet and undisturbed location for your study, and plan as far as possible to use the same period of time each day. Getting into a routine helps to avoid wasting time. Make sure that you have all the materials you need before you begin so as to minimise interruptions.

2. Store all your materials in one place, so that you do not waste time searching for items around the house. If you have to pack everything away after each study period, keep them in a box, or even a suitcase, which will not be disturbed until the next time.

3. Limit distractions. To make the most effective use of your study periods you should be able to apply total concentration, so turn off the TV, set your phones to message mode, and put up your 'do not disturb' sign.

4. Your timetable will tell you which topic to study. However, before diving in and becoming engrossed in the finer points, make sure you have an overall picture of all the areas that need to be covered by the end of that session. After an hour, allow yourself a short break and move away from your books. With experience, you will learn to assess the pace you need to work at. You should also allow enough time to read relevant articles from newspapers and journals, which will supplement your knowledge and demonstrate a wider perspective.

5. Work carefully through a chapter, making notes as you go. When you have covered a suitable amount of material, vary the pattern by attempting a practice question. Preparing an answer plan is a good habit to get into, while you are both studying and revising, and also in the examination room. It helps to impose a structure on your solutions, and avoids rambling. When you have finished your attempt, make notes of any mistakes you made, or any areas that you failed to cover or covered only skimpily.

6. Make notes as you study, and discover the techniques that work best for you. Your notes may be in the form of lists, bullet points, diagrams, summaries, 'mind maps', or the written word, but remember that you will need to refer back to them at a later date, so they must be intelligible. If you are on a taught course, make sure you highlight any issues you would like to follow up with your lecturer.

7. Organise your paperwork. There are now numerous paper storage systems available to ensure that all your notes, calculations and articles can be effectively filed and easily retrieved later.

Organisational Management and Information Systems Syllabus

First examined in May 2005

Syllabus outline

The syllabus comprises:

Topic	Study Weighting
A Information Systems	20%
B Change Management	10%
C Operations Management	20%
D Marketing	20%
E Managing Human Capital	30%

Learning aims

Students should be able to:

- describe the various functional areas of an organisation and how they relate to one another,
- apply theories, tools and techniques appropriate to a functional area in support of the organisation's strategy,
- prepare reports and plans for functional areas,
- evaluate the performance of functional areas.

Assessment strategy

There will be a written examination paper of three hours, with the following sections.

Section A – 40 marks
  A variety of compulsory objective test questions, each worth between 2 and 4 marks.

Section B – 30 marks
  Six compulsory short answer questions, each worth 5 marks. A short scenario may be given, to which some or all questions relate.

Section C – 30 marks
  One question, from a choice of two, worth 30 marks. Short scenarios may be given, to which questions relate.

Learning Outcomes and Syllabus Content

A – Information Systems – 20%

Learning outcomes

On completion of their studies students should be able to:

(i) explain the features and operations of commonly used information technology hardware and software;

(ii) explain how commonly used technologies are used in the work place;

(iii) identify opportunities for the use of information technology (IT) in organisations, particularly in the implementation and running of the information system (IS);

(iv) evaluate, from a managerial perspective, new hardware and software and assess how new systems could benefit the organisation;

(v) recommend strategies to minimise the disruption caused by introducing IS technologies;

(vi) explain how to supervise major IS projects and ensure their smooth implementation;

(vii) evaluate how IS fits into broader management operations.

Syllabus content

- Introduction to hardware and software in common use in organisations.
- Hardware and applications architectures (i.e. centralised, distributed, client server) and the IT required to run them (PCs, servers, networks and peripherals).
- General Systems Theory and its application to IT (i.e. system definition, system components, system behaviour, system classification, entropy, requisite variety, coupling and decoupling).
- Recording and documenting tools used during the analysis and design of systems (i.e. entity-relationship model, logical data structure, entity life history, dataflow diagram, and decision table).
- Databases and database management systems. (Note: Knowledge of database structures will not be required.)
- The problems associated with the management of in-house and vendor solutions and how they can be avoided or solved.
- IT – enabled transformation (i.e. the use of information systems to assist in change management).
- System changeover methods (i.e. direct, parallel, pilot and phased).
- IS implementation (i.e. methods of implementation, avoiding problems of non-usage and resistance).
- The benefits of IT systems.
- IS evaluation, including the relationship of sub-systems to each other and testing.
- IS outsourcing.
- Maintenance of systems (i.e. corrective, adaptive, preventative).

B – Change Management – 10%

Learning outcomes

On completion of their studies students should be able to:

(i) explain the process of organisational development;

(ii) discuss how and why resistance to change develops within organisations;

(iii) evaluate various means of introducing change;

(iv) evaluate change processes within the organisation.

Syllabus content

- External and internal change triggers (e.g. environmental factors, mergers and acquisitions, re-organisation and rationalisation).
- The stages in the change process.

- Approaches to change management (e.g. Beer and Nohria, Kanter, Lewin and Peters, Senge et al.).
- The importance of managing critical periods of change through the life cycle of the firm.

C – Operations Management – 20%

Learning outcomes

On completion of their studies students should be able to:

(i) evaluate the management of operations;
(ii) analyse problems associated with quality in organisations;
(iii) evaluate contemporary thinking in quality management;
(iv) explain the linkages between functional areas as an important aspect of quality management;
(v) apply tools and concepts of quality management appropriately in an organisation;
(vi) construct a plan for the implementation of a quality programme;
(vii) recommend ways to negotiate and manage relationships with suppliers;
(viii) evaluate a supply network.
(ix) explain the concept of quality and how the quality of products *and* services can be assessed, measured and improved.

Syllabus content

- An overview of operations strategy and its importance to the firm.
- Design of products/services and processes and how this relates to operations and supply.
- Methods for managing inventory, including continuous inventory systems (e.g. Economic Order Quantity, EOQ), periodic inventory systems and the ABC system (Note: ABC is not an acronym. A refers to high value, B to medium and C to low value inventory).
- Strategies for balancing capacity and demand including level capacity, chase and demand management strategies.
- Methods of performance measurement and improvement, particularly the contrast between benchmarking and Business Process Re-engineering (BPR).
- Practices of continuous improvement (e.g. Quality circles, Kaizen, 5S, 6 Sigma).
- The use of benchmarking in quality measurement and improvement.
- Different methods of quality measurement (i.e. operational, financial and customer measures).
- The characteristics of lean production: flexible workforce practices, high-commitment human resource policies and commitment to continuous improvement. Criticisms and limitations of lean production.
- Systems used in operations management: Manufacturing Resource Planning (MRP), Optimised Production Technologies (OPT), Just-in-Time (JIT) and Enterprise Resource Planning (ERP).
- Approaches to quality management, including Total Quality Management (TQM), various British Standard (BS) and European Union (EU) systems as well as statistical methods of quality control.
- External quality standards (e.g. the various ISO standards appropriate to products and organisations).

- Use of the Intranet in information management (e.g. meeting customer support needs).
- Contemporary developments in quality management.
- The role of the supply chain and supply networks in gaining competitive advantage, including the use of sourcing strategies (e.g. single, multiple, delegated and parallel).
- Supply chain management as a strategic process (e.g. Reck and Long's strategic positioning tool, Cousins' strategic supply wheel).
- Developing and maintaining relationships with suppliers.

D – Marketing – 20%

Learning outcomes

On completion of their studies students should be able to:

(i) explain the marketing concept;
(ii) evaluate the marketing processes of an organisation;
(iii) apply tools within each area of the marketing mix;
(iv) describe the business contexts within which marketing principles can be applied (consumer marketing, business-to-business marketing, services marketing, direct marketing, interactive marketing);
(v) evaluate the role of technology in modern marketing;
(vi) produce a strategic marketing plan for the organisation.

Syllabus content

- Introduction to the marketing concept as a business philosophy.
- An overview of the marketing environment, including societal, economic, technological, political and legal factors affecting marketing.
- Understanding consumer behaviour, such as factors affecting buying decisions, types of buying behaviour and stages in the buying process.
- Market research, including data gathering techniques and methods of analysis.
- Marketing Decision Support Systems (MDSS) and their relationship to market research.
- How business-to-business (B2B) marketing differs from business-to-consumer (B2C) marketing.
- Segmentation and targeting of markets, and positioning of products within markets.
- The differences and similarities in the marketing of products and services.
- Devising and implementing a pricing strategy.
- Marketing communications (i.e. mass, direct, interactive).
- Distribution channels and methods for marketing campaigns.
- The role of marketing in the strategic plan of the organisation.
- Use of the Internet (e.g. in terms of data collection, marketing activity and providing enhanced value to customers and suppliers) and potential drawbacks (e.g. security issues).
- Market forecasting methods for estimating current (e.g. Total Market Potential, Area Market Potential and Industry Sales and Market Shares) and future (e.g. Survey of Buyers' Intentions, Composite of Sales Force Opinions, Expert Opinion, Past-Sales Analysis and Market-Test Method) demand for products and services.
- Internal marketing as the process of training and motivating employees so as to support the firm's external marketing activities.
- Social responsibility in a marketing context.

E – Managing Human Capital – 30%

Learning outcomes

On completion of their studies students should be able to:

 (i) explain the role of the human resource management function and its relationship to other parts of the organisation;

 (ii) produce and explain a human resource plan and supporting practices;

(iii) evaluate the recruitment, selection, induction, appraisal, training and career planning activities of an organisation;

(iv) evaluate the role of incentives in staff development as well as individual and organisational performance;

 (v) identify features of a human resource plan that vary depending on organisation type and employment model;

(vi) explain the importance of ethical behaviour in business generally and for the Chartered Management Accountant in particular.

Syllabus content

- The relationship of the employee to other elements of the business plan.
- Determinants and content of a human resource (HR) plan (e.g. organisational growth rate, skills, training, development, strategy, technologies and natural wastage).
- Problems in implementing a HR plan and ways to manage this.
- The process of recruitment and selection of staff using different recruitment channels (i.e. interviews, assessment centres, intelligence tests, aptitude tests, psychometric tests).
- Issues relating to fair and legal employment practices (e.g. recruitment, dismissal, redundancy, and ways of managing these).
- Issues in the design of reward systems (e.g. the role of incentives, the utility of performance-related pay, arrangements for knowledge workers, flexible work arrangements).
- The importance of negotiation during the offer and acceptance of a job.
- The process of induction and its importance.
- Theories of Human Resource Management (e.g. Taylor, Schein, McGregor, Maslow, Herzberg, Handy, Lawrence and Lorsch).
- High performance work arrangements.
- The distinction between development and training and the tools available to develop and train staff.
- The importance of appraisals, their conduct and their relationship to the reward system.
- HR in different organisational forms (e.g. project-based firms, virtual or networked firms).
- Personal business ethics and the CIMA Ethical Guidelines.

1

Information Systems

Information Systems

1

1.1 Introduction

The increase in more sophisticated information and technological solutions has led to the emergence of e-commerce, the automated office, teleworking and the 'information superhighway' as facts of organisational life. It follows that information technology and information systems assume increasing managerial importance within the modern organisation.

In order to understand how information systems operate within organisations it is important to appreciate the information technologies used, and the possible ways these technologies can be structured to form a system. This chapter introduces the main elements of computer hardware, software and communications and indicates the different types of system configuration. This will help understanding of how the different types of hardware and software can support organisations' information communication requirements. Next, the major concepts of systems theory are considered, the relevance of which is that they can be applied to organisational information systems. Having explained the principles and concepts of the general systems theory (GST), management issues including system design and implementation are explored. Finally, perspectives are offered on IS as a vital functional area of business including its 'fit' with other areas.

A computer system consists of a number of components, including the computer hardware and software used. The consideration of these in turn forms the basis for initial study.

1.2 Hardware components of a computer system

Typically a computer system is likely to consist of several hardware devices such as the main computer (the central processing unit) and screen, a printer, a keyboard, a mouse and a scanner. These are now considered along with associated issues.

1.2.1 The central processing unit

The 'heart' of the computer system is its central processing unit (CPU), which in turn consists of three elements:

The control unit. The control unit directs the operations of the whole computer system. An instruction containing codes identifying the operation to be performed, and the data to be used in the operation is copied from the main storage to the control unit. The control unit reads the operation code of the instruction and carries out the operation on data contained in the main storage. The control unit has three main functions:

- to read and interpret program instructions,
- to direct the operation of internal processor components,
- to control the flow of programs and data in and out of memory.

The arithmetic logic unit (ALU). The ALU executes the operations identified by the control unit. The ALU is designed to perform all computations (addition, subtraction, multiplication and division), all logic operations (e.g. comparisons) and both numeric and alphabetic operations.

Main storage. The CPU's main storage has two functions:

- to provide a storage place for the executable instructions making up a computer program, and
- to provide areas for storing data processed by the program.

Main storage is also called 'primary storage' or 'main memory' and is made up of circuits such as the random access memory (RAM). RAM is known as a 'read and write' memory as it allows data to be both read and written to memory. RAM provides the processor with short-term storage from programs and data currently in use, which the processor then manipulates. All programs and data must be transferred to RAM from an input device or from secondary storage before programs can be executed or data processed. The major problem with RAM is that it is volatile, hence when the electrical power is interrupted, data may be 'lost'.

A special type of internal memory, called read only memory (ROM), cannot be altered by a programmer. As the name suggests, the contents of ROM may be read but not overwritten. The contents of ROM are more stable, and when a computer is switched on the program in ROM automatically readies the computer for use.

1.2.2 Input devices

Input devices are the communication links between the computer and the user. Input devices form a major aspect of the human/computer interface and represent much of the user's view of the system. The choice of input device must be suitable for the characteristics and purpose of the overall system. The main types of input device are:

Keyboard. Most modern computers use keyboard terminals as the primary data-entry method.

Mouse and trackball devices. These use the rolling motion of a ball to act as a cursor control or to move data around the screen quickly.

Voice data entry (VDE). VDE uses a microphone to accept vocal input. Although the natural language capability of computers is still restricted, significant developments in voice recognition software have taken place. A recent development in VDE has been language programs, designed to translate one language into another instantly, thus allowing the user to conduct international business correspondence.

Light pen and touch screens. These utilise the Visual Display Unit (VDU) screen to input. A light pen connected to the terminal is placed against the screen and a light-sensitive device recognises the position by X and Y coordinates. Touch screens are commonplace devices in high street cash withdrawal machines.

1.2.3 Data-capture devices

Direct-entry or data-capture devices are designed to allow input of large volumes of routine data, often with little human intervention. A number of direct-entry devices include:

Optical character recognition (OCR). This is the ability to read printed information into a computer system. OCR documents are printed on special stylised forms using standard type fonts.

Optical mark recognition (OMR). This is the use of documents that are designed so that a mark made in a particular position represents data. OMR documents work in conjunction with special software written to read and understand the position of each mark.

Scanners. These read and capture text, graphics and pictures from normal documents and can be used within the office environment to scan images into documents created by (for instance) desktop publishing software.

Magnetic ink character recognition (MICR). MICR systems use human-readable characters, which are pre-printed in special ink impregnated on to a form or document with iron oxide. A machine reader recognises the magnetised character, codes it and passes the data to the computer.

Bar-code readers. These display a unique identification code in a series of lines of differing widths. This sequence can be translated into digits that uniquely identify a product or unit.

Digital cameras. These allow the input of high-quality images directly into the computer which can then be manipulated as required by image-processing software.

✋ **Exercise 1.1**

Give examples of how each of the above input devices could be used within particular business contexts.

☑ **Solution**

Input device	Example
Optical character readers	Pre-printed fuel billing.
Optical mark readers	Multiple-choice marking on a questionnaire as part of a staff selection process.
Scanners	Web page creation and desktop publishing.
MICR	Chequebooks and other banking documents.
Bar-code readers	Supermarket checkouts.
Digital cameras	Newspaper or corporate documentation photography.

1.2.4 Output devices

The most common methods of supplying output information from a computer are identified here:

- The VDU allows the operator to monitor the input from the keyboard, etc., and display the machine-generated immediately on-screen. This enables the operator to verify the accuracy of input instantly and to check output before it is sent to an alternative output medium, such as a printer.
- Hard-copy devices, including printers and plotters, are the most common form of output device (even in this supposed age of the 'paperless' office). The range of performance and cost varies from one printer to another, so the choice must be made to suit the output requirements of the system.
- Audio output devices are speakers either inbuilt or attached which provide sound output often from CD-ROMs or voice recordings.

1.2.5 Storage devices

Most types of computer systems will have two types of storage – main (primary) memory (discussed earlier) and backing (secondary) storage. There is a variety of backing storage devices, most relatively inexpensive, including floppy disks, flash drives and DVDs (digital video/versatile disks) which have high-capacity storage and allow data access at high speed.

1.3 Software components of a computer system

Many of the decisions made in the design and specification of information systems are concerned with the hardware (e.g. the output speed, storage capacity, speed and cost of processing, etc.), but the hardware of the computer is virtually useless on its own. It is the computer software that brings the hardware to 'life' as software controls the activities of the hardware. The ultimate characteristics of a system and its successful operation will depend greatly on the decisions made about the software.

Software can be classified as either systems software, which allows the system to provide basic operational services to the user, or applications software, which carries out specific user requirements.

1.3.1 Systems software

Systems software includes three elements:

The operating system. This is a set of computer programs that directs the operations of the entire computer system. When the user first switches on the computer, the computer copies the operating systems software from a secondary storage device to the main storage. The operating system then takes control of the CPU and all of the connected peripherals (such as printers, monitors, mouse, keyboard). Examples of operating systems software include MS-DOS, Windows 95/98, Windows 2000, Windows XP, Linux, Mac OS, Unix and network operating systems such as Windows NT, and Novell Netware.

Utility programs. These are designed into the operating system by the manufacturer, primarily as a support to programmers (and possibly users), to help when writing, storing and running their programs. Examples of utility programs include Microsoft Visual Studio (program development tools), virus check programs, debugging programs, etc.

Communications software. This is primarily designed to support network computer systems (discussed later in this chapter). Communications software helps to select the best transmission medium across networks, then codes, transmits, receives and stores data.

1.3.2 Applications software

Applications software is designed to perform specific personal, business or scientific processing tasks such as word processing, sales invoice processing, tax planning, product design, desktop publishing, financial planning or entertainment (such as computer games). Applications software performs the specific functions that the user requires from their system.

Exercise 1.2

Reflection

Make a list of the different types of application software you use on an everyday basis either at home or at work.

1.4 Computer system configurations

Hardware and software components make up a computer system, but not all systems combine the components in the same way. The 'system configuration' (or hardware and applications architecture) describes how a specific organisation combines hardware devices to support the applications utilised by its computer system.

1.4.1 Centralised processing

Originally, all organisational computer systems were centralised. They used large mainframe computers to process data, connected to remote terminals that communicated with the central machine. The system required specialist staff to maintain it, as mainframes were often large, complex machines, sometimes requiring a controlled physical environment. These systems are usually designed for processing large volumes of data and transactions, and are still found in areas of business life such as banking.

1.4.2 Distributed processing

The basis of a distributed system is that it uses a data communications system to create and maintain a network of computers, which are equally capable of independent operation and of resource sharing as required. Sharing may involve the access of data on a remote file or the ability to transfer whole files or programs across systems. This trend for distributed processing in information systems development has become known as 'end-user' computing, which means that the responsibility for IT resources has been delegated to individual users and control over processing has been decentralised.

Table 1.1 compares the relative merits of centralised and distributed processing.

Exercise 1.3

What are the disadvantages of each processing approach?

Solution

Centralised processing:

Can be inflexible.

Changes in software can take a long time to implement and can be disruptive.

Mainframes can become technologically obsolete and it can be difficult and expensive to replace.

Encourages user dependency.

Requires the extensive use of IT experts.

Table 1.1 The merits of centralised processing versus distributed processing

Centralised processing
  There are economies of scale for large transaction-processing systems.
  Able to cope in terms of speed and capacity with large organisational databases.
  The routine processing is ideally suited for the type of software these systems use.
  Consistent with a centralised control philosophy.
Distributed processing
  Processing activities can be shared between computers.
  Allows for independence and flexibility for the users.
  Potentially a greater sense of personal ownership.
  Consistent with a decentralised devolved responsibility philosophy.

Source: Author (2004)

Distributed processing:

May be costly to maintain.

May result in duplication of effort as end-users develop their own systems.

Emerging systems may be similar to other (cheaper) end-user systems.

Responsibility and control becomes diffused and unclear.

1.4.3   Client/server computing

Client/server technology refers to the division of operations in a computer network between end-users (clients) and processors that provide services to them (servers). A client would be any workstation attached to the network. A server is another networked computer that provides a specific service, such as managing files (a file server) or routeing messages on the network (network server).

As client computers have become faster and more powerful, many functions have moved away from servers to the client, which makes the system more responsive to user needs. It gives users greater control of their own applications at their own locations. Many organisations have reduced the costs of executing routine accounting functions by moving these applications to clients while maintaining accounting data on a file server.

1.4.4   Peripherals

A 'peripheral' is a term for an optional hardware device that is added to a computer in order to expand its functionality (abilities). Types of externally hooked up peripherals would include printers, scanners, speakers and joysticks, etc. With the widespread adoption of personal computing over the past few years the boundaries beyond the base system and optionals have been redefined somewhat so that (screen) monitors, keyboards and mice are now so widely recognised as fundamental that they no longer are considered peripherals.

> Note: For more on peripherals refer to http://peripherals.about.com

1.5   Computer networking

A network is where a number of computers and other devices are linked in such a way that any one device can communicate with any other so enabling resource sharing between a number of users. Many organisations adopt a computer systems configuration that utilises a data communications network. Networks may link computers in different organisations and can involve widely distributed geographical sites (known as wide area networks or WAN), or computers within the same local site (known as local area networks or LAN). Where the WAN uses dedicated links it is called a physical network. Where a WAN uses a combination of links that are 'transparent' to the user, the network is called a virtual network.

1.5.1   Network topology

> The term 'topology' refers to the physical arrangement of a particular network. Possible topologies of networks include star, ring and tree.

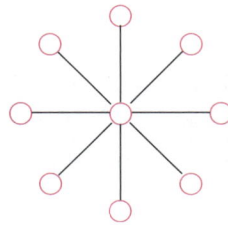

Figure 1.1   A star network

Star networks

The star configuration (Figure 1.1) consists of a single central computer as a server that transfers data among all of the other computers in the network. Each peripheral computer is linked directly to the central processor only, using a single data communications link. The peripheral computers do not have a direct link to each other, and must go through the central computer if they wish to communicate.

Ring networks

A ring network (Figure 1.2) consists of a number of computers, each connected to two others in the ring. Each may be dedicated to processing only one or a few related applications. Data containing a destination address are circulated around the ring when required, and each processor reads the message and passes on relevant data to other processors. Again, each processor has the ability to communicate to any other in the network, but only via a number of other computers (unless communication is with one of the computers on either side).

Tree networks

A tree network (Figure 1.3) is sometimes known as a hierarchical network because it contains a hierarchy of processors. The processor at the top is the most important and is usually a mainframe. The processors at lower levels in the hierarchy are smaller computers such as minicomputers or microcomputers. Processors at the second level transfer data to the lower levels and to the high-level mainframe.

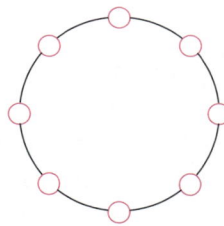

Figure 1.2   Ring networks

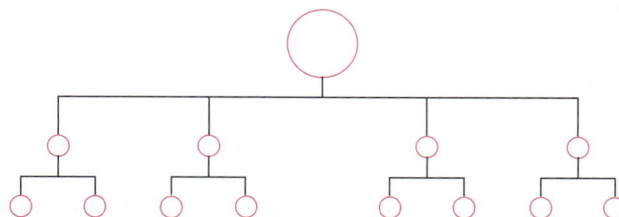

Figure 1.3   A tree network

1.5.2   Network components

A LAN usually contains five components:

- The network hub. A central point for physically connecting the other components of the LAN.
- One or more workstations, each may include a microcomputer, a keyboard, a disk storage device and a printer. A network user would enter data, execute the applications software and receive output at the workstation.
- A file server, a processor connected to a high-speed online form of secondary storage. All workstations on the LAN may place files on the file server.
- A print server, a device that controls the high-speed printers connected to the network and can again be used by all workstations on the LAN.
- A communications server, a processor on the LAN that handles communications with other systems or networks outside the LAN. Small organisations with only one LAN do not need a communications server.

1.5.3   Internet, Intranet and Extranet

The Internet is a public and global communication network that provides direct connection to anyone over a LAN. An example of a virtual network is the Internet. Access to it is open to all, which may result in an unruly proliferation of information. Common Internet tools include e-mail, World Wide Web (www), newsgroups, chatting, electronic conferencing, file transfer protocol (FTP), and Telnet (for remote computer logging in).

The significance of the Internet on organisations can be gauged by reference to some of its benefits, including:

- access competitors' information and intelligence gathering
- improved communication
- enhanced relationship with business partners
- reduced costs
- improved supply chain
- access to new markets
- enhanced customer loyalty and retention, including online customer services
- innovation in new products offered
- new way of doing business (facilitate e-commerce including internet marketing, online buying and selling)
- new way of gaining/sustaining competitive advantages
- online surveys and market research
- online contract tendering, etc.
- developing a new way of working, for example, home working.

An Intranet is an internal organisational network that is based on the Internet technologies, and can be accessed only by authorised employees. While the Internet has open access to the public, an Intranet is private and is protected by a 'firewall' (an access control system consisting of hardware and software that is placed between an organisation's internal network and external networks). One of the main advantages of an Intranet is that it allows confidential internal information sharing, for example, corporate policy, document sharing, telephone directories, training programmes, etc. It can also facilitate intrabusiness commerce including internal buying and selling.

An Extranet refers to an extended Intranet of an organisation that links to its business partners (e.g., customers, suppliers or other trade organisations). Only authorised users can access to the Extranet. Data transmitted over the Extranet is usually secured. One of the main advantages of an Extranet is to connect the dispersed networks together. It has great potential in enhancing inter-organisational communication, facilitating electronic data interchange (Internet-based EDI) and e-procurement. Conceptually it is not dissimilar from subscription-based internet sites that require password access.

1.6　The workplace: technology and systems

1.6.1　Organisational information technology

The office (like the factory before it) has been subject to huge technological advancements in recent years. These changes have affected how and where employees work. 'Office automation' is a term that refers to the use of computers, communications and network technology in managing the organisation's operations and information resources. In recent years this has resulted in the combination of data, text, image and sound into office-built multimedia systems. Two examples of office automation and their advantages are briefly described below.

Example 1

Teleworking (or telecommuting). One significant impact of office automation technology has been the increase in staff working from home, rather than being based in an office. By utilising a combination of communications technology such as phone, fax, e-mail and the World Wide Web (www), staff now have the ability to communicate with colleagues, customers and suppliers from their own homes. There are a number of clear advantages of teleworking not least reducing commuting to and from a fixed place of work. This means that less fuel is consumed and the environment is subject to less vehicle pollution. From the organisation's point of view there is no commuting involved and time savings, together with the reduction in office distractions and disruptions, should lead to improved productivity. Operating costs for the organisation are also reduced (through lower facilities costs). For the employee there is greater flexibility over precise working times and geographical proximity to colleagues is rendered less relevant.

Exercise 1.4

What are the disadvantages of teleworking?

Solution

- A potential loss of team cohesion and a sense of belonging.
- Potential control difficulties.
- The need to provide and maintain adequate levels of office equipment in a domestic setting.

Example 2

Electronic data interchange. Many organisations have made use of network technology, specifically electronic data interchange (EDI). EDI is the computer-to-computer transmission of data contained in standard business documents and reports, such as customer invoices and purchase orders. EDI is intended to replace conventional business documentation with structured data transmitted electronically over networks ('paperless trading'). Importantly, the data must be structured in a standard common format so that the documents are standardised at both ends of the transmission. Obvious advantages of EDI include:

- saving in clerical and administration costs/time;
- the speeding of transactions with potentially reduced lead times for material purchases, which may lead to reduced stock levels;
- better customer service and may improve the response to changes in customer demands. (An order to replenish stock reaches its destination in seconds rather than days.)

Corporate IT is recognised by many as the lifeblood of the modern organisation. Pesola (2004) comments:

businesses increasingly run their databases over office-wide networks, link employees' computers via office-wide wireless-LAN (local area network) connections, sell goods and run support services over the internet and rely on receiving customer commissions by e-mail

Various forms of automation and other technology are commonly found in most office environments. Some are discussed below.

Electronic mail (e-mail)

E-mail systems are intended to reduce the volume of paper movement by electronic transmission of graphical or textual information. Key advantages of e-mail include speed and versatility, allowing communication over long and short distances and immediate response. E-mail has the facility to send electronic attachments. A common difficulty is the risk of computer viruses being transmitted through the opening of rogue messages.

Facsimile (fax)

Fax transmission allows the user to send an exact copy of a document, which is digitally coded then transmitted, recorded and composed by the receiver's equipment. It appears that e-mails' popularity may be overshadowing the fax, however it remains an easy method of sending complex diagrams or pictures and is useful where verification of a signature is required.

Teleconferencing and videoconferencing

The ability to conduct meetings, business negotiations and presentations without the participants having to be at the same location has obvious benefits for organisations.

Teleconferencing is a relatively inexpensive means of communication, allowing a number of telephone participants to hold multiple-way communication. One potential difficulty is the lack of visible identification and recognition of speakers. Videoconferencing over-comes these problems but is still relatively expensive and requires special equipment. Teleconferencing allows two or more locations to be linked (using a number of transmission media, including the Internet and satellites) and is likely to become of increasing importance in business communication across the world.

Advantages of teleconferencing include savings in cost and time for attendants, fast communication and therefore timelier decision making.

The Internet (and the World Wide Web)

The Internet represents a virtual network that links millions of computers all over the world. The www exists on it and consists of pages of information that can be found at Websites, and can be accessed through the use of a Web browser (e.g. Internet Explorer, Netscape) by using a unique address called a universal resource locator (URL). Search engines are often used (such as google or Yahoo) to search for topics by keywords or by asking a question. The flexibility and accessibility of the Web makes it a particularly useful tool for business. Many organisations now use the Internet to advertise, trade and search for information about competitors, customers and suppliers (see later chapters in particular the relevance of the World Wide Web to marketing).

Exercise 1.5

Reflection

If you or your organisation uses the Web, take a few minutes to consider how it is used:

- to trade;
- for leisure purposes;
- for information;
- for marketing.

Make a list of both your personal uses and your organisational uses of the Web.

The Internet has transformed aspirations to join a global marketplace and in the process has reshaped the business world (Phillips, 2000). The electronic business phenomenon has over the past decade or so seen phrases such as 'e-commerce', 'e-business', 'digital economy', 'Internet commerce' and other besides becoming mainstream language. Phillips (2000) believes that they all mean similar things, drawing a slight distinction whereby:

- e-commerce (electronic commerce) represents the means by which companies communicate via digital transactions, but
- e-business (electronic business) also incorporates business being done throughout the value chain (with suppliers downstream and customers upstream) with early pioneers claiming a 20 per cent reduction in costs.

The competitive advantage to be gained from adept use of this potential to create new business models and to find new ways of doing things is easily apparent. He cites the strategic implications of e-business as including:

- The death of distance as a communication impediment
- The reality of virtual organisations able to make savings and operate differently
- The need for a redesign of traditional financial planning, control and evaluation techniques.

As the opportunities of new technology present themselves so too do the risks. Businesses typically spent 2 to 4 per cent of their IT budgets on contingency planning, others more. Such expenditure is easily justified. An hour of IT down time preventing a bank from trading can cost $6.5 million or a travel agent $90,000 in lost airline bookings (Pesola, 2004). One trap organisations fall into is apparently placing too much emphasis on hardware rather than the software architecture (the interconnection of software), as Pesola (2004) notes:

many applications are interconnected these days back-office stock inventories linked to front-office transactions software and so on-and the failure of one can easily take down the other systems as well

Accountants have been automating their practice management for decades, using all sorts of tools ranging from basic cost control systems such as Sage Time and Fees (www.sage.co.uk) and Time Sheet Professional (www.dsareen.com) to full blown professional services automation (PSA) systems such as Novient (www.solution.co.uk) and SharpOWL (www.sharpowl.com) via a range of practice management tools and systems. But this has left many with a mixture of disparate and disconnected systems that keep them tied up in knots and do little to improve their efficiency or effectiveness.

Of course, this is an issue for organisations of all shapes and sizes, not just accountancy firms. But the profession has been particularly hard hit of late, and the growing burden of bureaucracy threatens to bury many: Increased automation, and improved integration, could offer a non-merger route to survival.

By using integrated applications, and taking advantage of broadband technology, Bevan & Buckland has been able to improve communications between the 5 partners and 60 team members in its five offices across Wales, and enhance the service it offers clients.

As all of the firm's offices are now linked by a broadband-based wide area network, it has benefited from faster and cheaper access to applications. Partners can also dial in remotely from either a client's office or from home working from the same screens they would have in the office.

(extracted from the article Automation nation by Lesley Meall, *Accountancy*, March 2004, pp. 74–75. Reprinted with the kind permission of the author).

1.6.2 Organisational information systems

Information technology allows organisations to operate a number of different types of organisational information systems each designed to assist decision making. These organisational information systems can be categorised as follows:

- Data processing systems or transaction processing systems (DPSs/TPSs). These systems normally involve the processing of repetitive tasks using well-defined and structured information that is relatively easy to capture and store in large volumes. The system provides vital day-to-day information about efficiency of operations and activities, but is limited in supporting managerial decision making due to the inflexible nature of information produced. Examples: Payroll systems, purchase/sales order entry systems and Stock control systems
- Management information systems (MISs) provide middle-level managers with information to monitor and control the organisation's activities and to report this to the senior-level managers. MISs are often based upon report-producing packages that use information from the same source as the DPSs. Examples: forecasting, reporting, budgeting and control information (exception reports, variance reports, etc.).
- Executive information systems (EISs) provide senior-level managers with strategic-level information to help them make strategic decisions. EISs contain powerful software for supporting the types of high-risk, unstructured decisions that are made by strategic-level managers. EISs combine information from within the organisation and from its environment, then organise, analyse and present it. Examples: key performance indicators (KPIs) through user-friendly interface graphical user interface (GUI) using icons, drop-down menus and mouse/pointer facilities. A typical EIS presents output using text and graphics, such as bar charts and histograms, which can be tailored and customised by each executive.

- Decision support systems (DSSs) provide managers with information to support unstructured, one-off decisions by retrieving and analysing data. A DSS possesses interactive capabilities, assists in solving ad hoc queries and provides data-modelling facilities. The complex mathematical models used in DSSs are designed to simulate the behaviour of an organisational activity in an unpredictable situation. DSSs generate a number of potential solutions, enabling managers to carry out 'what if?' analysis.
- Expert systems (ESs). Many decision situations will require an even higher degree of support than that provided by the EIS or DSS. ES is a system that simulates the problem-solving techniques of human experts, by applying human expertise and knowledge to a range of specific problems about a particular area of expertise. The major benefits of expert systems include a preservation of knowledge, a distribution of knowledge and effective training. Examples: credit control systems, auditing, tax and investment appraisal.

1.6.3 The workplace: contemporary developments

In a thoughtful article in the CIMA journal *Financial Management* Camilla Berens (2006) reflects on the online auction house of eBay that becomes one of the largest UK marketplaces, claiming that the UK population spends 10 per cent of its web-surfing time on buying and selling goods. This seems to emphasise a new technology-enabled retail marketplace, and '... most retailers can't afford not to trade on the internet, particularly those based in the UK. According to analysts, online shoppers in the UK will spend £1,170 per head on the Web this year, compared with their US counterparts' £987. One of the factors behind this growth is thought to be the rapid take-up of domestic broadband services.'

In the same article, Berens (2006) identifies practical advice for building a commercial website:

- Ensure that your site works across all platforms (e.g, Apple Mac, PCs, Linux) and across browsers (e.g. Internet Explorer, Firefox and Opera).
- Inform users how secure their transactions are. Winning your customers' trust is vital.
- Be aware of Consumer Protection and privacy legislation (see www.oft.gov.uk/business /legal/dsr).
- Ensure that you know your obligations under data protection legislation. Draw up a privacy policy and terms of use for the site.
- Resist collecting too much information from site users, it might deter them.
- Try to stay in contact with your customers, maybe by getting them to sign up for e-mail newsletters.
- For detailed information support and advice visit Business Link at www.businesslink.gov.uk and Technology Means Business at www.tmb.org.uk.

The following short article describes the way in which some organisations are also exploring the potential for what is known as 'blogging':

Pub bores may be unbearable, but at least they come alone. Imagine a network of these narcissists, in love with the sound of their own opinions, computer-linked to each other's ramblings — it's enough to send right-minded news junkies cowering behind the Times.

But the network is spreading. Blogger.com began offering free blogs — short for weblogs, or online journals — in 1999. One is now created every second. According to Technorati, a website that monitors online activity, the 'blogosphere' now comprises 27 million blogs, peddling opinions on anything from bubblegum ice cream to censorship in China. Does anyone care? Well, yes. Boing Boing, a directory ranked by Technorati as the world's most linked-to blog, has an audience of 1.7 million and commands up to $8,000 a week for ad space; AOL last year bought blog hub Weblogs for $25 million; and the BBC and Guardian's websites now endorse blogosphere musings, giving credence to talk of 'citizen journalism'.

But the anti-establishment heyday of the blog could be over. The corporates have themselves begun blogging. GM's vice-chairman Bob Lutz uses his Fastlane blog to talk product development, while Microsoft lets employee Robert Scoble criticise its products in his popular Scobleizer blog. The blogosphere is a great way to track public opinion, but beware: bloggers will pounce on blatant PR and, like pub bores, their voices can be loud and persistent.

Source: It'll never fly: Blogging, *Management Today*, April 2006, p. 12

1.7 Databases and database management systems

Data needs to be stored, managed and retrieved. One method of simplifying matters is by means of an integrated dataset, whereby one set of data can be used by more than one application. This is known as a database, some appreciation of which is provided in this section. (Note that for examination purposes detailed knowledge of database structures will not be required.)

Traditional approaches to file management have taken an applications approach to data structure, whereby there is a concentration upon the processes or applications being carried out. For example, files based around accounting transactions, such as stock records, sales invoices and purchase orders, would be collected and stored in an accounting application. Under this approach each application collects and manages its own files and data, normally within separate files for each application. One outcome of this type of file structure is 'data redundancy' that may occur between various files. 'Data redundancy' is the duplication of data in two or more files, and may lead to inconsistencies of the same data and an increase in storage costs. For example, the accounting department may keep files relating to customers, as might the marketing department, but these records are likely to be kept separately within different departmental applications.

A database is a collection of structured data, and the structure of that data is completely independent of any one application. A database could be described as a collection of data files that are integrated to provide one single file system. The main aim of a database file structure is to provide one common dataset for a wide variety of users and their information needs.

1.7.1 Database management systems

A database management system (DBMS) is a set of integrated programs designed to organise and simplify the creation, management and access of data held within a database structure. A DBMS represents the way in which an organisation coordinates the complex activities carried out by its department into one data location. A DBMS should enhance the organisation's ability to provide reliable, relevant information to decision makers easily, efficiently and effectively.

1.7.2 Database objectives, advantages and disadvantages

A database should aim to:

- Provide data for a number of users and meet their individual information requirements.
- Allow multiple users to have shared access to the database to carry out their own processing, potentially accessing the same database at the same time if necessary.
- Maintain the integrity of the data (as there is only one dataset). It is important to restrict users from making unauthorised changes that could spoil the data for all other database users. However, users must be able to have access to the data so that they can update it when necessary.
- Be dynamic with an ability to develop and evolve as the organisation's information needs develop and evolve.
- Connect to a web server through a data access component (e.g. Microsoft ADO) to enable dynamic web database enquiry (see later).

Advantages of a database include:

- *Reduced storage costs.* Potential file storage requirements are reduced, resulting in file storage savings. (However, it must be noted that these cost savings are often matched by the additional costs of operating a DBMS.)
- *Reduction of data redundancy.* In a database structure, data is only stored once. Any application that requires an item of data can access and retrieve it from a central store.
- *Data integrity.* This again results from reduced data redundancy, as by keeping only one version of each data item within the database, inconsistencies in data between applications are eliminated.
- *Data independence.* The database approach allows multiple applications to use the same data at the same time. Additionally, the data can be accessed in a number of different ways according to what the user is doing (e.g. preparing a report, performing a query or through basic applications processing etc.).
- *Privacy.* DBMS software can provide sophisticated security features to protect the database from unauthorised access, alteration or data destruction.

Some disadvantages of databases should, however, also be acknowledged:

- *Data ownership.* A dispute over who 'owns' the data within the database may result in problems over who should carry out file maintenance.
- *Database failure.* With all of the organisation's data held in one location, should the power or the database fail, no processing or access to files is possible anywhere within the organisation. This is a significant risk for most organisations.
- *Contingency planning.* As all files are held in one location the risks of loss is an increased concern, therefore contingency planning is significantly more important, which may be costly and time-consuming.
- Some organisations may implement databases without really considering the benefits to their specific situation, and databases may not always be the best solution.

Exercise 1.6

Your organisation is considering changing to a database system. List the issues it would need to consider.

☑ Solution

- Specialist staff required (in implementing and running the new system, such as a database manager and administrators)
- Set-up costs of new software and possibly new hardware
- Training costs
- Security features
- Possible disruption
- Responsibilities
- Contingency and back-up facilities.

1.7.3 Database: contemporary developments

Fast evolving web database technology can enable web visitors from outside the organisation (such as potential customers) to make enquiries about product and price information, and to make orders and view shopping cart items from a web browser. For this to happen a database is connected to a web server by a database connectivity component, for example, Microsoft ADO and Open Database Connectivity (ODBC).

1.8 Systems Theory

There are several distinct approaches to understanding organisations and their management including the classical (scientific) approach, the human relations approach and the systems approach. Mullins (2005) establishes a relationship between the three as follows:

- the classical (scientific) approach emphasises the technical requirements of the organisation and its needs
- the human relations approach emphasises the psychological and social aspects and human needs
- the systems approach attempts to reconcile the two.

The systems perspective therefore considers the whole organisation as not so much a series of separate parts more an interrelationship of structure, behaviour and other variables. Such variables include the wider environment within which the organisation exists. This thinking is developed by the General Systems Theory (GST) approach that recognises that systems vary in complexity from a simple structural framework (such as an organisational charts) or a clock (dynamic but predictable and externally controlled) to humans and their social systems.

> 🖉 Note: For more on this thinking visit the following website: www.bsn-gn.eku.edu/ BEGLEY/GSThand1.htm

It should become apparent that this thinking that systems should be a central consideration for organisations and their use of information technology.

A system is a set of related parts coordinated to accomplish a set of goals. The function of a system is to convert or process inputs to achieve useful outputs. To take a simple example of a motor car viewed as a system, petrol is the input, the engine represents the process and movement represents the output (Figure 1.4). Using this example, the motor car is also subject to external factors in the environment such as the road surface, the steepness of the ground, the wind speed, etc.

1.8.1 Key features of a system

There are a number of key characteristics and components of any system:

- *Inputs*. Inputs may take the form of people, energy, materials, equipment, money or data: any raw materials in fact. These inputs may be received individually or in combination and can originate from a number of diverse sources.
- *Process results from receiving input*. Some form of conversion activity is carried out, with the aim of adding value to that input to produce an output. These processing activities may include (for instance) assembling, machining, shaping, melting, sorting, storing, calculating, etc.
- *Outputs*. Once processing is complete, the finished, processed product or service which results is passed out to the environment. This may involve the delivery of goods to a customer or the transmission of goods or information to a new system or subsystem. Typically, the value of the output is greater than the value of the input (i.e. the system adds value to the resources used). For example, an organisation will take in raw materials and labour, will utilise that to produce a product to sell to a customer, who then pays, normally at a higher price than the original cost of the raw materials.
- *Boundary*. The systems boundary separates the system and its components from its environment. Systems boundaries may or may not be physical, and sometimes may be not easily identifiable. Examples might include the garden wall or fence, the business unit, the organisation, the accounts office, etc.
- Environment. A system's environment is often defined as those external elements that have direct or indirect influence on the process and the elements of a system (Figure 1.4). Most systems operate within the context of an environment and interacts with it by receiving inputs from it and delivering outputs to it. The system is likely to deliver its outputs to a different part of its environment from that which it received its inputs. For example, a manufacturing company will receive its raw materials from specific component suppliers, but when these components are processed they will be delivered to the customer. That customer is unlikely to be the same as the supplier.

In systems terms when applied to the organisation, the environment can be viewed both internally (within the boundaries of the organisation) and externally. Even within the external business environment Johnson, Scholes and Whittington (2005) identify three layers of influence:

- Competitors and markets
- Industry (or sector)
- Macro environment (comprising political, economic, sociocultural, technological, legal, and environmental or PESTLE factors).

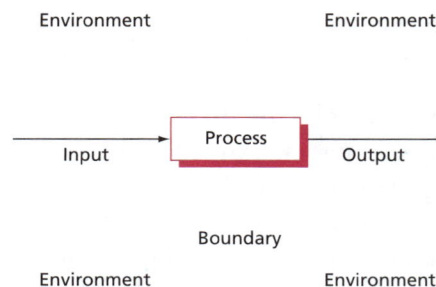

Figure 1.4 Elements of a system

Exercise 1.7

How has management accounting been affected by the changing business environment?

Solution

Consider the general and specific dimensions of the business environment:

- Technology factors, e.g. networking, Internet
- Regulation and deregulation on financial reporting
- Economic conditions
- Social and cultural changes
- Competition
- Customer demands and expectations
- Supplier
- Shareholder demands
- Other stakeholder demands.

Now choose an organisation to which you 'belong' (e.g. a church, a charitable group, a football club, a society, etc.) and assess which key factors are most affecting the organisation at the present time and which are likely to be most important in the next few years.

Two further concepts and definitions relevant to systems theory are as follows:

Subsystems. The system itself may contain a number of different smaller systems, called subsystems, each of which consists of a process whereby component parts are co-coordinated to achieve a set of objectives. The goals of subsystems must be consistent with the goals of the overall system, and should be designed to play a part in the achievement of the overall goals of the whole system.

Interfaces. Whenever systems or subsystem boundaries meet, an interface is created. This normally involves some form of resource exchange, often in the form of an input/output relationship.

Exercise 1.8

Think of examples from business to illustrate each of the above concepts.

Solution

Some examples are included here (they are unlikely to be exactly the same as those you have written down).

- *Subsystems*. An organisation will have many departments, each of which could be viewed as a subsystem. Each will have its own departmental objectives which, when put together, should achieve the organisational objectives.
- *Interfaces*. In a business context this may be a provision of raw materials for a reciprocal monetary repayment, or finished product or service provided to a customer in exchange for monetary remuneration.

1.8.2   Types of systems

Most systems will conform to a common classification, the most popular of which are illustrated in Figure 1.5.

Closed systems

A closed system is totally isolated from its environment. There are no external interfaces, the system has no effect outside its own boundaries and the environment has no effect on the processes of the system. A closed system does not receive inputs from or deliver outputs to its environment. It is difficult to find examples of systems that are truly closed other than inanimate objects such as hills or mountains. An isolated religious community might at one level be seen as a possible example.

Semi-closed systems

A semi-closed system is one that reacts with its environment in a known and controlled way. The system has interfaces with its environment, and it can control the effects of the environment on its process. This represents something of a bridge between the closed and the open systems.

Open systems

An open system is one that interacts with its environment in both a controlled and an uncontrolled way. As well as having inputs and outputs, an open system has disturbances (or uncontrolled inputs), that affect the processes of the system. If a hospital is seen as an open system a disturbance might be a government that needs to be taken into account. Open systems grow, develop and adapt. As such, most business systems would be considered to be open systems.

Dynamic (and static) systems

An open system can evolve towards a dynamic state, capable of reacting to external environmental changes through changing the structure and the process of internal components. Similarly it might attempt to influence its external environment in some way (e.g. by lobbying

CLOSED

OPEN

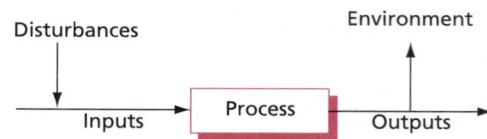

SEMI-CLOSED

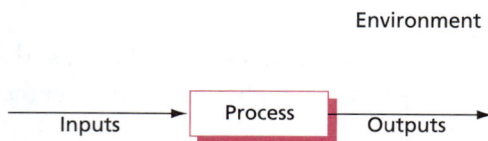

FEEDBACK CONTROL

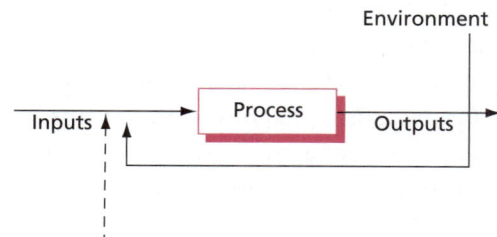

Figure 1.5   Types of systems

government over legislation). Later in this text 'learning organisations' are considered as examples of how to survive and prosper in a competitive environment, effectively dealing with external opportunities and/or threats. Conversely, organisations that resolutely refuse to change in relation to the environment might be viewed as static systems. The consequence of this sort of thinking is also explored as part of change management later. An example of an open system evolving towards a dynamic state is the accounting system. A typical accounting system interacts with the company's other systems, for example sales systems and stock control systems for new data input, and produces financial information as outputs to reflect and influence sales management and stock control. The future accounting system may be able to directly interact with the external environment for external financial information scanning, processing and reporting (an environment accounting system).

Feedback control systems

In feedback control systems, a part of the system output is returned as an input to the system as feedback. A system can be designed to provide feedback to help the system achieve its goals. Most accounting systems are designed to provide feedback for control purposes. Responsibility reporting systems provide feedback to managers about their performance in achieving organisational objectives. Managers can then make decisions that adjust their inputs to processes that will help them achieve their goals. Budgetary control systems will produce variance analyses and reports to cost centre managers, and they can then make decisions to change either input or processes.

Feedforward control systems

The environment and the processes and system output are monitored in order to provide corrective action if required. Feedforward control brings a predictive element into the control loop. Any corrective action taken is based upon both current and future predictions of events. Feedforward control is not as common as feedback control, because predictive information is not as easy to obtain as current or past information.

   Finally three further concepts are worthy of mention here:

Entropy. A concept developed elsewhere that within this context represents the amount of randomness in a system that may lead to system breakdown unless controlled in some way. Information systems can provide an important role in providing managers with information to ensure that objectives are met and order established. This might be done by establishing rules and enforcing them.

Requisite variety. Complex systems such as business organisations contain a large number of components and subsystems and follow a range of objectives. The law of requisite variety states that to survive, the system should contain variety at least equal to the system it needs to control. The effect of this is that a relatively simple control system in organisations (such as a budgetary control system) cannot be expected to control the complex activities of large multidivisional and multiproduct organisations.

   Here is an example of sufficiency of variety:

'The stuffy boardroom of Marks and Spencers did not have the requisite variety to understand the ecological changes going on in the environment (i.e. changes in middle-aged clothing preferences). . . . Examples of where good requisite variety has recently been available in companies. . . . (include) 'Yahoo'; Microsoft, Cisco, the Financial Times, Wal-Mart, Intershop'.
Source: www.syre.com/Requisite.htm

Coupling and decoupling. Coupling measures linkages between systems (or subsystems) and the extent of the speed of impact from one to another. Interfaces are often designed to provide decoupling between component parts and between subsystems. Therefore, components of a system have the ability to operate independently, so that the timing of the operations of one component does not rely on the operations of another.

1.8.3 Feedback control loops

Control within systems is exercised by feedback loops that gather information on past performance from the output side of a system, and then use it to govern future performance by adjusting the input side of the system. Systems theory gives special names to certain parts of the control and feedback cycle (Figure 1.6).

- Sensors are the measuring and recording devices of the system. (In organisational systems the usual sensor is likely to be a program or paperwork).
- Comparator is the mechanism by which actual results are compared with the plan. Typically in information systems, a clerk or a computer program checks for certain criteria in the data, normally against some kind of standard. (For example, in a budgetary control system, the budget itself is the standard).
- The effector is usually a manager acting on the report containing the results of the comparison between actual and standard, and issuing the instructions for adjustment to be made. An effector could also be an automatic process, such as an automated stock reordering system that checks stock levels and automatically reorders when the preset reorder quantity is reached.
- Single loop feedback implies that the existing performance standards and plans remain unchanged. This is the conventional feedback system and is normally associated with normal control systems at the tactical and operational levels of the organisation.
- Double loop feedback is a higher order of feedback designed to ensure that plans, budgets and the control systems themselves are revised to meet changes in both internal and environmental conditions. The business environment contains many uncertainties such as competitors, inflation, legislation, industrial disputes, changes in taste and technology, etc. The monitoring of these trends and performance is likely to be vital if the organisation is to survive in the long term.

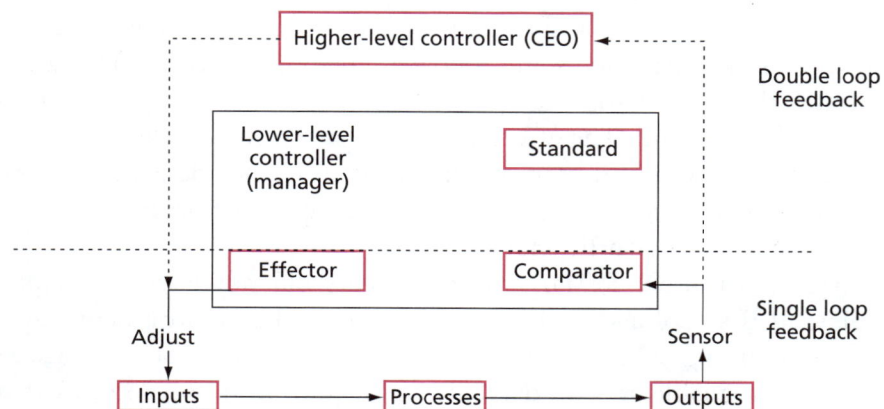

Figure 1.6 Control and the feedback cycle

The example of a typical production system demonstrates the relevance of these concepts, principles and theories to organisational information systems (as illustrated in Figure 1.7).

Having introduced the major concepts of systems theory, general theory and types of systems, these concepts are applied to information systems within organisations. Attention is now turned to tools used during the analysis and design of such systems.

1.9 Systems analysis and design

Systems analysis is a detailed analysis of the problem/system under review, to assess and develop potential options and to provide management with greater information to decide the most appropriate system options. This analysis consists of a set of procedures and processes involving the methodical investigation of a problem and the identification and ranking of alternative solutions to it, and is designed to gain more information in order to describe and explain the problem fully.

Systems analysis is a set of procedures and tools designed to create the specifications of a new system. One outcome of systems analysis is to produce the design specifications for the new system.

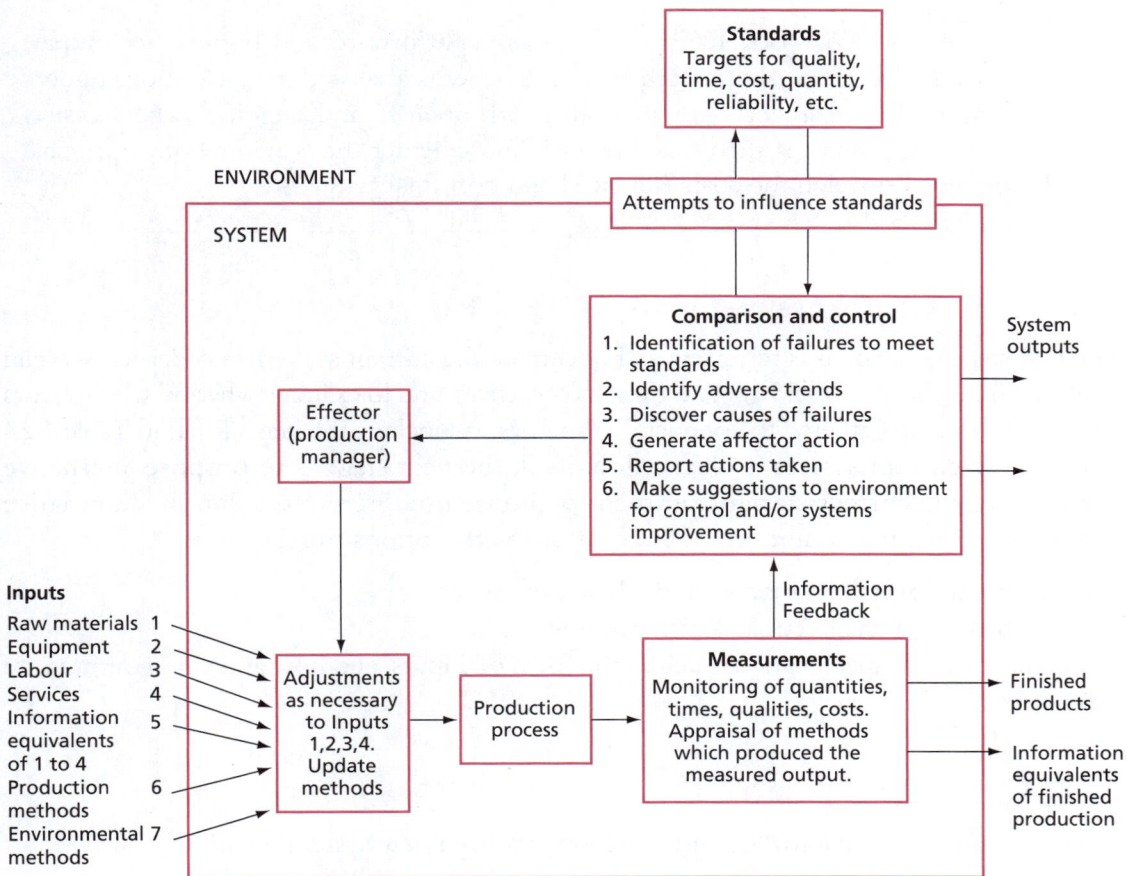

Figure 1.7 Production system example of GST. T. Lucey, Management Information Systems, 8th edition. Reprinted with permission of Taylor and Francis.

Once the current system has been clearly described, by means of interviews, questionnaires and data flow diagrams, the next stage is to propose alternative solutions to the current system, and then to choose one preferred solution.

The main aims of the systems analysis phase of development are as follows:

- Define the current problem in detail in order to understand it fully.
- Devise alternative design solutions that would solve the problem.
- Choose one of these alternatives and justify the choice, using techniques such as cost/benefit analysis, SWOT (a 2 × 2 cell matrix identifying strengths, weaknesses, opportunities and threats) and PESTLE analysis (see Table 2.4 later).
- Develop logical specifications for the selected option.
- Develop the physical requirements (file size and structure, screen layouts, response times, capacity, etc.).
- Develop a budget for systems development (including design, implementation and maintenance).

The final three elements of the list above generally form part of a single final document, produced by this stage and known as the approved systems analysis document. This sets out the scope, structure and functional requirements (in terms of finance, people, technology and equipment) of the final proposed solution.

> Note that: Cost/Benefit Analysis is a straightforward and popular technique used in decision making. Both costs and benefits are listed for the options under consideration. Financial costs are attached (both one off and ongoing) where easily apparent. A judgement is then made by deciding whether the benefits both financial and otherwise outweigh the costs (financial and non-financial).

1.9.1 Activities involved in systems analysis

The first stage of analysis is to review and document the current system, in order to ascertain how it operates, how it should operate given its objectives, and to examine why and where errors occur. Information gathered to conduct this analysis will include the items listed in Table 1.2.

Once the current system is clearly described, the next stage is to propose alternative solutions to the current system and then to choose one preferred solution. Alternative solutions will include a number of suggestions with options in relation to:

- which processes will be manual and which automated,
- which processes will occur at which event in the system,
- the final physical specifications such as the form of inputs, and how and when outputs are produced.

1.9.2 Requirements for a new system

Details of the functional (or logical) requirements for a new system include:

- Objectives and benefits of the new system.
- A narrative of each system function, including a description of work and data flow, user needs and interfaces between applications.

Table 1.2   Information-gathering techniques

Interviews	A range of staff (mainly direct users) to identify features and problems of current system
	Ascertain required features of new system
	Obtain direct response from users
Observations and narrative	Observe users at work on the system to see what actually happens (Note that there may be problems of users changing their behaviour.)
Documentation review	Review of existing system development documentation, manuals and narrative
Flowcharts and data flow diagrams	Allows graphical representation of the system, and aids clarification and understanding of movement of information and documentation
Questionnaires of users	Used to obtain a range of opinions
	Must be clearly set out and avoid ambiguities and misleading questions

- A description of each input, output and file in terms of volume, frequency, purpose, origin and major components.
- Specifications for features such as editing, file maintenance controls, backup and security.

These represent the 'logical' aspects of the system and concern its overall 'shape' and purpose.

Technical details required for a new system represent the 'physical' requirements, and include:

- Data storage (file structures, e.g. database)
- File size, access needs, update frequency, growth requirement
- Transaction volumes and growth, source
- Peripherals required (printers, scanners, etc.)
- Communications requirements
- Processing requirements (centralised, distributed, client/server)
- Output, distribution, formats
- Response times
- Layout of enquiry and input screens.

1.9.3   Systems selection and sourcing alternatives

Systems selection uses the new system's specifications obtained in the analysis phase to decide what resources will be necessary for the new system. Systems selection involves deciding upon a number of important issues, such as:

- the suitability of computer software to implement the logical specifications of the required system
- the suitability of computer hardware to satisfy the physical specifications of the required system (including the architecture, type, model, speed and capacity).

There are a number of alternative options for both hardware and software selection. Software can be purchased as a package externally or developed in-house. Hardware can be rented, leased or purchased. Table 1.3 identifies considerations involved in both internal and external sourcing options.

INFORMATION SYSTEMS

Table 1.3 Internal versus external hardware and software options

	Internal	External
Software features		
Quality	Must manage development effectively	contract must specify quality standards and performance criteria
Cost	Often costly	Usually less costly than internal
	Difficult to estimate if new software	More easy to determine final cost
Time	Need to wait for software to be developed – requires significant planning	If amendments not required – availability immediate
Compatibility	Should be completely compatible	May require amendments to fit in with current system
Support	Organisation must provide and perform training and maintenance programme	Vendor likely to support both own training and maintenance (built into contract)
Satisfaction of user needs	Maximum satisfaction as designed specifically for users	May not satisfy needs exactly – may require further tailoring to do so
Nature of development	Develop in-house if unique requirement	Purchase if industry standard
Hardware features		
Management	Organisation/user responsible for management	Managed by outside party
Support	Internal (IT department)	Available externally (for a fee)
Cost	Mostly fixed	Mostly variable
Satisfaction of user needs	Tailored – maximum satisfaction (within budget)	Less flexibility (more determined by cost budget)

Choice of supplier

If a decision is made to test the outside market or use an external supplier then an Invitation to Tender document (or request for proposals) is drawn up. This document invites potential suppliers to bid for provision of the hardware, software and specifications as proposed in the systems analysis phase. An organisation could ask one or numerous suppliers to submit a proposal, depending on reputation, convenience, past experience, time and cost, etc. The organisation may ask for very clear systems specifications. If the requirements are not fully understood or the organisation is wishing to rely on the supplier from their past experience and expertise, the request may be more general.

Exercise 1.9

What items do you think should be contained in a typical Invitation to Tender?

Solution

- A definition of the nature and scope of the request.
- Brief description of required hardware and software.
- Description of the logical functional specifications.
- Description of the physical specifications.

- System growth requirements.
- Criteria for supplier evaluation.
- Timescales.
- Financing alternatives.

Choice of computer

One of the more difficult choices for management actual relates to the actual purchase decision for hardware, and this will normally depend on a number of factors including:

The cost of the hardware. Cost will normally be justified in terms of benefits arising from the use of the computer. (Traditionally this has been expressed as staff time saved. More enlightened organisations take into account the value adding potential of the purchase).

The user requirements. This tends to be expressed in terms of applications to be used, processing power required, portability of the system, etc. More detailed requirements will normally have an impact on cost, so cost–benefit analysis is essential in determining the hardware that can be purchased.

Compatibility with existing systems.

Reliability and support of the manufacturer of the computer. Some manufacturers have a better reputation for producing high-quality computer systems, although reliability and price may have to be traded off in making the final decision.

The specification of the computer. The required specification will depend partly on the applications to be used both now and also in the next few years. It may also be worth purchasing a computer with larger RAM, hard disk and processing power than is necessary to allow for upgrades to software. (Almost every new release of software requires more computer processing power than the last, so purchasing a low-specification computer now may mean the computer will not be able to run some software coming onto the market in the near future.)

Appropriate built in security systems (examples include power-on passwords)

Availability of appropriate ports and expansion slots.

1.9.4 Systems design

Structured systems design converts the logical specifications into a workable design that can be implemented by the organisation. It includes outline designs, module designs, interface design, etc. Plans will also be designed at this stage for testing the system and training the users. The main aims of the systems design phase of development are as follows:

- To convert the specifications proposed in systems analysis into a reliable, workable design.
- To develop a test program to ensure completeness, accuracy and security of the system.
- To develop an implementation plan with testing procedures built in throughout, to ensure the integrity of the system throughout the whole life cycle.
- To develop a training programme and user manual to ensure full user support throughout and after the development process.

The final outcome from the systems design phase will be an approved systems design document, which should specify the following:

- Detailed descriptions and plans of the system's logical processes and functions, including a description of inputs, processes and outputs.
- An implementation plan, detailing a schedule of events, stages of implementation and a budget for each stage.
- A test plan, highlighting the test required at each stage of implementation, as each module of the system must be tested prior to operation.
- A training programme, outlining who needs to be trained and at what stage. Users will need to be trained prior to the final systems implementation, therefore it is important to plan in advance which users are critical to the operation of the system, and which parts of the system they must know in advance.
- A user manual, which will provide support to users during the training programme, and support users and non-users after implementation and training are complete.

1.10 Analysis and design documentation techniques

A number of tools and techniques used by systems analysts and designers have been developed in order to describe and summarise systems information. These have been particularly helpful in:

- Capturing the results of interviews or observations about a particular systems module,
- Communicating and documenting a description to others who may have different skills or levels of knowledge.

A number of these techniques are described below, specifically data flow diagrams, entity relationship modelling, entity life histories, and decision tables.

> Note that for examination purposes you will not be asked to reproduce these diagrams. You will however need to understand the range and nature of these techniques and their potential contribution to systems analysis and design.

1.10.1 Data flow diagrams

The purpose of data flow diagrams (DFD) is to describe the flow of data between entities, processes and data stores. Analysts use data flow diagrams to understand the flow of data into, out of, and within the organisation and to provide a basic understanding of how a system works. The highest-level DFD is called a context diagram. This defines the system boundary and shows how all information enters and leaves the system. DFDs can be used on both manual and computerised systems, and can be used to model the existing system in order to highlight any gaps in the current data flow or logic.

The four symbols used in data flow diagrams are as follows:

- *Data flow*. A data flow indicates the movement of data from one location in the system to another. A data flow could be a letter, a verbal message, a telephone call, an e-mail or a fax. It may or may not involve the transfer of a physical document.

- *External entity*. An external entity is either the destination or the source of data, which is external to the system. It may be people, groups or another organisation that either provide data to or receive data from the system.

- *Data store*. Data stores are where data is held within the system and which receive data flows. Examples of data stores are data files reports, documents and transaction records (manual or computerised).

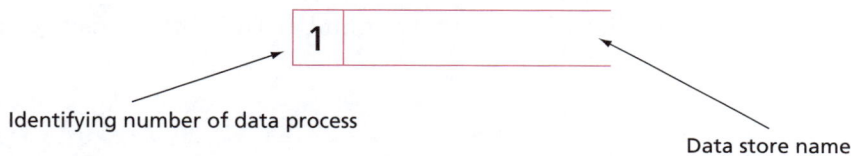

Identifying number of data process

Data store name

- *Data process*. Data processes are processing activities carried out from a data store or produce data for a data store (computerised or manual). A process simply uses data from storage and performs some kind of operation upon that data such as sorting, or recalculating the data, then sends the processed data back to storage or as output to an external entity.

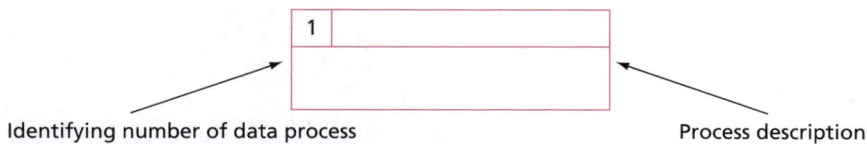

Identifying number of data process   Process description

1.10.2 Entity relationship modelling

Entity relationship modelling is a tool used within data analysis, mainly for database design, and is structured around three basic concepts:

- *An entity*. This is an item (person, product, activity, job, department or business) that is important to an organisation and about which information must be stored (e.g. customers, suppliers, employees, etc.)

INFORMATION SYSTEMS

- *Attributes.* An attribute is a fact or characteristic of an entity that the business records. For example, the attributes recorded about an employee could include name, address, qualifications, department and salary level.
- *Relationship.* These are the logical links between entities. The degree of relationship between entities may be one of three, as shown below:

One-to-one relationship (1:1) means that the entity only relates to one other entity.

That is, a student can only conduct one dissertation, and only one student completes a dissertation.

```
[ Student ]———conduct———[ A dissertation ]
```

One-to-many relationship (1:*N*) means that an entity can relate to one or more other entities.

One degree will contain many modules of study, a module is developed for one degree.

```
[ A degree ]———contains———<[ Modules ]
```

Many-to-many relationship (M:N) means that a number of entities may relate to a number of other entities.

```
[ Modules >———taught by———<[ Lecturers ]
```

A module is likely to be taught by a number of lecturers, and a lecturer can teach a number of modules.

✋ Exercise 1.10

Z Ltd has many departments containing a number of staff. Each department has only one manager, and these managers form the 'management board'. The managers are all salaried and therefore are on the monthly payroll. The other staff within the department can either receive a salary (monthly) or can be paid wages (received weekly).

Demonstrate the above using an ERM diagram.

☑ **Solution**

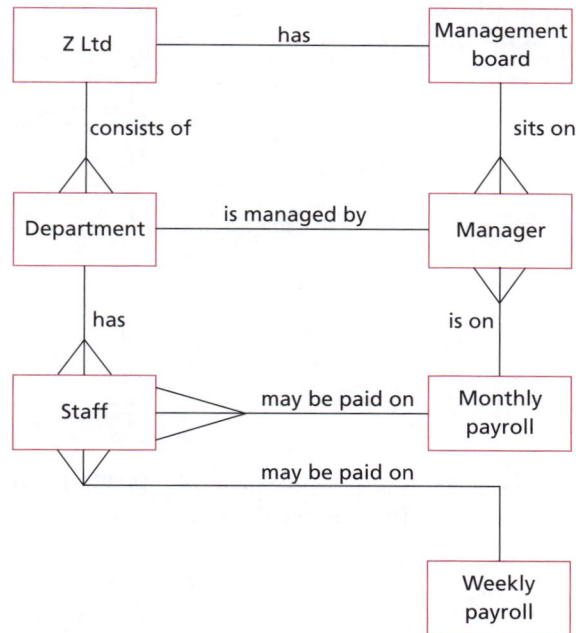

1.10.3   Entity life histories analysis

An entity life history (ELH) is a representation of the processes that occur in the life of each individual entity, and is designed to show the way in which information within a system changes over time. An ELH shows what happens to an entity between its creation and its termination. The entity can go through three phases of development: creation, amendment and termination. The important function of ELH analysis is the identification of the events and functions of an entity that cause the entity to change, rather than the analysis of the entity itself.

There are three main symbols used within ELH diagrams (see Figure 1.8): there is a rectangular box, within which can be placed either an asterisk or a small circle.

- The top level shows the entity itself, and at each subsequent level the boxes read from left to right (in order of create, amend, delete).
- At lower levels the boxes represent events that occur within the life of the entity.
- If an event affects an entity many times, an asterisk can show this.
- The boxes with small circles in the top right-hand corner indicate alternatives for particular events.

In the given example:

- The entity is the student
- At lower levels the boxes represent modules and examinations encountered by the student.
- The asterisks indicate that the student will study numerous modules during the life cycle. Similarly, testing will consist of a number of examinations.
- The boxes with small circles in the top right-hand corner indicate students may be learning or being tested but not at the same time. Similarly, for any examination, the student can either pass or fail, but not both.

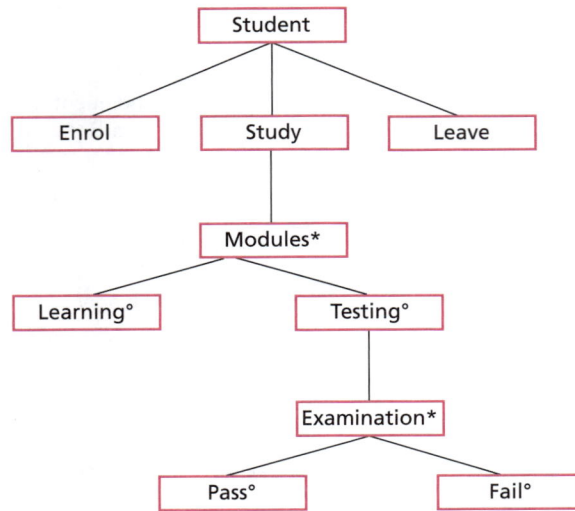

Figure 1.8   ELH for the entity 'student' (Ritchie et al., 1998). Reprinted by permission of Thomson Publishing UK.

1.10.4   Decision tables

Decision tables are used to describe the processing logic of a system. The most useful application of decision tables is in a situation where there may be a number of alternative conditions to evaluate.

A decision table contains four quadrants: the conditions quadrant, the conditions entry quadrant, the action quadrant and the action entry quadrant.

Conditions	Condition entry
Actions	Action entry

The decision table begins with the posing of a question. Starting with a basic example: do we offer credit facilities to our customers?

1. From the question, establish the conditions and then complete the condition quadrant of the table. The conditions need to be formulated into a question format that can be answered by yes or no answers only.

    Thus, for the above example, the conditions could be as follows:
    - Customers with orders under £100 do not receive credit facilities.

- Customers with orders valued between £100 and £249 receive credit for 1 year. Existing customers' rate of interest is 5 per cent per annum, and new customers' rate of interest is 7 per cent.
- Existing customers with orders above £250 are offered credit terms at 7 per cent for 1 year, but new customers with orders over £250 must undertake a credit check procedure.

Conditions Order under £100? Order between £100 and £249? Existing customer?	Condition entry
Actions	Action entry

2. The next stage is to fill in the condition entry quadrant. The condition entry should contain the answers in yes/no format that will cover every possible condition in the condition quadrant.

   The condition entry quadrant is completed in the form of 'columns' of combinations of yes and no answers. The number of columns is determined by 2 to the power of n, n being the number of questions in the 'conditions' quadrant.

   In this case, therefore, the number of columns is $2^3 = 8$.

3. The next stage is to methodically complete the condition entry quadrant by applying the 'halving rule'.

Conditions	1 2 3 4 5 6 7 8
Order under £100?	Y Y Y Y N N N N
Order between £100 and £249?	Y Y N N Y Y N N
Existing customer?	Y N Y N Y N Y N
Actions	Action entry

4. Now eliminate any impossible columns from the condition entry quadrant.

   In this question, the first two columns are impossible situations and can therefore be eliminated

Conditions	1	2	3	4	5	6	7	8
Order under £100?	Y	Y	Y	Y	N	N	N	N
Order between £100 and £249?	Y	Y	N	N	Y	Y	N	N
Existing customer?	Y	N	Y	N	Y	N	Y	N
Actions				Action entry				

5. The next stage is to complete the action quadrant, by listing the possible alternative actions that can be carried out.

Conditions	3	4	5	6	7	8
Order under £100?	Y	Y	N	N	N	N
Order between £100 and £249?	N	N	Y	Y	N	N
Existing customer?	Y	N	Y	N	Y	N
Actions						
No credit given						
Credit given 1 year at 5%			Action entry			
Credit for 1 year at 7%						
Credit check						

6. Now complete the action entry quadrant by considering each possible combination of conditions, and place an X in the action entry quadrant to indicate action to be taken.

Conditions	3	4	5	6	7	8
Order under £100?	Y	Y	N	N	N	N
Order between £100 and £249?	N	N	Y	Y	N	N
Existing customer?	Y	N	Y	N	Y	N
Actions						
No credit given	X	X				
Credit given 1 year at 5%			X			
Credit for 1 year at 7%				X	X	
Credit check						X

1.11 Managing systems implementation and operation

The implementation of Information System technologies can be highly disruptive. Poorly supervised projects may, without care, lead to the organisation operating in an ineffective manner. Managers must ensure that disruptions are kept to a minimum. Alternatively, one manager may need to supervise major IS projects to ensure their smooth implementation. Some of the issues associated with these situations are considered here.

The organisation will normally have agreed a programme of events for implementing the system and ensuring it is fully operational. Once operational a post-implementation review should be carried out to determine that the user's requirements (as originally identified) have been satisfied and that the development process has been carried out in an efficient and effective manner.

1.11.1 Systems implementation

Systems implementation is sometimes treated as a separate project involving formal project management techniques and the designation of a named project manager. An implementation schedule needs to be created, and the activities required for successful implementation carefully planned. The type and quantity of equipment that needs to be purchased and installed depends on the degree of change and type of system being implemented. Some projects could involve the complete replacement of the existing system with either a new mainframe or a large local area network, if this is the case:

- the site for the new equipment may need to be selected and prepared
- hardware will need to be ordered, delivered, installed and tested
- staff accommodation may also need to be selected, redesigned and fitted out
- standby equipment, such as generators and back-up computers, may also need to be installed
- software will need to be sourced, installed and tested.

1.11.2 Testing

A critical activity prior to changeover is testing the new system to ensure that it is working correctly before going live. The system programmers will develop a test plan for each program within the system. Testing must be carried out using test data that the program could be expected to handle when operational. Preparing for system testing includes the following activities:

- constructing test data
- identifying personnel involved in testing
- establishing a testing procedure and schedule
- developing criteria for measuring test results.

Ultimate users should be involved in the process. The tests should be of several kinds, and carried out possibly in the sequence indicated:

- Realistic tests present the system with a realistic example of the environment in which the system is to operate. This tests the system and the understanding and effectiveness of training of users. It also gives users confidence before they take over the system.

- Contrived tests present the system with as many unusual and unexpected events as possible, such as incorrect codes, wrong amounts, inappropriate commands, and so on. The intention is to see how the system reacts, and whether all conceivable anomalies have been catered for in the system.
- Volume tests present the system with a large volume of transactions to see how it reacts, particularly in operating and response times. This is a good test for database access concerns.
- The users undertake acceptance testing after all other systems testing is complete. It is designed to test the complete system, and to ensure that it is satisfactory from the users' point of view.

1.11.3   Training

Decisions will need to be made over the training needs of those who either operate the new system and those who manage operators. The training requirements of the new system users are likely to involve the following:

- Training in basic computer literacy and user skills if the system is a move from manual to computerised one.
- Learning how to use specific applications and modules quickly and in detail, examining important procedures, commands and data-entry requirements.
- On-the-job training, (i.e. training while staff are actively using the new system).
- Training updates as the users become more familiar with the system and require further knowledge and skills development or consolidation.

In addition to users, management training will also be necessary. Middle management is likely to require training on those elements of the system for which they are responsible. It is unlikely that they will require detailed user knowledge but they will need an understanding of the particular business issues and security and control features related to a particular system. Senior management will be trained in a less structured manner, with training being at a more general level. Training is likely to take the form of:

- short demonstrations of particular business-related features of the new system;
- DVD or video demonstrations to provide an overview;
- formal executive training seminars on systems features such as executive information systems.

1.11.4   Changeover approaches

Once the organisation is satisfied that all testing is complete and that file conversion has been carried out accurately, the next stage is to make the system operational. The main methods of changeover are described below. Selecting an appropriate changeover approach can greatly determine the success of conversion to the new system.

- The Parallel approach is probably the most common, whereby old and new systems operate together for a period of time, processing the same current data. The outputs of the two systems can then be compared to determine whether the new system is operating as expected and that no processing errors occurred. The advantage of this approach is that it allows for greater control, as the new system is not fully operational on its own until the organisation is satisfied that it is working correctly. The problems with parallel conversion is that new system implementation is delayed, possibly indicating a lack of confidence in the new system, and a requirement for greater resources to operate two systems instead of one. It is important that if this approach is taken the organisation decides upon a time limit for final changeover so that continual delays do not occur.

- Direct approach. This approach to conversion has the highest risk, as at a predetermined point in time the old system entirely ceases to operate. There is no opportunity to validate the new system's output with the old, so management must have complete confidence in the new system. This kind of changeover should be carried out during a slack period, such as a weekend or bank holiday, when minimum disruption is likely.

- The 'pilot approach' to changeover can be implemented in two ways:
  - A restricted data pilot involves taking one whole part of the complete system and running it as the new system. If this operates correctly, then remaining elements of the system can be transferred gradually. For example, one group of stock records could be transferred and run on the new system as a first stage.
  - A retrospective pilot, by comparison, involves operating the new system with old data already processed by the existing system. The results produced by the new system can be readily crosschecked with the results already processed by the existing system.

- The Phased or Modular approach involves gradual implementation and is often used in large systems projects or in organisations that are geographically dispersed. This will involve implementing one subsystem at a time or the whole system into one organisational unit at a time. For example, an organisation may implement a new accounting information system by first converting the sales order subsystem, then the customer accounts subsystem, then the purchase order subsystem, etc. Alternatively, an organisation may implement a complete system, but in one geographical location at a time, for instance the implementation of a new banking customer enquiry system branch by branch. Implementation at any branch could be direct or parallel. A modular approach allows pilot testing to be carried out on a system or subsystem prior to full implementation.

1.11.5 Systems operation

Once implemented, the organisation should periodically examine the system to ensure that it is continuing to operate as expected and that it still satisfies user needs. The organisation is likely to undertake two different types of systems review: post-implementation review and systems maintenance.

- The post-implementation review is a thorough review of a new system carried out soon after implementation, in order to establish whether the system is operating as expected and whether the user's needs are being satisfied (Table 1.4). Post-implementation should consider whether development objectives have been met. If not, the reasons should be established and future changes should be proposed.

  Post-implementation review should be carried out as soon as the system is fully operational and functional, possibly between 1 month and 1 year after changeover. It is important not to leave post-implementation review too late, as the advantage of a quick response to improvements may be lost.

Table 1.4 The goals of post-implementation review

Establish whether the new system satisfies user needs.

Evaluate the actual performance of the new system compared with anticipated performance.

Make recommendations for improvement if necessary.

Ascertain the quality of systems project management.

Recommend improvements to the systems development procedures if necessary.

Recommend improvements to project planning procedures by examining project costs and project team activities.

Review original cost/benefit analysis to ascertain if costs have been met/exceeded and whether perceived benefits have been achieved.

Suggest any other changes that might improve systems development and systems project management in the future.

The findings and recommendations from the post-implementation review should be formalised into a final report. This report may include the following:

- The system's goals and an analysis of how successfully the new system achieved these.
- A summary of the system's overall quality.
- A summary of those areas where the system is considered to be unsatisfactory, together with recommendations for improvement.
- An assessment of overall systems performance, (including throughput, number of errors, and processing costs, etc.)
- An assessment of the quality of the project management and recommendations where necessary.
- A cost/benefit analysis comparing the costs and benefits identified at the feasibility study stage, with actual costs and benefits.
- A summary of recommendations for improving the performance of the system and improving future systems development projects.

● Systems maintenance can be performed in response to specific user needs or as a result of ongoing systems development. Systems maintenance is the repair, correction or further enhancement of systems once in operation. The goals of systems maintenance are to:

- ensure systems changes are carried out quickly and effectively;
- ensure that systems changes are appropriate to the organisation's current processing environment;
- perfect systems maintenance and development procedures by collecting and using information about systems change requirements.

Systems maintenance can take several forms:

Corrective maintenance relating to the correction of residual faults. This process corrects errors within the existing system, normally identified as a result of some problem occurring. Corrective maintenance is reactive by nature and its main function is to ensure that the system can continue to operate. It has been estimated that typically this represents 20 per cent of all maintenance time.

Adaptive (or adaptative) maintenance is carried out in order to adjust applications to reflect changing business operations or the wider environment. This type of maintenance is unlikely to immediately follow implementation, rather it is likely to be a more mid- to long-term maintenance process. It has been estimated that typically this represents 20 per cent of all maintenance time.

Perfective and preventative maintenance that represents a broader form of maintenance than corrective or adaptive maintenance. Processes aim to prevent possible failures in the future or to make the system more perfect, possibly in terms of efficiency.

1.11.6 Managing systems implementation: an overview

On the subject of implementing new financial systems software, Denton (2002) makes the following points:

'It isn't difficult to find presentations, articles and conferences that tell you what financial systems do. The tendency has always been to major on the functionality of these systems – yet this is only part of the story for decision-makers.

Whether the new system is replacing existing software or being installed at a 'green field' site, the actual installation process is the key to success.

And while the process of deploying a piece of financial software may vary in terms of time, resource and general upheaval – depending on the type of system and the size and complexity of the organisation – the steps that you need to go through are almost always the same.

These steps are:

- *Justification, definition and planning of the project.* This should be concerned particularly with whether the business value of acquiring the new system has been adequately justified.
- *Requirement analysis* is concerned with the degree of customisation of the software in order to meet business requirements, and the change of business process due to introducing the new system.
- *Implementation*: A number of factors could be critical during the implementation stage, these include:
  - executive support
  - user and manager engagement
  - changes in the behaviour of users
  - aligning the new system and business process
  - education and training
  - data migrating
  - systems changeover
  - user support
  - system evaluation.
- *Support*: Monitoring system performance when financial system transfers to live operation, and user support.

If these steps are properly executed there will be successful implementation'.

1.12 Post-implementation challenges

Occasionally implementation produces difficulties and challenges for the manager of a human rather than technical kind! Implementation may be met with employee resistance either direct or passive. Inevitably there may be a variety of reasons for this and every individual case is unique. Reasonable speculation as the likely reasons can, however, be made in the most general of terms. These reasons could be:

- the chosen methods of implementation may be felt to be inappropriate.
- there may have been faulty communication.
- there may have been a lack of adequate training (see earlier).

Exercise 1.11

Suggest potential problems that might arise if there is either inadequate or inappropriate user training with the introduction of new systems.

Solution

Problems

- Fear of new system's effect on jobs
- Fear of the unknown
- Reluctance to use the new system
- Errors in processing (either deliberate or accidental)
- Slower processing due to a lack of confidence, unfamiliarity or covert sabotage
- Staff turnover or increased absence arising from avoidance of the new system.

Training methods may include the following:

- Attending training courses (either provided externally by systems consultants, or internally by experts and trainers).
- Reading the user manual.
- Online computer-based training (possibly using disk- or web based training packages).
- Help lines and dedicated support teams.
- Lectures and discussion forums held internally for users to discuss problem areas.

Resistance in the wake of the implementation of an IS system should be acknowledged as little different by nature to the resistance met by implementation of any form of organisational change. In all cases there needs to be an anticipation of difficulties beforehand and tactics evolved to deal with these. Kotter, Schlesinger and Sathe (1992) identified six main methods of exercising influence to overcome resistance, namely:

- education and communication
- participation and involvement
- facilitation and support
- negotiation and agreement
- manipulation and co-optation
- explicit and/or implicit coercion.

It is likely that the managers facing the problem of resistance to the new IS system could use their individual judgment and apply one or more of these tactics to good effect. (Ethically there are concerns about the application of the final two tactics in this listing.)

If the manager discovers that there are instances of non-usage of the systems this might be interpreted as being a result of a number of reasons:

- An expression of resistance. In this case appropriate influencing measures should be applied (see above).
- A lack of confidence in the new system, in which case enhanced communication is required and system modification should be applied where appropriate.
- Employees may lack confidence in their abilities to cope with the new system. In this case training and other support mechanisms should be addressed.

INFORMATION SYSTEMS

It is interesting to note that just as change management thinking can be successfully applied to an IS situation so the use of information systems can assist in change management ('IT-enabled transformation'). This is particularly so where technological change can form a focus for a significant organisational change including its culture. Chapter 6 deals with these and other associated issues in some detail.

1.13 Information systems and the organisational 'big picture'

IS must not be considered in isolation: it represents only one of an organisation's functional area. As such it should complement and support other areas including marketing, finance, human resourcing and operations. Examples of IS contributions in supporting other organisational roles includes:

- The development of a DBMS to support all functional areas
- Use of the Intranet in supporting operations and meeting customer support needs
- Use of the Internet to support marketing activity and providing enhanced value to customers and Suppliers
- Online technology-supported learning as part of HR training and development efforts.

Later in this study system, reference is drawn to a number of these potential contributions.

1.13.1 Information systems alignment with corporate aspirations

When taking a management perspective of the IS function, one should remember that the main customers IS normally interfaces with directly are internal customers. This implies that it serves others in the organisation who serve the true 'external' customer. This means that the function should take trouble to understand the needs of their colleagues and seek to satisfy these through policies, practices and developments.

Undoubtedly, effective information management through IT solutions can be a source of organisational strength. It can help support as well as transform business organisations to enable them to operate effectively and competitively in a sometimes hostile environment. There is an essential role to be played in automating business processes, finding networking business and providing information for management decision-making and planning.

Cohesive IS strategies are developed in many organisations and these should be consistent with and contribute to the achievement of corporate aspirations. In terms of overall corporate performance, above all the benefits of IT systems should outweigh the costs associated with them.

Clegg (2003) offers some valuable reflections on developing strategies as follows:

- An information strategy is a plan for ensuring that information is appropriate, accurate, available and timely: in short effective.
- Do not confuse information strategy with Information Technology: Technology is just the delivery option (it is feasible to have a viable IS strategy without computers), quality of information is more important than technology.
- Do not leave information strategy to experts: the business managers know what type of information they need.

He also points out that organisations must choose between two opposite approaches to strategy development:

1. Top-down, where the starting point is the organisation, and the information it needs to operate effectively
2. Bottom-up, where the starting point involves taking stock of all the information currently in the organisation, and then overcoming duplication and inaccuracies.

1.13.2 Managing outsourced solutions

The organisation corporately holds certain values and broad policy ideas. For some there may be an enthusiasm for outsourcing while others may feel strongly that services should be retained in-house. Advocates of outsourcing may point to cost savings whilst proponents may argue that additional monitoring mechanisms might be costly in themselves.

Systems development does not necessarily have to be carried out by in-house development staff. Organisations may give responsibility for control and management of their information systems to external organisations. The problem with 'outsourcing' is that the external vendor may not understand the business process, or the organisation may lose control over its information systems. It also runs the risk that cost could be high, as the vendors may charge extra services to keep updating technology. Therefore careful planning and monitoring will be required to ensure that systems development objectives are achieved by the external organisation.

Differing management problems are associated with in-house and vendor solutions. In-house, the difficulties tend to centre on the assembly and maintenance of an adequately skilled and motivated workforce to deliver IS solutions. The emphasis for outsourced facilities tends to focus on contract compliance and adherence to predetermined standards.

1.14 Summary

This chapter has covered a number of information system topic areas and relationships between IS and other management functions within an organisation should now be apparent. A managerial perspective has been taken throughout in dealing with issues such as the features and operations of commonly used information technology hardware and software, implementation and running of the information system. The significance and scope of office automation as well as computer networks and DBMS has been emphasised, in addition to the likely challenges arising from new system implementation.

References and further reading

Anon (2006) It'll never fly: Blogging, *Management Today*, April, p. 12.
Berens, C. (2006) Windows of opportunity, *Financial Management* (UK), November, Vol. 12, No. 5.
Clegg, B. (2003) Deciding factors? *Professional Manager*, September.

Denton, A. (2002) Stepping out – a four-step guide to implementing new financial systems, *Conspectus*, April.

Kotter, J. P., Schlesinger, L. A. and Sathe, V. (1992) *Organization: Text, Cases, and Readings on the Management of Organizational Design and Change* (3rd edn), Homewood, IL: Irwin.

Johnson, G., Scholes, K. and Whittington, R. (2005) *Exploring Corporate Strategy: Text and Cases* (7th edn), Financial Times, Prentice Hall.

Long, L. and Long, N. (2004) *Computers* (12th edn), Harlow: Pearson Education.

Lucey, T. (2004) *Management Information Systems* (9th edn), Thomson Learning.

Meall, L. (2004) Automation nation, *Accountancy*, March, pp. 74–75.

Mullins, L. J. (2005) *Management and Organisational Behaviour* (7th edn), Harlow: Financial Times, Prentice Hall

Phillips, P. (2000) E-business: what is it and does it matter to accountants? *Management Accounting*, February.

Pesola, M. (2004) Network protection is a key stroke, *Financial Times,* March 8.

Ritchie, B., Marshall, D. and Eardley, A. (1998) *Information Systems in Business*, (2nd edn) Thomson Learning.

Revision Questions

This first question is relevant to the learning outcome *explain the features and operation of commonly used information technology hardware and software.* While the scenario seems quite simple, it gives you the chance to think about the hardware and software requirements without having to be too concerned about the company itself.

? Question 1

The S Company operates 86 retail supermarkets selling a wide variety of food to the general public. Each supermarket maintains its own computerised stock system, with all deliveries and sales being recorded in the online and real-time computer system.

   The computer system is updated for goods being sold from one of the 30 point-of-sale checkouts. Customers take their purchases to the checkout where an assistant records the purchases into the computer system using a unique bar code located on each product. Payments for the food purchased can be made by cash, cheque, or by debit or credit card.

   The main computerised database provides real-time stock balances for all goods sold in each supermarket. Both deliveries and sales of goods are reflected in the stock balances as they occur.

Requirements
(a) Explain the computer input and output devices that are required at each point-of-sale terminal.
(b) Explain the computer hardware that will be required to maintain the online database of goods in stock. **(16 marks)**

? Question 2

This question is relevant to the learning outcome *evaluate, from a managerial perspective, new hardware and software and assess how new systems could benefit the organisation.*

Requirement
Describe the most important properties that a database system should have in order to be successful. **(10 marks)**

This question is relevant to the learning outcome *recommend strategies to minimise the disruption caused by introducing IS technologies*. This question investigates some of the problems that can occur during a systems changeover. As with any question, read the scenario carefully to identify the key problems and then explain these in the answer.

? Question 3

The R company is about to implement a new management information system. This MIS will replace an existing system, although this provides little more than a daily summary of the information maintained on the transaction processing system. The new MIS will still access the TPS data, but will provide more comprehensive analysis including historical statistics and limited comparison to prices charged by competitors.

The system will be implemented by direct changeover, because the network servers have insufficient capacity to maintain both systems on the hard disks. The installation will also take place over a weekend to minimise disruption to managers. The system developers believe that the new MIS is so intuitive that managers will be able to use it straight away.

Requirement
Identify and discuss the risks with the implementation of the new MIS.   **(10 marks)**

? Question 4

4.1   Bar code readers, scanners and keyboards are examples of:

    (A)   hardware input devices
    (B)   software input devices
    (B)   systems processing devices
    (D)   hardware processing devices.   **(2 marks)**

4.2   Local area networking is used for:

    (A)   communication between computers within a limited geographical area
    (B)   structuring an organisation within a division or business unit
    (B)   exchange of information through a trade association or region
    (D)   managing a complex operational issue by global interface with trade associations and professional bodies.   **(2 marks)**

4.3   Many large organisations have established a computer intranet for the purpose of:

    (A)   providing quick, effective and improved communication amongst staff using chat rooms
    (B)   providing quick, effective and improved communication to staff
    (C)   providing quick, effective and improved communication to customers
    (D)   providing quick, effective and improved ordering procedures in real time.
    (2 marks)

4.4   The main advantages of a database management system include:
    (A)   the development of separate data sources
    (B)   unlimited access and open communication
    (C)   end user flexibility and a devolution of responsibility
    (D)   data integrity and elimination of duplication.   **(2 marks)**

4.5 An expert system describes:

(A) a database built upon past knowledge and experience
(B) a powerful off-the-shelf software solution
(C) an online library of operating advice and handy hints
(D) an electronic version of working papers assembled by the research and development
department.   **(2 marks)**

Each of the sub-questions below require a brief written response and are worth 4 marks each. This response can be in note form and should not exceed 50 words.

4.6 Explain why a phased system change-over for a computer development might help employees cope better with technological change.   **(4 marks)**

4.7 Describe the main benefits of in-house developed information systems.   **(4 marks)**

Solutions to Revision Questions

✓ **Solution 1**

Guidance and common problems

- Ensure completeness of answer. Even though the system may be familiar to you, imagine yourself at a supermarket checkout, and think what input and output devices there are.
- Check that hardware is explained in section (b) and not software. Remember the need to focus on specific sections of a computer system as required by the question. As usual, there is a need to plan your answer to check that the content is appropriate before writing it out in full.

(a) Input devices required are:
- *Bar-code scanner* to read the codes on each item being purchased. This will provide quick and accurate input, which is essential where many relatively low-value products are being purchased. The scanner needs to make some form of 'beep' to confirm that the input has been accepted.
- *Keyboard* allowing both alphabetical and numeric input. Some bar codes may be damaged and so the scanner will not be able to read them. Similarly, the computer system itself may not have been updated for specific goods and so no match for the bar code will be found. In these situations, manual input of the product will be required, either entering the bar code number by hand or recording the error in the transaction and entering all information on the product.
- *Magnetic-card reader* to validate credit- and debit-card purchases online. The supermarket will need to check that the card being used by the customer is valid. Most supermarkets have 'online referral' to the banking system to confirm the card is valid and check that the customer has sufficient funds to purchase the goods.

Output devices required are:
- *VDU* or smaller dot matrix display to confirm details of the product purchased and its price. It is important to check that the bar code on the product actually relates to that good. With product details displayed on the VDU, both the customer and the checkout operator can check the product being purchased is the one recorded on the shop's database.
- *Printer* to provide for the customer a list of the goods purchased. The customer may need a list of food purchased for later reference and checking to ensure that

prices charged are correct, etc. A specialised printer is therefore required to provide this list. The printer may also incorporate printing of credit-card receipts, as noted below.

- In some locations, a separate printer is needed to produce a credit-card receipt for the customer. Although the credit card will be validated online, a customer signature is still required to confirm the transaction. Some form of receipt is needed to print out the total amount charged and the credit-card details, prior to the customer signing it to confirm the sale. A second copy will also be needed for the customer most simply by providing another copy of the credit-card receipt.

(b) The computer hardware required is:
- *A large hard disk.* The hard disk will need to be large enough to store the operating system software, the online real-time stock system, the data files being used and the daily transaction files as well as additional temporary working space to minimise processing time.
- *Random access memory.* An online real-time system will require a significant amount of RAM due to the intensive processing that will take place. Having 30 online terminals for sales, and an undisclosed number for recording purchases, will also add to the RAM requirement. The minimum RAM is likely to be in the region of 256 megabytes.
- *Cabling.* High-volume/speed cabling will be needed to connect the different items of hardware together. Cables should be capable of running at 100 megahertz at least, due to the high volumes of data being moved around. Appropriate routers and other hardware will also be required.
- *Backup device.* While not strictly necessary for the day-to-day running of the stock system, an appropriate backup device will be required. Given the importance of the data, offsite backup will be needed and possibly disk mirroring during the day to ensure all transactions are backed up as they occur.

☑ Solution 2

The essential feature of a database approach is that data is regarded as a central resource of a company. Data, like other assets, should be owned and maintained for the use and benefit of the business as a whole. To be successful, a database system must have the following properties:

- Data independence – the data must be defined and exist independently of the programs that use it. The logical definition of data in the database is different from the physical organisation and storage on the disks – physical independence. The logical data in an application is viewed from the perspective of that application, this is, different from the logical definition of data in the database – logical independence. As the data and programs are independent of each other, either can be amended without changing the other.
- The database must be capable of being shared. Different users, using different application programs, must be able to access the same data, often at the same time.
- Duplication of data and data redundancy can be reduced as only one entry per record or transaction is needed in the database. Data inputs may also be reduced as data is only required to be input once to update all files.
- Integrity of the data in the database must be maintained. Controls need to be implemented to ensure that the data remains accurate at all times.

- The database should be flexible and able to develop or evolve with the organisation. The database needs to change and develop to meet the future needs of the company.
- The database should be able to connect to web server to support dynamic e-commerce transaction.

✅ Solution 3

Guidance and common problems

Having found the problems in the question scenario, remember to provide an explanation to show why these areas may result in the new MIS failing. The examiner is looking for direct and practical comments, so keep your answer to the point and explain clearly what the problems are and what can be done to resolve them.

The risks associated with implementing the new MIS will include:

Lack of user acceptance testing. There is no indication that users have actually been involved with the system development or even seen the new system prior to installation. If users have not been part of the system development testing, then they may not accept it when it goes online. (People like to be involved in the development process rather than have new systems imposed on them). Lack of user involvement also carries the problem that the system may not meet user requirements, which will add to the temptation for users to reject it.

At the very least, some user representatives should review the system to make sure it does meet their requirements and provides information in a format that they can understand.

No parallel run. The changeover between the old and new MIS will be direct; that is, one system will no longer be used and the new is made available immediately, so there is no time when both systems are available. While this approach has some benefits in terms of staff time and costs, there are risks that errors may occur in transferring data between the two systems. The errors will be difficult to identify because the output from the systems cannot be compared. This may have significant effects for R, for example transferring the price of a product incorrectly will give a wrong comparison with another company. An incorrect price adjustment could be made to R's product causing it to be sold below cost.

Providing a parallel run will be appropriate to ensure that data is completely and accurately transferred.

Direct implementation. It is not clear from the question whether there has been any testing on the company's hardware systems. If this has not been carried out, then stopping one system and implementing another may have a significant negative impact on the company if the new system does not work.

If there is insufficient server space, then R must consider purchasing or hiring a duplicate server to test the new MIS in parallel with the old to confirm that it does work correctly.

Lack of training and user documentation. The suggestion that the new system is easy to use may be correct. However, even if this is the case, it is quite possible that users will not be aware of the most effective or efficient method of using the system. Significant amounts of time can be lost through 'trial and error' as managers attempt to obtain information without detailed guidance on how to do this.

Some form of training, or at least provision of user documentation, is advisable. This will show to users that their requirements have been considered and will enforce good system use from the beginning. Trying to amend work methods at a later date will be difficult as managers will tend to see training at this stage as a waste of time.

✅ Solution 4

4.1 (A)

4.2 (A)

4.3 (B)

4.4 (D)

4.5 (A)

4.6 A phased system changeover:

- allows employees time to adjust
- appears less pressured and stressful
- appears less extreme potentially reducing resistance
- allows time for retraining & staff displacement, and so on to be addressed.

4.7 In-house development benefits:

- Information system is likely to match the needs of users more closely (greater staff acceptance/involvement?).
- Development team is local and immediately available.
- Greater focus on progress/success?
- Development team gets user acceptance more readily?

2

Marketing

Marketing

2

2.1 Introduction to marketing

This chapter provides some basic frameworks and ideas to help appreciate the importance of marketing within the business environment. It describes the marketing tools an organisation will need to compete successfully in contemporary, dynamic and often chaotic markets.

> **!** An excellent source to enhance your understanding of this subject can be found by accessing the UK's Chartered Institute of Marketing (CIM) web site www.cim.co.uk.

Newspapers and other media tend to use 'marketing' as an alternative to selling, advertising, or retailing. Marketing is however a much broader concept embracing all these areas plus many others besides. Marketing is in evidence all around us, from the packaging on the products we buy, to our recognition of companies through their logos and symbols, or the television advertisements we watch. The choices we make as consumers are likely to be shaped in some way by marketing. So what exactly is marketing?

The UK's Chartered Institute of Marketing (CIM) when answering this question suggest that many organisations either knowingly or unknowingly engage in marketing to some degree:

Think about what you do. You probably make a particular effort to know your customers well. Your instincts tell you that getting to know what your customers want on an individual basis and giving it to them is what will keep you in business. You know that you can't stand still, and that you need to improve and extend existing products and sometimes develop new ones. If this description rings true, then your marketing activity closely fits the classical definition of marketing

CIM defines Marketing as:

> 🔑 the management process responsible for identifying, anticipating and satisfying customer requirements profitably.

This definition acknowledges the importance of the customer, their requirements and the careful planning processes needed to achieve the organisations goals. It follows that marketing is a business activity that should be at the core of any organisation. Marketing is relevant to any business irrespective of its size or nature of operation. Kotler (2003) is not alone in believing it is key to achieving organisational goals.

It is all about getting the right product or service to the customer at the right price, in the right place, at the right time. Business history and current practice both remind us that without proper marketing, companies cannot get close to customers and satisfy their needs. And if they don't, a competitor surely will.

(CIM, 2004)

2.2 Marketing as a business philosophy

Satisfying customers is at the heart of marketing. Who then assumes responsibility for this important function? Possibly the marketing department or the sales force? True, such personnel can have an influence on customer satisfaction, but marketing as a philosophy is wider than this narrow group of employees. Employees outside the marketing department or sales force can also play an important role in determining customer satisfaction.

Marketing is more than a range of techniques that enables the company to determine customer requirements, rather it is a shared business ethos. The marketing concept is a philosophy that places customers central to all organisational activities. The long-term strategies of an organisation might be centred on profit maximisation, market share growth, or growth in real terms but none of this can be achieved without satisfying customers. Without customers there would be no business.

Organisations who put customer needs first and provide products and services that meet these needs in this way are said to be 'market orientated'. Some organisations however still reject or ignore such a philosophy. For these organisations making products assumes prime concern followed by an attempt to 'get customers'.

Boddy and Paton (2002) summarised alternative organisational philosophies into four categories. These are given here with the main benefits and disadvantages of each:

- Product-orientated organisations have a main focus of product features. This could result in the production of goods with high quality features. Little or no research to identify a demand for the product beforehand means that the organisation risks their products not selling in sufficient numbers.

- Production-orientated organisations have a main focus of production efficiency and low costs. Production levels and process changes have no regard to the customer. This means that either too much may be produced (and left unsold) or customers might associate low cost with low quality leading to lower sales.
- Sales-orientated organisations have a main aim of selling their good or service. This implies the need for a keen sales force with clear targets and a focus on short-term cash flow. Ethicaly questionable, high-pressure sales techniques might not be sustainable longer term as there may be adverse publicity and past customers maybe left feeling dissatisfied.
- Marketing-orientated organisations have a main focus of the customer and their demands. The benefit is that products offered are determined by consumer demands. Although this may seem preferable it should be conceded that there might be a need for a heavy initial investment of time and effort in achieving such an orientation.

Exercise 2.1
Reflection

Under which market conditions could product orientated organisations best succeed?

Solution

Where demand far exceeds supply and the consumer is not discerning due to the shortage of this product or service. Twenty years or so ago this was particularly true within the former Eastern bloc countries where queues formed to buy food and goods irrespective of quality. In some cases those queuing did not know the precise goods they were queuing for!

Stages in the evolution of marketing can be identified within the UK linked to periods in history:

- *The production era.* The rapid growth in production from factories towards the end of the Industrial Revolution gave rise to this thinking. Rising standards of living fuelled demand, but customer preferences were not accounted for, instead output was maximised wherever possible.
- *The sales era.* 'The depression' due to the downturn in the world economy through to the immediate post Second World War period provided a background. In order to stay competitive firms needed to *sell* goods rather than just *produce* them. A growing expertise in sales techniques developed including more attention being paid to advertising.
- *The marketing era.* When in the early 1960s demand for goods was matched by supply, organisations began to try to better understand their customer base, and the use of segmentation and differentiation strategies heralded a new era. (Segmentation and differentiation as topics are dealt with later in this chapter.)

Exercise 2.2
For reflection

Does the pace of technological change and heightened customer demand mean another era is about to unfold?

2.3 The marketing mix

It is obvious from the preceding sections that successful marketing strategies and plans can only be crafted with a clear focus on satisfying (meeting) customer needs and wants. Customers must be central to everything an organisation does.

Approximately 30 years ago it became accepted that in this quest for a customer driven approach, organisations had four basic marketing dimensions. These became known more commonly as known as the Four Ps;

- Product (or service)
- Price
- Promotion
- Place (distribution).

Marketing guru Philip Kotler would add at least one, P, that of people, and more recently other factors have been added to this basic listing. However, the Four Ps are used in the following sections as a starting point to discuss marketing tools, other Ps including people are dealt with later in the chapter.

The term 'marketing mix' was first applied at the Harvard Business School, USA to explain the range of marketing decisions and elements that must be balanced to achieve maximum impact. The Marketing mix represents the 'tool kit' for marketing practitioners who attempt to 'blend' the four Ps. The apportionment of effort, the precise combination, and the integration of all four elements to achieve organisational objectives represent an organisation's own marketing programme or 'mix'. The marketer therefore is a mixer of these ingredients, a mix of procedures and policies to produce a profitable enterprise.

Kotler and Lane Keller (2006) define the marketing mix (Table 2.1) as: '. . . the set of controllable variables and their levels that the firm uses to influence the target market.'

The manager must address these fundamentals areas, so that all 'Four Ps' combine to emphasise marketing as a total system of coordinating organisational activity focused on satisfying customer needs. For the majority of private sector organisations the aim of marketing is, generally speaking, synonymous with the overall purpose of maximising financial returns. There are clearly a wide variety of possible combinations of marketing variables which management can select. Inevitably some combinations will earn greater financial returns than others. The crucial combination of factors comprising the marketing mix is therefore of high significance.

Table 2.1 The variables of the marketing mix

Variable	Examples
Product	Features, quality, durability, design, brand name, packaging, range, after-sales service, optional extras, guarantees, warranties
Place	Distribution channels, distribution coverage, the types of transportation vehicle, locations of sales outlets, the arrangements of sales areas, stock levels, warehouse locations
Promotion	Advertising, personal selling, publicity, sales promotion
Price	Levels, discounts, allowances, payment terms, credit policy, etc.

The 'design' of the marketing mix will normally be decided on the basis of management intuition and judgment, together with information provided by market research. It is particularly important that management understand the image of the product in the eyes of the customer. There are number of different considerations when formulating the marketing mix. For instance:

- The time of year might be relevant to the manufacturers of seasonal products: indeed most products are seasonal to some extent.
- Altering one component impacts upon another, for instance the quality of advertising may need to be raised if the selling price of products is increased.
- A manufacturer may need a marketing mix for the end consumer, and an additional mix for the retailers who they actually sell the product to.
- The mix will change as the marketing environment changes. The growth of Internet stores and warehouses has persuaded some booksellers like W. H. Smith to switch to an internet café approach in some of its stores.

The 'Four Ps' are now discussed in more detail including the specific tools and techniques associated with each.

2.4   Product

Product embraces product quality and durability, product design, brand name, logo, packaging, the product range, after-sales service, optional extras, guarantees and warranties, etc. (Product in this context also includes associated service). Marketing a product involves product design, concept testing and product launch. For service rather than product based organisations this category includes the nature of the service including its key features.

The starting point should be of course being not with the product, but instead with the customer. By understanding their needs and wants an appropriate product or service can be developed to fulfill these desires. Potential customers need to be satisfied with an organisation's product or service or they are unlikely to buy it. This means that the product or service must fulfill their need and should clearly be of a quality that fits its purpose. This final sentence has two implications for the organisation:

- it needs systems to monitor customer perceptions of the product or service,
- product quality must meet the 'fitness for purpose' test. Developing a sophisticated software package with many applications might be inappropriate for a market that just wants to write business letters (an electronic typewriter might suffice).

It is worth noting a key marketing concept, namely that the customer does not so much buy a product as satisfies a need or a want. This is important for the organisation to understand so that it can concentrate on the *benefits* of its product rather than its *features*.

Useful questions from a marketing point of view include:

- Are customers satisfied with existing products and services?
- Do these products or services fulfill their future needs?
- How are competitors addressing themselves to the same questions?
- Can competitors fulfill customers' future needs?

✋ Exercise 2.3

For reflection

As customers buy the benefits of a product not its features identify a recent purchase you have made and consider both its features and benefits.

In terms of generic competitive strategy, Porter (1980) argued that an organisation could compete on the basis of price or by differentiating its product from the competition in some way. It might then choose to address itself to the whole market or just a narrower part (segment) of that total market. If the chosen competitive strategy is differentiation clearly the features of the product assume added significance as part of the marketing mix.

2.4.1   The product life cycle

Classically marketing explains products as passing through a cycle of life. Most products are said to have a life cycle, which has distinct stages:

- *Introduction*. An organisation starts to produce and sell a new product. Initially, demand is low. Heavy advertising or other selling costs are needed to make customers aware of the product. High prices can be charged, because the product is new and supply is limited. Only a limited distribution network exists for the product. There is likely to be a single or limited product range to avoid confusing the customer and there will be a need to induce product recognition amongst potential customers.
- *Growth*. Demand for the product builds. Product design improves as producers gain production and marketing experience. Advertising and sales promotion are still important. The distribution network expands. Competition between rival producers intensifies. The most significant feature of this stage is increasing complexity as rivals enter the market and the range of products widens as producers seek to attract customers from each other with novel features. The marketing focus switches to seeking to differentiate the firm's product and brand in the minds of customers. Prices fall, but profits improve because of the higher volume of sales.

  Some marketers consider that an addition phase (shakeout) occurs when sales growth begins to dip and market is saturated by providers. The weakest providers are 'shook' out and exit the business.
- *Maturity*. This is the longest stage in the life cycle of most successful products. This is where purchases settle down into a pattern of repeat or replacement purchasing. For consumer goods food these may be habitual purchases. For durables such as televisions changing technical features, fashions and wearing-out of old product will influence the frequency of repurchase. Demand has reached its limit. In general, prices fall. A good distribution network has built up, and advertising costs per dollar, euro or pound of sales are low. Further advertising, product design changes, and segmentation can extend the maturity phase of a product's life.
- *Decline*. The product declines into obsolescence as technically superior alternatives replace it. The existence of such alternatives will cause sharp profit reductions among producers of the product. Many firms will have already found alternative industries, while those remaining will be looking for an orderly way to exit the industry. As demand starts to fall, so too do prices (and profits). Eventually the product disappears from the market.

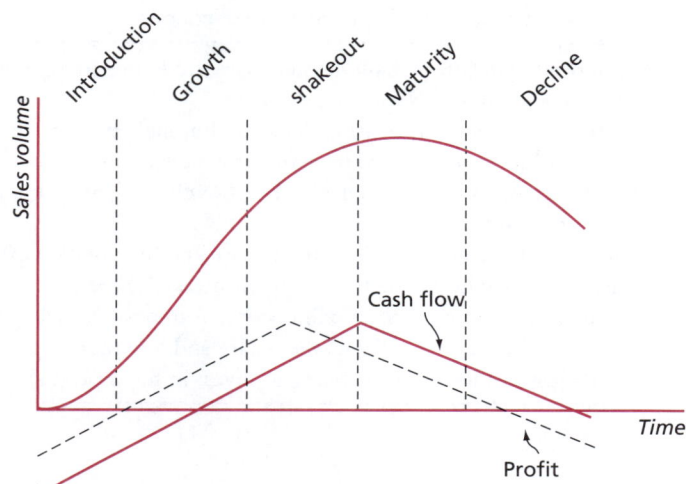

Figure 2.1 The product life cycle

The product life cycle (Figure 2.1) can be used to help determine appropriate strategies for the organisation and help inform decisions over investment in products.

Exercise 2.4

What are the practical problems associated with the model?

Solution

- It is not possible to forecast precisely where the product is in practice.
- It assumes that all the stages are inevitable yet certain products (e.g. Kellogg's cornflakes) have existed in their present form for many which years seem to disprove this.
- It considers a product singly and not as part of a portfolio of products.

The marketing mix will change over time as the product goes into different stages of its 'life'. When a product is in its 'growth' stages of life, the marketing mix might emphasise the development of sales outlets and advertising. In its 'mature' phase, there might need to be more concern for product quality. To postpone the eventual decline, it may be necessary to reduce prices and spend more on advertising.

(Note that product life cycles and their relationship to business strategy will be considered later in the business management learning pillar).

Exercise 2.5

Review the commentary earlier on the four stages of the product life cycle and identify the implications on the variables of price, promotion and place.

2.4.2　Investing in products

An organisation will need to determine how much funding it allocates to each product within its portfolio of products (or services). Decisions such as which products to discontinue, promote more, conduct further research into, etc. are all essential considerations.

Table 2.2 BCG product classifications

Cash cow	Characterised by relatively high market share but low market growth. Function: generating cash for use elsewhere
Problem child	Characterised by relatively low market share but high market growth. For these products to succeed investment is needed to improve market share. If insufficient funds are available choices will need to be made over which to invest in and which to let go.
Star	Characterised by relatively high market share and high market growth. Although investment may be needed to maintain market share it is worthwhile as the market size is growing. Stars will become tomorrow's cash cows.
Dog	Characterised by relatively low market share and low market growth. There may be little justification for continuing to invest in these products.

One popular framework for assisting in these decisions is known as the Boston Consulting Group (BCG) matrix, which plots in a 2 × 2 cell all products according to the growth rate of the market served and the market share held. Products are then classified as being 'stars', 'cash cows', 'a problem child' or a 'dog'. Table 2.2 summarises the possibilities.

2.5 Place

Getting 'place' right in marketing terms means effective distribution: getting the right products into the right places at the right time. The movement of goods from production to consumption points is key. Place therefore refers to distribution channels, distribution coverage, the types of transportation vehicle, locations of sales outlets, the arrangements of sales areas, stock levels, warehouse locations, etc. Research indicates that delivery performance is one of the main criteria for businesses choosing a particular supplier. Questions from a marketing point of view include:

- Is the place of purchase convenient to customers and does it fulfill their needs?
- Is the means of distribution appropriate?
- Is the product available in the right quantities?

Contemporary developments have dictated that there is a changing emphasis for 'place' within the marketing mix with advances in direct marketing and interactive marketing.

2.5.1 Direct marketing

The links in a distribution channel involve the manufacturer selling to retailers who then act as an intermediary to the final customer. Under this model the customer would have no direct dealings with the manufacturer. Where there is only one intermediary link in the chain the activity is referred to as a 'one level channel'. This generally applies to most consumer goods such as branded foodstuff and clothing.

Often there are several intermediaries in the chain ('two level channel') making manufacturer and ultimate customer contact even more unlikely. The further the manufacturer is from the final customer the less control the manufacturer has over marketing effort. (See later references to the value system).

Direct marketing refers to a 'zero level channel' where the manufacturer interacts directly with the customer. Under these conditions 'place' becomes cyberspace. Examples include the web-based company Amazon.com and the direct booking of air travel on line. The Chartered Institute of Marketing (2004) comments that direct marketing 'is becoming increasingly important, particularly as technology advances. It involves such techniques as direct mail shots, telesales, etc.'

2.5.2   The internet and marketing

Technological advances and the introduction of large organisational databases have enabled companies to identify customers, their behaviours and characteristics and build profiles of individual households including how they are made up and their collective interests. This has led to more accurate targeting of marketing communications and direct marketing to take place. (Thus direct marketing impinges on two aspects of the marketing mix: place and promotion.)

Chapter 1 dealt with technological advances including the growth of the internet and the world wide web and this has clear implications for marketing and 'place' in particular. With the adoption of personal computers in the home, increasingly firms are dealing directly with customers who can buy virtually anything online without leaving their home. Supermarket shopping, for instance, need not be a physical event instead it can involve a 'mouse to house' transaction (borrowing the strap line from a supermarket chain). This has been facilitated by adoption of the technology in the home, acceptance of credit cards, and organisations developing efficient supply and distribution systems.

Exercise 2.6

Identify what you believe to be some of the advantages of the Internet as a marketing channel.

Solution

- Speed
- Flexibility
- Convenience
- Attractive use of time
- Potential for lower prices
- Potential for shopping around easily
- Potential for databases.

2.5.3   Teleshopping

Developments in communication technology, specifically cable, satellite and digital technologies has provided a platform for another form of home shopping via the television. Advantages over web-based selling include complete user familiarity with the equipment (the TV) and the ability to extensively demonstrate/advertise the products visually on a dedicated channel.

2.5.4 Telemarketing and M-marketing

Telephone technology is not new but ownership is more widespread than ever. Within the UK virtually all businesses, most homes and increasingly all teenagers and adults have a telephone. This provides the potential for contact to be made by telemarketing to either stimulate product interest, sell directly or arrange for a visit to be made by a salesperson. There has of late been great emphasis in providing specialist training for telesales personnel including coaching on accent and responses to questions raised by customers. A contemporary trend is also the development of large call centres sometimes based overseas. ('M-marketing' refers to the technique being adopted using mobile telephones).

This type of selling involves the initiative being taken by the vendor and is unsolicited. As such it may be unwelcome, intrusive even and naturally ethical concerns can surface. Impolite approaches or 'pushy' sales techniques being employed are particularly distasteful.

2.6 Promotion

Promotion includes the tools available to communicate with customers and potential customers about a product or service. A clear focus on customers and communication is central to modern marketing. Increasingly organisations attempt to understand customers and design communications to effectively and efficiently meet their needs. Once the organisation has determined what they believe the customers see as the main benefits of their product or service (see earlier) these aspects are focussed upon when promotion takes place.

Communications can take many forms and generally operates at one of three levels:

- non-personal and mass, typically aimed at a market segment at large
- personal and direct, typically one way communication with a potential customer (e.g. by sending a letter)
- personal and interactive, involving some one-to-one dialogue between the salesperson and the potential customer.

Promotion (irrespective of form) involves persuasion: ways of communicating convincingly the benefits of an organisation's products or services to customers and potential customers. There are many individual promotional tools available and possibly these constitute the most visible dimension of marketing. These communication mechanisms need 'blending' by an organisation to develop its own promotional mix. The main promotional tools are briefly considered here.

- Advertising is the non-personal presentation and promotion of ideas, goods, or services but targeted at a specific market through some media channel. The mass media such as TV, press, radio or newspapers might be used as well as more traditional forms such as posters, billboards and fliers.
- Sales promotion is impersonal and short term by nature, involving the offering of incentives to encourage sales. Sales promotion is therefore a marketing activity aimed at stimulating consumer purchasing. It can involve the use of coupons, offers, giveaways, discounts, competitions, or BOGOFs (buy one get one free) products. Other non-routine promotional events include displays, exhibitions, demonstrations, and product sponsorship.
- Publicity and public relations is 'non-personal stimulation of demand for a product, service, or business unit by planting commercially significant news about it in a published medium, or obtaining favourable presentation of it upon radio, TV or stage. Whilst it is not paid for by the sponsor in the way that media time or space is paid for advertising,

there may be costs in informing journalists and other types of opinion leader.' (The Chartered Institute of Marketing, 2004). This is an often-underestimated tool that can also include company open days, press releases and conferences.

- Personal selling often involves one to one contact with potential customers most commonly by telephone. The salesperson verbally presents the benefits of the product or service in the hope of making a sale.
- Direct mailing of promotional literature. Databases allow messages to be personalised to include the prospective customer's name. Normally, messages are personally targeted using either the traditional mail systems (often referred to as junk mail) or the e-mail media (often referred to as SPAM mail).

There is also a case to include direct marketing and packaging into this listing as both tools can contribute to the communication of the products benefits. (Packaging includes package, label, and description design). Other promotional activities include branding and producing literature and brochures.

Just as promotional tools need to be blended to form a promotional or communication mix, so promotion itself needs to be blended with the other Ps comprising the marketing mix. For instance, a reduction in promotional activity may be possible if a wider range or larger number of sales outlets is developed. (This implies a heavier mix of place at the expense of promotion).

2.6.1 Promotion: push and pull policies

The traditional 'push' marketing policy is concerned with transferring goods out to wholesalers and retailers who then have the task of selling them to ultimate final customers. The emphasis of a 'push' policy is therefore on getting dealers to accept goods.

A 'pull' policy by comparison is one of influencing final consumer attitudes so that a consumer demand is created which dealers are obliged to satisfy. A 'pull' policy usually involves heavy expenditure on advertising, but holds the potential of stimulating a much higher demand. For example, producers of convenience food and alcohol advertise their products nationally rather than relying on supermarkets to promote these products.

This represents consumer advertising as part of consumer marketing, and should be distinguished from trade and corporate advertising. Lancaster and Withey (2005) differentiate advertising according to uses and types as follows:

- advertising products and services (e.g. Ford cars)
- advertising ideas and issues (e.g. Greenpeace)
- advertising people (e.g. Jennifer Lopez)
- trade type (e.g. C&Q: 'warehouses for professional decorators')
- consumer type (e.g. Robinson Barley Water: 'refresh your ideas')
- corporate type (e.g. Shell: 'the caring company').

> **!** Procter and Gamble has been active in supermarkets assisting in the merchandising (displaying) and just-in-time supply of their goods. This effort is linked to EFTPOS (electronic funds transfer at the point of sale) and manufacturing scheduling at the Procter and Gamble factories. This had led to lower inventories at both locations, and greater team working resulting in shared ideas for point-of-sale promotions. As a result, Procter and Gamble managers are now more involved in the entire supply process.

MARKETING

2.6.2 Advertising

It is estimated that within Western Europe every adult has up to 3,000 'advertising encounters' every day. With so much expenditure on advertising it is perhaps surprising that there is any controversy over whether a company advertises or not. Lancaster and Withey (2005) articulate the diverse opinions surrounding the value of advertising as part of an organisation's promotional mix. Although most marketeers agree that advertising has a role to play, some believe that it is an ineffective way of getting customers to purchase products. Two polar opposite positions can be identified as follows:

- Advertising is ineffective and a waste of money, only adding to company (and hence eventually customer) costs. Brands such as Body Shop, Pizza Express and Red Bull do not see a need to use advertising in their promotional campaigns relying instead on other sources of information in order to form positive attitudes towards their products. In any case some might think that advertising demeans a particular product or company. In some cases advertising may seem unethical.
- Advertising is so powerful and effective as to be essential. Consumers, it could be argued, will rarely purchase unadvertised brands so by not advertising a company will be at a serious disadvantage compared to competitors. The results of advertising campaigns have been undeniably successful including for brands such as Orange, Walkers Crisps, Tango and French Connection.

Lancaster and Withey (2005) conclude that some brands may be strong enough to sell on their own merits only if they are long-established and have strong brand-loyal users. For advertising to be successful it needs to be

- well planned and executed
- part of an effective promotional mix
- effective as a communication tool
- consistent with the values and mission of the organisation.

Exercise 2.7

For reflection

You may wish to reflect on why two of the companies cited, Body Shop and Pizza Express can afford not to advertise. Hint: (Think of the other compensating aspects associated with their operation such as PR within the promotional mix and place visibility.)

2.6.3 The selling mix

The selling mix concentrates on point-of-sale activity and involves several dimensions of promotion including:

- Logos, special storage and branding
- Locally devised packaging
- A personal selling approach

- Merchandising and display
- Point-of-sale advertising
- Distribution policy, especially dealer areas and competition limitations.

2.6.4 Emerging trends in promotion

The following extract is from a journal article which reports on a US conference of the Association of National Advertisers. In the article the author reflects on both the medium of Google for advertising (apparently it is a '$ 3billion player') and the different views on how best a promotional budget might be spent:

At the conference, execs from some of the most traditional companies (who control some of the biggest marketing budgets) described big shifts away from traditional media. Wachovia Chief Marketing Officer Jim Garrity said his research on ad effectiveness would sadden broadcast TV execs but gladden employees of Yahoo! and – yup – Google. Joseph V. Tripodi, a good-humored old-school salesman, is Allstate's chief marketing officer. He told me Allstate's spending on "nontraditional media" – from the Internet to sponsorships – increased from 5 to 25 per cent of its marketing budget in recent years.

Titans of traditional media are all too aware of this shift. Vanity Fair Editor-in-Chief Graydon Carter last month told an audience of advertisers that while he often used Google, he never remembered the ads. Schmidt countered by using Vanity Fair as Exhibit A: Its circulation is around 1 million, he said, and a full-page ad for a Prada bag costs around $100,000. So that ad in Vanity Fair costs 10 cents per impression. How about paying about 20 cents per impression, he offered, for a link to a Web site where you can buy the bag?

In truth, Vanity Fair's ad is cheaper per impression if you measure by the magazine's total audience, but Schmidt's point is nonetheless clear: Which gets you closer to commerce, and how much do you pay for that?

(*Source:* extracted from Hard Questions from Google; Asking advertisers: What's the right amount to spend? By Jon Fine, *Business Week*, October 24, 2005 i3956 p. 28 The McGraw-Hill Companies, Inc.)

2.7 Price

Of the four Ps comprising the marketing mix, price is the one most directly linked to revenue levels. Price setting is all-important especially for a financially orientated firm. Pricing includes basic price levels, discounts and allowances, payment terms and credit policy, etc.

The accountant within us may force us to view price from a mathematical viewpoint and culminate in fixing a product price based on 'cost plus'. Undeniably the need to recover total costs plus necessary profit is a powerful and legitimate consideration. However, customers need to see price as 'fair' (not necessarily cheap). Pricing, therefore, needs to meet both the organisation's financial and marketing aspirations. It is perhaps illuminating to consider the issue from three perspectives (Lancaster and Withey, 2005):

MARKETING

Table 2.3 Approaches to pricing

Competitive	Setting a price by reference to the prices of competitive products
Cost plus	Adding a mark-up to costs of production which may incorporate desired return on investment
Market based	(or perceived value). Setting a price based on the value of the product in the perception of the customer
Penetration	Setting a low selling price in order to gain market share
Predatory	Setting a low selling price in order to damage competition
Premium	Achieving a 'high' price due to differentiation of the product
Price skimming	Setting a high price in order to maximize short-term profitability (e.g. the introduction of a novel product)
Selective	Setting different prices for the same product maybe in different markets
Selective: category	Cosmetic modifications to allow variations to take place
Selective: consumer group	Modifying the price to take account of certain groups (e.g. junior or OAP area)
Selective: peak	Setting a price which varies according to level of demand (e.g. happy hours, premium rate calls, etc.)

Source: Based on CIMA Official Terminology (2005)

- *The economic view.* Suppliers are in the business of profit maximisation. A market is a place where supply and demand comes into contact. Price is the mechanism whereby demand and supply are brought into equilibrium.
- *The accountancy view.* Price is set to recover costs and make profit. Pricing should be guided by the use of ratios and techniques such as breakeven analysis.
- *The marketing view.* Price is only one factor influencing demand, it does however have an impact on an organisations competitive market position, including sales, and market share. A good price measure might be what 'the market will bear'.

In practice all these viewpoints should be considered to some degree. In addition an appropriate blending of the three other factors of the marketing mix (place, product, promotion) will also help establish the price. Table 2.3 summarises the range of methodologies that can help determine selling price.

2.7.1 Customer attitudes to price

Customers' feelings about a product or service are reflected in what they are prepared to pay, so getting pricing 'right' is crucial. Ultimately the manager must address the issue of whether customers believe the price is fair commensurate with the quality of the product or service.

CIM make the point that existing customers are generally less price sensitive than new ones. (This is one reason why it is vital to retain existing customers. A truism is that it is preferable to retain existing customers rather than having to find new ones.)

For the customer price can imply quality. Pricing that is too low can have a detrimental effect on purchasing decisions and overall sales levels. Conversely, the higher the price, the more customers will expect in terms of product and service (whether packaging, the shopping environment, or promotional material, etc.)

2.7.2 Pricing strategies

Reference was made earlier to generic competitive strategy and the possibility of an organisation competing on the basis of price. If this is the chosen strategy it is important that excess production costs are squeezed with the overall aim that the organisation will be cost leader within their market. These savings should be passed on to the customer and will be reflected in low prices. Larger, well-established businesses are better able to compete on price. This is generally as a result of two basic concepts:

- *The experience curve.* Reductions in the average unit cost price as a result of learning from past experiences.
- *Economies of scale.* Reductions in the average unit cost price as a result of size of operation.

There can after all only be one price leader in a market. It may be more advisable therefore to add value to the product so differentiating it from the competitors offering in some way. Alternatively, part of the market (a segment) might be identified where the competition will find it hard to access. Here the organisation is in a position to price on the basis of 'what the market will bear'.

2.7.3   Price and the product life cycle

Pricing can be explained by reference to the product life cycle. (Refer back to Figure 2.1.)

Exercise 2.8

For each of the four stages of the product life cycle describe the pricing considerations.

Solution

- *Introduction.* High prices might be charged, because the product is new and supply is limited also initial set up costs need to be recovered.
- *Growth.* Competition between rival producers intensifies so prices will reduce in the hope of penetrating the existing market and either retaining or increasing market share at the expense of competitors.
- *Maturity.* Prices fall mainly in order to beat competitors but the experience curve and scale economies should come into play. Market segments are sought where higher prices can be charged.
- *Decline.* The product declines into obsolescence so it may even be sold off below cost price to clear stocks and exit the market.

Two forms of pricing might also be applied particularly in the introduction stage of the product life cycle, namely:

- *Skim pricing* reflecting high prices but low profit due to high fixed costs.
- *Penetration pricing,* deliberately entering a market to build market share and pricing so as to deny the competitors those opportunities.

2.7.4   Price: other considerations

There may be several other considerations when fixing price and some of which include:

- The nature of competition. If the competitor is the price leader pricing levels may be determined by 'follow the leader' pricing. So, for instance, if the largest oil company cuts the price of fuel, others are likely to follow suit.

- The nature of the market. By way of example, a company may find itself in the fortunate position of being the sole producer of a product due to a monopoly of 'know-how', resources or raw materials, etc.
- Pricing as a result of a short-term promotion. This may lead to 'loss leader' pricing on certain items to generate either customer loyalty or more sales of other products. This is particularly popular in pricing consumables in supermarkets.
- Pricing as a competitive weapon. The pricing of product may be set in order to crush competitors rather than achieve returns in revenue.

2.8 Beyond the four Ps

The co-ordination of the four elements of the marketing mix is crucial to the success of the overall marketing strategy. Some thinkers believe that other factors could also usefully be considered. The number of factors augmenting this basic categorisation varies but arises mainly as recognition that service organisations are 'different' to production organisations in marketing terms.

2.8.1 People

People include both staff and customers. An organisation's people come into contact with customers and can have a massive impact on customer satisfaction levels. In the customers' eyes, staff are generally inseparable from the total service. This implies the need for well-trained, motivated staff mindful of the adage 'the customer is always right'. It is important therefore that every member of staff contribute to the marketing philosophy and support the firm's external marketing activities.

As organisations introduce streamlined hierarchies and more flexible working practices, marketing offers the opportunity for their employees to operate in interdisciplinary teams furthering an overall marketing philosophy. Corporate investment in their most valuable asset, employees, through training and development supports the processes of creating and defending competitive advantages gained from successful marketing.

In terms of customers, good research should reveal vital, personal, cultural, social and psychological profiles of potential customers. This data can be exploited when applying other aspects of the marketing mix.

> **!** Many supermarket chains offer regular customers 'loyalty cards'. These cards allow sophisticated databases to record purchasing profiles of customer groups and enable better targeting of their products.

2.8.2 Processes

Processes refer to systems involved in providing a service focussed upon 'identifying, anticipating and satisfying customer requirements.' So for instance, useful considerations might include the processes implied by the following questions:

- Do customers have to queue or wait to be dealt with?
- How are customers kept informed?
- Is the service conducted efficiently?

Processes assume greater significance in certain sectors such as banking and financial institutions.

2.8.3 Physical evidence

As one of the features of a service is that it is intangible by nature it cannot (unlike a product) be experienced before it is delivered. This means that potential customers may perceive greater risk. To overcome these feelings service organisations can give reassurance by way of testimonials and references from past satisfied customers as a substitute for physical evidence.

> **Table 2.2 An example of a client testimonial appearing on a website of an HR consultancy practice**
>
> 'I have been very impressed with the service provided by Reed Consulting's strategic research team. Our account manager took the time to gain a thorough understanding of the issues we face, and designed and delivered research which has fully met our requirements. The analysis report was clearly presented and has been influential in driving our strategic decision-making.' (source: www.reedconsulting.co.uk/index.php?sectionid=75 &contentid=78)

2.9 Product placement

According to Campbell (1997), product placement combines two main aspects of marketing:

- identifying the customer group to be aimed at;
- identifying the best method available to reach this target market.

This section deals with these and associated issues.

> Note: In certain contexts the term 'product placement' can have an alternative meaning. It can be used to describe the visibility of branded products in TV programmes and films, such as watches, clothing, motorcars and drinks. The film-maker is paid for displaying these items, and the product is advertised as part of a storyline in return.

2.9.1 Market segmentation

A market is rarely a mass, homogeneous group of customers, each wanting an identical product. 'Market segmentation' is a technique based on the recognition that every market consists of potential buyers with different needs, and different buying behaviour. These different customer attitudes may be grouped into segments and a different marketing approach may be taken by an organisation for each market segment.

Market segmentation may therefore involve the subdividing of a market into distinct subgroups of customers, where any subgroup can be selected as a target market to be met with a distinct marketing mix.

The important point of market segmentation is that although the total market consists of widely different groups of consumers, each group consists of people (or organisations) with common needs and preferences, who perhaps react to market stimuli in much the same way. For example, the market for hats might be segmented according to the gender (as women and men prefer hats of different styles). The men's market might be further subdivided into age or occupation (e.g. professional classes, commuters, golfers). Each sub-division of the market (or sub segment of a market segment) will show increasingly common traits. Golfers, for example, appear to buy baseball hats.

Any market segment can become a target market for a firm, requiring a unique marketing mix if the firm is to exploit it successfully. Recognition of segmentation will enable a company to adopt a more refined approach to selling to a given group of potential customers.

Exercise 2.9

When might market segmentation prove difficult or inappropriate?

Solution

When the total market is so small as to make segmentation unprofitable sometimes consumer differences may exist, but it may be difficult to analyse them into segments. Finally, a total market may occasionally be homogeneous but this is likely to occur only rarely.

2.9.2 The bases for segmentation

The choice of marketing strategy may depend on the existence of clearly distinguishable market segments. These segments would also need to be sufficiently large to promise satisfactory returns, and would need to be readily accessible through distribution, selling and marketing efforts. Kotler and Lane Keller (2006) suggest that since the purpose of segmentation is to identify target markets, segments must be:

- measurable – segmentation by 'personality' for example, might be difficult to measure
- accessible – the market must be easily reached by the organisation
- substantial – the costs of reaching the target market must be weighed against potential demand for the uniquely-marketed product.

An important marketing task is the identification of segments within the total market.

Segmentation may to some extent be a matter of subjective analysis, but typical market segments might relate to:

- geographical area
- end use (e.g. some types of paper are specially made for drawing offices)
- age (e.g. market for classical or pop music)
- gender (e.g. clothes)
- family size or family life cycle (e.g. the market for housing)
- income (e.g. the market for luxury goods)
- occupation (e.g. the market for briefcases)
- education (e.g. the marketing of magazines)
- religion or religious sect (e.g. marketing by mail-order by religious booksellers)
- nationality, race, and culture (e.g. the market for food)
- social class
- lifestyle (a general category based on differences in personality, peer social class, groups, etc.).

Segmentation may be quite complex. There are many different bases on which segments can be analysed; one basis will not be appropriate in every market, and sometimes two or more bases might be valid at the same time. One basis or 'segmentation variable' might be 'superior' to another in the hierarchy of variables; for example, market segments may exist on the basis of gender sub-segments may then be age group within gender, and sub-sub-segments may be geographical region within age group within gender. On the other hand, if a market can be segmented both by marital status (unmarried, married) and by religion (say, Protestant and Catholic) then the market might be divisible into two at times; with separate segments (married Protestants, unmarried Protestants, married Catholics and unmarried Catholics, etc).

The following extract from an article illustrates the increasing significance of a market segmented on the basis of age within the UK and the way in which products might be promoted to appeal to a mature age group:

She's back. Isabella Rossellini, the actress and model who was allegedly dropped as the face of cosmetics brand Lancôme because she was too old at the age of 40, is making a new foray into the world of celebrity endorsements. Now 52, the elegant Italian will act as brand ambassador for Silversea Cruises and is to feature in print ads and brochures for the company as well as making appearances aboard the line's ships 'to create a photographic journal of her travels'.

Silversea says Rossellini was hired for her 'timeless beauty' and ability to represent the brand's Italian heritage. But a spokesman admits that her mature years will strike a chord with people aged over 50 who make up the bulk of the market for cruises.

The issue of how to promote brands to the burgeoning mature market is set to become a major concern for marketers over the next 20 years.

Cruises, coach tours, financial products and medicaments are age-specific and can be directly targeted at the senior market. But the bigger question is how best to promote products such as packaged groceries, new media, cars and clothes, which are bought by people across the age spectrum, when declining childbirth and increased longevity mean there are fewer consumers under 35 and more over 50.

The population is rapidly ageing. In 2020, there will be 5.2 million more people in the 45-to-74 age-group than there are today, according to census analysis by Future Foundation. In the 2001 census, it was revealed that for the first time there were more people over 60 (21 per cent of the population) than under 16 (20 per cent). By 2041, the over-75s will outnumber those aged between 55 and 74.

The Government is being forced to grapple with the demographic time-bomb as it addresses the pensions crisis and the realisation that many people will be heading into retirement with insufficient provision for their old age. One important question will be how to unlock the enormous spending power in retired people's homes. Another will be how marketers should tap into this income.

(*Source:* extracted from Marketing's age concern by David Benady, *Marketing Week*, October 28, 2004. Reproduced with Permission).

2.9.3   Segmentation of the industrial market

Identifying the significant bases for segmentation in any particular market is a matter of judgement. A new company entering a market may be able to identify a potentially profitable target market segment that existing firms may have 'missed'.

Segmentation can also be applied to industrial markets possibly by the nature of the customer's business. Component manufacturers specialise in the industries of the firms to which they supply components. In the automotive industry, companies specialise in the manufacture of car components, sometimes for a single firm. (In the industrial car market, there are only a few major buyers, and segmentation may mean providing an individual marketing service for each buyer.) By way of example Pirelli Tyres supply their tyres already fixed to the wheels of Jaguar and other cars, and so form a larger part of the Jaguar supply/value chain. (See supply chain partnerships Chapter 5).

2.9.4 Distributions channels

Some products such as fresh foodstuff clearly benefit from short distribution channels. In the countryside it is often possible to buy produce directly from the farmyard. Alternatively, the farm may deliver daily to the supermarket. A specialist foreign car might, however, need to be imported, here the distribution is relatively lengthy and may take time.

The precise method of distribution chosen will vary dependent upon the nature of the product and the degree of market exposure required. The greater the market an organisation wishes to access the longer and more complicated the distribution channel.

Campbell (1997) identified the most commonly observed channels as follows:

- producer to consumer
- producer to retailer to consumer
- producer to wholesaler to retailer to consumer
- producer to agent to wholesaler to retailer to consumer.

Now refer to 2.6.1 promotion policies earlier in this chapter to reinforce your understanding. This idea of the distribution chain is returned to later in this chapter when particular marketing contexts are considered.

2.10 Market positioning

If the company wants a leadership position, and cannot achieve that in an entire market, it can attempt to gain leadership in a single segment or in several segments. The market segments selected for a leadership position would ideally:

- have potential for future growth
- show a distinctive customer need for 'exploitation'
- be accessible and substantial
- be without a direct competitor of similar size.

Taking the last of these, it would be unusual to enter a market segment where there is no direct competitor. This being the case a firm will probably need to make its product 'different' by creating some form of product differentiation (real or imagined) as part of the marketing mix. This competitive positioning requires a firm to develop an understanding of what kind of offer it will make to the target market in relation to what the competitors are offering.

Segmentation forms the basis of strategies for targeting markets, and the consequent positioning of products within markets in terms of quality and price. The alternative strategies are:

- Undifferentiated positioning involves a targeting of the entire market with a single marketing mix. The undifferentiated policy is based on the hope that as many customers as possible to buy it. In essence this approach ignores segmentation entirely.
- Differentiated targeting involves a targeting of certain market segments and then applying distinct marketing mix to each. This can be complex and time consuming but should be ultimately rewarding. The company may attempt to introduce several product versions, each aimed at a different group of potential customers, (e.g. the manufacture of different styles of the some article of clothing adapted to different world climates and national cultural tastes).
- Concentrated positioning involves a targeting of a single market segment with an ideal product for that one segment of the market (e.g. Rolls-Royce cars). This would possibly be the best approach for a small player within the market place.

The major disadvantage of a differentiated marketing strategy is the additional costs of marketing and production (more product design and development costs, the loss of economies of scale in production and storage, additional promotion costs and administrative costs, etc.). When the costs of further differentiation of the market exceed the benefits, a firm is said to have 'lower differentiated'. Some firms have tried to overcome this problem by selling the same product to two market segments. For example, Johnson's baby powder and Heinz baby apple food is sold to many adults for their own use.

The major disadvantage of concentrated marketing is the business risk of relying on a single segment of a single market. On the other hand, specialisation in a particular market segment can give a firm a profitable, although perhaps temporary, competitive edge over rival firms.

Decisions are generally made on the relative attractiveness of segments and the capability of the organisation itself. The position the product or service has in the market must be carefully weighed against the positioning of competitors.

The choice between undifferentiated, differentiated or concentrated marketing as a marketing strategy will depend on the following factors:

- The extent to which the product or the market may be considered as uniform in its requirements. 'Mass' marketing may be 'sufficient' if the market is largely homogeneous (e.g. the market for safety matches).
- The company's resources must not be over-extended by differentiated marketing. Small firms may succeed better by concentrating on one segment only.
- The product must be sufficiently advanced in its 'life cycle' to have attracted a substantial total market. Without such a substantial market, segmentation and target marketing is unlikely to be profitable.

2.11 Marketing and business contexts

Hopefully, the business contexts within which marketing principles can be usefully applied are apparent. A few of these contexts are discussed here in order to give a flavour of the particular considerations including buying decisions and consumer behaviour. These contexts are:

- fast-moving consumer goods
- business-to-business marketing
- services marketing.

2.11.1 Fast-moving consumer goods

Consumer goods can take two forms:

- durable goods,
- fast-moving consumer goods (FMCGs).

The decision to purchase high cost durable goods such as televisions, computers, cars and furniture and the frequency of repurchase will be influenced by changing technical features, fashions and wearing-out of the old product.

FMCGs are by comparison purchased for personal reasons and generally involve relatively low financial outlays. For FMCGs like canned foods, soft drinks and confectionery there may be habitual purchasing but products tend to have short life cycles. It follows therefore that the marketing mix will differ considerably between both types of consumer good. Understanding consumers involves appreciating the factors that affect buying decisions as well as types of buying behaviour. In the context of FMCG, Lancaster and Withey (2005) identify a consumer decision process as having five stages that organisations need to understand:

- *Problem recognition (as purchasing is a problem solving process)*. The consumer identifies the need or problem. The firm must orientate the promotional aspects of the marketing mix to convince the consumer that the product could be the answer.
- *Information searching*. The consumer may perform this search informally in terms of memory of past experiences or by conversations with others. When selling FMCGs there must be a sufficiency of information provided through promotional activities.
- *Evaluation of alternatives by the consumer*. The firm needs to understand on what basis this choice is made (e.g. price, weight, value for money, packaging) and this should be reflected in the marketing mix.
- *Purchasing decision*.
- *Post purchase evaluation*. The firm will be interested to know if the consumer is satisfied with the choice they have made. Increasingly consumers are written to or telephoned to determine this information.

Of particular relevance to FMCG is advertising, branding and packaging. Lancaster and Withey (2005) identify the following key factors influencing FMCG purchasing behaviour:

- personal factors (age, gender, income, etc.)
- psychological factors (perceptions, motives, attitudes)
- social/cultural factors (family influence, reference groups, etc.).

2.11.2 Business-to-business marketing

For organisations that market goods and services to other intermediary organisations (rather than direct to ultimate consumers), the implication of buyer behaviour, the assessment of marketing opportunities and industrial market segmentation take on heightened significance.

Business-to-business (B2B) marketing differs from business-to-consumer (B2C) marketing in a number of key respects, not least the purchaser makes purchasing decisions for organisational rather than personal reasons. In addition many people are involved in the B2B buying decision including:

- Initiators who start the buying process. (It might be for instance a department who identify a need to replace a piece of equipment).
- Influencers who affect the buying decision often based on their particular technical expertise.
- Buyers who raise orders and sanction payment and although they may enter into negotiation they may be guided heavily by others in the organisation.
- Users who ultimately operate the equipment (using the earlier example).

Exercise 2.10

On what basis are B2B purchasing decisions made?

Solution

- Economic/task factors (price, delivery, location, quality, reliability, customer care, after care)
- Non-task factors (personal risk or gain, previous decisions, politics, those influencing the purchaser, perception)
- or probably some combination of both.

Significant B2B marketing mix features include quality assurance, reliability, delivery, price and after sales service.

2.11.3 Services marketing

Recognition should be given to the fact that there are fundamental differences between products and services; hence the marketing of a service assumes a different emphasis. Mullins (2005) identified the main differentiating features as:

- The consumer is a participant in the service process.
- Services are perishable. If there is no sale on Monday it cannot (unlike a tin of fruit) be sold on Tuesday: that sale is lost forever.
- Services are intangible, so communication is made more difficult when explaining the benefits.
- Services are people orientated and the characteristics of the workforce determine the effectiveness of the service.
- Output measurement is less easy to evidence.

Exercise 2.11

Using the above features identify examples of services and the implications this has on service marketing.

MARKETING

✅ Solution

- The consumer is a participant in the service process. Environmental surroundings of the service operation need attention, for example, the décor of a hairdressers, the cleanliness of the hospital ward, etc.
- Services are perishable therefore consideration might be given to differential pricing, for example, seats left unsold on airplanes one hour before flight might have to be heavily discounted.
- Services are intangible, communication might recognise that feelings and emotions are important (e.g. 'sleep safely with house cover from Royal Life').
- Services are people orientated and the characteristics of the workforce determine the effectiveness of the service. The implication is that attention must be paid to key human resourcing issues such as recruitment and training.
- Output measurement is less easy to evidence, therefore multiple indicators might be stressed, for example, length of hospital stay, cost of operation, post-operation support, etc. This thinking can be directly applied to the marketing mix, for instance:
  - The 'product' will consider in particular issues of type and range of service offered.
  - Pricing will be mindful of persishability of the service.
  - Promotion might emphasise personal selling.
  - Place will take account of the fact that the consumer is a participant in the service.

For service organisations it is worth noting the heightened emphasis on the augmentation of 'four Ps' already identified namely:

- *People*. As employees interface with customers and can have a massive impact on customer satisfaction levels.
- *Processes*. Systems involved in providing a service.
- *Physical evidence*. Organisations can give reassurance by way of testimonials and references from past satisfied customers as a substitute for physical evidence.

Lancaster and Withey (2005) explain that the banking industry took a long time to wake up to the need to be customer oriented and the benefits of using the marketing tools and techniques in the same way that fast-moving consumer goods did. They identify a dramatic change over the past decade concluding that 'the global banking sector is one of the success stories in recent years of the application and implementation of the marketing concept'. Some of the changes include:

- market research and analysis designed to keep in touch with customer needs and customer satisfaction levels
- organisational and marketing structures based around customer requirements
- marketing planning and control systems including market segmentation and targeting
- a need for increased quality, service and customer care
- an awareness of wider environmental factors, including its ethical and social responsibilities towards customers.

There are many of examples of organisations that have effectively marketed their services, sometimes globally with huge success. For other service organisations, such as Not for Profit (NFP) organisations including charities, hospitals, political parties and Universities and Local Authorities, marketing has been embraced with varying degrees of enthusiasm and success. It is beyond the scope of this study system to discuss the marketing implications of each in turn but it is worthwhile perhaps highlighting the particular features associated with NFP organisations, namely:

- NFPs are subject to tighter legislative requirements;
- heightened issues of achieving value for money often arise;
- customers may be a different grouping from those paying for the service to be provided.

> ❗ To reinforce your understanding of service organisations distinguishing features refer to Table 5.5 which appears later in this learning system.

2.12 Market research

Market research should be distinguished from marketing research. Market research is a concentration on one the market alone while the wider brief of marketing research involves investigating all marketing activities (see later).

Success often depends on organisations exercising control over markets or market segments. Such control allows organisations to reduce costs and benefit from economies of scale in production. Important strategic decisions such as this have to be taken with the confidence afforded by relevant and comprehensive information resulting from effective market research.

Many management decisions are made under conditions of uncertainty and risk, hence the need for good research. The use of market research is one of the few highly developed areas where management research approaches a scientific quality. Market research concentrates on quantifying information about potential sales and is therefore based on the use of mathematical and statistical techniques.

To be comprehensive, research must show an awareness of the PESTLE factors (Table 2.4) that may affect supply and demand for a product.

Changes in these influences should wherever possible be anticipated. For example, redundant corporate executives in their 50s with 'golden handshakes' represent a new market for luxury goods and leisure pursuits, activities but specific problems may arise which can be very costly. Typically, these research studies include investigation of demand:

- in a particular market segment or geographical area
- through the cyclical or seasonal pattern of demand
- by analysis of sub-segments by age, gender, etc.

When undertaking market research there is a need to:

- define the problem
- establish the type and amount of information needed
- decide on the type of data (secondary or primary)
- determine the collection method to be used (postal questionnaire, personal interview, etc.)
- identify an appropriate organisational resource or select a research agency
- determine the sample
- collect the data
- interpret the data and report.

Table 2.4 The PESTLE factors framework

Political Government stability Regulations (e.g. concerning foreign trade) Taxation policies	**Technological** Spending on research Industry focus on technological effort New discoveries/developments Speed of technology transfer Rates of obsolescence.
Economic Inflation Unemployment Trade cycles Interest rates Levels of disposable income	**Legal** Competition laws Employment laws Health & safety laws Product safety
Sociocultural Demographic trends Income distribution Life-style changes Attitudes to work, leisure, consumption, etc. Consumerism Social mobility	**Environmental** Environmental protection laws Waste disposal Energy consumption

Source: Based on Johnson, Scholes and Whittington (2005)

2.12.1 Market research and IT

Technological advances and the potential offered by IT have assisted data gathering techniques considerably. The Internet can access secondary research data sources, and Universities typically have effective databases allowing for research and analysis of customer behaviour. Primary research that is generated by the organisation itself (because such data does not currently exist) can emanate from a number of sources. Leading research companies can be employed for the purpose and methods of data collection and analysis are again helped by technology (for example the use of scanners, observational equipment and sophisticated databases all may have a role to play).

Exercise 2.12

Suppose that you are asked for your advice on how to prepare a forecast of your company's sales turnover next year. Your company expects to introduce some new products or services to sell at the beginning of the year. How would you suggest that the sales forecast should be prepared?

Solution

For existing products or services, it might be sufficient to forecast sales by using statistical techniques to analyse sales in the past. A statistical forecast could be compared with sales forecasts that are drawn up for their own area by the company's salesforce and some adjustment made based on 'local knowledge'.

Forecasting turnover for new products or services might be based on information already provided by a market research survey into the sales potential of the products (at given prices and with given levels of expenditure on advertising and sales promotion).

2.12.2 Market research and sales forecasting

Market research information can be used to help in the preparation of sales forecasts. Sales forecasting can be based on statistical techniques using historical sales data from the previous years or months. These techniques are not described in detail here, but include extrapolation by judgment, linear regression analysis, trend line analysis with adjustments for seasonal variations in sales, and exponential smoothing.

Market forecasting can focus on either the present or the future.

The focus of market forecasting current demand for products and services, includes:

- Total market potential
- (Geographical) area market potential
- Total industry sales
- Relative market shares between main competitors.

Market forecasting methods of future demand for products and services include:

- Surveys of buyers' intentions.
- A composite of sales force opinions. Straightforwardly this involves asking sales staff for sales forecast estimates for their area or region and then cumulating these forecasts.
- Expert opinion: obtaining estimates of future sales from 'experts'.
- Estimates based on past-sales analysis.
- Estimates based on other factors (e.g. monthly house sale figures can be correlated to purchases in DIY stores).

2.12.3 Market research in non-consumer products industries

You should be aware of some of particular aspects of market research in industries other than those for consumer products:

Service industries. Research on behalf of financial institutions such as banks or insurance companies requires data that may be considered personal and confidential. For example, it may be necessary to know details of the respondent's income. Given that respondents may be wary about the improper use of confidential information, great care and tact are required to conduct a survey.

Industrial marketing research. The researchers must have some understanding of the industry or industries in order to design a research survey. In addition, it may be possible to carry out a census instead of a sample. It may be difficult to identify the person (or persons) in a customer firm who makes the buying decisions; therefore care must be taken to ensure that the researcher goes to the appropriate person (see B2B buying decisions earlier).

Not for profit organisations. A considerable amount of market research is carried out on behalf of the national or local government. Social problems concerning the elderly, disabled, unemployed, etc., may call for information about their opinions and circumstances to help inform policy decisions. The possible disadvantage of market research for smaller NFP bodies such as charities is the cost of conducting a 'professional' research project. There might be a temptation for an organisation to use its own staff to do research, with the result that the findings might be incomplete, biased or misleading.

2.12.4   Market research and sales potential

Sales potential is an estimate of the part of the market that is within the possible reach of a product. The potential will vary according to the price of the product and the amount of money spent on sales promotion. Market research should attempt to quantify these variations. Sales potential also depends on:

- how essential the product is to consumers;
- whether it is a durable commodity whose purchase is postponable;
- the overall size of the possible market;
- competition.

Whether sales potential is worth exploiting will depend on the cost of sales promotion and selling that must be incurred to realise the potential. Sales potential will influence the decisions by a company on how much of each product to make (its production mix). The market situation is dynamic, and market research should reveal changing situations. A company might decide, for example, that maximum profits will be earned by concentrating all its production and sales promotion efforts on one segment of a market. Action by competitors might then adversely affect sales, and so market research might reveal that another market segment has become relatively more profitable. The company might therefore decide to divert some production capacity and sales promotion spending to the new segment in order to revive its profits. Estimates of sales potential are required in deciding whether to invest money in the development of a new or improved product.

2.13   Technology in modern marketing

Advances in technology mean that marketing techniques, applications and systems can be significantly enhanced. So far reference has been drawn to some applications for the internet, web marketing, teleshopping, telemarketing and M-marketing. The potential of new technology in promotional activities and market databases has also been recognised and practical examples of the use of EFTPOS (electronic funds transfer at the point of sale) and IT assisted market research approaches have been cited. This section completes this consideration of technology in modern marketing with specific reference to

- e-business (e-commerce)
- marketing information systems and marketing planning.

2.13.1   E-business (e-commerce)

General and applied marketing knowledge can be found within the specialised area of E-business, a collective term for all electronically based systems and technologies of doing business (including most significantly the internet). Here use is made of electronic technologies and systems to facilitate and enable transactions to take place.

Using the Internet as a platform a rapid growth in so-called 'dot.com companies' took place about a decade ago, most taking advance of e-marketing. Although not all of these start-up companies survived more established organisations have since invested in this technology and thinking to enhance their existing marketing efforts.

Berens (2006) explains:

'The dot-com boom was led by start-up companies that had unproven records, but the latest growth is being led by established retailers who understand their customers, have brands that people trust and see the web as a bolt-on', says Nick Gladding, senior retail analyst at Verdict Research. 'Lots of businesses that were sitting on the sidelines have now taken the plunge. It has been a difficult time for the retail industry, but there seems to be more confidence now and e-retailing is one area that has a lot of potential for attracting new business.'

Grocery shopping has become one of the key interests for UK consumers. Tesco's and Asda's online services have had a dramatic impact, the former controlling two-thirds of the Internet groceries market. Other big names among the country's top 20 Web retailers include Argos, B&Q, Comet, Currys, John Lewis, Marks & Spencer and Next.

But not all UK retailers that reigned on the high street have found going online easy. Waterstone's and HMV, for example, are struggling to contend with the likes of Amazon and the rapid development of the market for downloading music in MP3 format. 'Some brands were very slow off the mark and are now finding it hard to compete in an increasingly aggressive environment', Gladding says.

Conventional retailers must also adjust to the fact that the Web has redefined how people shop. It's enabling consumers to choose goods that meet their requirements precisely, empowering them to find the lowest-priced product and allowing them to go shopping at any time that suits them.

So what are the keys to successful online trading? 'You have to provide something extra in terms of the product, the service and the price,' Gladding says. 'With the advent of comparison sites such as Kelkoo, prices are very visible online, particularly those of electrical goods. But established retailers still have the edge, because customers find that a reputable brand provides a lot of reassurance.'

With the incredible uptake of use of the Internet a number of benefits present themselves in marketing term (for example, in terms of data collection and providing enhanced value to customers and suppliers). It should, however, be noted that there are potentially a number of drawbacks of internet trading (e.g. financial security issues, computer disruptions, and a possibility of organisations ceasing trading).

E-business has its roots in B2B transactions that sought to do away with paperwork concerning reorder levels, delivery schedules and invoicing. The obvious advantages of E-business to the customer in a B2C context has helped fuel a rapid growth in this area, including:

- One-stop shopping
- Convenience of place
- Ability to shop around
- Speed and flexibility
- Reduced impulse buys
- Direct communication over issues of delivery and complaints.

It has become difficult for firms to survive on domestic business alone. To achieve scale economies, firms need to develop new markets and e-marketing has allowed organisations to trade more easily globally and seek out and exploit new markets. This trend is evidenced by the fact that the last 20 years has seen world trade has grown at twice the rate of world GNP.

MARKETING

2.13.2 Marketing information systems and marketing planning

Market research is viewed as a component of total system of marketing information aimed at supporting marketing decisions. The collection of data to solve a one off marketing problem through the market research represents one part of the marketing information system. According to Lancaster and Withey (2005) three sub-systems feed into a marketing database:

- market research,
- marketing intelligence,
- internal organisational information.

From this database the system is able to offer Marketing Decision Support (MDS) to the marketing decision maker. The purpose of a system could be viewed as aiding the decision maker in the following ways:

- improving problem-solving capacity,
- dealing with unstructured or semi structured decisions,
- helping manage knowledge.

This is particularly so when technological advantages are maximised to support these processes.

Gray (2004) illustrates the advantages of IT in promotional campaigns by citing the example of the Carlson Marketing Group, which apparently:

- Plans campaigns using desk research including the Internet and reference guides.
- Maintains a database for all the venues visited, including demographic and volume details.
- Uses geographical information software to give detailed local marketing targets including customer profiles to pinpoint areas of the country that have a high concentration of the customer profile looked for.

The effect is to reach the targeted segment more effectively and accurately, so improving response rates and sales.

2.14 Strategic marketing

Developing a Marketing Strategy is vital to help the organisation manage in a dynamic, volatile and complex environment. Strategy will not emerge from a simple aggregation of the different elements of 'marketing mix' although these aspects will be key considerations.
The strategy itself should:

- be consistent with other organisational business planning processes,
- develop key priorities identified in the overall corporate strategy,
- cohesively plan and co-ordinate elements in an integrated fashion. It is vital that these factors are blended together to ensure that their product or service satisfies (or exceeds) the benefits demanded whether as consumer or business buyer,
- be realistic in terms of capability of the organisation and finance available.

The Chartered Institute of Marketing (2004) state that

A marketing plan (strategy) defining objectives, targets and performance measures is . . . developed with a financial budget. And when specific goals have been defined, then strategic alternatives to the current position can be discussed, and ways to achieve those alternatives can be chosen. The marketing strategy is then formalised within a specific plan of action, which is constantly revised and updated and the marketing campaign progresses.

2.14.1 Process involved

The process of developing a Marketing Strategy begins with an environmental audit involving:

- A detailed investigation of the market and targeted segments.
- The development of a PESTLE analysis that considers trends influencing the market (see earlier).
- A consideration of the position of the organisation relative to these PESTLE factors including potential realistic ways in which the organisation might influence this environment.
- Discussions centred on developing an appropriate marketing mix to achieve corporate aspirations.

Marketeers use several analytic frameworks shared by strategists when considering environmental factors. The most common start point is to use a SWOT (strengths, weaknesses, opportunities and threats) analysis usually depicted by a four-cell matrix where SW factors are internal and OT external factors. Internal factors are controllable. External issues are beyond the control of an organisation, however potentially influence might be exercised to some degree on some of these factors.

Analysis of internal factors should be guided by the following questions:

- What portfolio of products or services do we offer?
- What is our capability?
- What are our expectations?

The external environments in which an organisation operates can have a major impact upon its performance either positively or negatively. It is vital that these influences are understood in order that opportunities might be seized and threats compensated for. A PESTLE analysis (see earlier) represents one framework for considering the macro environment and relevant external factors. Results arising from this scanning should clearly indicate marketing implications.

Analysis is required of all external factors including:

- *Customers*: Their buying habits, nature, expectations, etc.
- *The market*: What research suggests, segmentation possibilities, the organisation's market position and potential for future development.
- *Competition*: Who they are and the basis upon which they are competing, also their distinctive strengths, weaknesses, track record, etc. Some organisations go to great lengths to discover more about their rivals and their products and services. In this context 'reverse engineering' involves taking apart and analysing a competitors' product '*in order to determine how they are made, costs of production and the way in which future development might proceed*' (CIMA, 2005).

Strategically considering marketing issues involves asking a series of basic questions such as:

- Product: What is being 'sold'?
- Place: Where is it sold?
- Price: How much for?
- Promotion: How do we engage our customers?

This naturally leads on to future considerations: what could be done and how do we bridge the gap from where we are now?

The Chartered Institute of Marketing (2004) note that:

Marketing focuses on the most fundamental requirements of companies to identify customers, research their needs and preferences, analyse their attitudes to promotion and other factors that influence their purchasing decisions and persuade them to buy products and services from you rather than a wide range of competitors.

2.14.2 Developing the strategy

All these aspects should be reflected in the marketing strategy. A strategy can ultimately be developed incorporating:

- clear marketing goals and objectives,
- targets, measures and performance indicators,
- the costing of the plan and the development of a revenue budget,
- an identification and costing of any capital requirements,
- identification of strategic alternatives,
- a detailed action plan-incorporating SMART (specific, measurable, achievable, realistic time bound) targets.

2.14.3 Coordination within the organisation

Strategic decisions made about marketing will impact on all other functional areas, for instance:

- *Finance:* Cash flow implications, finance for marketing campaigns, etc.
- *Human Resourcing:* Training requirements, specialist recruitment, etc.
- *Operations:* Cost and volume implications of switching production, etc.

The strategy itself should be developed in conjunction with as wide a body of individuals as possible. This will help coordinate marketing with other aspects of the organisation and 'ground' strategies within local realities. Additionally, two very good further reasons exist for such an approach. First, these individuals will need to implement the strategy and will therefore need to be committed to it. Second, the involvement of others leads to a greater depth of shared knowledge and understanding in order to produce a robust strategy.

2.14.4 Agreement and monitoring

Marketing research is the investigation of the marketing activities of a company (the entire marketing mix). It looks into how far all these activities are consumer-orientated, and how they might be planned in the future. This therefore includes branding, product mix, pricing, advertising, sales promotion, public relations, packaging, and distribution. In this way, the importance of marketing research is to provide information that will enable the correct marketing decisions to be made. One of these key decisions must be the commitment of funds to marketing itself, including research costs, advertising costs, promotions, etc. Marketing research can therefore be used in two contexts:

- To provide a basis for developing a new strategy
- To review the existing strategy.

The processes and techniques used in monitoring, implementing and controlling a marketing plan are arguably as important, if not more important, than the processes involved in formulating the strategy.

Once developed, the strategy should be approved by top management and communicated to staff to ensure effective implementation. This will extend beyond those involved in the marketing function and will include colleagues in others areas such as finance, production and research and development. Marketing is not an island and the strategy will not succeed without the cooperation of others.

Inevitably factors will alter and the action plan should be used for progress monitoring and should be continually reviewed, revised and updated as the marketing campaign progresses. With a greater emphasis being attached to measuring and monitoring performance more sophisticated tools are being developed. This control information is helpful in both coping with volatile environments and also ensuring greater internal accountability.

2.14.5 Social responsibility in a marketing context

Accountability can also be viewed as a corporate concept, in this case the organisation being accountable to society at large. As with all areas of business, ethics and responsibility to society is a relevant issue. Certain ethical questions naturally arise in relation to marketing including:

- To whom do we sell?
- Are our products of an appropriate standard, safe and produced to environmental standards?
- How do we advertise: is it fair balanced and truthful?
- Do we have policies that support dissatisfied customers?
- Is our pricing policy exploitive of any groups in society, etc.?

The basis of social responsibility is the premise that an organisation enjoys certain benefits of society and therefore in return should engage in practices that supports and does not exploit society. One organisation that is renowned for ethical trading and marketing practices is the Body Shop and Table 2.5 below outlines both their values and how this translates into community involvement.

Table 2.5   The Body Shop: a strategic approach to social responsibility

'*Our values*

We consider testing products or ingredients on animals to be morally and scientifically indefensible

We support small producer communities around the world who supply us with accessories and natural ingredients

We know that you're unique, and we'll always treat you like an individual. We like you just the way you are

We believe that it is the responsibility of every individual to actively support those who have human rights denied to them

We believe that a business has the responsibility to protect the environment in which it operates, locally and globally

Community involvement

Community involvement is nothing new to The Body Shop – it is a concept that has always been an integral part of our business and is vital to us going forward into the 21st century. As a socially responsible business we campaign for the protection of the environment, human and civil rights and against animal testing within the cosmetics and toiletries industry.

Volunteering supports this work enabling us to positively contribute to the local, national and global communities in which we operate. We are proud of our employees' enthusiastic involvement in their local communities and actively encourage their participation at the same time as considering the changing expectations of society and the growing environmental and ethical concerns. In understanding this we realize that our support is fundamental and continually explore imaginative new ways of working.'

Source: www.thebodyshop.com. Reprinted with the kind permission of The Body Shop International plc.

It is interesting to note that one aspect of promotion, public relations (PR) and community involvement, is entirely consistent with a marketing strategy that reflects social responsibility. Sponsorship of local events, community projects, sports and charitable donations can broadly be classified as community involvement. While the aim may be to enrich the community at the same time it might also provide a valuable source of PR as part of the promotional mix.

The following article extract illustrates an interesting dilemma for the fast food giant McDonald's as it considers whether it should adjust one aspect of its marketing mix (product) or not in the USA.

Exercise 2.13

As you read this short passage make notes on the significant factors in the Macro environment (PESTLE factors) and the ethical issues arising.

Why McD's hasn't cut the fat. Fast-food leader fears oil change will leave bad taste among its fry fans

When McDonald's corp. announced it would move to a trans-fat-free oil, the impact was immediate as consumers flooded the fast feeder with complaints that its fries didn't taste as good. But in actuality the taste was the same, the company hadn't yet switched oils, and some four years later it still hasn't.

Now the share leader is still struggling to make good on its 2002 vow as the pressure mounts from rivals such as Wendy's and KFC, which have cut trans fats from their menus and Burger King, which will start testing new oil within 90 days. McDonald's, meanwhile, has yet to put an end date on its super-secret tests.

It's understandable that McDonald's would be ambivalent about changing its signature fried potatoes, which helped shape the Golden Arches. Fries rank second only to beverages as the chain's margin-leading item and are the undisputed leader in quality and taste among McDonald's peers, said executives close to the marketer.

'In a category where there are low quality ratings of food, the fries are always rated high, and they are inexorably linked to the brand, perhaps more than any other product', said one executive, comparing McDonald's trans-fat conundrum to New Coke. 'That would be the one thing you wouldn't want to mess with if you didn't have to.'

Yet McDonald's has to, unless it wants to go toe-to-toe with municipalities mandating that it has to go trans-fat-free.

And that raises the specter of a public-relations nightmare, no matter what McDonald's does. If it changes its oil, the company will likely encounter the same kind of consumer push back it felt in 2002. If it keeps trans-fat oil, the chain could get lambasted by health advocates.

(*Source:* extracted from *Why McD's hasn't cut the fat*, by MacArthur, Kate, Advertising Age, 11/6/2006)

☑ Solution

You could have made notes in the following areas:

- *Socio-cultural trends.* A desire for fast food as part of a busy lifestyle. Fast food has become an American way of life. There is still a taste by customers for full fat fries (chips). Generally in society there are concerns over healthy eating and concerns about obesity which is being led by a vocal health lobby.
- *Political.* The desire by municipalities (government) for trans-fat-free oil to be used.
- *Legal.* Possible legislation over the use of trans-fat-free oil.
- Ethical issues:
  - McDonald's announced it would move to a trans-fat-free oil in 2002 does this make it honour bound to keep its public promise? Is the delay ethical?
  - Is it ethically defensible that McDonald's should continue to sell food that it knows is unhealthy? Is it right that vulnerable groups (children, those in a hurry) should have easy access to food that may lead them into having health difficulties?
  - Do McDonald's sell the customer what they want even if it is harmful to them?
  - Are McDonald's prepared to break the law and continue with production of fries (chips) as present?

2.15 Summary

This chapter has covered much of the basics of marketing in practice, including the marketing concept and its relationship to organisation's functioning and systems. The notion of the marketing mix and its associated tools has been discussed. Throughout understanding has been built of the applicability of marketing to many types of organisation and the particular considerations associated with them. Finally, attention has been given to issues of both technology in modern marketing, and practical considerations associated with producing a strategic marketing plan.

References and further reading

Berens, C. (2006) Windows of opportunity, *Financial Management* (UK), November, p. 12(5)

Benady, D. (2004) Marketing's age concern. *Marketing Week*, October 28.

Boddy, D. and Paton, R. (2005) *Management. An Introduction* (3rd edn), Harlow: Financial Times, Prentice Hall.

CIMA (2005) *CIMA Official Terminology*. Elsevier.

Fine, J. (2005) Hard questions from Google; Asking advertisers: What's the right amount to spend? *Business Week*, October 24, p. 28.

Gray, R. (2004) Right people, place, time, *Marketing* (UK), August 1, p. 23.

Johnson, G., Scholes, K. and Whittington, R. (2005) *Exploring Corporate Strategy: Text and Cases* (7th edn.), Harlow: Financial Times, Prentice Hall.

Kotler, P. and Lane Keller, K. (2006) *Marketing Management*, (12th edn) Prentice Hall.

Lancaster, G. and Withey, F. (2005) *Marketing Fundamentals*, Oxford: Butterworth-Heinemann.

MacArthur, K. (2006) Why McD's hasn't cut the fat, *Advertising Age*, 00018899, 11/6/2006, Vol. 77, No. 45.

Mullins, L. J. (2005) *Management and Organisational Behaviour* (7th edn), Harlow: Financial Times, Prentice Hall.

Porter, M. E. (1980) *Competitive Strategy*. New York: Free Press.

also

The Chartered Institute of Marketing (2004) (www.cim.co.uk)

The Body Shop (2004) (www.thebodyshop.com)

Revision Questions

2

? Question 1

In the last few decades, companies have moved increasingly towards the targeting of particular customer segments rather than seeking to sell a single product range to all customers. Explain the advantages that a company might hope to gain by targeting particular segments of the market. **(10 marks)**

? Question 2

H Company, a high-street clothing retailer, designs and sells clothing. Until recently, the company name was well-known for quality clothing at an affordable price, but the situation has changed dramatically as new entrants to the market have rapidly taken market share away from H Company. One marketing analyst has commented that the problem for H Company is that it has never moved from being sales orientated to being marketing orientated and that this is why it has lost touch with its customers.

Requirements
(a) Describe the difference between a company that concentrates on 'selling' its products and one that has adopted a marketing approach. Advise H Company on how to develop itself into an organisation that is driven by customer needs. **(10 marks)**
(b) Explain how the management in H Company could make use of the marketing mix to help regain its competitive position in the clothing market. **(10 marks)**

? Question 3

Describe three variables you think would be useful as a basis for segmenting the market for clothing sold by a large retail chain, and two variables for segmenting the market in paint sold to other businesses by a paint manufacturer. Explain your reasons for the choice of all five variables. **(10 marks)**

? Question 4

Hubbles, a national high-street clothing retailer has recently appointed a new Chief Executive. The company is well established and relatively financially secure. It has a reputation for stability and traditional, quality clothing at an affordable price. Lately, however, it has suffered from intense competition leading to a loss of market share and an erosion of customer loyalty.

Hubbles has all the major business functions provided by 'in house' departments, including finance, human resources, purchasing, strategy and marketing. The Strategy and Marketing department has identified a need for comprehensive review of the company's effectiveness. In response, the new Chief Executive has commissioned a review by management consultants.

Their initial findings include the following:

- Hubbles has never moved from being sales-oriented to being marketing-oriented and this is why it has lost touch with its customers.
- Hubbles now needs to get closer to its customers and operate a more effective marketing mix.
- Additional investment in its purchasing department can add significantly to improving Hubbles' competitive position.

The Chief Executive feels that a presentation of interim findings to senior managers would be helpful at this point. You are a member of the management consultancy team and have been asked to draft a *PowerPoint* slide presentation of some of the key points.

On a single sheet of paper prepare a slide outline and a few notes in response to following sub-questions:

(a) Describe the difference between a company that concentrates on 'selling' its products and one that has adopted a marketing approach.   **(5 marks)**
(b) Explain how Hubbles might develop itself into an organisation that is driven by customer needs.   **(5 marks)**
(c) Explain what is meant by the 'marketing mix'.   **(5 marks)**
(d) Identify examples of ways in which the management in Hubbles could make use of the marketing mix to help regain its competitive position.   **(5 marks)**

Solutions to Revision Questions

2

✔ Solution 1

Companies have a number of alternatives as to where they will focus their marketing effort. They can adopt an undifferentiated marketing stance in which they make a product offering to the market as a whole. They can alternatively seek to cater for the needs of each individual customer, a bespoke approach, finally they can focus on particular segments of the market. The idea of dividing the market into segments is to identify groups of potential consumers who have similar needs and will respond to a particular marketing mix in broadly similar ways.

The undifferentiated or mass marketing approach is inefficient in many ways because much of the marketing effort is wasted on consumers who have no interest in purchasing the product or service and are unlikely to do so whatever the efforts of the marketing staff.

The alternative of targeting and catering for the different needs of every individual customer is costly and impractical for most organisations. Resources in organisations are limited and the task of dealing with each customer on a one-to-one basis is too costly for most companies to contemplate.

The advantage of market segmentation is that it allows a company to concentrate its resources on meeting the needs of consumers who have been identified by market research as those who are most likely to purchase the product or service. This is, of course, if the product or service is of an appropriate quality and is offered at the right price, in the right place at the right time.

In addition to the advantage of being able to concentrate resources in a way that will bring the greatest return, segmentation has other advantages. These include easier analysis of customers, a better understanding of the competition and more effective market planning.

Segmentation allows a company to gain a better understanding of customer needs, wants and other characteristics because of the sharper focus it allows on the personal, situational and behavioural factors that characterise customers in a particular segment of the market. This detailed knowledge allows marketers to respond quickly to any changes in what the target customers want.

Competitor analysis is also assisted by knowledge of market segmentation because it enables a company to develop an understanding of the nature of the competition they face. By focusing on particular segments, it is much easier for a company to identify its competitors and at which segments it is targeting its products. If the company observes that competition is severe in a particular segment, it may be that this knowledge of market segments will allow the company to focus on a different segment and so avoid head-on and costly competition.

MARKETING

Finally, knowledge of market segments assists with marketing planning. Dividing markets up allows organisations to develop plans that give special attention to the particular needs of customers in different segments. The time scale of such plans can also be facilitated because some segments change more rapidly than others and such changes need to be anticipated in any planning operation. The markets in ladies' fashions and in recorded music are examples of rapidly changing markets and of the need to anticipate and to plan accordingly.

✓ Solution 2

(a) The claim that H Company concentrates on 'selling', implies that the company is not focussed on customer needs. Instead of finding out what the customer wants, H Company is trying to sell whatever items it happens to have in stock. Sales orientated organisations are so-called because of their aggressive selling, advertising and sales promotion. But selling is not marketing. As all the textbooks make clear, marketing is about trying to get the company to supply what the customer wants rather than getting the customer to accept what the company supplies.

In order to become customer led, H Company needs to adopt the marketing concept. This involves several key changes to the way it conducts its business. The first and most important is for H Company to focus on the need of its customers. This shift in orientation will require H Company to change the way it defines and investigates its markets, prices its products and communicates with its customers.

One of the first steps for H Company therefore is to identify the needs of potential customers and how these needs can be satisfied. This is the main purpose of market research. Only when the customer's needs are known can the company develop a range of clothing to meet them.

The greatest opportunity for H Company lies in meeting needs that have not been met by the competition, so market research should also cover competitors' products so that H Company knows exactly what is on offer in the market place and what gaps if any exist.

Being customer-led, involves more than a change in the marketing department: it also involves the adoption of a new way of thinking by the whole organisation.

The critical people in the customer led organisation that H Company is seeking to develop, are the front line staff because it is they who the customer comes into direct contact with. They need to be trained to be responsive to customers and to provide the best possible service and image for the company.

Marketing cannot be left just to the marketing department. It requires all departments to adopt the marketing philosophy if it is to succeed. This means that the design department of H Company must take note of the findings of market research and seek to design clothing that fits the needs of the customer. Similarly, the supplier must recognise the need to sell clothing at a price the customer can afford to pay. This customer-led focus should, in fact, permeate every department through production, packaging and merchandising so that at all times the needs of the customer are kept in focus.

In a company that adopts a marketing approach, it is the task of middle and senior management to help front line staff by providing the right products and resources and by helping remove obstacles.

A further aspect of the marketing concept is to meet customer needs better than competitors. In order to do this, they must measure themselves against competitors by some kind of benchmarking system that compares customer satisfaction indicators with those of key rivals. H Company can then use this kind of information as a basis for possible improvements to the design of its products, its manufacturing processes, customer service, and means of display.

(b) When H Company has adequately identified its target market by Market research it will be in a position to develop its marketing mix. The marketing mix consists of four major components: product, place (distribution), promotion and price. Increasingly, 'people' are becoming the fifth component particularly for service organisations. These components are called marketing mix decision variables because a marketing manager must decide how to create and maintain a marketing mix that satisfies consumers' needs.

Marketing mix variables are often viewed as controllable variables because they can be changed. There are, however, limits to how much these variables can be altered because changes in sizes, colours, shapes and designs of most tangible goods like clothing are expensive. Nevertheless, in a world of rapidly changing fashion, there is a need to make changes quickly to meet changing customer needs. This is also true of promotional campaigns and the methods used to distribute products. Staff will also require training and motivating, and all this takes time.

The management at H Company must develop a marketing mix that precisely matches the needs of the potential customers in the target market. Before he/she can do this they have to research the market about these needs. The information required will include data about the age, income, gender and educational level of people in the target market, their preferences for product features and their attitudes towards competitors' products. With these kinds of data, the management at H Company will be better able to develop a product, promotion programme, distribution system, and price that satisfy the people in the target market.

The product variable is the aspect of the marketing mix that deals with consumers' product wants and desired characteristics. It also involves the creation or alteration of packages and brand names and may include decisions about guarantees and arrangements for returns. To maintain a satisfying set of products that will help H Company achieve its goals, the organisation must be able to develop new products, modify existing ones and eliminate those that no longer satisfy buyers or yield acceptable profits

In dealing with the distribution (place) variable, the management in H Company must seek to make products available in the quantities desired to as many customers as possible in the right place and keep the total inventory, transport and storage costs as low as possible. This may involve the motivation of suppliers and dealers and a review of inventory control procedures and transport systems. The retail outlets, as the place where customers buy clothes should be designed to reflect the values of the H Company's brand and positioning. This could be achieved through signage, layout of stores, display of clothes and location.

The promotion variable relates to activities used to inform people about an organisation and its products. Promotion can be aimed at increasing public awareness of an organisation and of new or existing products. In addition, promotion can serve to educate consumers about product features and indicate H Company's position as a retailer of quality clothing at affordable prices. It may also be used to keep interest strong in an established product that has been available for many years.

The price variable is concerned with establishing pricing policies and determining product prices. Price is a critical component of the marketing mix because consumers are concerned about the value obtained in an exchange. Price is often used as a competitive tool; in fact, extremely intense price competition sometimes leads to price wars, so H Company will have to be particularly careful with this variable.

People, particularly the staff in the retail outlets, can influence buyer behaviour, so H Company should ensure that they are given appropriate training and support.

✔ Solution 3

In the segmentation of consumer markets the availability of information on demographic, socio-economic and geographic location variables have made their usage popular.

Demographic variables include age, gender, family, race, and religion; socio-economic variables include income, occupation, education and social class; geographic location variables include country, region, type of urban area, and type of housing. The use of lifestyle, motives and personality are also increasingly used for segmentation purposes.

There is no single best way of segmenting a market and few if any market segments can be regarded as timeless but experience tells us that a number of variables have been found useful as a basis for segmenting particular markets.

Some of the useful bases for segmenting the market for clothing include the following:

Differences in the clothing worn by males and females is so evident that it hardly needs to be mentioned. Males and females do, however, wear different styles and items of clothing so it is necessary to design, promote, price and place male and female clothing according to the demands in each market segment.

A second useful variable is that of age. Common observation tells us that retailers segment the population according to age. So it is common in a retail department store to see not only men's and women's clothing displayed separately but also clothing for children, young teenagers, older teenagers, and young adults to mature adults.

Another variable that may be used is that of occupation. Professional, managerial and administrative workers tend to wear business suits to the office while other occupational groups tend to wear more casual attire.

The clothing market can be segmented by other variables related to occupation such as income. High-income earners can afford more exclusive and expensive clothing than middle-income earners who in turn can afford better quality clothing than low-income earners. The above variables represent the more common bases for segmentation.

The segmenting of organisational or industrial markets is less frequently carried out than segmentation in consumer markets but nevertheless, companies find it increasingly useful.

Organisations may segment markets according to personal characteristics of buyers, situational factors such as urgency and size of order, purchasing approach, technologies applied by buying organisations, and demographic aspects like location, industry and size.

An example of segmentation according to personal characteristics of buyers might be a paint manufacturer who segments potential customers into several different groups such as paint wholesalers, do-it-yourself retail outlets, housing developers, contracting decorators, and vehicle manufacturers.

Segmenting according to situational factors such as order size can also be illustrated by the example of the paint manufacturer. The size of container and packaging of the paint will vary according to the user needs of the customer. Contracting decorators, for instance, may need large containers, but will not be particularly concerned about packaging, while do-it-yourself outlets may require containers of various sizes with attractive decoration.

✅ Solution 4

(a)
Slide 1:
Features of sales-orientated organisations:

- Aggressive selling, advertising and sales promotion.
- A concentration on selling not marketing.
- A strong sales department.

  Marketing is about:

- Supplying what the customer wants.
- An organisation-wide philosophy.

Notes to Slide 1:
The claim that Hubbles concentrates on 'selling' implies that it is not focussed on customer needs. Instead of finding out what the customer wants, it is trying to sell whatever items it happens to have in stock.

(b)
Slide 2:
Adopting the marketing concept:

- focus on potential customer needs (and how these can be satisfied);
- greatest opportunity = meeting needs (gaps) not currently met;
- implies market research, competitor product research;
- possible future benchmarking;
- NOT a change to the Marketing department: a new way of organisational thinking;
- training for all staff;
- management to help by providing the right products & resources.

Notes to Slide 2:
Reorientation means Hubbles to change the way it defines and investigates its markets, prices, products and communication with its customers. The critical people are the front-line staff that customers come into direct contact with. This customer-led focus should permeate every department so that the needs of the customer are kept in view at all times.

(c)
Slide 3:
Components of marketing mix:

- *Product.* Customers' product wants and desired characteristics;
- *Place* (distribution). Desired quantity available at the right place and time;
- *Promotion.* Increasing awareness of products; inform about product features; keep interest;
- *Price.* Is critical and can be used as a competitive tool.

Plus sometimes added for service organisations:

- *People*. Staff decisions, image and actions central to the other marketing mix components.

Notes to Slide 3:

After Hubbles has identified its target market, it will be in a position to develop its marketing mix. Components are decision variables that can be changed and Hubbles must decide how to create and maintain a marketing mix that satisfies consumers' needs.

(d)
Slide 4:

- *Product*. Develop new products, modify/enhance existing ones and eliminate others.
- *Place*. Improve inventory, transport and storage to serve market. Well-sited premises redesigned to reflect brand, and so on.
- *Promotion*. Rebranding, advertising campaigns, using different media to target groups.
- *Price*. Revise pricing structure to convey value, or price below competitors.
- *People*. Training programmes, monitoring systems and on going support can influence buyer behaviour.

Notes to Slide 4:

Must develop a marketing mix that precisely matches the needs of potential customers in the target market. First research the market for data about the age, income, sex and educational level of target market, preferences for product features and attitudes to competitors' products.

3

People Issues:
Motivation, Rewards
and Ethical
Considerations

People Issues: Motivation, Rewards and Ethical Considerations

3

LEARNING OUTCOMES

This chapter contains detail on broader themes that underpin many areas of organisational management. It provides some background to issues of motivation, the relevance of 'Taylorism' and ethical considerations that are particularly relevant when dealing with people. Completing this section should help you to:

► evaluate the role of incentives in staff development as well as individual and organisational performance,

► explain the importance of ethical behaviour in business generally and for the Chartered Management Accountant in particular.

3.1 Introduction

The issues covered in this chapter represent something of a foundation for study of the next chapter specifically and the subject matter of organisational management and information systems in general.

This chapter provides an underpinning of understanding in issues relating to 'fair' and legal employment practices and ways of managing these. Attention is given to the role of incentives and issues in the design of reward systems. These arise out of understanding of certain key theories derived from the work of several writers including Taylor, Schein, McGregor, Maslow, and Herzberg. Finally, specific attention is drawn to personal business ethics and the CIMA Code of Ethics.

3.2   Motivation in overview

Motivation is vital to human resource management; it does after all influence employee productivity and quality of work. Mullins (2005) defines motivation as 'the driving force within individuals by which they attempt to achieve some goal in order to fulfill some need or expectation'.

The study of motivation involves many complexities and difficulties, need least because it involves behaviours, individuals and internal processes. As a consequence, there are several different theories of motivation. This chapter will outline some of the principal ones.

Exercise 3.1

Motivation is not the only factor influencing employee productivity and quality of work. What are some of the other factors you would expect to be important?

Solution

Other organisational factors, such as the availability of technology, raw materials and financial resources will also have an important effect on productivity and quality.

Much of a manager's functioning concerns performance management. As such a manager operating to an ethical code will attempt to improve performance in a way that is both legitimate and fair. Attempts to improve performance should start by addressing the question of whether there is a problem of motivation. The simplest way of viewing motivation is in terms of how much effort an individual puts into a particular course of action. The outcome of the course of action, however, depends on other attributes of the individual besides effort including ability, skills and support.

Exercise 3.2

Reflect and make notes on a manager's ability to influence the variables of effort, ability, skills and rewards. Which in your opinion are easiest to influence positively?

Mullins (2005) identified distinct broad classifications that could be applied to understanding motivation, namely:

- Economic rewards such as pay, security, perks of the job, etc.
- Intrinsic satisfaction, derived from the nature of work, interest in the job, self development, etc.
- Social relationships, such as friendships, being part of a team, etc.

Note: Motivation – a case in point

A summer heat wave was met with an innovative response by the management of Volkswagen (VW) Group UK. The 500 plus staff were invited to cool down, both morning and afternoon, with ice cream, watermelon and anything else restaurant staff could come up with. This contrasts with a tale of a large financial institution who had a rule that employees could only remove their jackets if temperatures soared above 80 degrees (F) for 3 days or more. By the time the memo granting permission had got to staff, temperatures had usually gone back down. Volkswagen looked at what staff needed and someone was able to make the decision right away. Undeniably an inexpensive treat, it was well received by staff because it showed they were valued as people. The Head of HR explained: *we're just the organisation in the middle, so all our value added has to be through our people. This means they have to be as motivated as possible.* People may be still driven by cash rewards, but these are recognised by VW as not enough. In addition to being a good payer, VW also boasts a good pension scheme and exceptional maternity benefits. (Source: Carrington, 2004)

Clearly this is a complex area of study. In an attempt to better understand this subject, the sections immediately following introduce various motivation theories and theorists. These are of relevance when considering motivation and its associated implications for HR practice.

3.3   Money as a motivator?

An appropriate starting point is the consideration of money as a potential motivator. Many of the assumptions that underpin HR policies and practices are founded on an assumption that money motivates individuals.

3.3.1   Taylor

Early writers such as Frederick W. Taylor (1856–1917) looked at maximising productivity. Taylor's long working experience in industry led him to conclude that:

- workers varied their pace at work to suit the conditions
- managers made little effort to specify what made up a 'reasonable day's work'
- no effort was made to identify the best methods, nor to train the workers in them.

Taylor reasoned that the prime objective of management should be to secure the maximum prosperity for both employer and employee. He established four principles:

- The development of a true 'science' of work. This was the assessment of what constituted a fair day's work, as well as a fair day's pay.
- The scientific selection and progressive development of workers, involving careful recruitment and training to ensure that the worker was capable of achieving output and quality targets.
- The bringing together of the science of work and the scientifically selected and trained men. This was referred to as the 'mental revolution', as the workforce were encouraged to develop to their full potential including their brains.
- The constant and intimate co-operation between management and workers, for instance over the allocation of work.

Taylor believed that workers would be motivated by obtaining the highest possible remuneration so work should be organised in the most efficient way. Perhaps too readily he assumed the view that the individual is a rational animal, calculating both effort required to work and reward.

More positively, Taylor recognised that if specialised knowledge and skills were concentrated in the hands of well-trained and able employees, there would be an improvement in productivity. He therefore broke jobs down into separate functions and then gave each function to an individual. Sometimes this meant that as many as eight functional foremen were giving instructions to other workers. Taylor believed that it was only through the effective use of control by specialists that best use would be made of the resources available to increase the size of the incentive surplus to be shared between efficient staff.

With modern trends including the need for flexible working and 'multi-skilling' it would be easy to dismiss Taylorism as outdated. It is still very evident, however in many areas including the development of 'call-centres': a classic application of scientific management principles of division of labour and specialisation of function.

Taylor's thinking has clear implications for a number of areas not least providing a challenge to consider the benefits of:

- Work measurement and study
- Fair expectations of the individual
- Training
- Job design
- Financial rewards
- Operations management as a subject (see Chapter 5).

Interestingly Lawrence and Lorsch's (1984) research supports delineation of work particularly when an organisation operates in a complex environment. Functions within organisations should be structured as a response to the environment in which they operate. (To succeed however the integration of these sub departments is essential.)

3.3.2 Schein

Edgar Schein's contribution to motivation concentrates on the behaviours of people not as individuals but as social groups. In his work on culture, Schein (2004) showed how behaviour altered to suit varying circumstances in organisations. This work links to other theories in terms of conformance and the predictability of individual behaviour. Four useful categories of worker (referred to in a sexist manner as 'man') are generally applied in this area:

- 'Rational Economic Man'
- 'Social Man'
- 'Self-actualising Man'
- 'Complex Man'.

   Rational Economic Man. This view has its roots in the economic theories of Adam Smith. It states that the pursuit of self-interest and the maximisation of gain are the prime motivators of people. It lays stress on a person's rational calculation of self-interest, especially in relation to economic needs. Schein assumes people can be classified according to two extremes: the untrustworthy (money motivated and calculating) and the trustworthy (more broadly motivated, moral elite who must organise and manage the mass).

   Social Man. In categorising social man, Schein draws heavily on Elton Mayo's work and the Hawthorne experiment, which saw how 'socialisation' at work motivated people (see later). Based on this thinking managers should pay attention to people's needs and move from being a controller to becoming a coordinator, guide and facilitator. Morale at work is seen as a way of levering superior performance.

   Self-actualising Man. The concept of self-actualising man is based in Maslow's theory of human needs (see later). Self-fulfillment is seen as the prime driving force behind individuals, not money. Such individuals need challenge in tasks at work, and be given responsibility and a sense of pride in their work.

Complex Man. Schein sees motivation very much in terms of a 'psychological contract' based on the expectations that the employee and the organisation have of each other, and the extent to which these are mutually fulfilled.

Exercise 3.3

As part of a 'psychological contract' what reasonable expectations do you have of your employer?

3.3.3 McGregor

Managers make assumptions about what employees are 'like', their needs and what motivates them. The manager may not articulate these assumptions explicitly, but their beliefs and prejudices will impact on their methods of managing certain individuals and groups.

Douglas McGregor suggested that there are two different sets of assumptions that managers might have about their subordinates, calling these Theories X and Y:

- Theory X. Work is inherently distasteful to most people. The average person prefers to be directed, wishes to avoid responsibility and wants security above all else.
- Theory Y. People want to contribute to meaningful goals they have helped to establish. The average person learns under the right conditions not only to accept but to seek responsibility.

Each of these assumptions has different implications for how people should be managed. Theory X implies that the manager must control people's work tightly, supervise them closely and give simple, repetitive tasks to do. The key 'motivators' are economic rewards and punishments. Theory Y, on the other hand, suggests that the manager should seek to create a participative environment in which each person can contribute to the limits of his or her ability, and to encourage self-direction.

Theory X is clearly inconsistent with contemporary enlightened thinking and yet many managers still approach their task from a Theory X perspective. It is not difficult to see the limitations of an uncritical application of a Theory X approach to management:

- The assumptions is invalid for those who are disinterested in economic rewards and unafraid of punishments.
- Individuals may resent strict controls and close supervision and this may cause conflict.
- Individuals that are treated in a Theory X manner may respond in this way by showing no initiative and nothing better than minimal compliance. (The danger of a 'self-fulfilling prophecy' arises.)
- It might be more effective and pleasant to encourage self-motivation and commitment.

It is worthwhile considering the application of a Theory Y approach that attempts to provide greater self-direction and satisfy individual needs at work. In order to understand the 'needs' that might be important to satisfy, it is useful to consider content theories of motivation.

The following journal extract addresses both motivation and money by synthesising recent research into the area. It comes to the conclusion that financial gain is overestimated as a staff motivator, but that money is still important:

More than money

There have been many thousands of studies over the last decade that have looked at incentives and rewards. These have overwhelmingly found that while motivation is determined by both monetary and non-monetary factors, money has come to play an overly important role in our thinking about the causes of behaviour. In most companies, very limited time and effort are spent on considering non-monetary sources of motivation.

But with regard to money as a reward, what have we learnt from these decades of research? Four key findings emerge.

First, money is important at work not simply because of what it can purchase, but also through the status it signifies in comparison with others, particularly with colleagues in our immediate proximity. For both monetary and non-monetary rewards, what may be crucial is not the absolute amount, but rather the distribution. Second, our perceptions of justice and fairness play a crucial role in this comparative process. In fact, the evidence supports the idea that most people prefer more equal distribution of rewards. Third (and perhaps reassuringly given the previous finding), there is little evidence that higher rewards or bonuses have an effect on subsequent performance. Finally, with regard to who gets what, the process of allocation can be as important as what is actually allocated. Specifically, people prefer procedures that are involving.

(*Source:* extracted from More than money by Lynda Gratton, *People Management*, January 29, 2004, Vol. 10, No. 2, p. 23).

3.4 Content theories of motivation

Content theories of motivation seek to describe and categorise the needs that influence behaviour. They assume that behaviour is caused by, and is directed towards, the satisfaction of these needs. Psychologists have suggested many needs, and there are several different theories. Among others, two of the most influential are considered here: Abraham Maslow's hierarchy of needs and Frederick Herzberg's dual factor theory.

3.4.1 Maslow

Abraham Maslow constructed his theory of motivation as a result of his experience as a clinical psychologist. The theory is founded on several assumptions, the first of which is that the individual is 'a perpetually wanting animal'. Secondly, only relatively unsatisfied needs are capable of motivating behaviour. Finally, five levels of needs can be arranged in a hierarchy of potency. This means that at any one time, the lowest level of relatively unsatisfied need will be the one that motivates current behaviour, and the less it is satisfied the more it will motivate. The individual will act primarily in order to satisfy that need, then move on to the next level and so on. The hierarchy of needs is as follows:

Higher-order needs

Self-actualisation
Esteem
Affiliation (social)
Safety
Physiological

As each need is satisfied, so the individual moves up the hierarchy, with successive levels of need dominating behaviour. If conditions are favourable, the individual will progress towards self-actualisation, unless a lower-order need again becomes unsatisfied, in which case behaviour will revert to seeking satisfaction of this need.

Maslow's theory has been widely accepted by many management writers, but it does have a number of limitations, including:

- It is very difficult to test empirically.
- It assumes all individuals have the same needs organised in the same way.
- It is difficult to predict actual behaviour from the theory.

Nevertheless, Maslow's theory provides a general explanation of motivation that many can relate to.

For reflection

F.W. Taylor's thinking on motivation is economic by nature, and this of course fits with the lower levels of Maslow's theory.

3.4.2   Herzberg

The central idea of Frederick Herzberg's motivation-hygiene, or dual factor, theory is that the opposite of job satisfaction is the lack of job satisfaction, and not job dissatisfaction. Similarly the opposite of job dissatisfaction is, by the same logic, an absence of dissatisfaction. It is not simply that satisfaction and dissatisfaction are different but, in Herzberg's view, that they are affected and caused by different factors. Factors associated with job satisfaction are called 'motivators', factors that cause dissatisfaction are called 'hygiene factors', (from the idea that good hygiene does not cause health, but rather serves to prevent ill health or sickness). As a result of an original study of accountants and engineers, and subsequently of further groups of employees, Herzberg suggested that the main motivator and hygiene factors can be categorised as follows:

Motivators	*Hygiene factors*
Recognition	Status
Achievement	Pay
Possibility of growth	Interpersonal relations
Advancement	Supervision
Responsibility	Company policy and administration
Work itself	Job security
Personal life	Working conditions

The parallels with Maslow's theory should be apparent, although Herzberg argues strongly against confusing the two approaches.

Although other research evidence gives some support to this separation of satisfaction and dissatisfaction, a number of serious problems with the approach have emerged:

- The theory is, essentially, one of job satisfaction, and not of motivation. It is not made clear what exactly is the linkage between increased satisfaction and job performance.
- Herzberg clearly believes the two to be connected, and advocates a policy of job enrichment, whereby motivation factors are built into jobs. Some experiments with job enrichment have been successful, but others have not.
- It ignores individual differences in needs and motives.

Despite these criticisms, Herzberg's theory and, particularly, its job-enrichment applications, has also been very influential and popular across a wide range of jobs, organisations and countries. The limitations of Maslow's and Herzberg's theories do not invalidate them, but simply indicate that individual motivation is not as straightforward as these theories might suggest. A particular problem is that there is no necessary connection between improving an individual's satisfaction or morale and increases in productivity or other dimensions of job performance. This is because individual needs and goals will not always be fully compatible with organisational objectives. These points can be developed more fully by looking at another category of theories of motivation that concentrates on explaining the process of motivation.

3.5 Process theories of motivation

A particular need can be satisfied in many different ways, and by a variety of forms of behaviour. This clearly limits the predictive value of content theories of behaviour. Process theories attempt to address this issue by explaining how individuals choose between alternative courses of action that might satisfy needs.

The most influential type of process theory is probably expectancy theory. In its simplest form, this approach postulates that when faced with a choice between alternative courses of action an individual bases his or her selection on the following two factors:

- The value placed on achieving the outcome of each alternative (in the terminology of expectancy theory this is referred to as 'valence'),
- The likelihood or probability of being able to achieve each outcome (this is 'expectancy').

Choice is then based on a multiplicative relationship between valence and expectancy, because if either is nil there will be no motivation, with the individual choosing the alternative that results in the highest or best outcome.

Exercise 3.4

You are faced with the need to choose between two job offers, one of which offers a salary of £20,000 and a very high probability (say 0.8) that you could do it to a satisfactory standard or better; the other carries a salary of £50,000, but you are very worried that you might not be able to meet the acceptable performance standards (say 0.2 chance of success) required to continue in the position. In every other respect, the jobs appear equal. Which would you select?

✓ Solution

The above example obviously oversimplifies the issues involved in choosing between the jobs, but it can be used to illustrate the basic choice principle of expectancy theory. Job 1 offers a salary of £20,000 and this is its valence. The 'expectancy' of being able to carry out the job responsibilities is 0.8. The expected value of this job to you is £20,000 × 0.8, which is £16,000. For Job 2 the expected value is £50,000 × 0.2, which is £10,000. According to expectancy theory the rational choice would, therefore, be to go for Job 1. In reality, the choice between the two jobs would depend on many more factors than just the salaries they offered: the individual might also attach importance to things such as opportunities for professional training, promotion prospects, the type of work involved and distance from home, etc. This requires expectancy theory to be expanded beyond the simple model used so far to take into account a third factor in addition to valence and expectancy: this factor is termed 'instrumentality', and measures the likelihood that a first-level outcome will be associated with a second-level outcome. This can be illustrated with a second example.

✋ Exercise 3.5

List the things that would be associated with you putting maximum effort into revision between now and your next set of professional examinations (option one). Next identify the things that will be associated with you adopting a policy of not doing any revision until a week before your examinations, when you will then start to put maximum effort into your revision (option two).

✓ Solution

Not everyone will identify the same factors in the above example and this is one of the strengths of expectancy theory; that is, it recognises the existence of individual differences. For purposes of illustration the following outcomes will be assumed:

Option One	*Option Two*
(second-level outcomes)	(second-level outcomes)
Good exam results	Moderate/poor exam results
No social life	Active social life
Little social expenditure	High social expenditure
Stress before exams	Relaxation before exams
Relaxed during exams	Stress during exams
and so on	and so on

The next step is to attach a value to each outcome and again there will be individual variations here, with some people seeing, for example, no social life as a major disadvantage, while others might see it as a small price to pay. There will also be variations in the

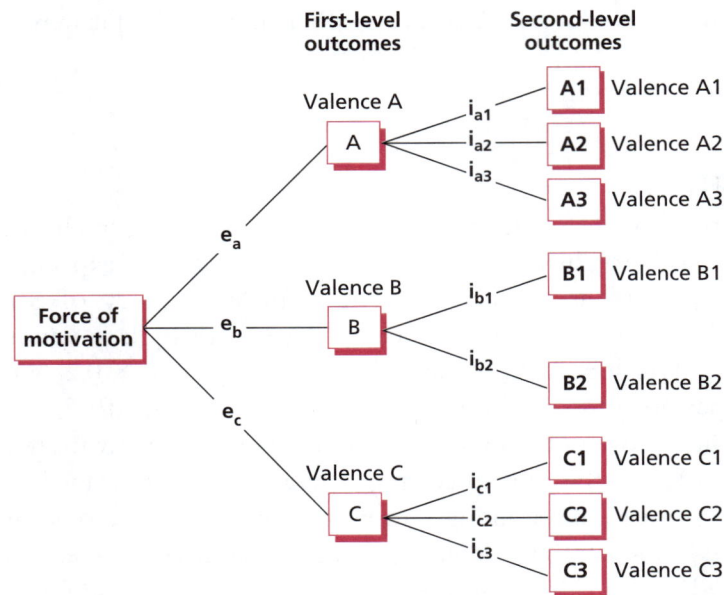

Figure 3.1 Vroom's expectancy theory

risk assessments (instrumentalities) of each of these second-level outcomes; one person might believe that option one will be associated with a high probability of good exam results, while another sees only a low probability of success. If these second-level outcomes and instrumentalities are included in the expectancy equation the model inevitably becomes more complex. This is illustrated in Figure 3.1 and the value of each first-level option now depends on the sum of the instrumentalities and values of its second-level outcomes.

Some models of expectancy theory go even further and take into account additional variables such as individual abilities and perceptions. Inevitably there is a trade-off between ease of application/understanding for such theories and their complexity/comprehensiveness. All expectancy theories assume a high degree of rationality in individual choice decisions. They also suggest that managers ought to take the following steps to improve employee motivation:

- determine what each individual values
- identify the type of behaviour desired by managers
- ensure that the desired levels of performance are perceived to be attainable
- find ways of linking outcomes valued by individuals with behaviours desired by managers
- ensure that improvements in performance result in changes in valued rewards that are large enough to motivate individuals
- try to make sure that reward systems are seen to be fair and equitable.

These prescriptions for improving motivation are not easy to implement. This highlights one of the paradoxes associated with the theories of motivation outlined so far: the content theories oversimplify motivation, but are easy to understand and apply to work situations, whereas process theories recognise the complexity of motivation, but are more difficult to apply and understand.

3.6 Reward systems

3.6.1 System aims

A reward system might be viewed (dependent upon the individual's perspective) as a hygiene factor or alternatively as a motivator. The goals of a payment system are recruitment (from the marketplace), retention (keeping up within the market) and reward (paying for performance). Armstrong and Murlis (1998) suggested that reward systems consist of two elements:

- Pay ranges, with a method for moving through (progression) or up (promotion).
- The benefits package (pensions, sick pay, medical and other insurance, car schemes, etc.).

Typically, organisations have grade structures that put jobs into grades based on the job value to the organisation. Small organisations may only pay spot rates for the job based on market prices, but larger ones tend to determine a pay range for each grade that takes into account market rates and the need for retention and reward fairly and systematically.

The managerial aims of reward systems are as follows:

- To provide a fair and consistent basis for motivating and rewarding employees.
- To further the objectives of the organisation by a logically designed framework of equitable and externally competitive rewards for similar work.
- To reward performance by progression or promotion via developmental pathways and career ladders.
- To recognise the various factors apart from performance such as job/role size, contribution, skill and competence.
- To control salary costs.

The design of reward systems should be appropriate to the characteristics and needs of the organisation, (e.g. size, stability of the environment, competitors' policies, local pay rates, and internal culture)

3.6.2 Design considerations

When managers create a climate in which people are motivated, this is likely to encourage compliance and to bring about commitment. Clearly the culture of the organisation will be a major factor influencing the particular motivational climate. However, there are other important contributory factors:

- *Money and reward systems.* Herzberg's theory sees money as a hygiene factor, but in terms of expectancy theory it could be an instrument for gaining several desired outcomes. In principle money can be a good motivator and there is no doubt that it is the main reason for most people go to work or run their own business. However, with some exceptions, it is difficult to use money as a direct motivator to improve performance, because of the difficulties associated with accurately measuring the amount and quality of an individual's or group's work. Attempts to introduce 'performance-related pay' into more organisations represent efforts to establish closer links between results and rewards. Interestingly, these attempts seem to be at odds with much of the literature on quality management and learning organisations, which stress the importance of intrinsic motivation, rather than extrinsic rewards such as money.

- *Job design.* Traditionally, jobs have been designed on the basis of the scientific management approach with a high degree of specialisation and strict controls. This is highly effective for bringing about conformity in many situations, but is hardly conducive to commitment. A number of other approaches to job design attempt to build more interest, variety and challenge into jobs.

- *Groups and teamwork.* The potential impact of work groups on individual motivation has long been recognised and was famously illustrated by the Hawthorne Studies. Whereas F.W. Taylor is acknowledged as the father of the 'scientific' movement, Elton Mayo holds similar status within the 'human relations' movement. Mayo's research, over a 5-year period at the Hawthorne Works of the Western Electric Company in Chicago indicated that work satisfaction depends to a large extent upon the social relationships. These are both informal between workers in a group and between workers and their bosses. The effects of the group proved more powerful than altered working conditions, new payment systems, rest breaks, varying the length of the working day, and offering food and refreshments. Most recently in many manufacturing organisations there has been a move towards groups and cellular production as part of programmes of quality improvement. Indeed 'Total Quality Management', which seeks to move the emphasis away from detecting faults to preventing them, stresses employee involvement and team working as important ways of achieving this (see later).

- *Management style.* The approach adopted by a particular manager can in many situations have a significant effect on efficiency, effectiveness and motivation.

- *Competencies and goal setting.* At the strategic level, it is important for an organisation to identify the core competencies needed for success. These can provide a framework for identifying more specific competencies in particular areas of the business. Some believe that it is possible to specify competencies for individuals or jobs (this approach lies behind much of the work of the National Council for Vocational Qualifications in Britain) (Table 3.1). Even if the competency approach is not followed, there is evidence that setting and agreeing clear, challenging goals for an individual can itself have a motivating effect. Without goals there can be no meaningful feedback for learning and enhancing motivation. (Budgets are one form of target that can act as a challenging objective if set at the level where they are demanding but achievable).

(You may wish to visit this web site www.dfes.gov.uk/nvq/what.shtml for more information on NVQs)

Table 3.1 The National Vocational Qualification (NVQ): some facts

- NVQs reflect the skills and knowledge needed to do a job effectively
- NVQs are classified according to the competence levels attained (expressed as levels 1 to 5).
- NVQs represent national standards recognised by employers throughout the UK
- NVQs evidence competency of the individual to do a job
- NVQs are based on standards that include current best practice, the ability to adapt to future requirements and the knowledge and understanding that underpin competent performance.

(*Source:* Based on information from the Department for Education and Skills www.dfes.gov.uk/nvq/what.shtml)

Exercise 3.6

Why might managers now have to pay more attention to employee commitment rather than just compliance? What are the implications of expectancy theory for achieving highly motivated, committed employees?

Solution

Compliance is concerned with meeting minimum standards and is typically based on tight formal controls. This may not be enough to ensure effectiveness in dynamic environments where a premium is placed on quality and innovation. Such situations demand self-motivated employees who are committed to outstanding performance and continuous improvement.

Expectancy theory of motivation suggests that to encourage highly motivated, committed employees a manager should:

- find out what each employee values
- determine what employees are meant to achieve
- ensure that required performance standards are perceived by employees as achievable
- devise a system to link performance with what employees value
- make sure that rewards for good performance are worthwhile
- pay attention to fairness and equity as these can be a key consideration when employees compare their rewards with those of colleagues.

3.6.3 Job evaluation

Relativities or 'differentials' in levels of pay can be methodically defined through job evaluation. There is often a need for different career structures according to the level or category of employees. A number of organisations have two levels: one for the staff and one for manual workers, Some have three: one for the managers, one for the professional staff and one for the junior staff and manual workers. In many cases, top management or directors may be left out of the main structure with their remuneration being agreed individually.

External comparisons made through market rate surveys and decisions on external relativities tend to follow the organisation's policy on how its pay levels should relate to the market rate.

There are at least two main forms of job evaluation schemes, namely 'Points-factor evaluation' and 'Ranking/market rate method'. The main features of each are as follows:

Points-factor evaluation scheme

- Plot the evaluation job scores against the current rates of pay for every jobholder to produce a scattergram.
- Draw a line of central tendency or 'best fit'.
- Obtain whatever information is available on market rate for 'benchmark' jobs and plot the upper and lower quartile and median trends.
- Decide the desired pay policy line and plot this on another graph.
- Decide on the overall shape of the pay structure in relation to the policy line.
- Define the pay ranges for each grade, taking into account the considerations affecting the size or span of pay ranges and the provision to be made for pay progression.

Ranking/market rate method

- Rank 'benchmark' jobs and plot their actual rates of pay to give the pay practice line.
- Plot market rate information on the benchmark jobs on the chart and derive a 'best fit' pay policy.
- Using the pay policy line as the midpoint guideline, plot the upper and lower limits of the pay range for each benchmark in accordance with range size policy.
- Develop the grade structure.
- Define the pay ranges for each grade.

3.6.4 Types of pay structure

Numerous types of organisational pay structures exist, the most common are identified here.

- *Graded pay* structures which consist of a sequence of job grades against which is attached a payment range.
- *Broad-banded* structures in which the range of pay in a band is significantly higher than in a conventional graded structure. The structure usually covers the whole workforce from the shop floor to senior management.
- *Individual job ranges* are used where the content and size of jobs is widely different. For example, at senior levels an individual job grade structure may be preferable to a conventionally banded structure. This approach avoids the problem of grouping number of jobs with widely different job sizes into a grade, with the inevitable consequence that some jobs are underpaid and others are overpaid.
- *Job family structures* consist of jobs in a function or discipline such as research scientist, development engineer or personnel specialist. Jobs will be related in terms of the fundamental activities carried out and the basic skills required, but will be differentiated by the level of responsibility, skill or competence involved.
- *Progression/maturity curves* are a development of job family structures. A pay curve system recognises that different methods of handling pay determination and progression may have to be used in some job families, especially those containing knowledge workers.
- *Spot rates* in their simplest form allocate a specific rate for the job.
- *Pay spines* consist of a series of incremental points extending from the lowest to the highest paid jobs covered by the structure. Pay scales or ranges for different job grades may then be superimposed on the pay spine. This method is favoured particular within the UK for most NHS and central and local government employees.
- *Separate pay structures* for manual workers relate to the rates paid to employees who work on the shop floor, in distribution, transport, and anywhere else where the work primarily involves manual skills and tasks. It is similar to any other pay structure in certain respects. It incorporates pay differentials between jobs, which reflect real and assumed differences in skill, and responsibility. Inevitably pressures from local labour markets influence it, as well as custom and practice and various settlements reached between management and trade unions.
- *Integrated pay structures* cover groups of employees who have traditionally been paid under separate arrangements. There may be one grading system which includes all employees, excluding senior management.
- *Rate for age* provides a specific rate of pay or a pay bracket to be linked to age for staff in certain jobs.

3.6.5 Profit-related pay

Profit-related pay schemes attempt to produce a sense of shared ownership and commitment. They are not as popular as they once were, for a number of reasons including:

- the tax implications of share purchase and share option schemes, etc. making this a technical area that requires the expert advice of specialist firms and management consultants
- the problem of 'free-riders' benefiting from the scheme
- the restricted use of the scheme to only a few groups (e.g. directors and senior managers) in some companies leading to resentment by other groups.

An example of profit sharing:
In May 2005, Royal Mail announced a record of £537 million profit on its operations with quality of service to customers hitting the highest levels in a decade. As a reward for this turnaround postal workers received a 'Share in Success' payment of £1,074 amounting to £218 million of the company's profit. This represented one of the biggest profit shares with employees in UK corporate history.

3.6.6 Performance-related pay: piece rates and sales bonuses

In the early days of industrial mechanisation, the Taylorist philosophy of paying employers on the basis of output alone was straightforward as output was clear and easily measurable. Payment was referred to as 'piece rates' because employees were remunerated based on the number of manufactured pieces they completed.

The modern organisation has, however, changed considerably and individual labour inputs are less likely to be traced as direct outputs. Group and team incentive structures have been pioneered in some new manufacturing plants and car dealerships in order to recognise staff cooperating to achieve shared outputs. However new challenges such as rewards shared by free riders (those who shirk work and unfairly rely on others in the team) have caused ill feeling and have been counterproductive.

Where direct output data can easily be measured and attributed mainly to one individual (e.g. in sales), management have continued to operate individual, quantitative, performance-based rewards ignoring factors that might have contributed to outputs such as managerial support and advertising outputs.

The employment relationship is built on a 'wage-effort bargain', however motivation theories have questioned how far individuals will go just for additional pay. Further, if targets are not met a demotivating affect might set in, and a dramatic fall-off in performance may result (Otley, 1987).

Exercise 3.7

Under which circumstances might reward based purely on sales within an area be perceived as 'unjust'?

Solution

- Areas might be unjust e.g. rural area or urban area, mature territory, etc.
- Where the previous salesperson was ineffective/particularly effective.

- Other marketing efforts and levels of support from the centre
- Expense account levels
- The suitability of the products being sold.

3.6.7 Appraisal based performance-related pay (PRP)

Appraisal based performance-related pay (PRP) is a method of payment where an individual employee receives increases in pay based wholly or partly on the regular and systematic assessment of job performance.

It is argued that performance-related pay, in the right context, can be of potential benefit to both employers and employees. It can, for example, help employers improve the efficiency and effectiveness of their workforce by emphasising the need for high standards of job performance. It is further argued that it can offer the flexibility to help motivate and retain valuable employees by targeting higher pay at better performers. Employees in turn may welcome a system that rewards extra effort by extra pay.

The introduction or revision of PRP is often linked with other organisational and HR changes including:

- greater decentralisation of the responsibility for pay determination
- the introduction or extension of appraisal schemes
- moves towards harmonised terms and conditions of all the workforce
- the greater use of flexible working arrangements, for example in skills acquisition.

The way in which payment systems are modified to take account of pay for individual performance include:

- replacing part or, occasionally, all of general pay increases with PRP awards.
- strengthening the link between pay and performance by introducing additional payments above the scale maximum to recognise high performance.
- introducing PRP in place of incremental pay increases which is based on length of service, age or qualifications.

Although PRP is more commonly used in larger firms, it can also be found in smaller firms and public bodies. As PRP can be time-consuming to both implement and manage, and involve a substantial change to an organisation's culture, it is often restricted initially to a particular group of employees (usually senior management) before consideration is given to extending it to other parts of the workforce. Such a gradual approach has certain advantages:

- Senior managers need to be committed to achieving improved performance from their employees. Experiencing a scheme first hand will help to foster such a commitment.
- Restricting PRP to specific groups of workers allows an opportunity to test whether the scheme is appropriate, meets its objectives and contains sufficient safeguards to be fair (a pilot scheme).

Before introducing PRP, employers should consider whether it will be appropriate to their organisation and should clarify their objectives. A PRP scheme should be introduced only if the primary reason is to improve performance. Employers should consider whether any change is needed in the existing payment system by measuring it against certain criteria, such as:

- Is it fair?
- Does it enable the organisation to recruit and retain on equal terms in the labour market?

- Does it accommodate change?
- Does it measure performance adequately?
- Does it motivate employees?
- Does it encourage productivity?
- Is it controllable?

PRP should be based on the foundation of a sound payment system and accepted salary levels. It should not be introduced if what is really required is a general increase in wage rates. PRP is not an effective substitute for adequate basic rates of pay.

Exercise 3.8

What are the benefits of PRP?

Solution

As organisations seek to compete more effectively to meet customer requirements they are increasingly examining methods of improving workforce flexibility and engendering a culture of high performance. By making a distinction between individuals' pay on the grounds of properly measured criteria and linking reward more closely to performance, employees may be encouraged to increase productivity. Resources can be better targeted to recognise effort and achievement, and to reward and retain more effective employees. Properly introduced, PRP can be used as a mechanism for promoting greater employee involvement and commitment to an organisation. Improved quality and customer service can be additional benefits.

Employees may welcome the introduction of well-designed and managed PRP schemes as a fairer means of recognising that more effective performers should receive higher pay. There is, in short, a more direct link between effort and reward that may in turn lead to an improvement in morale.

There are undeniably difficulties with PRP, normally stemming from poor design and/or introduction. PRP may not only fail to motivate but may cause dissatisfaction if:

- employees are not aware of the levels of performance they need to attain
- PRP awards are not applied consistently across the eligible participants
- financial constraints by the use of budgets or 'quotas' restrict the amount of awards
- there is subjectivity in assessment
- there is divisiveness in operation.

Any PRP scheme should be designed to avoid any 'drift' – a tendency to mark higher each year. If there is drift any beneficial link between performance and reward may be lost with pay costs rising without a corresponding rise in performance.

Employers considering PRP should take account of the following:

- how the scheme will fit the management style and organisational culture (e.g. many employers emphasise the need for teamwork and cooperation).
- how the scheme will continue to encourage and reward individual accountability within the team
- a reluctance among some employees to change roles where learning the skills required by a new job may jeopardise their PRP awards

- trade unions and employee representatives hostility as PRP may be seen as running counter to the principles of collective bargaining
- the degree of negotiation, consultation and additional management required.

3.7 Total reward packages

Competitive salary and benefits are important, but two other factors are even more critical, according to a survey 'Why Employees Walk: 2005 Retention Initiatives Report' (Anon, 2005). Employees are more likely to look for a new job:

- when their needs for career advancement or training aren't being met, or
- when their relationship with their manager is poor.

The report concludes that employers looking for ways to hold on to workers should consider training managers and implement more flexibility in pay and conditions.

The past few years have seen organisations put a name to the whole range of benefits they have offered for a while, cash and non-cash, and for the first time publicise the fact more fully. 'Total reward packages' originated in the US and represents a bundling together of all cash and non-cash motivators an organisation has to offer.

The concept recognizes that money is not the only motivator and that employees, prospective employees and other stakeholders might find the organisation more attractive because of its total reward package. This development marks a changing attitude to reward from both employers and employees. The package might include non-cash benefits, such as flexible working, flexible hours, training, career progression and a pursuit of green policies but must not be seen as a way of keeping pay rates down.

Carrington (2004) explains that a range of factors have driven the initiative including:

- talent wars because of the shortage of skilled staff during the 1990s, leading to employers' attempts to maximise their organisation's attractiveness
- the need for a mechanism to develop organisational vision and culture.

According to Carrington (2004) total rewards have the advantage of:

- making positive statements to stakeholders about the organisation and its culture
- helping employer branding so that retention and recruitment is enhanced
- breaking down the them and us attitude in the workforce.

The following short extract is from an article that explores approaches to rewarding and 'incentivising' employees at a time when it seems more difficult than ever. In purely financial terms the factors cited are low cost, but in outcome terms they are apparently high-impact:

Andrew Sellers, corporate business manager at John Lewis Direct, agrees that companies are using incentives in a broader way. 'In the call centre environment, where call-handlers are employed at roughly the same salary across the industry, it's the small things that make a difference to the workforce.'

Vodafone used John Lewis Direct to send a bottle of champagne to a team that had achieved a project ahead of time and on budget. Such a discretionary approach allows employers to target incentives more widely to reward attendance, productivity, customer service and good ideas.

The key to reward and recognition in this environment is to make awards as instant as possible. This spontaneity is hampered when rewards have to be ratified and paperwork completed, risking resentment rather than goodwill.

John Lewis relaunched its vouchers last year with an online redemption element. The innovation addresses two issues, says Sellers. 'We want to grow our online business and when people are in front of a screen all day, the PC is their interface with the world, so they can spend their reward there and then.'

Successful schemes are not prescriptive, so despite a sometimes dull reputation, vouchers are the most popular choice of reward after cash.

'The problem with cash is that no one ever remembers what they did with it, so its motivation effect is lost', says Sellers. 'With vouchers, people will treat themselves and tell their colleagues about it.'

(*Source:* extracted from Incentives: The rewards of work by Stuart Derrick, *Marketing*, July 13, 2005 p. 37, Haymarket Business Publications Ltd).

Sherman's (2005) research into female business owners concludes that they may not offer more perks to the workplace than men, but the perks they offer employees 'often have a decidedly feminine touch'. She cites Hillary Kelbick, president of MKP Communications a $5 New York million marketing and consulting firm . Flexible working and telecommuting is commonplace, untypically MKP allow staff to bring their young children to work when day care is difficult. Kelbick also funds staff to purchase new outfits for important client meetings. The reasoning is faultless: perks' such as these enabled MKP to compete with larger, more established companies in hiring and keeping the 'right' people.

> **Note:**
>
> Two examples are given here:
>
> ### Example 1
>
> Ofcom's attempts to attract female professionals and those with caring responsibilities included, as part of the employment package:
>
> - flexible working including term-time working, nine-day fortnights and an opportunity to trade annual leave for paid work.
> - career development to help people develop their CVs including university access (some paid).
>
> ### Example 2
>
> Nationwide Building Society began its total reward strategy by overhauling its pay and benefits. When some jobs were linked to the marketplace some were underpaid so a progression system was introduced to make wages comparable within 3 years. From having 78 per cent of staff paid below the market rates for their job pay rates became more generous than many of its competitors. The importance of communicating the entire package to the workforce was obviously key. An intranet allowing staff explore everything on offer such as pay, pensions, flexible working, career development and other rewards was developed.
> (Source: Carrington, 2004)

The issues of changing attitudes to reward on the part of employees, the challenges posed to reward managers and the cultural impact of rewards are all apparent. There are also ethical implications of 'being a good employer' and treating the workforce as more than a mere resource.

Prickett (2006) explores the fact that firms are realising that flexible benefits are a practical and affordable way to reward their staff, and in so doing identifies what incentives she feels are growing in importance and those that are not:

Growing	Static	Declining
Schemes such as home PCs, bicycles and childcare vouchers. (all are tax-efficient)	Concierge services, (e.g. shopping and dry-cleaning) These are mainly confined to large City firms.	Final-salary pension schemes
More flexible pension schemes that offer choice	Store cards/vouchers.	Golden parachutes.
	Gym membership.	Bonuses
	Health insurance	Share schemes, (stock prices, which are easily affected by external events, do not accurately reflect the performance of an individual or team).
	Optional extras such as dental insurance and pet cover.	

3.8 Ethics in management

Reference has made throughout this chapter to 'fairness'. Mention has also been made of the psychological contact based upon an employee/employer relationship of mutual expectation. Fairness and reasonable expectation can embrace many aspects of people management including recruitment, dismissal, and redundancy. Compliance with the law, local agreements and moral considerations all relate to ethical management approaches.

The term 'ethics' refers to the code of behaviour considered correct by a particular group, profession or individual. Managers of organisations face many situations that require ethical judgements, and the question of what criteria these judgements should be based on is one that requires careful attention.

Unsurprisingly, CIMA expects the highest standards of ethical behaviour from its members and students. They make the points that *good ethical behaviour may be above that required by the law. In a highly competitive, complex business world, it is essential that CIMA members sustain their integrity.*

The CIMA Code of Ethics for Professional Accountants sets out the key principles of professional behaviour and provides comprehensive guidance in support of this. The code makes clear that members and registered students have a duty to:

- *Observe the highest standards of conduct and integrity,*
- *Uphold the good standing and reputation of the profession,*
- *Refrain from any conduct which might discredit the profession.*

These guidelines must be observed by CIMA members and students alike *irrespective of their field of activity, of their contract of employment or of any other professional membership they may hold.*

3.9 Summary

This chapter has dealt with a number of complex areas, not least motivation theory and its relationship to organisational management. This thinking has been applied in one area of human resourcing, reward strategies and the way these might translate into practice. Finally, some underpinning ethical considerations have been highlighted. With the foundation established by this chapter attention turns next to the subject of human resources.

References and further reading

Anon (2005) Money talks, but not that loud (retention) (Brief Article), *Work & Family Newsbrief*, October, Vol. 1, p. 3.

Armstrong, M. and Murlis, H. (1998) *Reward Management: A Handbook of Remuneration and Practice* (4th edn), London Kogan Page.

Carrington, L. (2004) Just desserts *People Management*, January 29, Vol. 10, No. 2, p. 38.

Derrick, S. (2005) Incentives: The rewards of work, *Marketing*, July 13, p. 37, Haymarket Business Publications Ltd.

Gratton, L. (2004) More than money, *People Management*, January 29, Vol. 10, No. 2, p. 23

Lawrence, P. R. and Lorsch, J. W. (1984) High-performing organisations in three environments. In Pugh, D.S. (ed.), *Organisation Theory*, Harmondsworth: Penguin

Mullins, L. J. (2005) *Management and Organisational Behaviour* (7th edn), Financial Times, Prentice Hall

Otley, D. T. (1987) *Accounting Control and Organisational Behaviour*, London : Heinemann in association with CIMA

Prickett, R. (2006) Pliable and viable, *Financial Management*, April, p. 19(4).

Royal Mail Group plc (2005) Press release issued by Postmen praised for delivering record Royal Mail profit and the best customer service in a decade [17/05/2005] http://www.royalmailgroup.com/news/expandarticle.asp?id=1512&brand=royal_mail_group

Schein, E. H. (2004) *Organisational Culture and Leadership* (3rd edn), San Francisco: Jossey-Bass.

Sherman, A. P. (2005) Central perks: women use unique benefits to show employee appreciation, *Entrepreneur*, September, Vol. 33, No. 9(1), p. 34.

(www.dfes.gov.uk/nvq/what.shtml)

Revision Questions

3

? Question 1

The following is a brief profile of three persons working for a small company which provides maintenance services:

- **Bookkeeper, Anne**, 50, widowed, living in a small house with garden, one son working abroad, married daughter with two children living in another town. Had several years' bookkeeping experience with a larger company before her marriage.
- **Maintenance engineer, Ben**, 23, unmarried, son of a senior manager in an oil company, shares house with three friends, has one motorcycle for transport and one for racing.
- **Maintenance engineer, Charles,** 38, married, two children and one from a previous marriage, bought his council house a few years ago at the insistence of his wife who is a primary school teacher. Father was a semi-skilled engineer.

Requirement

Explain how the factors that affect performance are likely to vary among these people, by reference to a process theory of motivation. (A description of the theory is not required.)

(20 marks)

? Question 2

Norman is a recently qualified management accountant. He chose this profession because he understood that successful accountants in senior positions could earn high salaries.

After training in various departments of a large firm he was offered a position in the consultancy division in a department concerned with advising companies in the London area on management accounting systems. The department is growing, partly because its expertise in management accounting systems is widely known. The department is therefore well provided with technical support and other resources. He enjoyed the analytical work involved and received high merit ratings in each of his two annual reviews. These resulted in substantial pay increases.

Norman is married, has a 2-year old son and another baby due shortly. He loves playing with his son, and is a keen member of a choir, which practices twice a week. He has purchased a house with a mortgage that is just within his financial means, and he enjoys making do-it-yourself improvements to the house.

A large organisation which has over 100 establishments throughout the country has asked Norman's employers to advise them on the management accountancy systems in each of these establishments. Each of the establishments differs in its structure, due to varying local environments. Because Norman's performance has been so good, it has been suggested that he should take charge of a small new department which will be specially set up for this business.

Requirement

Analyse Norman's personal motivation and how it may be affected by the suggested change of job. **(20 marks)**

? Question 3

3.1 Abraham Maslow's theory of motivation is often represented as:

(A) a hierarchy of needs
(B) individual tendencies labelled X or Y
(C) a scientific relationship between work and reward
(D) a series of negative and a series of positive factors. **(2 marks)**

Solutions to Revision Questions

3

☑ Solution 1

A process theory of motivation concentrates on how the motivation process works rather than on what motivates people. A variety of process theories exists, including Equity theory, Reinforcement theory, Social Learning theory and Expectancy theories. The process theory which will be applied to the three cases in this question is a version of the expectancy theory developed from Vroom's initial model by L. Porter and E. E. Lawler.

The likely motivation of the three people profiled in the question is as follows:

First, bookkeeper Anne who lives alone is likely to value the social contact, which she will derive from work since it is clear that she is widowed and living alone. She is unlikely to expect promotion but will possibly enjoy employing her expertise obtained from her years of experience in bookkeeping. In terms of the key factors of effort, performance and reward, she is likely to perceive that her efforts will result in a reasonable performance because she has the requisite skills and experience to do the job. Furthermore, she will expect that rewards will follow in terms of intrinsic satisfaction from doing the job well and in terms of extrinsic rewards in the form of a modest salary and a degree of social recognition. Her perception that her performance will bring these rewards should result in her making sufficient effort to do an adequate to good job.

Maintenance engineer Ben is likely to value money very highly as a reward because of his expensive hobby of motorcycle racing. His socialisation, as the son of a successful senior manager, is likely to have given him some insight into the connection between effort, performance and promotion and so he is likely to make the effort to succeed. On the other hand, his interest in racing may deflect him from seeking promotion in the company to seeking success on the track. He is likely to enjoy the satisfaction of maintenance work, since his hobby also requires the exercise of similar skills in the repair and upkeep of his two motorcycles. In terms of expectancy theory, he is likely to make the required effort because he has the skills for the job, values the reward, and is likely to appreciate the close links between effort, performance and reward.

Maintenance engineer Charles, at 38 years, should be experienced in his work by now and so have the requisite skills. Though he may be paying maintenance for the child of his first marriage, he has security in having bought his home, and his second wife, a teacher, will bring in a useful second income. He will value money as a reward since he will need this to sustain a reasonable living standard with two or three children to maintain. He has already matched and exceeded the achievement of his father and therefore his desire for promotion may be saturated, though it is impossible to say without additional information. Again, Charles has the skills and will value money as a reward, but with a young family will have alternative sources of interest and satisfaction. He will expect effort to produce the required performance and the reward of money and so he will make the effort. On the information available, however, other assumptions are possible and more information is required.

✅ Solution 2

Vroom's Expectancy Theory of Motivation is based on the following formula:

Valence × expectancy = motivation

'Valence' refers to the strength of a person's preference for a particular outcome, and 'Expectancy' to that person's belief that that outcome will satisfy their needs.

In other words, the perception that effort will lead to effective performance, and that performance will lead to rewards. The recipient must consider the rewards available attractive before he/she is willing to make the necessary effort.

The main motivating factors for Norman from a work point of view are:

- high salary
- analytical work
- high merit ratings and
- substantial pay increases.

These are the rewards he may be looking for; the high salary and promotion being of an extrinsic nature and the personal satisfaction more intrinsic.

On a social level, Norman enjoys:

- family life
- the church choir and
- DIY in the home.

With the new job the main considerations are:

- the recognition he has gained resulting in the job offer
- the challenge of setting up the department and being in charge.

The question is what are Norman's valences and expectations? It is clear that he wishes to be successful; but the fact is that he thinks he is already there, so would this new job add anything more to that feeling? If the considerations noted above, i.e. recognition, challenge and being in charge, are what he wants (valence), and he believes that through the new job he can get them (expectancy), then he will be motivated in the new job.

However, there are other social considerations outlined above that need to be examined. If these play a part in Norman's expectancy formula, i.e. that he wants to have enough time and money to be able to actively pursue his social interests (valence), then the question is, does he think that the new job fills the expectancy part of the equation? If the new job is going to mean long working hours, then it means less time to spend with his family or doing DIY work. If he has to travel a lot, then again his family and social time will be sacrificed.

If achieving even more recognition is what Norman wants, then the new job will tempt him away from his social pleasures and he will be willing to sacrifice these in order to fulfil his career needs. If, on the other hand, he believes that he has nothing more to gain, recognition-wise, by taking the new job, then he would not be seriously interested at the end of the day. The question is that of Norman's role perception. If his role as family member is of more importance than that of successful accountant, then the new job may not appeal quite as much.

✓ Solution 3

3.1 (A)

4

Managing Human Capital

Managing Human Capital

4

4.1 Introduction

This chapter builds on the thinking developed so far in this study system in particular Chapter 3. It explores the relationship of the employee as part of the business plan and determinants and content of a HR plan or strategy. Practical issues associated with implementing plans, recruitment, selection, induction, development, training and appraisals are then reviewed. Finally, the chapter considers practices in different organisational forms and structures.

4.2 Human resource management – overview

This section distinguishes human resource management (HRM) from personnel management and explains the development of thinking in this area.

Organisations at their most basic level are nothing more than collections of people. The policies, procedures and practices associated with people are commonly referred to either 'personnel' or 'human resource' matters. Since organisations came into being it has always been the case that people issues have been significant. These issues have involved management in the considerations of matters such as resource planning (or manpower planning in a less enlightened era), recruitment, training and so on.

Armstrong (2003) defined Personnel Management as:

Obtaining, developing and motivating employees and making best use of their skills.

Most agree Personnel Management to be concerned with the ongoing issues associated with managing people and hence it is an integral part of most managers' work. For organisations of any size however specialists also provide support. Personnel Management is an administrative support function helping to ensure consistency and fairness of treatment and the operation of organisation wide initiatives such as appraisal or job evaluation. Personnel Management is concerned with imposing compliance with organisational rules and procedures among employees.

Personnel is a management function but distant from the line management of an organisation. This specialist function attempts to grasp the perspectives of non-managerial employees without actually representing their views. For this reason personnel often mediate between both sides. By nature personnel specialist perform a 'firefighting' function dealing with problems as they occur. In addition, the Personnel Management function reacts and responds to changes in employment law, labour market conditions, trade union actions and other environmental influences.

Human resource management (HRM) emerged as a concept during the 1980s representing a major shift of emphasis in the way in which employees were viewed. Armstrong (2003) defined HRM as 'a strategic approach to the acquisition, motivation, development and management of the organisation's human resources.' Bratton and Gold (2003) offered a more detailed definition of HRM:

That part of the management process that specialises in the management of people in work organisations. HRM emphasises that employees are critical to achieving sustainable competitive advantage, that human resources practices need to be integrated with the corporate strategy, and that human resource specialists help organisational controllers to meet both efficiency and equity objectives.

HRM forms part of a more strategic approach to planning and resource deployment within the context of the external environment. HRM is essentially a strategically driven activity, not only as a major contributor to the strategic process but also a determining part of it. Although prescriptive by nature it is concerned with developing initiatives articulated in various planning documents including business plans. HRM determines general policies for employment relationships. It has long-term perspectives and seeks to coherently integrate all the human aspects of the organisation. It needs to help develop an organisational culture that produces employee commitment and co-operation. Unlike Personnel, the HRM starting point is not with people, but with the organisation's needs for human resources.

Some would view Personnel Management as a narrower dimension of a fuller function recognised as the Human Resource Management. So in contrast to traditional personnel management, which many be seen as standing between employer and employee, HRM staff are more part of the management team, shaping and delivering corporate and business strategies.

Table 4.1 Eras in managing People

The Industrial Revolution 18th & 19th centuries	Factory owners improved their methods of recruitment, training and other related activities by trial and error.
	Early, factories often characterised by the harsh treatment of employees
	Philanthropic employers contributed to improvements in working life by running 'model factories' and appointing industrial welfare workers to 'look after' their employees.
First World War	Large numbers of women in factory environments.
	Thousands of women supervisors appointed to observe and regulate conditions of workforce.
	At the end of the war in 1918, the establishment of the industrial welfare officer reflected in the setting up of the Welfare Workers' Association.
1918–1939 interwar	Pressure to cut costs and increase efficiency encouraged the use of the ideas of scientific management and, later, the use of human relations techniques to secure the commitment and motivation of workers.
Second World War	Demand for the productivity maximisation led to a strengthening of personnel specialists role
1945–1980s	Personnel management established as a profession with own institute and examinations.
	Growth and increasing influence of trade unions seeking to improve the pay and working conditions of their members
	Management of industrial relations and personnel issues dominate
The 1980s	HRM became fashionable with more strategic thinking.
	Less conflict with trade unions

Exercise 4.1

Re-read this section and list five key differences between Personnel Management and Human Resource Management. Table 4.1 indicates the developments in this area over time within the UK and elsewhere.

Gratton (2004), when reviewing what an HR function actually does, suggests that a significant amount of time is spent on 'traditional' activities associated with rewards, job descriptions, appraising and measuring performance and so on. Research indicated, however, that time spent on strategic HR and organisational development issues (for example, change management) was more highly valued by chief executives.

It may be that HR professionals should also to be taking on additional responsibility particularly in the ethical treatment of employees. The issue of ethical behaviour has already been discussed in the previous chapter, but the article that follows develops some of these themes. Specifically it argues why rules cannot ensure ethical behaviour when it comes to human resource management.

Why do corporate scandals such as the recent Hewlett-Packard Co. (HP) debacle continue to come to light in the post-Enron climate of increasingly stringent government regulation? HP used 'pretexting' – impersonating people to obtain information – to acquire phone records in an effort to discover who at the company had leaked confidential board of director discussions to the press.

'The heightened regulation has reassured some that people's behaviour has changed' as a result of the new regulations, says Constance Dierickx, senior consultant at RHR International. 'That is a false and dangerous assumption', she warns. 'Human behaviour is not governed by rules and regulations. What governs human behaviour is reinforcement and relationships and social and cultural norms.'

Dierickx says each board has its own climate and culture that need to be intentionally cultivated through interaction and dialogue. When boards reach the 'cloak-and-dagger state of HP', she says, it means there are systemic issues and the board is dysfunctional.

Dierickx, who works with directors and senior management, says HR is uniquely positioned to 'put the issues on the table'. She points out that a critical part of HR's role is to be an adviser to senior management, 'and make sure they don't oversimplify problems and derive overly dramatic but too-targeted solutions that aren't going to solve the problem.'

For example, Dierickx says many boards conduct their own self-assessments and, not surprisingly, usually find that 'we're doing pretty well': Instead of focusing on self-congratulations, she says, boards need to have 'messy, complicated discussions' about the way they work, the subjects of their agendas and the quality of the discussion.

'And every director on every board should have an ethics hat on all the time', she says. 'HP's problems were not technical problems; they were behaviour problems.'

(*Source:* Rules can't ensure ethical behaviour (Executive Briefing), HR *Magazine*, November 2006)

4.3 Human resource management as strategy

Human Resource planning represents a rational, logical approach to the recruitment, retention, utilisation, improvement and disposal of the human resources of an organisation. Its purpose is to secure the organisation's employees in order to enable corporate plans to be carried through successfully. HR planning seeks to define what the organisation's needs for people are, where they are to be found, and how they are to be obtained. It is concerned with the flow of people into, within and out of the organisation. It involves line managers as well as specialists such as HR Managers.

An HR strategy can only make sense when related to business objectives. The demand for human resource comes from the organisation's need to continue to supply goods or services to its customers. It is also true that human resources themselves can have a vital influence on organisational objectives. Plans for training, promotion and productivity all indicate the importance of obtaining the right type of staff as well as the right numbers. However, larger or more complex organisations need a more strategic approach.

The demand for labour can be more or less continuous in most organisations. It has its short-term aspects, that is, the clearly defined requirements for specific skills or positions that need to be filled in the context of existing budgets. This usually means periods of about 6–9 months. It also has medium-term (9–18 months) and longer term needs (18 months and beyond) in line with the market and financial targets of the corporate plan.

A longer-term view of labour is essential for ensuring that the organisation is supplied with skills that take time to be developed. Most professional jobs, for example, require a training period of 3–5 years before the trainee can claim even the basic competencies of the profession. If an organisation decides to develop its own electronics engineers, it needs to

HRM stategy	HRM practices	HRM outcomes	Behavioual outcomes	performance outcomes	Financial outcomes
Differentitaion (innovation)	Selection	Commitment	Effort/ motivation	High productivity, Quality, innovation	Profits
Focus (quality)	Appraisal		Co-operation		
	Rewards	Quality	Involvement	Low: Absence,	Return on investment
Cost (cost reduction)	Job design			Lobour, Turnover,	
	Involvement	Flexbility	Organisational citizenship	Conflict, Customer complaints	
	Status and security				

Figure 4.1 The Guest model of HRM

Source: Guest (1997) Reprinted by permission of Taylor and Francis UK.

look ahead for at least 5 years from the time the first apprentices are appointed. If the organisation decides it will not train its own engineers, but buy them in from the market place, then it has to be reasonably assured of the forecast availability of trained engineers at the time they will be required.

One model that clearly demonstrated the relationship between HRM activities and strategy was proposed by David Guest (1997) and comprised six components:

- An HRM strategy.
- A set of HRM practices.
- A set of HRM outcomes.
- Behavioural outcomes.
- A number of performance outcomes.
- Financial outcomes.

The relationship can be depicted in the form figure similar to that in Figure 4.1.

The central idea of the model is that HRM practices should be designed to lead to a set of positive outcomes including high staff commitment and high quality, highly flexible employees. The main features are:

- high commitment as a vital outcome.
- a goal of binding employees to the organisation and obtaining behavioural outcomes of increased effort, co-operation, involvement and organisational citizenship.
- high-quality employees, involving workplace learning and the need for a capable, qualified and skilful workforce to produce high-quality services and products.
- flexibility concerned with ensuring that workers are receptive to innovation and change and operation.

The right-hand side of the model focuses on the link between HRM and performance. According to the model, only when all three HRM outcomes (commitment, quality and flexibility) are achieved, can behaviour change and superior performance outcomes be expected. These HRM goals are a 'package' and each is necessary to ensure superior performance and financial outcomes depicted on the right-hand side of the model. Guest (1997) argued that:

only when a coherent strategy, directed towards these four policy goals, fully integrated into business strategy and fully sponsored by line management at all levels is applied, will the high productivity and related outcomes sought by industry be achieved.

An alternative model developed by Devanna et al. (1984) emphasised the interrelatedness and the coherence of HRM activities. The HRM cycle in their model consists of four key constituent components: selection, appraisal, development and rewards (Figure 4.2). These four human resource activities aim to increase organisational performance. The model emphasised the coherence of internal HRM policies and the importance of matching internal HRM policies and practices to the organisation's external business strategy. The cycle represents a simple model that serves as a useful framework for explaining the nature and significance of key HR practices and the interactions among the factors making up the complex field of HRM.

It is important to note that the overall performance of the organisation depends on efficient and effective operation of each of the four components and the co-ordination of each with the organisation's strategy:

- The selection process is important to ensure that the organisation obtains people with the right skills and/or the potential to develop such skills.
- Appraisal is a pivotal process enabling managers to set targets for future performance in line with an organisation's strategic objectives. It also enables managers to assess the gap between the competences already possessed by staff and the skills and knowledge that the staff will require in order for the organisation to attain its strategic objectives.
- Training and development are essential to ensure that staff can compete with the best in the industry in terms of their ability to develop key competences. It is in this sense that their skills are a key source of competitive advantage.
- The reward system has to be such as to motivate people and to ensure that those key employees do not leave the organisation and join the competition.

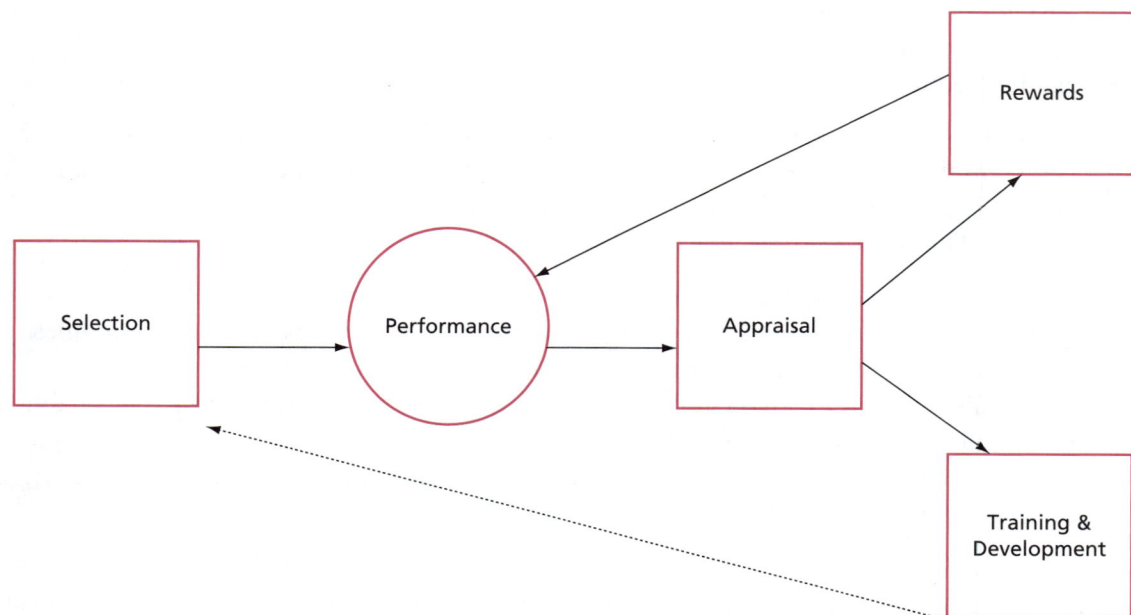

Figure 4.2 The human resource cycle. Reproduced from Devanna et al. (1984); © 1984 John Wiley & Sons, Inc. This material is used by permission of John Wiley & Sons, Inc.

Useful though each of these models is in explaining the relationships between different HRM practices and the role of each in organisational strategy, they do have limitations. Neither sufficiently takes account of external factors that can translate into opportunities or threats (or even all the internal organisational factors which represent strengths and weaknesses). External factors include industry characteristics such as type of business and technology employed, level of trade union influence, nature of the competition, extent of change and country/regional characteristics (e.g. political and economic conditions, legal requirements and socio-cultural conditions). Internal factors include company structure, competitive strategy employed and the organisational culture.

An additional complication in understanding HRM is that human resource specialists and line managers often have different approaches to HRM. The so-called 'hard' approach to HRM version emphasises the term 'resource' and adopts a 'rational' approach to managing employees by aligning business strategy and HR strategy, and viewing people as any other economic factor, and a cost that must be controlled. Conversely the 'soft' HRM model emphasises the term 'human' and thus advocates investment in training and development and the adoption of 'commitment' strategies to ensure that highly skilled and loyal employees give the organisation a competitive advantage. The 'soft' version also emphasises the importance of workplace learning and enlightened leadership. Most 'soft' HRM models assert that the organisation's 'human resources' are valued assets, not a variable cost, and emphasise the commitment of employees as a source of competitive advantage. Assumptions about the nature of human potential and the ability to tap that potential are based on organisational behaviour theories developed by psychologists like Maslow and Herzberg (see chapter 3).

A further dimension to HRM is that of national (and sometimes regional) cultural differences, where specific traditions and economic and legal environments shape HR practices. A major factor is the degree of state interference, meaning that:

- in countries with centralist control orientated traditions, like Eastern Europe and China, law and politics largely determine HRM, leaving less choice for individual organisations.
- in Western Europe, welfare and educational systems act as strong influences on the labour market (implying high state intervention again).
- in Japan and USA, state interference is relatively low. In Japan, this lack of a legal structure is partly compensated for by cultural factors, especially notions of collectivism.

4.4 Planning human resources

✋ Exercise 4.2

What does planning involve?

☑ Solution

Planning involves:

- Capturing a present state and making a position statement
- Identifying a future desired position
- Establish how to achieve change from the present to the future.

CIMA (2005) define planning as

'(the) establishment of objectives, and the formulation, evaluation and selection of the policies, strategies, tactics and action required to achieve them'

One definition of a human resource plan is:

a strategy for the acquisition, utilisation, improvement and retention of an enterprises human resources. (UK's Department for Education and Employment definition)

Such a plan must be integrated into the other organisational plans in order that HR can be effective and contribute properly to the achievement of organisational goals. The planning process requires management to think ahead and encourages a climate of awareness of issues key to organisational success such as:

- What has to be done to attain the objectives of the business?
- Who is to be responsible for the various stages of the plan?
- When will these stages have to be completed?
- How will they be accomplished?

4.4.1 Why undertake human resource planning?

There are a number of compelling reasons why organisations should plan their human resourcing, including:

- A need to establish cost and develop budgeting, especially in new projects to control costs and numbers employed.
- To rationally plan recruitment.
- To provide a smoother means of coping with redeployment, redundancies and retirements.
- To provide structured education, development and training needed by a future workforce.
- To allow a degree of succession planning.
- To adapt more quickly to ever changing circumstances.

Before beginning a human resource planning exercise a considerable amount of data, both internal and external, must be collected and analysed (Table 4.2).

Forecasts of people requirement are based on predictions. Most organisations estimate the demand by asking each manager to project their people needs over the planning period. These can then be reviewed in the light of:

- Future output/volumes/sales/product projections
- Future methods of production and IT usage
- Likely external influences such as competitor action, trade unions, government and other pressures.
- Changes in corporate strategy.

An analysis of labour supply needs to commence with a positional assessment of the organisation's current employees (see table above). Staff turnover raises a number of issues such as:

- historic rates and those expected in similar businesses
- the rate at which staff are leaving and their reasons for leaving
- numbers retiring and likely future projections based on age profiles.

Table 4.2 Human resource planning: some data requirement

Internal
Employee analysis: numbers, gender, qualification, trade and job, skills, experience, etc.
Categories of staff
Staff suitable for promotion or redeployment
Overtime levels and trends
Labour turnover analysis and reasons
Absence level by category and trends
Productivity ratios and trends
Comparison with national/regional/industry trends

External
Regional employment trends and unemployment levels
Demographic projections
Skill levels and shortages
Education levels and proposals
Transport and planning proposals
Labour mobility
Migration and immigration trends
Growth of competing firms in the area

Source: Author

If a significant cause of turnover is due to a lack of promotion opportunities, inadequate training, low morale or poor management, then these problems need to be addressed within the strategy. Consideration should also be given to the organisation's ability to continue to attract suitable recruits into its various operations. Can the organisation count on filling vacant posts satisfactorily when it goes into the market place? Are some posts more difficult to fill than others, and can anything be done about this?

Reputedly Nissan and other car firms where high-intensity teamwork is necessary rely on a high turnover rate of employees to enable fresh recruits to be brought in at regular intervals. By comparison other organisations expect a considerable degree of stability among their workforce, and build this expectation into their planning assumptions (such as the UK's Civil Service).

Exercise 4.3

For reflection

According to one HR consultant in the USA, 50 of the country's biggest companies anticipated losing half of their senior management in the next 5–6 years (Byrnes and Barrett, 2005). At what level does the staff turnover rate become acknowledged by your organisation as unacceptable?

Having considered the existing supply of labour, an organisation will need to project a view of what the workforce will need to be like in the future in order to fulfill its strategic plans. If the organisation cannot meet its future HR needs internally, then it must look to the external labour market. There are a number of important questions to be asked, for example:

- What will the overall employment situation likely to be over the planning period?
- How is this situation likely to affect our local labour market?

- What competition for labour is likely?
- Are there any trends in the wider environment (e.g. in education) which might affect recruitment plans?
- Are there factors in our strategic plans that might speed up the voluntary leaving rate?

The answers to these questions will indicate the likely prospects of meeting future labour needs from external sources. For example, labour (particularly skilled) may be an extremely scarce resource in most advanced industrialised nations during times of economic prosperity. Another reason to recruit externally is driven by changes in technology or production processes which bring about changes in the numbers and types of employees required. Improved technology can (for instance) lead to less work for machine operators on the one hand, but more jobs for skilled maintenance technicians on the other.

The difference between the two projections of supply and demand can be made ('gap analysis') and plans developed accordingly, for example, retraining, part time workers, use of consultants overtime, computerisation recruitment, redundancy policy, etc.

Since employees are probably the most unpredictable organisational resource, the best plans will be those that allow the greatest flexibility. Most HR plans are developed on a rolling 3-year basis, which means that forecasts for next year and the succeeding years in the cycle are updated every year in the light of this year's experience. Detailed plans for securing sufficient and suitable employees for current needs are made for a 1-year period, in line with current budgets. Less detailed plans are made for the 3-year period, prepared in line with the organisation's corporate strategy.

Mullins (2005) captures all elements involved in planning (Figure 4.3) and articulates the HR plan and consequent action programmes as a means of reconciling supply and demand.

One issue that arises as part of this process is arriving at a method for assessing likely workload. The 'Taylorist' approach is traditional, especially in manufacturing environments, and can be a simple, straightforward way of forecasting if the organisation has reliable data. This method involves separating the work to be done into discrete parts. Each part is then forecast and converted into staffing requirements by a conversion factor, for example the number of hours required to do each job is then multiplied by the number of forecast jobs:

- Classify the work into tasks.
- Calculate hours per task.
- Forecast work in terms of number of each task.
- Convert the above into jobs.
- Convert number of jobs into people required on the basis of the organisation's annual hourly contract commitment per employee.

A range of methods might be used from simple observation or comparisons with other similar organisations, through to rigorous work-study methods.

> **!** This method may seem outdated but the large petrochemical firm BP/Amoco has used this approach when developing chemicals plant through a 10-year programme of new capital construction and some 5,000 to 10,000 workers at different times. For contractors, labour costs are the prime cost of running the business and so effective planning at this level of detail is essential. Teams from BP/Amoco and contractors, together with trade unions, were set up to find out the various ways in which this exceptional demand for labour could be met.

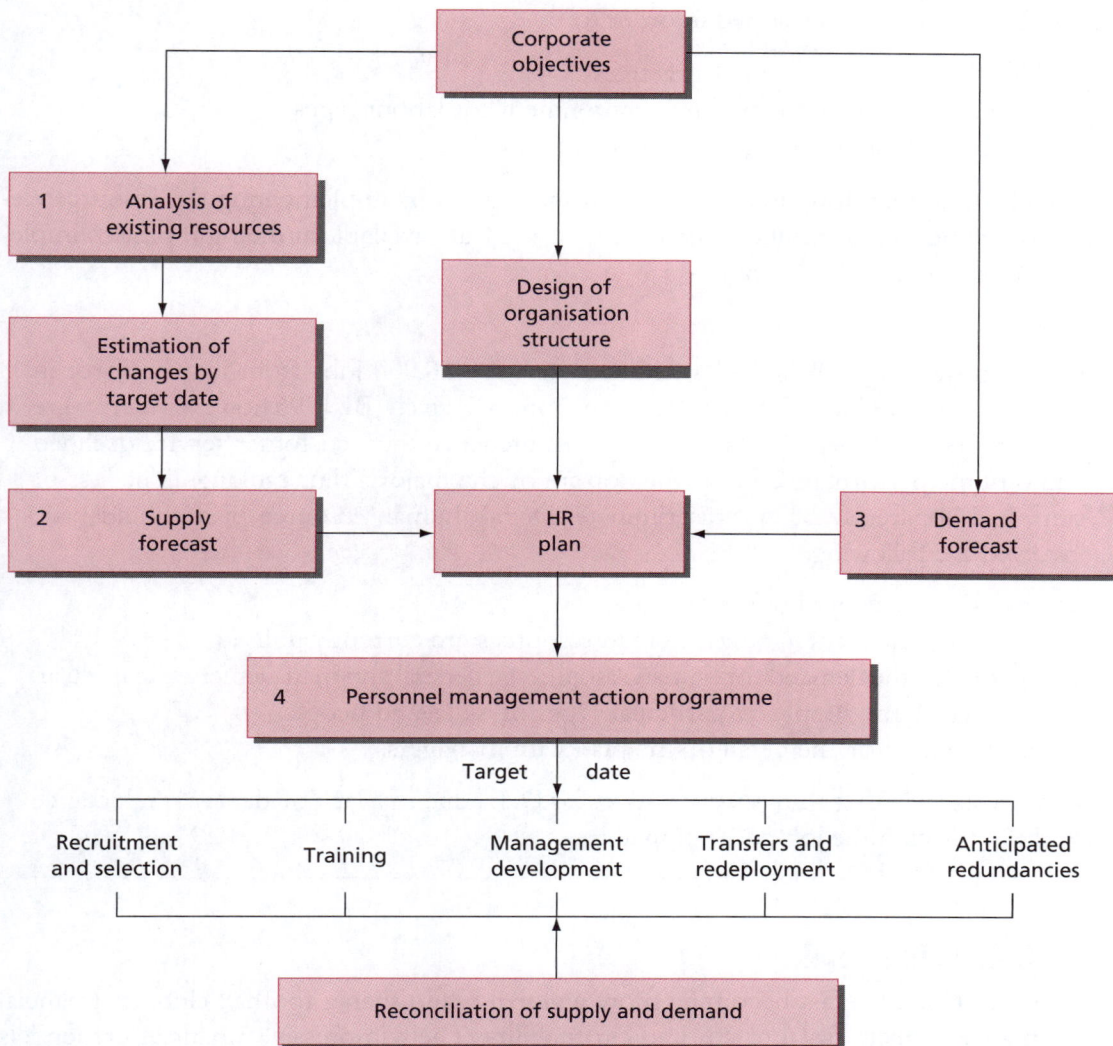

Figure 4.3 Main stages in human resources planning
Source: Mullins (2005) © Laurie J Mullins 2002. Reprinted with permission of Pearson.

4.4.2 Planning: some influencing factors

Planning is complicated by factors such as the nature of the organisational environment (e.g. stable and predictable or fast changing and unpredictable) and the lifecycle of products and services (see 2.4.1 earlier).

The following factors also significantly impact on the planning process:

- Overall corporate plan and the implied demands upon human resources.
- Changing output of the organisation.
- Developments in technology.
- Availability of new technology.
- Access to finance.
- Organisation of work.
- Productivity trends.
- Employee (industrial) relations atmosphere.

The HR plan must be developed in order to:

- be able to implement intended strategies
- protect fluctuations in the external environment for labour types
- effectively compete for labour against competitors.

HR planning therefore links to other business plans by implementing the resource element so that necessary numbers and quality of staff are available at the right time to implement the business's other plans.

> In the early 1990s, Delta Airlines cut some 10,000 jobs from its workforce in order to reduce costs and compete more effectively. By 1995 however there were clear shortages of baggage-handlers and maintenance staff, customer service declined and on-time performance fell to the bottom of the major airline rankings. The loss of staff had apparently been indiscriminate. Delta's human resource plan should have involved the following:
>
> - Analysis of current human resources.
> - Review of the ways in which human resources are currently utilised.
> - Forecast of the demand for human resources in general and management in particular.
> - Forecast of the supply of particular types of skills and people.
> - Development of the detail of the plan with managers.
>
> It is unclear whether things went wrong for Delta due to a lack of data or a reluctance to think through the job cuts rationally.

Exercise 4.4

Manchester United is fast becoming more a global brand than a football club. Its financial performance reflects fast growth and profitability. Their impressive financial credentials made them until recently the world's largest club (generating well over £100 million revenue per annum 'before a ball is kicked'). Players enjoy huge salaries and the club is better placed than most to pay the top dollar in terms of transfer fees and wage demands. This means they could recruit the best footballers from anywhere in the world. Yet the club continues to spend heavily on their youth policy. Why should this be the case?

Solution

It partially insulates the club from the transfer market and also importantly brings loyalty and commitment to the playing staff. The first team itself represents a combination of expensive buys and players who have progressed through thanks to the club's youth policy. The average age of the talented professional playing staff is a youthful 25 years old. The youngsters continue to benefit from the best training facilities money can buy at the purpose built multi million pound Trafford Training Centre, Carrington set in 70 acres. (Source: Perry, 2005)

4.4.3 Dimensions and content of a human resource plan

This section deals with some of the practical issues associated with developing a human resource plan.

Organisational growth rate

Human resource demand estimates arise from a number of factors, including:

- Priorities identified in the corporate plan.
- The orientation of the organisation in terms of labour and technology (from the use of labour-intensive, low-skill workforce to highly skilled and capital-intensive employment).

  If expansion is planned, an organisation might need to:

- draw heavily on the local labour-market
- identify new sources of labour
- identify new approaches might need to be sought.

To overcome labour shortages some European employers around have chosen to base part of their operations overseas with areas such as Asia proving popular thanks to a relatively cheap and a plentiful labour source.

Insight:

Within the UK's National Health Service (NHS) key skill gaps remain unfilled, despite best endeavours of HR specialists. As a result there is recruitment from overseas, so much so that up to 30 per cent of the workforce in some areas are occupied by employees born overseas, mainly Africa and Asia. The effect of this immigration is that key skills are lost to countries that cannot compete with the recruitment packages offered by the NHS. This raises clear ethical concerns.

Increasingly, to provide for workforce flexibility (possibly during periods of growth), new forms of employment terms are being adopted. These include fixed-term or part-time contracts or a system of 'annual hours' to smooth the use of staff over critical periods such as year-end or seasonal shortages around Bank Holidays. Other organisations have chosen to outsource certain functions preferring to rely on outside contractors rather than attempt to provide an adequate internal provision. Such an initiative involves an appreciation of the availability, suitability and reliability of contractors.

Charles Handy's (1999) concept of the 'shamrock' organisation is of some relevance here. The three leaves of the shamrock are symbolic of an organisation's human resource usage, namely:

- a core of professional workers paid through the payroll
- a contractual fringe of people outside the organisation who provide specialist and non-essential services
- a flexible labour force of part-time and temporary workers who are used during busy periods.

If contraction rather than growth of the business is planned, staff turnover rates and the age profile of the workforce are of relevance. Under these circumstances it might be an advantage to have an ageing workforce so that redundancy is less of an issue. Any redundancy costs that are likely to arise can reasonably be planned for and be factored into the main business plan. (Under these conditions profit warnings may have to be given and 'restructuring costs' may emerge within financial statements.)

Technology and productivity

The influence of technology on organisations can be over-estimated. The Economist reported research in 1999 that showed little evidence of a productivity increase in the USA due to automation, except in the computer-manufacturing firms themselves. The whole economy, however, was more productive, suggesting other reasons for improved efficiency.

The skill level required of the workforce (and in turn its market price) is often influenced by the level and sophistication of technology. The organisation needs to ensure that remuneration is sufficient to attract and then retain the workforce. A strategic consideration when developing an HR plan involves issues such as:

- The plans for technology development in the organisation
- The revised skill sets demanded by these developments
- How high-cost groups of key employees might be accommodated
- The use of funds released by improved output per employee or other productivity indicators.

Productivity is often dependent upon perceived incentives and clearly the reward structure needs to be maintained to ensure that these incentives are working. There is ample evidence that faulty pay-for-productivity plans aimed at maximising 'output per employee' create the wrong type of outcomes whereby measured outputs are maximised at the expense of vital but unquantifiable ones (such as cooperation). In addition quality often suffers as a result. (See previous chapter)

Skills

Skills requirements come from the basic operations of the organisation. Traditionally skills were thought of in terms of 'trades' and 'professions'. Increasingly, however, new skills are being demanded. The growth of the service sector and the 'knowledge economy' has led to a surge in new skills such as 'Web Authors' (those who design web pages) a job unheard of until relatively recently. Similarly, political and legal factors create the need for additional skills.

> Within the UK local authorities have identified a need for managers skilled in competitive tendering and contract compliance. This is as a result of the government's use of 'best value' (formerly compulsory competitive tendering) placing the onus on them to find competitive sources of contract work rather than relying on direct labour forces without testing their competitiveness in the market.

Training

When developing an HR plan issues including a concept of what the basic job requires and professional training needs should be provided to prepare new and existing staff to fulfill their roles satisfactorily. Special programmes may need to be established to deal with retraining or updating and traineeships and apprenticeship training may need to be accounted for.

Less enlightened organisations may choose not to invest in training believing that improved qualifications merely improve the employees' marketability. Such an organisation may believe it can save costs by simply recruiting another's trained employees at a slightly higher rate of pay, obviating the need for a training department, plans and systems and the employment costs of trainees.

Training may be closely linked to both recruitment and career development. Training itself can take many forms (see later).

> In Japan there is a tradition of lifetime employment with one organisation. This is reinforced by the system of pay-for-seniority (nenko-juretsu) meaning that employees wishing to leave have to take a pay cut at the new firm as they are then on the bottom of the new ladder.

Recruitment and selection

There is a section later in this chapter giving details of recruitment and selection procedures here it is considered as part of HR planning. A number of fundamental planning questions arise such as:

- How do we ensure our anticipated needs for replenishing or adding to our workforce are best met?
- Do we want to recruit trained and experienced people or develop our existing staff?
- How much provision should be made for recruiting part-time and more flexible staff?
- What steps should be taken to promote our organisation in schools, colleges and universities?
- What use, if any, should we make of recruitment consultants?
- What improvements could be made to our selection procedures?

These questions should be addressed within the HR strategy.

Development, promotion and succession planning

In this area there are considerable variances in practices between organisations. Some offer no real prospects for increased variety or responsibility at work. Others build reputations as 'good' employers claiming career development to be an integral part of their approach. Arguably organisations taking the latter approach can expect greater internal receptiveness to organisational change.

Development, promotion and succession planning depend on good systems of appraisal and job evaluation. These allow organisations to promote workers to more demanding situations to enhance their overall learning and development. For a large multi-level organisation there are large numbers of jobs and staff movement so giving scope for development within job roles or by switching roles. (The redesign of a job by adding more demanding tasks is refereed to as job enrichment.) For a smaller organisation this would be impossible, and self-career development may only be possible by an individual leaving a company and moving to another employer.

An assessment of individual's knowledge and skills needs to be accurately assessed and the demands of the current job need to be known before a range of future jobs can be identified. The essence of job evaluation is precisely to identify these demands and these must be accurately assessed if development is to work well.

> **! Insight:**
> In a study conducted in the USA, 10,000 workers were polled (Anon, 2005) with some telling findings emerging:
>
> - half expected to change companies within the next 5 years
> - more than one-third expected to change companies in less than 3 years
> - one-third were currently looking for another company career.
>
> Does this indicate an end to company succession planning?

Natural wastage

Provision in the HR plan should be made for those reaching retirement age. Natural wastage also includes 'turnover' of staff leaving for different reasons. It may also be possible to accurately estimate the extent to which maternity leave will affect a workforce based on past experiences. In many countries leave and career break concessions for paternity leave are being granted and this may need to be factored into calculations. Natural breaks of service like this can become extended and in many cases and the leavers may never return, or take some years out of the employment market.

> ⚠ Within the UK the National Health Service (NHS) spends considerable sums on nurse training. Despite this there often remains an excess of demand over supply for nurses due to very high wastage levels. Some leave the profession entirely or take career breaks never to return. To solve this difficulty the NHS has over a number of years pursued a number of initiatives including enticing ex-nurses back through advertising campaigns and financial inducements for returners.

4.4.4 Implementation and review

HR planning is a corporate activity across all divisional and departmental boundaries of an organisation. It is not the preserve of any one group of specialist managers (e.g. Personnel), even though such specialists may well play a key co-coordinating role in the implementation and review. Major reviews of progress will usually take place annually and possibly half-yearly or quarterly. The principal vehicle of the monitoring process is the monthly budget statement. These can be expressed in a number of ways (e.g. costs, headcounts or person hours, etc.) The costs identified will be the total labour costs for each category of staff for the period concerned, and will also indicate the running totals to date. Current totals will be compared with budget targets and any variances noted. 'Headcounts' are usually made against establishments, which are target employee numbers fixed for a given period. This is probably the most popular method of controlling employee numbers. 'Person hour' methods are more likely to be used for employees whose work can be measured in this way.

   HR review activities are important for generating feedback information. This information tells the organisation not only how well it is achieving its HR plans, but also points out the necessary changes that must be made at one or more points in the cycle. Some changes need only be made at the tactical level, (e.g. to amend next year's plans). Other changes may have to be made at the highest strategic level where longer term plans may need to be modified.

4.4.5 Criticisms of a planned approach

Human resource planning shares criticisms similar to that directed at any formal rational strategic planning processes when environments seems uncertain. The attempt to plan human resources in a highly rational manner in a seemingly chaotic environment was best illustrated by one issue of the magazine (*Management Today*) that had a cover headline of (in relation to managerial jobs) 'No Stability, No Security, No Careers'.

✋ Exercise 4.5

How can an organisation plan rationally in an unstable environment?

✔ Solution

- By planning flexibly
- By taking greater account of external factors
- By more sophisticated monitoring and control mechanisms
- By planning in shorter time frames.

Problems in achieving plans might to a degree be predictable and in the past have also traditionally centred on:

- Retention especially when employees are well trained or have specialist skills
- Slow promotion leading to staff turnover
- Difficulties associated with putting succession planning into practice
- Unexpected vacancies arising in very senior positions or in vital skills areas.

Byrnes and Barrett (2005) summarise what they see as a century of innovations and fads aimed at 'trying to get the workforce right', extracts are shown in the Table 4.3.

Table 4.3 HR Innovations through the years

1881 BUSINESS GOES TO COLLEGE

- Joseph Wharton, co-founder of Bethlehem Steel, persuades the University of Pennsylvania to launch an undergraduate business education program so saving company costs

1900 MBAs

- First graduate business school. By 2002, there were 120,875 MBAs awarded in the U.S., and many schools have opened overseas.

1911 TAYLORISM

- Frederick Winslow Taylor argues that there is only one objectively correct way to perform industrial jobs.

1943 EXECUTIVE MBAs

- University of Chicago offers the first MBA for working managers.

1956 CORPORATE CLASSROOMS

- Leadership development goes in-house at General Electric when the company opens its own management 'school' in Ossining, NY.

1959 'KNOWLEDGE WORKERS'

- Drucker describes the declining importance of manual labour and describes a new type of employee.

LATE 1980s 360 DEGREES FEEDBACK

- Managers are exposed to critiques from those below them in the hierarchy.

1990 PAY FOR PERFORMANCE

1999 JOB JUMPING

- Online job search

2005 ACTION LEARNING

- A growing training practice is based on the premise that it makes more sense to put promising people to work on real business problems. They get trained and the company gets a problem solved.

Source: Based on Byrnes and Barrett (2005)

4.5 The human resource cycle

An individual's relationship with an organisation can be viewed as a series of staged processes that extend from the arrangements made by the organisation for the post to be filled through to that individual completing their engagement with the organisation and leaving. This section deals with certain of these dimensions and gives some background and detailed discussion of the process and associated techniques. (Table 4.4)

4.5.1 Job analysis

When a decision is made for the first time that a particular post should be created, some form of job analysis should take place. Job analysis is also useful when an organisation wishes to assess whether or not a post that is due to fall vacant should be filled. The process of job analysis will form a basis for the subsequent preparation of job descriptions and person specifications (see later). Methods of analysing and defining jobs could include:

Direct observation. Several drawbacks exist to this approach. A skilled and experienced worker can make a job look easy or difficult, depending on their disposition. Additionally, some manual tasks are so fast or intricate that accurate observation can only be achieved by the use of video recording.

Interview the existing post holder. Again this can cause problems, if the post holder exaggerates or depreciates the importance of the job. An employee's attitude towards the job, organisation or supervisor may influence their responses. Even if co-operative, the post holder may forget some important details and merely recall the most recent events. There is also the potential difficulty of the employee not being able to communicate effectively.

Interview the immediate supervisor. The value of this approach can be variable, as the supervisor is often out-of-touch with the details of the job. The description of the job may be influenced by the supervisor's opinion of the current jobholder. As with the jobholder, the supervisor may exaggerate the importance of the job in order to increase his or her own importance.

Manager trying the job. This obviously has a high opportunity cost and in any case may be only useful if the job involves simple tasks.

Previous studies. Training, job evaluation, work-study records, manuals and information obtained in other ways are sometimes available. These can be brought up to date or added to produce a job description.

Table 4.4 The human resource cycle

Activity	Description
Job analysis	Analysing and defining jobs
Job description	Purpose and the main tasks of the job
Person specification	Personal characteristics, experience qualifications, etc. of post holder
Recruitment	Attracting a pool of suitable applicants
Selection	Making a choice
Induction	Making the settling-in period easier
(Ongoing processes)	Appraisal, training, development
Termination	Promotion, resignation, retirement, redundancy

Source: Author

Questionnaires. These can be useful but are frequently unreliable. Employees may not understand the questions, or the questions may be too restrictive.

Work diaries. These are useful chiefly for managerial and complex technical jobs. The current post holder is asked to record their activities over a period of up to 3 months. The diary is analysed on a weekly basis to obtain an understanding of the tasks, contacts and frequency of the activities. Problems occur should the jobholder forget to make entries and it can be very tedious to complete, therefore the use of pre-printed forms covering the most common activities is preferable. The purpose of this analysis is to identify the key result areas or the critical incidents, which is of particular value in defining complex jobs.

4.5.2 Job descriptions

The job description defines the overall purpose of the job and the main tasks to be carried out within the role. Existing job descriptions and terms and conditions of employment should be checked and confirmed to ensure they are up to date. Where a job description does not exist one can be created following a job analysis.

A robust job description is essential to successful recruitment and selection since it is the foundation upon which other processes are based. The job description should be considered as a quasi-legal document, since once issued to an employee, it may be viewed as contractual. The person specification, advertising copy and assessment procedure will be based on the job description.

The main points to be covered in the job description include the following:

- The location of the job within the organisation structure (division, department and section).
- Title of the job, and the job code if available.
- Job title of the person to whom the jobholder is responsible.
- Job title(s) of the person(s) responsible to the jobholder, and the number of staff directly supervised.
- Brief description of the overall purpose of the role (listed chronologically or in order of importance, preferably using action verbs).
- Details of any technical procedures, tools, machinery or equipment used by the jobholder.
- Any special requirements to liaise or deal with contacts of high significance inside and outside the organisation.
- Physical location of the job and the amount of travelling required. Special circumstances (if any) attached to the job, such as shift, night work, on-call, degree of overtime commitment, weekend working, physically demanding activities, etc.
- Responsibility for budgets, etc.

It is also useful to set out the terms and conditions of employment such as salary, normal working hours and holiday entitlement, etc. separately in a letter when making a formal job offer.

4.5.3 Person specifications

The person specification defines the personal characteristics, qualifications, and the experience required by the jobholder in order to do the job well. Any other special demands or requirements such as physical aspects and unusual working hours should be included. The information relating to qualifications and experience demanded by the job can only be derived following a thorough job analysis that identifies the knowledge, skills and other behaviours required. The list of personal characteristics needs to be as precise as possible so that the assessment process can identify what a candidate knows and can do. A danger in overstating the qualifications and experience demanded by the job is that it could lead to appointing a new employee who quickly becomes dissatisfied with the lack of challenge and subsequently leaves.

When the job requirements have been agreed with the line manager, they should be analysed using a suitable structure. The Five-Fold Grading System (Munro Fraser) and the Seven-Point Plan (Alec Rodgers) are the most familiar instruments used in the UK. The Five-Fold Grading System is simpler and places greater emphasis on the dynamic aspects of the job and a candidate's career. Line managers, however, generally find the Seven-Point Plan easier to complete as it is more structured (Table 4.5). Both structures provide a framework for the selection process.

Increasingly some UK organisations also utilise a list of specific or generic competencies based on in-house research or national competency frameworks such as National Vocational Qualifications (NVQs). These competencies attempt to specify the cognitive and social skills required by the organisation.

4.5.4 Recruitment

It is important to note that although the term 'recruitment' is often used conjunction with 'selection' however the terms refer to two separate processes. Recruitment is a set of activities designed to attract a qualified pool of applicants to an organisation. (The process of selection, involves choosing from a pool of applicants the person or persons who offer the greatest performance potential). Typically, there are three steps in the recruitment process:

- advertisement of a job vacancy
- preliminary contact with potential job candidates and
- initial screening to create a pool of suitable applicants.

The issue for an organisation is to decide how best to fill the gap created by a vacancy. The internal process begins with the existence of a vacancy (normally because of a resignation or transfer). To find a replacement, there needs to be some kind of description of the job

Table 4.5 Example Seven-Point Plan for a shift process operator

Essential	
Physical make-up	Good health record (from references)
	Acceptable bearing and speech
	Smart appearance
Attainments	GCSE English language and Maths grade C or equivalent, e.g. GNVQ
General intelligence	Average
Special aptitudes	Manual dexterity and reasonable facility with figures, experience of extended shift work
Interests	Mechanical – cars, model airplanes, etc.
Disposition	Calm, self-reliant
Circumstances	Living within ten miles
	Own transport (no public transport operators at shift change times)

and of the personal attributes required or desired in the ideal candidate, possibly in the form a person specification. The external process begins with accessing the channels by which applicants might be found.

Recruitment need not involve advertising, but if it does it must be effective. External advertising is expensive and may account for up to half the year's salary for some jobs. Too loose or glamorous an advertisement may result in an unnecessarily large response that becomes time-consuming to deal with.

It is necessary for a continuous review and evaluation of advertising practices to ensure their effectiveness and efficiency. The appropriate media needs to be selected depending on the target audience and the speed with which the position needs to be filled. Professional journals, for instance, may be more precise in targeting the audience but are expensive, have long intervals between issues, a long lead time, and a subsequent slow response rate.

It is important to choose an appropriate and cost effective method of recruitment (Table 4.6).

In instances where difficulties in attracting or retaining staff arise or are anticipated, it may be necessary to conduct a preliminary investigation of the factors likely to attract or deter candidates. A list of those factors most likely to be most appealing to potential applicants (key selling points) should be identified. It is important to consider (regardless of the labour market) that while candidates may be 'selling' themselves, they are also 'buying' what the organisation has to offer. Some of the key factors include:

- national or local reputation of the organisation
- total reward package offered (see section 3.7)

Table 4.6 Recruitment mechanisms and media

MOST POPULAR
Press

- Regional: for local markets, evening papers
- Specialist: trade journals or quality press

Job centres
Employment agencies

- Government operated. Employment agencies in the UK include Government-funded initiatives such as Jobcentres and Jobclubs, which aim to help the unemployed get back to work.
- Private sector. Private sector agencies often deal with temporary support staff such as secretaries, or specialist staff such as computer programmers.

Recruitment Consultants

OTHER
- Executive Search consultants
- Careers conventions. Exhibitions, fairs and conferences – to target highly selective groups
- Open days
- University Milk Rounds for graduate recruitment
- Radio. Often used locally, particularly for opening new stores or for temporary jobs, as it has an immediate effect
- Cinema. Still used for local jobs. Often advertises agencies rather than vacancies
- Posters. A low-level method that does not target applicants in a helpful way (used by small retailers, etc.)
- World Wide Web.
- TV. Unusual unless local or large numbers needed as it is expensive
- Locally maintained registers. There is some cost associated with maintaining these records and drop out rate of candidates tends to be high. Registers can be compiled from the data of previously unsuccessful candidates and those who unsolicited have forwarded their CVs to the organisation.

- working conditions
- intrinsic interest of the job
- security of employment
- opportunities for training and development
- career prospects.

Except in special circumstances, the final advertising copy should be written to complement the assumed aspirations of the target population and include, in suitably abbreviated form:

- the job description
- person specification
- organisation's key selling points such as compensation
- instructions for applicants
- deadline.

> **! Insight:**
>
> There were 14,700 agencies in the UK alone in 2004 (Marketing Week, 2005) performing a wide range of services, including:
>
> - Specialist temporary staff. Many charge a month's salary for a permanent placement of a temporary employee ('temps') subsequently hired.
> - Executive services. Larger employment consultancy firms tend to be managed from a corporate headquarters and are selective whom they represent. They may maintain the CVs of executives looking for future developmental moves. They may provide a more complete service including a shortlisting of candidates but may not be organisationally culture-sensitive. Executive searches undertaken by such firms involve consultants maintaining an informal network of contacts and keeping track of the careers of those likely to be in demand. Candidates for unadvertised vacancies are approached directly and the job (probably not the firm) discussed in outline, then in detail. The candidates' motivations and preferences can be discussed without the individual knowing the organisation's location or industry. This is however a high-cost, high-risk method, partially because the new recruit may be 'headhunted' again. Many search firms are members of the professional bodies that regulate activity, however fairness and ethical concerns persist.
>
> **! Insight:**
>
> One UK example of web recruitment is www.jobs.ac.uk which claims to be 'the top recruitment site in its sector the research, science, academic and related professions' and claims the following impressive statistics:
>
> - over 30,000 jobs advertised each year
> - each job advert page being read around 500 times on average
> - over 350,000 unique users each month.
>
> A further website is http://jobs.candidateone.com/ which is growing in popularity as it offers a free service to both recruiters and jobseekers.

Exercise 4.6

What standards in recruitment should an ethically driven organisation adhere to?

Solution

Standards in recruitment should be (but often are not) determined by company policy. Issues include standards of behaviour, cost, time, fairness, user-friendliness, validity, reliability, applicability and overall acceptability to both candidate and organisation.

4.5.5 Selection techniques in overview

Steps in a typical selection process include:

- completion of a formal application form
- interviewing
- testing
- reference checks
- medical examination
- final analysis and decision to hire or not to hire
- official job 'offer' letter.

Any techniques used in selection should be (but often are not):

Reliable: give consistent results.

Valid: accurately predict performance.

Fair: select employees in a non-discriminatory way, particularly in terms of race, age, and gender. This may be to fulfill legal requirements and the ethical frameworks under which the organisation operates (see previous chapter).

Cost-effective: the costs of devising and operating the selection methods must be justified in terms of the benefits of selecting good applicants for the particular jobs in question.

Increasingly, however, organisations are introducing measures to try to ensure that selection processes are as objective as possible. The outcome of a faulty selection process can involve:

- rejecting applicants who would have been suitable and
- employing people who turn out to be unsuitable.

Beaumont (1993) reported a further dimension to the selection decision as follows:

. . . (it has become) less about matching an individual employee to the fixed requirements of an individual job at a single point in time (and) as a consequence, immediate skills and employment background . . . and more about willingness to learn, adaptability, and willingness/ability to work as part of a team. These changes are concomitant with moves away from Tayloristic work organization which involved a hierarchy of narrowly designed and highly specialised job tasks to each of which was attached the rate for the job and moves towards a reduction in the number of individual job classifications, team working . . . and the integration of all responsibility for quality control

Precise selection techniques can take many forms, and the main ones are considered in the sections that now follow.

4.5.6 Selection techniques: interviews

Once a shortlist has been drawn up, the most common way of selecting a candidate is by interview or series of interviews. Under the right conditions, selection interviews may give reliable and valid results, but these 'right conditions' will not occur automatically. Interviewers should determine before the interview the criteria against which they are judging applicants and then after interview assess how each applicant 'measured up'.

Selection interviews have been extensively researched and much derided but very few selection decisions are made without an interview, even for internal promotions where the candidates are well known. Repeated research shows that the interview used in isolation is unreliable as a selector, however when it is used along with other methods greater reliability is achieved. It is important therefore to consider all methods of selecting staff and to use those that seem appropriate in each circumstance.

Some believe that the main value of an interview is to provide a two-way dialogue in exploring the motivation and enthusiasm of a candidate.

The problems with interviews include the following:

- *Reliability*. This may be interpreted as repeatability (i.e. if others conducted the interview, would the same applicant be selected?) In this context there are several ways in which reliability can be impaired. The so-called 'primacy effect' is where interviewers make up their minds too early in the interview (sometimes in the first few minutes). The early part of the interview consequently can have considerable importance. This means that the order of presentation of questions and the structure of the interview have to be controlled and consistently repeated in all interviews if all applicants are to be treated fairly. It follows that structured interviews should be the 'norm' rather than unstructured open-ended discussions.
- *Validity*. In this context, validity means ensuring the 'right' candidate being placed in the 'right' post, however the interview if used in isolation is notoriously ineffective in this respect. Interviews may be an efficient way of eliminating the very poor performers, but less good at distinguishing between the moderately good and the moderately poor.
- *Fairness*. The content of interviews may be inappropriate. Some interviewers can concentrate on areas where they themselves are experts which may mean that the interview fails to explore all the applicant's relevant expertise properly. Standard questions need to be used in order to treat all interviewees fairly. Interviewers who apply stereotypes or have inappropriate prejudices can damage the integrity of the process and breach legal, organisational, professional and other ethical frameworks. Personal biases should be avoided at all costs.
- *Accuracy*. The accuracy of factual data revealed in interviews is reasonably high, but never complete. Inaccuracies may arise from embellishment of claims, deliberate deception and/or misunderstandings on the part of the interviewer.

Other problems, which can affect the quality the interview experience include interviewers who are poorly trained or inexperienced. Such interviewers may fail to make use of an accurate person specification, or may forget that selection should be a two-way process that gives applicants an opportunity to find out about the job and the organisation. Training the interviewers and careful preparation for the interviews will help to reduce interviewer error.

There are several types of interview:

- The individual or 'one to one' interview is the most familiar method involving face-to-face discussion and provides the best opportunity for the establishment of a rapport between the interviewer and the candidate. If only one interviewer is used, there is more scope for a biased or superficial decision to emerge.

- Tandem interviews involve two interviewers per candidate. Rapport may be reduced but so is the possibility of bias. Typical interviewers would be the personnel or HR officer and the relevant line manager.
- Panel interviews consist of a number of people who interview the candidate together. The interview is conducted on a very formal basis but it does enable a number of different people to have a look at applicants and compare notes in 'real time'. The disadvantage is that a single member of the panel could dominate proceedings. In addition confident, articulate candidates may be more comfortable with this approach.
- Sequential interviews involve the candidate being passed from one interviewer to another until several one to one interviews have taken place. The advantage here is that several people may see the candidate but the disadvantage is that interviwers may vary in their opinions when results are collated.

4.5.7   Selection techniques: tests

Reliability is an important consideration in the context of selection testing, in this case the consistency with which a test produces the same score through a series of measurements. If the same person is asked to take the test on a number of separate occasions, approximately the same score should emerge each time.

Validity is the extent to which the test measures what it is intended to measure. There are several sub-classes of validity, specifically:

- *Face validity*. The test must give the impression of measuring relevant characteristics.
- *Concurrent validity*. The extent to which the scores of a test relate to the performance of employees currently undertaking the kind of work for which candidates are being evaluated.
- *Predictive validity*. The extent to which the scores of a test relate to some future measure of performance.

The main types of test that can be used in selection are as follows:

- *Cognitive tests* which relate to thinking processes and include tests of intelligence, ability, aptitude, communication, numerical skills, etc. Usually *intelligence tests* are described to candidates as 'aptitude' or 'skills' tests and normally comprise of mathematical or number skills, communication or verbal skills and a general logic or problem-solving testing. Originally they were work-related, such as typing tests, but gradually more abstract forms were developed (especially by the armed forces and government employment agencies) for aptitudes seen to be important for some jobs. Manual dexterity, mechanical, numerical ability and spatial testing are included in this category. Research shows that these have only a modest degree of predictive accuracy concerning job performance.
- *Personality tests*, which involve assessing non-cognitive and non-intellectual characteristics of an individual, usually the emotional make-up, reflected in the style of behaviour. Beaumont (1993) noted that 'there is probably no subject more controversial in occupational psychology than the merits and demerits of personality assessment'. Results from personality tests have to be interpreted carefully alongside the applicant's other known attributes. Many categories of personality tests exist, including questionnaires, which have doubtful validity as candidates may attempt to predict likely required answers. Another test is where a candidate is presented with some ambiguous material and asked to freely respond to it by, for instance, word association or sentence completion and this involves the psychologist interpreting the response. Such

MANAGING HUMAN CAPITAL

techniques tend to have low reliability and less predictive validity. Further, tests devised to observe candidates' behaviour in a standardised situation that will throw light on aspects of their personality crucial to the job concerned. Examples include leaderless group discussions. These tests can be both reliable and valid providing they are focused on particular job requirements.

> ### ! Insight:
>
> The most-well known personality test is the Cattell 16 PF (Personality Factors) which provides 16 basic dimensions, such as extrovert/introvert, tough-minded/tender-minded, along which individuals score from 0 to 10. These standard-ten or 'sten' scores can be aggregated to produce higher-level factors such as leadership or toughness. This test has norms against which candidates can be compared, and also has a 'lie-detector' scale or 'motivational distortion' score, which can be used to assess how far the candidate has tried to manipulate their responses. There are several books interpreting the scores of such tests and computer software that can produce written narratives explaining the results.
>
> - *Psychometric testing* is sometimes also undertaken in this context. The term 'psychometric' derives from 'psyche' meaning the mind and 'metric' meaning measuring so psychometric applies to both personality and cognitive testing. The quality of tests used ranges from good to of dubious quality. Others are expensive to administer and score, often requiring the involvement of the commercial consultants. Organisations intending to use such tests should first seek guidance from the British Psychological Society, the American Psychological Society (Table 4.7) or other reputable agencies in other countries.
>
> In psychological testing, ethical considerations should be applied to critical aspects of the science. Since administration, scoring and interpretation of tests is a skilled operation only qualified people are entitled to use them. The British and American Psychological Societies require proper training of test administrators and interpreters and there is a strong recommendation to give the candidates feedback on their results. Tests are available from psychological publishers but the applicant must be registered and have The British Psychological Society's Level A and/or B testing certificate in order to be able to administer and scope the test and if necessary interpret the scores accurately. Both the reliability and validity of personality tests provided by some commercial organisations in particular should be questioned.

Table 4.7   The British Psychological Society, the American Psychological Society

British Psychological Society

'The Society is a learned and professional body controlled by our Royal Charter. This means that our primary duty is to preserve and nurture the discipline on behalf of the nation. Our main objective is to advance and diffuse knowledge of psychology. This combines with our charitable status which says that as an organisation we are not permitted to do anything outside of the objectives as specified in the Charter.' (source: http://www.bps.org.uk)

American Psychological Society

'The American Psychological Society's mission is to promote, protect, and advance the interests of scientifically-oriented psychology in research, (and) application' (source: www.psychologicalscience.org/)

4.5.8 Selection techniques: other issues

This section deals with important areas associated with staff selection, assessment centres and group selection methods.

An assessment centre involves 'the assessment of a group of individuals by a team of judges using a comprehensive and interrelated series of techniques'. An assessment centre does not necessarily mean a physical centre but is a particular approach and philosophy. It is important to ensure that jobs have been analysed and the results classified to provide a list of criteria or competencies around which the assessment centre should be designed. These assessment instruments such as 'in-tray' exercises, negotiations or presentations, can be designed or bought off the shelf, but it is important to ensure that there are a sufficient number of the right type of activities to measure all relevant criteria. It may be helpful to combine interviews with other selection techniques such as some of the tests described earlier, group exercises and simulations. A typical assessment centre will involve applicants attending for 1 or 2 days and being subjected to a 'battery' of selection techniques. Trained assessors observe candidates and at the end pool their judgements of the applicants based on their performance on the range of selection devices so that an overall assessment of each individual's suitability will then be reached. Although assessment centres can be very accurate methods of selection, they are expensive to design and administer and can only be justified for certain types of jobs.

Where reliable past data is available on performance (e.g. in sales) assessments are really not necessary, nor for jobs where significant factors are already known. Managerial jobs or those where the field of applicants are unfamiliar with the new setting (such as University graduates, or line managers applying for consultancy) often require the assessment centre approach.

Group selection methods are relevant if the emphasis on selection is placed less on technical ability and more on social skills, influencing, communication, intellectual ability, attitudes and personality. Using group exercises involves the evaluation of individuals by several assessors trained in observation and activities scoring. Applicants receive individual briefings, usually relating to a wider problem of issue. Time is provided for individual preparation and each candidate puts forward a recommended course of action or solution and then defends and debates proposals with other members of the group. Exercises include leaderless group exercises and group problem-solving exercises. Group selection is often included as part of an assessment centre (Table 4.8).

Table 4.8 An example of an assessment centre

A leaderless group exercise. Candidates are given a group task to undertake in a given time, for example in the form of a business game. Observers judge performance under pressure and look for leadership and team working abilities

A report-writing exercise. Participants under time pressure, write a report on some aspect of business. Here time management, written communication skills and understanding can be assessed

An in-tray exercise. This consists of issues that a manager might find on a day performing the job for real. Ability to work under pressure, delegate, analyse and problem solve might be tested by this method

Other tests

Formal interview

Research suggests generally positive findings about group selection methods and high validity correlations have been achieved between assessments and subsequent job performance achieved. Candidates are, however, aware of why they are participating in the assessment exercises and might feel expected to tailor their behaviour accordingly. On the other hand, the individual may well feel highly stressed by the experience and fail to reveal positive and relevant aspects of themselves.

It is suggested that the case for using group selection methods is strongest with younger applicants who generally offer little experience to probe in interview, and also with senior managerial appointments where the individual's inter-personal and group skills are crucial.

4.5.9 Post-interview considerations

Selection is a two-way process and, if offered a position, the candidate also has a decision to make. Applicants have an understanding of expectations about how the organisation will treat them, and recruitment and selection represents an opportunity to confirm and clarify issues. One method of strengthening understanding suggested by Herriot, are 'realistic job previews' (RJPs) which can take the form of case studies of employees and their work, the chance to 'shadow' someone at work, job sampling and videos. Research found that RJPs lower initial expectations about work and an organisation, causing some applicants to deselect themselves. Conversely, they can increase levels of organisation commitment, job satisfaction, performance and job survival.

As in all forms of human selection, non-objective factors influence the interviewee. Candidates respond to appropriate interpersonal behaviours on the part of interviewers as well as useful information about the post at the point of selection. Several studies found that the image projected by the selectors was the candidate's primary motivating factor in accepting the job offer. Such 'recruiter behaviour' affected the candidate's decision, and the probability of job acceptance not only concerned the adequacy of job information but the candidate's perceptions of the selectors' personalities and manner, especially where candidates liked the selector. A friendly interviewer translates as a friendly company, dynamic interviewers translate as a dynamic company, and so on.

From a management point of view it is important to present a professional business-like image so that candidates can concentrate on information rather than impressions. This might include some better analysis and questioning of the candidates' motivations about the type of work, the organisation's industry or sector, its technology, the location and so on. There may be little negotiation about salary as recruiters may be careful to make this clear in advertisements.

Candidates who are offered a position can be flattered and do not always check the detail of the package or assume they will be allowed to continue with and be financially supported in their studies, (CIMA for example). The employer often wants the potential employee to negotiate the finer details so that expectations are not raised, which later prove a source of dissatisfaction. Issues might include the following:

- Training
- Pension transfer values
- Relocation assistance conditions
- Use of cars
- Annual leave

- Location of workplace
- Fringe benefits such as personal telephone calls, using mobile phones, the use of computers and other ancillary equipment.

So far rational processes have been described. Realistically one should acknowledge however that humans are involved hence there is often the issue of whether the individual is likeable or not. This may not be explicitly acknowledged as a factor amongst interviewers as it is a purely subjective (and potentially unfair) measure. This feature, which asks, 'will the person fit in' possibly, accounts for the popularity of interviewing as a method despite all the evidence that it is an unreliable method.

Finally, the medical examination is a type of test that may be used to provide valid information for selection purposes. A physical check up by a medically qualified person or the completion of a health check form covering the matters to be assessed in the examination may be given to candidates.

4.5.10 Obtaining references

The purpose of a reference is to obtain in confidence factual information about a prospective employee and opinions about his/her character and suitability for a job. Employer references are essential but unreliable. A satisfactory reference has to be treated at its face value – all one can be reasonably certain of is that factual details are likely to be correct. A glowing reference may arouse suspicion and it is worth comparing it with one from another previous employer. Poor references should be treated with alarm if only because they are so infrequent. Allowance should be made for prejudice and a follow-up telephone call may clarify the issue.

If a reference is not satisfactory but all other factors about the applicant are acceptable, the employer has to make a decision on the whole case.

4.5.11 The process of induction

Induction involves all arrangements meant to familiarise a new employee with the organisation, including safety rules, general conditions of employment, the work of the section/department, etc. (Table 4.9). Many definitions also mention the importance of helping employees 'settle into their new jobs', welcoming them and arranging for

Table 4.9 Indicative elements in the induction package

Terms of employment, such as information about hours of work, shift arrangements, timekeeping and clocking-on and -off systems

Housekeeping and security issues, such as catering facilities, energy conservation and speed limits on site

Health and safety regulations, such as safety procedures, protective clothing and hazards of office equipment

Remuneration and benefits, holiday and sick pay, profit sharing, expenses claims, welfare

Organisational rules and policies, such as disciplinary and grievance procedures, trade union membership, works rules, time off for statutory or trade union duties, equal opportunities

Employee development opportunities, sports and social amenities

Information about the company and the industry, such as a mission statement, history, product markets, organisation structure and communications;

Job performance issues, such as standards, appraisal and role within the department

them to get to know others. A formal induction programme need not be expensive, and the benefits far outweigh the costs of recruiting more staff if new staff fail to settle and leave.

Induction can be viewed from a number of perspectives:

- From the *administrative* perspective the principal issues appears to be what topics to include and when to deal with them so as to prevent information overload. The role of the HR specialist is seen as particularly relevant in maintaining quality standards during the induction process, as well as in delivering some parts of the programme, (such as information about welfare, wage and salary administration, grievance and disciplinary procedures, etc.) Induction may be carried out informally but should be systematic enough to ensure that essentials are covered. The overall plan should be drawn up in consultation with those usually involved, such as supervisor, training officer, safety officer, human resource manager and trade union representative. Induction procedures must be designed with the perspective and needs of the new employee in mind. To ensure that this has been achieved, it will be useful to review systematically the experiences of newcomers and other relevant employees (e.g. supervisors, training and HR specialists) in order that unsatisfactory elements can be changed. Irrespective of whether or not a formal, structured programme is in place, all employees go through an induction phase on joining a new organisation or department. In many organisations the formal phase can be little more than a rudimentary greeting before being shown to their place of work. New recruits may be told to ask questions if they need assistance.

- The *welfare* perspective argues that during the 'period of after-care' when people start employment with an organisation, the manager must try to settle the new person in quickly, almost as an act of benevolent paternalism. There may be some who are lacking in confidence (e.g. school leavers who are entering employment for the first time, women returners who are coming back into the labour force after a long gap, etc.) for whom such a philosophy is particularly appropriate. Other workers may face particular problems at work and need some initial assistance, for example, employees with disabilities will need to know immediately where and how special arrangements can be made for them, and members of minority groups may need to be put in touch with support mechanisms soon after taking up employment.

- The *strategic* human resource management perspective views induction in more stark terms in which employers make use of various techniques to 'educate' employees about the organisation's ethos, aiming to integrate them culturally. This view is rarely to be found in mainstream publications, in which induction is regarded as a value-free device for helping employees to settle down in a new job. This more strategic view of induction is that it aims to engender feelings of belonging and hence a commitment to organisational goals. The employer then maximises the contribution of the workforce and gets a 'faster return on investment'. This should not lead to organisational cloning, but should produce individuals who function effectively. Harrison (1992) suggested that 'dialogic learning' is a major element of induction in that new recruits are 'oriented to the mission and culture of the organisation, to its beliefs and ways of doing things'. By placing some interpretation on the policies and practices which are administered by the employer, new recruits are able to appreciate the meaning and purpose of them in practice. With reference to diversity issues or quality service, for example, employees are provided with a clear understanding of what this means in practice, and the fact that this is an important aspect of organisational life.

> **!** Organisational loyalty is a major component in the employment strategies and practices of many Japanese and US companies, exemplified by artifacts such as similar uniforms, badges, and company credit cards. New recruits at Fujitsu are invited to join the 'family of employees' and at Honda, to be 'associates'. Some organisations use a process known as 'intensive induction' during which new recruits are developed into loyal and trusting members of staff, which, as well as learning about the philosophy and motives of the company, involves team activities and physical exercises. Some leading UK employers have copied this approach.

4.6   Developing the human resource

HRM's emphasis on employee commitment and flexibility implies the importance of investing in employee development and training. (This is consistent with the notion of viewing human resources as an asset rather than as a cost). The problem is that this training seems to be heavily concentrated on particular groups such as those who already have qualifications, those in higher-level jobs, new employees and young people.

Hendry (1995) suggested that in part the differences in training and development between jobs and sectors are due to the different forms of labour markets that govern them. The various service sectors, for example, have tended to operate internal labour markets in which they have been able to rely on retaining trained employees with some form of career progression. By way of contrast many manufacturing industries have depended on the apprenticeship system, which helped to sustain an external, occupational labour market. This has limited the ability of firms to deploy staff flexibly and to retain the people they have trained. This hypothesis concerning the relationship between types of labour markets and training provision is given some support by reference to international comparisons. The forms the labour market takes have a significant impact, then, on the nature and extent of training which organisations undertake and training and careers interact. In countries where occupational labour markets predominate (such as Australia), in-firm training (in the absence of state intervention) is likely to be relatively scarce. By comparison, in Japan, with strong internal labour markets, the pattern is for in-company training.

Training is a learning process whereby individuals acquire knowledge and/or skills to aid in the achievement of specified goals. These goals may be defined in very specific terms, such as the ability to use a particular software package to produce business reports, or much more broadly, as would be the case in improving leadership skills.

Development, on the other hand, can be seen as a longer-term continuing process, more often associated with moving jobs (either sideways or upwards as a promotion), with both organisations and the individual jointly determining the detail.

Some organisations devise well-thought out mechanisms to aid development and career advancement such as formal mentoring. A mentor is (according to Daft 2000) 'a higher ranking senior organisational member who is committed to providing upward mobility and support to a protégé's professional career'. Mentors under such arrangements can act in a number of roles, including:

- Coach
- Counselor
- Sounding board
- Facilitator.

Note: In some organisations the learning benefiting from, mentoring is referred to as a mentee, in others a protégé.

Both training and development might also be seen as part of the reward system, possibly in a short-term way (e.g. the exotic location of a training course) or longer term as developmental assignments (especially overseas).

Exercise 4.7

Outline the steps you would follow to devise an appropriate management development programme for a group of qualified accountants. What activities other than formal training courses might be appropriate for such a management development programme?

Solution

A systematic review of the management development programme appropriate to a group of qualified accountants would involve:

- determining their management development needs
- identification of the organisation's management development objectives
- developing criteria against which to assess performance
- finding ways of selecting the appropriate people for the training programme
- identifying methods of management development to encourage learning
- making arrangements about location, type and duration of training
- devising ways of monitoring effectiveness.

Other than formal training courses the programme could include an emphasis on self-development so that the accountants pay systematic attention to learning opportunities on and off the job.

4.6.1 Learning

Learning is a complex process that despite a vast amount of research, is still not fully understood. One perspective on learning first developed by David Kolb (1984) captured it as involving a problem-solving cycle (Figure 4.4). Effective learning usually involves completing this cycle rather than just accessing one point. Formal lectures for example have little real effect on

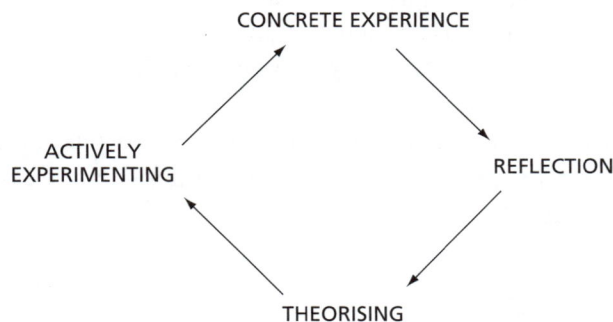

CONCRETE EXPERIENCE

ACTIVELY EXPERIMENTING

REFLECTION

THEORISING

Figure 4.4 Kolb's learning cycle

learning if they are simply concerned with imparting knowledge which students may not reflect on, or see any relevance of, in terms of their actions. This learning cycle has important implications for training and development, which has to be an active process if it is to be effective. The matter is further complicated by the fact that individuals have different preferred learning styles with, for example, some favouring analytical reflection, while others may strongly prefer active, practical problem solving, etc. Nevertheless, the following general principles can guide the design of effective learning programmes:

- Participants should have both the ability to learn the required skills/knowledge and the motivation to learn (this will be influenced by the perceived relevance of the training).
- It usually helps to provide an overview of the tasks to be learned before dealing with particular, specific aspects.
- The availability of timely, accurate feedback greatly enhances the effectiveness of most forms of training.
- There should be positive rewards or reinforcements when activities are carried out correctly. These rewards may be internal (e.g. a feeling of accomplishment) and/or external (e.g. the issue of a certificate, a compliment from the trainer, etc.).
- Active involvement is usually associated with more effective learning rather than passive involvement such as simply listening or reading.
- Most training will involve a learning curve which may be initially very flat as the learner struggles to acquire basic competence or in other cases quite steep when the skills required for modest competence are learned more quickly, but all learning will involve periods when there seems to be no improvement in performance (a learning plateau).
- Training should be as much like the job as possible to minimise problems of conceptualising theory to the workplace.

Learning underpins development, education and training.

4.6.2 Management development

Significant relationships exist between management development activities and other aspects of HRM such as HR planning, selection, appraisal and reward systems. Management development is sometimes thought of as an activity that only takes place in certain special situations, such as a short course or studying for an MBA, but in fact it can and does take place in a much wider variety of contexts. This point can be understood most clearly if the process is seen as one of self-development which is based on the premise that 'any effective system for management development must increase the managers' capacity and willingness to take control over and responsibility for events, and particularly for their own learning' (Pedler et al., 2006). This highlights the possibilities for learning and management development sometimes being accidental (unconscious) as well as planned (conscious), and that it may take place on-the-job as well as outside the normal place of work. This variety of learning opportunities is illustrated in Figure 4.5.

The importance of self-development is reinforced by the emphasis many professional bodies (including CIMA) are placing on continuous professional development (CPD), which recognises that being admitted to a professional body does not guarantee proficiency forever. Individual members of the profession must take responsibility for their own post-qualification continuing development and updating. In this way individuals can ensure they remain up to date in a rapidly changing world and can facilitate career planning.

```
                                    ON-THE-JOB

              Accidental          Making and taking
              learning at         learning opportunities
                 work                   at work

UNCONSCIOUS ─────────────────────┼───────────────── CONSCIOUS

              Accidental          Structured learning
              learning at home    e.g. formal courses,
              and socially        workshops etc.

                                   OFF-THE-JOB
```

Figure 4.5   Learning opportunities

4.6.3   Education

Education can be seen as a more generic kind of development. In management terms this often applies specifically to accredited training and development leading to a certificated course often through use of a local University. By utilising local case study material and data assignments help focus learning on the candidate's own organisation.

Self-education is often evident in the ranks of senior managers who can be surprisingly well read. The benefit of an accredited course is that the learning is focused and progressive, and leads to a definitive end-stage. Managers also educate themselves specifically in the workplace by learning by rote the names and background of subordinates, colleagues in affiliate organisations overseas and so on. Many managers take the business press such as the *Economist* and *Financial Times* in order to keep generally abreast of business developments.

Either training or development or both can be accredited by internal or external sources to produce vocational or generic managerial qualifications, though some of this more general process may be termed education as it is not so goal-specific as either training or development.

Some occupational groups, such as lawyers and accountants, have a tradition of education and training controlled by professional bodies and this enables them to take advantage of external labour markets (often national and international rather than just local). Managers as a group, however, have not succeeded in establishing themselves as a recognised profession, in large part because of the sheer diversity of managerial roles and responsibilities.

4.6.4   Training

Training can be seen as a formal, often short-term process where the organisation attempts to increase an individual's ability to better perform a particular set of tasks. It can take place off or on the job, or be a combination of both. Much management training is 'ad hoc' based on a specific training need identified in the appraisal process. Many organisations are moving to preferred suppliers for training in order to control cost and outcomes more closely. In this way the value adding effect of training is increased.

'On-the-job' training from others can be effective if the existing employees have time to devote to the process, and are themselves competent and know how to impart the necessary skills. Unfortunately these conditions are often not satisfied in practice therefore, other methods such as simulations, class or laboratory-based training or off-site training may be more effective.

One development in the UK is competence-based training linked to a system of NVQs. The essence of competence-based training is that it assesses the ability of the trainee to carry out specified activities to predetermined standards rather than concentrating directly on an individual's knowledge and understanding. This development can be seen as a consequence of the collapse of the traditional apprenticeship system and the uncoordinated proliferation of vocational qualifications. NVQs operate at five levels from basic training to professional level and provide the basis for national training targets specifying the proportion of young people and employees who will have obtained these NVQs by specified dates.

Whatever form of training or development is used it ought to be part of a systematic overall training system involving:

- determining training needs
- identifying training objectives
- development of criteria against which to assess performance
- developing methods to determine current levels of proficiency among potential trainees to enable the right people to be selected for training
- making arrangements for the location, type and duration of the training
- devising methods for carrying out the training and encouraging effective learning
- monitoring the effectiveness of the training and comparing outcomes against criteria.

Regrettably much training is not subject to systematic planning, and careful evaluation is the exception rather than the norm. This implies that time, effort and money will be expended on training programmes without a clear understanding of benefit achieved as a result. The issue of how best to evaluate training should be considered before training begins. It is generally recognised that there are four levels at which training can be evaluated using the Kirkpatrick (1998) model:

- Reaction – evaluates how well the trainees liked the training.
- Learning – measures the extent to which trainees have learned the principles, facts and theories covered in the training.
- Behaviour – concerned with the extent to which behaviour changes as a result of the training.
- Results – considers what benefits (e.g. better quality, reduced costs, etc.) result directly from the training.

These levels will not necessarily be independent of each other, but each dimension represents a rigorous evaluation. When designing methods of evaluation the most common approach is simply to measure outcomes at one or more levels after the training. The limitation of this design is that it makes it difficult to know whether the outcomes being measured are a result of the training or not. This can be overcome to an extent by measuring outcomes before and after the training: a pre/post measure evaluation.

Most learn best when they genuinely are motivated to do so. Any training is most likely to be effective, therefore if the individual is involved in agreeing his or her training plan and in choosing the method or means by which the training is to be provided. There are potentially many training methods that an organisation may wish to develop and these are listed in the (Table 4.10).

Table 4.10 Training methods that an organisation may wish to develop

Action learning: learning by doing, for example, participation of person with others in project work or group assignment, or by secondment to another section/department.

Briefing group: short exposition by manager to a workgroup, followed by questions and answers, and discussion

Business games: board games or computer-assisted evolving case studies in which managers assume roles in a fictional business and see the consequences of their decisions in a given situation

Case studies: write-up of a real management situation, with questions for analysis

Coaching: a manager maximises training opportunities in the course of everyday work with their staff

Computer-assisted learning (CAL) or computer-based training (CBT): essentially programmed learning via interaction with a computer

Delegation: manager actively delegates parts of their own job to subordinates and coaches them in its execution

Demonstrations and guided practice: supervisor (trainer) shows employee (trainee) how to (e.g. operate machine); then trainee attempts it with guidance. Films, DVDs and/or video can also be used to demonstrate off the job

Discovery or experiential learning: essentially learning by doing it for yourself, but within some structured logical sequence

Distance learning: learning at a distance with interactive texts and exercises

Job or work rotation: involves the employee moving to a new job or new area of work for short periods to widen experience

Lectures: delivery of a prepared exposition

On-the-job training: training while the job is actually being carried out in the normal work situation

Programmed learning: book/machine that paces reader and checks knowledge through periodic questioning

Role play or behaviour role modelling: person puts him/herself in 'someone else's shoes' for purposes of practical exercise, usually to develop inter-personal skills, and receives feedback on behaviour (often via closed circuit television/video)

Rote learning: by oral repetition (could be useful in some instances for non-English speakers or young trainees)

Seminar or workshop: a meeting of several employees in which all attempt to improve their knowledge in a specific area by sharing information and practice (Seminars usually have an 'expert' to lead)

'Sitting next to Nellie': learning by copying someone doing the same job

Simulations: attempt to reproduce the conditions of work (e.g. flight 'simulators' for pilots, war games for the armed services or desk-top in-tray exercises for executives)

Special projects or assignments: manager/supervisor asks subordinate to research, report and make recommendations on specific topic (or as part of a group project)

Structured work experience: a specific programme of work activities (drawn from the job description), structured in priority order and to be experienced within set time limits

Trainee logbooks: books/diaries in which a record is kept of a trainee's work programme, performance and progress

Training manuals: written collection of instructions (e.g. how to operate a machine)

The various methods identified in the table are not unique to any specific location or type of training organisation. Often a programme of structured training, whether it is a one-week course or a series of quite separate days or parts of days spaced at intervals will utilise a number of different techniques. Each technique or method has its own advantages and disadvantages most importantly the considerations should be:

- how effective the method or methods are in meeting the specific training need, and
- how suitable or acceptable the method is for those concerned.

Exercise 4.8

To increase effectiveness of a training programme, what issues should be addressed before, during and after the course?

Solution

Before the course

- Choose the best location: should it be on- or off-site? Is the physical environment conducive to learning? Can it house the equipment you will need (e.g. Smartboard, white board, wall board, flip charts, data projection facility and PowerPoint presentation overhead projector and screen, closed circuit television or video and camera, tape/slide or projector)? Does it allow for flexible seating, rather than fixed rows, to promote participation?
- Prepare thoroughly and rehearse your instructional presentation (but not to the point of boredom!) Prepare your visual aids and your active exercises for the group to actually participate in the learning.
- Motivate your audience beforehand. Gain their interest and enthusiasm so that they are looking forward to the time with you.

During the course

Start with a 'lively opener' and state the objectives clearly to reinforce your staffs' motivation and enthusiasm, and help them to feel at ease. Continually look for, and use, feedback. If your audience have gone to sleep, look bored or puzzled, or are fidgeting, they are not learning (and you are probably talking too much!). Respond to their non-verbal signals and change the pace or style of presentation. Turn the responsibility for, and involvement in, learning back onto them by getting them actively doing; re-check their understanding; get them to express what they think or feel about the session or content so far.

After the course

- Obtain detailed feedback on the extent to which your presentation achieved its objectives.
- Modify any future presentations in the light of feedback.

Training delivery can be provided either in-house, through use of external trainers or by means of open learning, with corresponding advantages and disadvantages. In-house training could also include the 'buying in' of an external trainer specifically to meet the organisation's own needs either on or off site. (Table 4.11).

External provision can include all the courses available at local Colleges/Universities or provided by specialist training companies. Although courses are unlikely to be wholly specific to an organisation's own needs it does overcome many of the difficulties associated with in-house provision. In particular, participants can mix and share problems and experiences with like-minded people from other organisations. The greatest disadvantage is that such training is usually provided to all-comers, on an unselective basis, across different types of industry and every level of ability. It will inevitably be difficult, therefore, to make it immediately relevant to the in-company situation and to the particular needs of selected staff.

Open learning has two meanings. One interpretation is learning for which no rigid entry qualifications are required. Increasingly it is used to mean learning that enables people to learn at the time, place and pace which meets their needs and their requirements. It can take the form of a whole range of updating and training facilities that can be used

Table 4.11   In-house training

Advantages

Course content and timing can be tailor-made to the organisation's needs

An organisation's specific technical equipment, procedures and/or work methods can be used

More economical (provided there are sufficient personnel with the same training needs, and the necessary resources, expertise and trainers to meet these)

Easily monitored

Can involve expert sessions from own senior managers or technical staff

Can generate a team spirit and develop culture

Can be linked to specific outcomes that are then monitored by participants

Can be enhanced by incorporating work-based projects

Disadvantages

Participants are not exposed to outside influences

Participants may be called away at short notice to deal with work problems

Participants more likely to withdraw at short notice than for an external course with non-returnable fees

Inhibits open discussion if immediate colleagues or bosses are present

in the workplace, at home or in some combination of the two. Employees can be offered a range of study packs or courses, in print, video, audio and/or computer-based programmes, selected according to the individual's training needs. Open learning can be fitted around workplace operations and does not involve any absence from the site. Open learning can complement an existing training provision and assist greatly in your training role. With the increasing growth in numbers of DVDs, video recorders and computers, both at the workplace and at home, open learning is becoming increasingly available to everyone. However, developing good open learning material is expensive. Usually it will only be financially viable if the same material is appropriate to large numbers of people.

While developing technology has the potential to play a large part in the process of learning and training, it is unlikely to eliminate personal contact entirely.

Information technology and particularly the Internet and Intranet systems have provided new opportunities for training and development at relatively low cost (Prithcard, 2003), for example:

- UK DIY products retailer B&Q (with 20,000 staff) uses computer-based training with locally run DVD-ROMS. Also B&Q uses networked management tools to keep track of training progress.
- Car producer Ford uses E-learning powered by an intelligent search and retrieval system (Ford Learning Network). This allows all its 335,000 employees worldwide to access training material in a wide range of subjects from engineering to finance. It also contains a search facility to assist with work-related problems.

Finally, managerial control needs to be exercised over training just as for any other activity. A professional service from those who provide it should be insisted upon. There are five dimensions to this control:

- Drawing up training plans
- Checking that training takes place according to these plans
- Checking on the quality of training and success in achieving the stated objectives
- Managing the tasks of the learner back in the work situation so that the effects of training are reinforced
- Checking that the results of training justify the resources allocated to it.

4.6.5 Job redesign

Job redesign can be used to help develop individuals and groups within the workplace. Experience of different jobs increases an individual's understanding, skills and empathy with others.

The job characteristics model (as shown in Figure 4.6) sets out the links between characteristics of jobs, the individual's experience of those characteristics, and the resultant outcomes in terms of motivation, satisfaction and performance. The model also takes into account individual differences in the desire for personal growth and development, (what Maslow called 'self-actualisation'). The strength of the links in the causal chain set out in the model are determined by the strength of the individual's personal growth need, so the model does not apply to everyone. The heart of the model is the proposition that jobs can be analysed in terms of five core dimensions as follows:

- Skill variety is the extent to which a job makes use of different skills and abilities.
- Task identity is the extent to which a job involves a 'whole' and meaningful piece of work.
- Task significance is the extent to which a job affects the work of other organisation members or others in society.
- Autonomy is the extent to which a job gives the individual freedom, independence and discretion in carrying it out.
- Feedback is the extent to which information about the level of performance attained is related back to the individual.

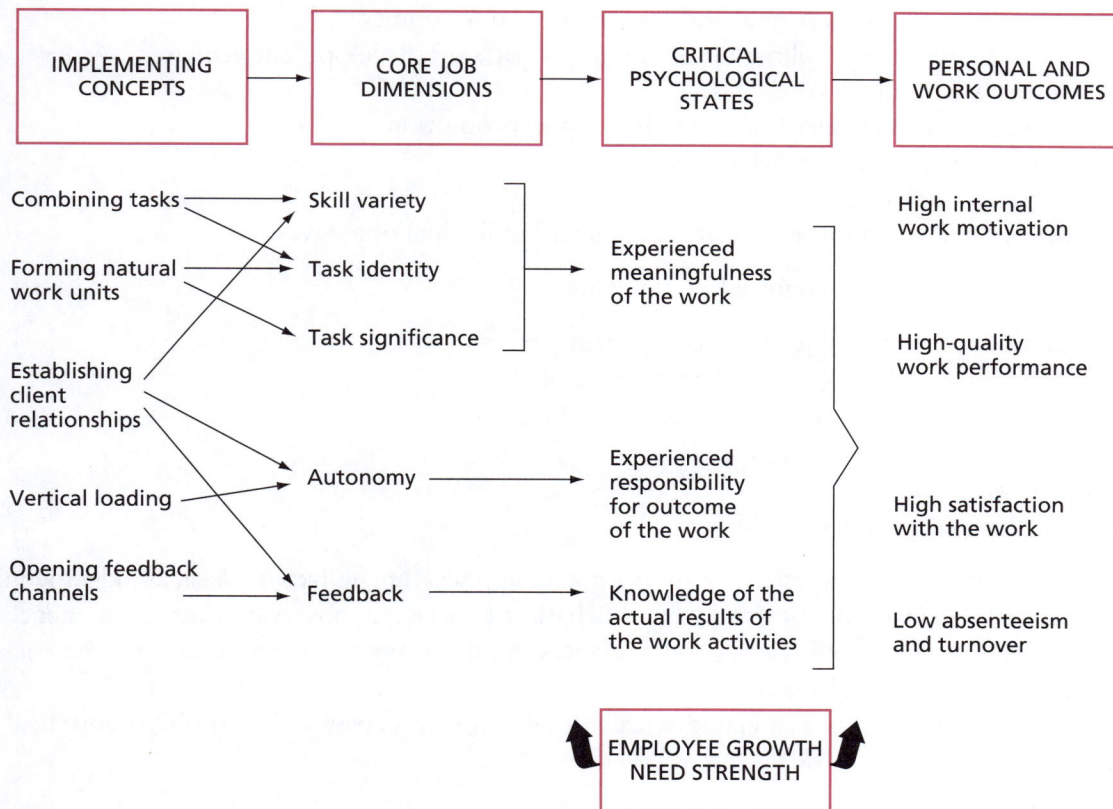

Figure 4.6 Job characteristics model

These five core dimensions induce the three psychological states critical to high work motivation, job satisfaction and performance. These three states are defined as follows:

- Experienced meaningfulness is the extent to which the individual considers the work to be meaningful, valuable and worthwhile.
- Experienced responsibility is the extent to which the individual feels accountable for the work output.
- Knowledge of results is the extent to which individuals know and understand how well they are performing.

Jobs that have high scores are more likely to lead their incumbents to the experience of these critical psychological states than jobs that have low scores. Expectancy theorists argue that all three critical psychological states must be experienced if the personal and work outcomes on the right-hand side of the model are to be achieved.

4.7 Appraisals

Appraisal of performance is a vital part of the HR cycle. Most appraisal systems should provide the individual with valuable feedback on their performance and focus on future activities. Most schemes rely on an annual meeting between the employee (appraisee) and his or her appraiser. The purpose of appraising may be seen as:

- aiding technical, professional and management development
- allowing a systematic follow-up of the results of staff development activities
- a source of motivation
- enabling the achievement of rewards (such as promotion)
- feeding into a wider reward system
- increasing performance
- helping achieve important organisational and individual objectives.

Other benefits are recognised as including:

- a mechanism to set objectives for the next period
- identifying good prospects for promotion or transfer
- developing psychological dependence on the manager
- fostering an open atmosphere
- developing relationships
- enhancing corporate cultural norms.

In small firms, formal systems of performance appraisal are unlikely to exist, as judgements about performance will be made on the basis of personal observation and experience. Irrespective of the organisation, good managers should ensure these judgements are fed back to employees on a regular basis.

Many of the pitfalls associated with the selection interviews also apply in appraisal, including:

- a lack of preparation on either side
- an appraiser talking more than the appraisee, and asking leading questions to which the answer is obvious and important aspects may be left unexplored

- appraisers being just as nervous as the appraisees
- little or no appraiser training.

Appraisers can improve the quality of interviews considerably if they keep in mind the overall objective, which is to get an accurate ideas of performance and improvement needs. The first task is to try to overcome the rather unnatural circumstances of the formal interview and to encourage the applicant to relax and speak freely. To do this the interviewer must keep the conversation flowing, while speaking no more than is necessary. By careful questioning the interviewer should bring out how well (or badly) the employee has matched the requirements of the job. The interviewer should always retain control of the situation.

Some factors present in effective appraisal systems include:

- Careful planning which ensures the purpose and objectives of the system are widely understood.
- Skill in carrying out the appraisal interview.
- Selecting the most appropriate method of appraisal.
- Setting challenging targets which the appraisee can influence.
- Adopting a participative system that enables those being appraised to have a meaningful input to the system.

Good interviews are well prepared and conducted in an orderly and thorough manner. Table 4.12 indicates some of the detailed considerations that an appraiser should take into account.

The scheme must be consistent with the organisation's reward and other systems, otherwise major problems will be caused if development activities identify one set of behaviours whilst others are rewarded in practice. Certain approaches will be adopted to make judgements and provide a basis for discussion in the appraisal interview, such as:

- Trait-orientated ratings of the individual on a number of personal-related dimensions, such as timekeeping and attitude towards work. A systematic appraisal of a subordinate's performance attempts to make inherent problems 'visible' and overcome them by focusing on the job rather than just the individual's personality. It attempts to be current rather than considering past experience.
- Result-orientated or 'performance appraisal' whereby appraiser and appraisee agree objectives and review progress of achievement accordingly.
- Some combination of both approaches.

Table 4.12 Detailed considerations that an appraiser

- Be properly organised and allow enough time
- Make sure there will be no interruptions, (divert telephone calls, etc.)
- Discuss issues of principle beforehand with senior manager and/or HR expert
- Identify possible reasons for unusual performance, particularly if it is possibly 'below par'? (Problem recruitment, inadequate training or experience, qualifications, etc.?) Check beforehand the policy to address poor performance
- Plan questions to be asked (they should be designed to probe performance and the training or development needs arising)
- Identify mechanisms to address individual training needs (e.g. refer to corporate training programme)
- Identify potential rewards for high performance (promotion policy, levels of salary increase, opportunity available for job moves).
- Identify opportunities for sideways development moves or job enrichment
- Anticipate the information needed to meet likely questions from the appraisee.

Overell (2003) reports on research into employee appraisals and identifies that most large companies use such a system. This does, however, vary according to the industry, (for instance in financial services, 80% of employees have them compared with 50% in retail). Private sector appraisals are conducted mainly to identify training needs, with evaluating performance secondary, and only 8 per cent of companies use appraisals for while tackling poor performance. Surprisingly perhaps only 15 per cent of companies use appraisals to determine pay.

Overell also reports that disturbingly it was once found that in the UK's Civil Service that the appraisal system was felt to discriminate against ethnic minority and disabled workers. (As a safeguard Management have since set up an independent assessor system, allowing staff a right of appeal.)

The question of who should appraise and when depends on determining the goal of appraisal and who is best placed to evaluate the employee's performance or needs against these. Managers often save up bad news rather than 'disciplining' staff at the time so that they will have 'ammunition' if necessary at the annual appraisal. Moves to more frequent appraisals run against the problem of time. Nevertheless, some managers do have weekly team briefings or individual discussions with staff as part of their ongoing managerial role that can be specifically aimed at assessing progress towards objectives.

Setting objectives as part of a performance appraisal (Table 4.13) involves agreement on SMART objectives (specific and challenging, measurable, but achievable, relevant and realistic and time-bound). A system of 'management by objectives' (MBO) is helpful if the employees are participants in their own objective setting. Otley's research into managers in the budget-setting process indicated that performance collapses if objectives have been set inappropriately. This means that appraisal of performance is potentially a very damaging activity for managers who treat it lightly or for organisations who do not consider the implications. This is particularly true of systems that apply pay to performance (PRP) based on appraisal interviews. These systems are treated with great suspicion by trade unions wary of unfair application and treatment.

The problems in coming to an accurate judgement of realistic objectives, and then the rating of the employee against those objectives are the main cause of subsequent feelings of unfairness among the workforce and accusations of favouritism. Damage done to individuals selected as poor performers can spread as others sympathise.

Finally, a number of types of appraisal exist:

Self-appraisal. This often takes place in preparation for a supervisor/appraisee meeting. This can save managerial time but the value may be questionable (if the appraisee is too self-critical or too lenient or critical incidents have been omitted).

Supervisor/appraisee. Normally the person who allocates work and establishes priorities and standards appraises. In some cases where there are many workers this may not be possible.

180 degree. Often managers, especially those in project teams or matrix organisations and professional bureaucracies, do not 'know' the appraisee sufficiently well. To some extent collecting anonymous or named views of colleagues can solve this. This can also be performed in the open groups session with the emphasis on first how the group performed and then the individuals' contribution (or the lack of it).

360 degree. This is where the appraisee prepares feedback on the appraiser as well as getting 180-degree feedback from colleagues. Problems include potential conflicts, power, influence issues, time and bureaucracy.

Table 4.13   Guidelines for setting performance standards

Clearly identify the individual's main result areas (e.g. finance, communication, staff development, supervision)

Select the vital key tasks from the result areas which, when performed well, ensure that the required objectives are being achieved

Set standards of performance against each of the key tasks which, when met, are acceptable to all concerned. Use information from past experience, present conditions and any foreseeable future changes. Standards must be valid in terms of result in the job

Ensure that standards are realistic and not too easy but present a challenge that is within the jobholder's capability

Strive for a clear definition at all times; standards that can be defined clearly minimise doubt and ambiguity

4.8   Termination

4.8.1   Dismissal

Dismissal is termination of employment with or without notice by the employer. Dismissal without notice is usually wrongful dismissal because it breaches the contract of employment. For a dismissal to be fair, the employer must show that the reason for dismissal is of a type acceptable under statute. In the UK a second consideration involves whether the employer acted reasonably in the circumstances in treating that reason as justifying dismissal. Factors it is reasonable to consider include both the interest of business efficiency and the likely effects of possible courses of action on someone's behaviour. It is important to find out as much about the case as possible, to follow agreed procedures wherever they exist, and to treat people consistently and reasonably. To defend itself against claims of unfair dismissal, an organisation also needs to have kept a written record of all of the stages in any disciplinary procedure.

If an individual's employment contract is terminated it must be done in a way which follows the correct procedures otherwise the employee may be able to claim compensation for unfair dismissal. In the case of 'constructive dismissal', resignation by the employee occurs because the conduct of the employer was sufficient to be deemed to have terminated the contract by the employer's actions.

When analysing whether dismissal is fair or a breach of contract, a number of issues are relevant, including:

- *Conduct*. A well-documented and fair disciplinary procedure is the best way of handling conduct problems. Large organisations especially need to demonstrate why they did not transfer the employee or counsel them.
- *Capability*. Normally an employer would have to demonstrate what standards there were, how the employee failed to meet them, detail the informal/formal warnings and any remedial action it tried to take, for example, extra training, or transfer. It is difficult to show that loss of efficiency has had an effect on the business.
- *Breach of statutory duty*. Continuing the employment might place the employer in breach of a statutory duty, e.g. under health and safety legislation. In such cases, there may be a valid ground for dismissal.
- *Some other substantial reason*. Possibilities include dishonesty, refusal to transfer overseas, loss of trust, etc.
- *Redundancy*. A dismissal on the grounds of redundancy may be justified on any of the following grounds: cessation of business; cessation of business in the place where the employee was employed; cessation of the type of work for which he or she was employed.

4.8.2 Redundancy

Before any employee is declared redundant, 'good' employers will have considered and discussed all possible alternatives with the relevant trade unions or staff representatives such as:

- reducing overtime (with excess work passed instead to other under-utilised employees)
- limiting future recruitment for vacancies that arise
- retraining (for new roles)
- transfers (to jobs in other departments)
- job-sharing (between two or more people)
- a shorter working week
- more effective HR planning in the future.

If despite these measures redundancies are still inevitable, then an organisation may decide to:

- offer early retirement to eligible employees (provided that the rules of the occupational pension scheme allow it).
- target part-time and temporary employees first.
- ask for volunteers by offering attractive terms (often known as a 'voluntary severance' or voluntary redundancy scheme). This option may attract older workers, since cash incentives tend to be linked to length of past service.

An employee's post can be made redundant if the employer ceases to need it. This should however be viewed as a last resort.

A claim of 'unfair dismissal' due to redundancy may be justified if:

- other employees in similar circumstances within the organisation were not dismissed (i.e. the selection for redundancy was unfair), or
- an inadmissible reason for redundancy was used, (e.g. such as the person was chosen because he or she was member of a trade union or took part in legitimate trade union activities), or
- the organisation did not follow an agreed procedure or an agreement justified by 'custom and practice'.

Selection for redundancy must be fair, carried out according to an agreed procedure laid down beforehand and consistently applied. Past practice when applying criteria for redundancies has popularly been selection on the basis of 'Last-In, First-Out' ('LIFO'). LIFO is easily applied and subject to potentially less dispute. Many organisations base redundancies on other principles, such as the skills that will be needed for the contracted operation. What is important is that the criteria must be clearly stated, agreed beforehand and incorporated into a written redundancy policy or employees' redeployment procedure. This should be negotiated with all the respective parties well before it is needed.

An employee who is under notice of redundancy does not have to work this period if it is agreed (with management and the trade unions) that they shall receive any due payment in lieu.

In the UK, legislation demands that redundancies are fair and consultation must take place. There is complex case law on what constitutes fair selection and UK managers are advised to contact ACAS for advice. Once employees and the relevant trade unions have been consulted, managers may also wish to contact the local newspaper, as an informed controlled press release is better than stories based on rumour and speculation which could be damaging to the organisation's reputation and image. The best method to inform any employee of redundancy is to tell them personally. Since any person who is to receive a redundancy payment must be given a statement in writing detailing the full amount to be paid and how it was calculated, it is probably best to give them the full letter of dismissal including these details at the same time. Employees eligible for redundancy pay are entitled in some countries to reasonable time off work, with pay, to look for other work. Managers may also like to invite local Job Centre or employment agency advisers to come to the premises, or to contact other local employers who may be able to take on excess staff and let them conduct interviews at the place of work. In addition a good counselling service to support individuals should be provided wherever possible. By helping redundant employees both to explore the range of options open to them and their own response real benefits have resulted. A study once carried out by the UK Government's Manpower Services Commission showed that unemployed executives were more likely to find jobs if they received counselling than if they had only 'technical' help, (e.g. preparing a curricula vitae, interview, techniques, etc.).

4.8.3 Job insecurity

Employees whose jobs become redundant are entitled in most countries to some compensation (redundancy payments) based on their length of service. Even where an employer pays generously, these 'golden handshakes' do not give most redundant people the financial means to survive for very long without working. The payments, in fact, go a little way towards providing compensation for the real (and sometimes long-term) social, psychological and economic effects of the experience.

For the individual redundancy is normally met by frustration and anger, followed by diminished self-esteem. If another job cannot be found, long-term unemployment can damage both physical and mental health, as well as carrying obvious financial penalties.

Redundancy is likely to be unpleasant not only for the individual and for the organisation. The manager may have a role to play in maintaining the morale and performance of those employees remaining, as well as dealing with potentially the damaged external image.

One consequence of redundancy may be a loss of some of the valued and most experienced employees. Management should act as honestly and as sympathetically as it can throughout (it will have to work with the survivors who have seen their work colleagues lose their jobs). It is as important for a manager handling redundancies, just as in handling discipline, to be seen to be fair in the treatment of individuals and adhere to recognised procedures.

For the individual a threat of redundancy and job insecurity can potentially manifest itself in stress, lost productivity, conflict and a lowering of loyalty to the organisation. It may also lead to individuals rethinking their career development opportunities and aspirations (see later).

Like most other electronics companies in the 1980s, STC had to radically restructure its workforce. By careful planning ahead and providing retraining opportunities, it was able to re-employ 97 per cent of people whose jobs had been made technologically redundant. The company claims high levels of employee motivation and certainly there were the process was less traumatic than it might have been.

4.9 Career development

Career planning has traditionally been viewed as principally an organisation-based activity that enables human resource managers to concentrate on jobs and building career paths so providing for logical progression of people between jobs. These career paths, particularly for people such as management accountants, have tended to be mainly within one specialised function and represent ladders on which individuals could progress within their functional specialism. Organisational career planning suffered severe setbacks from the layoffs during the recession of the late 1980s and early 1990s. In addition these core concepts have increasingly been challenged due to a number of other developments including:

- Non-traditional organisational structures emerging. These flatter organisation structures have removed some career paths entirely and reduced opportunities in other areas. Additionally these structures imply a need for multi skilling and teamwork at the expense of promotion 'ladders' found within traditional hierarchies. Increasingly workers are seeking to be 'multi-skilled' often developing a good understanding of more than one function rather than specialists.
- The development of general management skills and the concept of cross-functional career paths long been accepted as the norm in Japanese firms.
- Increasingly, career development has become led by the individuals themselves. An individual philosophy of building a portfolio of experience qualification and networks arose in order to develop a career outside a single organisational structure. This individual career planning focuses on individuals' goals and skills. It considers ways in which each individual might expand his or her capabilities and enhance career opportunities both within and outside a particular organisation. (Within the UK the Association of Graduate Recruiters recently warned that career paths no longer exist: only crazy paving that the individual lays himself or herself!)

Given this background, it is unsurprising that succession planning as an alternative to external recruitment may be seen as of decreasing HR significance. Problems have in any case always been associated with succession planning, including:

- *Retention*. Unlike other assets that have received investment, employees who are well trained especially those who are over-trained in anticipation of future developmental moves and are highly marketable.
- *Individual failure*. A failed assignment damages the individual, the company and the working relationships. 'Failure' may be attributable to one of a number of HR defects including poor control or managerial judgement, the over-promotion of individuals, and defective appraisal monitoring systems.
- *Timing*. One person failing to move because of personal circumstances can hold up the development of others unless some other kind of arrangement can be made. Slow promotion or development can lead to frustration and (for instance) graduate staff leaving shortly after becoming useful to the organisation. As the process depends on political expediency, many talented staff find that their present manager is reluctant to release them.
- *Size of organisation*. For a multi-national organisation, extensive relocation can be financially costly and for the family potentially distressing, demotivating and stressful. For many in small organisations a feeling of 'waiting for dead people's shoes' (as the old expression has it) may exist.
- *Overseas postings*. The issues of combining multi-cultural groups and three types of employee (the parent country nationals (expat), the home country national and the third country national) may prove problematic. Planning the correct combination of these staff is virtually impossible because of competing priorities and so many firms merely rely on the ability of all employees to 'mutually adjust' to each other and the new situation.

Exercise 4.9

List the advantages and disadvantages of:

(a) recruiting leaders from outside the organisation
(b) developing leaders from within.

Now read the article that follows. The extract argues strongly for developing leaders from within and identifies a number of things that an organisation might do. (Note that the use role-play and psychometric testing is normally associated with an assessment centre used in selection, and 360 degree feedback with performance appraisal, here the techniques are suggested within the context of career development).

In the war for talent, identifying and nurturing the bright young things under your nose is not just a strategic manoeuvre, it's your lifeblood.

Fail in this and your most promising people will achieve their potential elsewhere, leaving you with a vacuum at the top of your organisation.

But where to start?

Do it once a year . . . . .

Bring on the scouts. Line managers are the best-placed people to spot talent, says Lucy McGee, a director of HR consultancy DDI. 'Historically, HR has tried to own the process, but the guys at the edge of the pitch are the best placed to identify tomorrow's stars.'

. . . . . .

Identify the X-factors. 'Current performance doesn't always predict future potential', says Dr Maria Yapp, MD of business psychologists Xancam.

. . . . .

Look to the future. 'Don't assess high potentials for what you need now or what has worked in the past – think about the business's future needs', says Yapp. IBM used to make computers, now it's all about services.

Evaluate your assets. Once you've conducted your trawl, establish just how good the chosen few really are. Role-playing, psychometric tests and 360-degree appraisals are often used.

. . . .

Fast forward. The next job is to create an accelerated development plan that brings them up to speed in the required areas. They'll need extensive support.

Keep it open. If the process is secretive, people will think it's unfair.

. . . .

Don't write anyone off. 'It's largely a question of readiness,' says McGee. Some high-flyers are just a bit slower to take off.

(*Source:* extracted from Brainfood: Crash course in . . . developing future leaders, *Management Today*, September 1, 2005 p. 24 Haymarket Business Publications Ltd).

4.10 Flexibility and HR

4.10.1 Flexible structures

HR practices inevitably vary dependent upon the specific organisational size, culture and availability of specialist HR or personnel managers to support management in carrying out their duties. Organisational structures, particularly those engineered to achieve operational flexibility are another important dimension impacting on HR practice. The need to respond to a fast moving environment has led to organisations moving from traditional hierarchies to adopting more flexible organisational structures including fluid matrix or project-based firms. Alongside these virtual or networked firms have grown up. (Such issues are discussed in more detail in Chapter 6.) Inevitably these non-traditional structures have presented new HR challenges and required managers to adapt traditional approaches to these local contexts. Throughout this chapter reference has been made to the need for HR thinking and practice to evolve in responses to these challenges of flexibility and environmental uncertainty, specifically in the areas of:

- Planning horizons
- Staff appraisal where there may be no formal supervisor/subordinate reporting relations
- Remuneration strategies (see previous chapter) where outputs are not easily attributable to individuals alone
- The structure of the workforce and the use of consultants and contractors
- Development, promotion and succession planning.

4.10.2 Flexible employment

There is nothing new about flexible employment as casual work, 'by the hour' or 'by the day' has long typified many industries enabling them to match the volume of labour exactly with the level of demand. Some management practitioners and theorists have accorded a renewed interest in workforce flexibility in recent years. The following reasons may explain why this should be so:

- Lower labour costs through operating at lower staffing levels.
- Growing international competitiveness making flexibility a necessity.
- Improved responsiveness to market changes.
- Greater utilisation of equipment.
- Higher quality output.
- Lower batch sizes tailored to specific market segments.
- Organisational flexibility to adapt, innovate, diversify and divest.
- Greater control of labour processes and costs.

Superficially an impression might emerge of widespread changes in employment patterns and working practices aimed at lowering wage costs and raising productivity. Blyton's (1992) review of research led him to the following conclusions:

- There has been a growth in various forms of flexibility in all areas, public and private sectors and manufacturing and services.
- Different types of flexibility are prominent in different sectors and similar forms are being pursued for a variety of reasons.
- Flexibility agreements with unions have been important but many of the changes have been introduced by unilateral management action.

Exercise 4.10

What are the main organisational disadvantages of employment flexibility?

Solution

- Potentially reduced commitment and/or quality.
- Potential loss of stability.
- Problems with continuity and team working.
- Training expenditure. Flexibility implies a necessity to significantly increase expenditure on training and yet temporary working implies minimal training commitment.
- Conflict with the workforce and trade union opposition.
- Resistance, especially from crafts people who are unlikely to willingly give up time-honoured job definitions.

Reference was made earlier in the chapter to Handy's concept of the shamrock organisation, and it is perhaps helpful at this stage to return to the concepts of 'core' and 'periphery' work-forces. (Core employees possess key and scarce skills and enjoy relatively high status positions with good prospects of security and promotion. Periphery workers on temporary or part-time contracts act as a buffer against changes in demand.)

The use of these distinctions may be challenged as some industries rely almost exclusively on 'periphery' workers and these groups become more central rather than peripheral. In addition, groups of employees who might be classified as 'core' do not nec-essarily enjoy the status that is suggested by the framework (e.g. skilled manual workers). Nevertheless, these concepts provide a background against which consideration can be given to the different forms of flexibility, namely task, numerical and financial (Atkinson, 1984).

Task or functional flexibility

There is evidence that traditional demarcations between jobs are being eroded and employees are being required to undertake a wider range of tasks. In white-collar employment functional flexibility has been facilitated by IT developments that cut across previous job classifications. There is also considerable evidence of organisations significantly reducing the number of job grades and this, of course, implies that individuals are undertaking a broader range of tasks. The integration of tasks can be viewed in two ways:

- Horizontally, involving employees undertaking a broader range of tasks at the same level as their original task(s).
- Vertically, involving undertaking tasks that were previously carried out by employees at higher or lower levels.

Numerical flexibility

Temporary, part-time, short-term contract working and sub-contracting combined with 'hire and fire' policies have been in the ascendant in recent years and have been adopted by organisations as a means of responding to demand fluctuations.

The evidence of increasing sub-contracting is relatively widespread but the trends in temporary working are more ambivalent. Numerical flexibility can be achieved by using both contractors and agency staff. There is some research evidence of a general trend in some sectors towards greater use of agency staff mostly in ancillary services such as maintenance, cleaning, transport, catering, computer services and security.

Financial flexibility

The growth of individualised and variable systems of reward has been noticeable and performance related pay schemes are now widely in use. Fees for service payments are used for increasing numbers of self-employed sub-contractors.

4.11   Summary

Human Resourcing is a detailed and complex subject worthy of study in some depth. Inevitably there is a limitation in coverage within the confines of a single chapter in a study book, however, many aspects have been considered here. An understanding of HRM has been established and the determinants content and implementing issues of a HR plan discussed. In so doing the relationship of the employee to other elements of strategy should be understood.

This chapter has built on the concepts of business ethics and fair and legal employment practices as well as motivation theories when outlining key dimensions of the 'employment cycle'. Specifically managerial and contextual considerations relating to recruitment selection channels, induction appraisals, development and training dismissal, and redundancy have been highlighted.

References and further reading

Anon (2005) Brainfood: Crash course in . . . developing future leaders, *Management Today*, September 1, p. 24 Haymarket Business Publications Ltd

Anon (2005) Money talks, but not that loud. (retention)(Brief Article), *Work & Family Newsbrief*, October, Vol. 1, p. 3.

Anon (2006) Rules can't ensure ethical behaviour, HR *Magazine*, November, Vol. 51 No. 11, p. 14.

Armstrong, M. (2003) *A Handbook of Personnel Management Practice* (9th edn), London: Kogan Page.

Atkinson, J. (1984) Manpower strategies for flexible organisations, *Personnel Management*, August.

Beaumont, P. B. (1993) *Human Resource Management: Key Concepts and Skills.* London: Sage.

Blyton, P. (1992) The Search for workforce flexibility, in Towers B. (ed.), *The Handbook of HRM.* Oxford: Blackwell.

Bratton, J. and Gold, J. (2003) *Human Resource Management, Theory and Practice* (3rd edn), Basingstoke: Macmillan Business.

Byrnes, N and Barrett, A. (2005) Star Search; How to recruit, train, and hold on to great people. What works, what doesn't, *Business Week*, October 10, No. 3954, p. 68.

CIMA (2005) *CIMA Official Terminology.* Elsevier

Daft (2000) *Management* (5th edn), Dryden

Devanna, M. A., Fombrun, C. J. and Tichy, N. M. (1984) A framework for strategic human resource management, in Fombrun, C. J. et al. (eds), *Strategic Human Resource Management*, Chichester: John Wiley.

Gratton, L. (2004) More than money, *People Management*, January 29, Vol. 10, No. 2, p. 23

Guest, D. (1997) Human resource management and performance: a review and research agenda, *The International Journal of Human Resource Management*, Vol. 8, No. 3, pp. 263–276.

Handy, C. (1999) *Inside Organisations: 21 Ideas for Managers* (2nd edn), Harmondsworth: Penguin.

Harrison, R. (1992) *Diagnosing Organisational Culture*. San Francisco: Jossey Bass/Pfeiffer.

Hendry, C. (1995) *Human Resource Management: A Strategic Approach to Employment*, Oxford: Butterworth-Heinemann.

Hofstede, G. (1980) Motivation, leadership, and organisation: do american theories apply abroad? *Organisational Dynamics*, Vol. 9, No. 1, pp. 42–63.

Kirkpatrick, D. L. (1998) *Evaluating Training Programs: The Four Levels*. New York: Pfeiffer Wiley.

Kolb, D. A. (1984) *Experiential Learning: Experience as the Source of Learning and Development* London; Englewood Cliffs [NJ]: Prentice-Hall.

Marketing Week (2005) Changing workforce is just the job, *Marketing Week Fact file*, January 13.

Mullins, L. J. (2005) *Management and Organisational Behaviour* (7th edn), Financial, Harlow: Times Prentice Hall.

Otley, D. T. (1987) *Accounting Control and Organisational Behaviour*, London: Heinemann in association with CIMA.

Overell, S. (2003) Employee appraisals, *Financial Times*, March 6, p. 13.

Pedler, M., Burgoyne, J. and Boydell, T. (2006) *A Manager's Guide to Self-Development* (5th edn), London: McGraw-Hill.

Perry, B. (2005) Manchester United, Brand of Hope and Glory in Johnson, G. and Scholes, K. (eds), *Exploring Corporate Strategy – Text and Cases* (7th edn), Pearson Education Limited.

Prithcard, S. (2003) DIY programme suits DIY staff, *The Financial Times*, April 2, p. 3.

www.jobs.ac.uk

MANAGING HUMAN CAPITAL

Revision Questions

4

? Question 1

M Ltd employs between 200 and 300 people. It was formerly part of a large group of companies with a centralised HR function. The responsibilities of this function were:

(a) recruitment services, including preparing person specifications, and interviewing;
(b) appraisal procedures, including the design of forms and maintenance of records;
(c) determining salary scales, including job evaluation.

   M Ltd has now become independent, through a management buy-out. The new managing director is considering whether to establish a central personnel department to take responsibility for the above matters or whether to devolve the responsibilities to the managers of the operating departments.

   You are required to explain the implications of decentralisation versus centralisation for each of the functions above;

(a) recruitment services	**(6 marks)**
(b) appraisal procedures,	**(8 marks)**
(c) determining salary scales,	**(6 marks)**
	(Total marks 20)

? Question 2

T plc has a large number of subsidiaries in the high-technology field. An element in its management staffing policy consists of determining, from the resource plan, the number of recruits required each year and the calibre in terms of academic achievement. As far as graduates are concerned, the policy is implemented by:

- asking subsidiaries to notify the central personnel department of vacancies at junior level for which a graduate qualification would be desirable;
- publicising the group's requirement of graduates in specific disciplines through the normal channels;
- a team from the HR department touring the universities, interviewing applicants and referring those with appropriate management potential to the relevant subsidiary;
- the local HR officer and the graduate's future manager making a final choice by interviewing a short list of candidates.

For the last 3 years the vast majority of the applicants chosen have declined the offers of employment by the group but have accepted jobs in competitor companies.

You are required to

(a) give your analysis of the situation; **(5 marks)**

(b) list five possible causes of this situation, suggesting a remedy
   in each case. **(15 marks)**

(Total marks 20)

? Question 3

3.1 Charles Handy's vision of a 'shamrock' organisation suggests a workforce that comprises of three different types of worker, namely:

(A) Strategic, operational and support
(B) Qualified, trainee and unskilled
(C) 'White collar', 'blue collar' and e-worker
(D) Core, contractual fringe and flexible labour. **(2 marks)**

3.2 The set of activities designed to attract a suitable pool of candidates to an organisation is called:

(A) job analysis
(B) recruitment
(C) selection
(D) induction. **(2 marks)**

3.3 Three hundred and sixty (360) degree feedback is normally associated with

(A) exit interviews
(B) quality circle activity
(C) appraisal processes
(D) reflection as part of a cycle of learning. **(2 marks)**

? Question 4

A year ago, the owner-manager of a taxi service also moved into a new business area of fitting tyres. This came about as a result of the experience of using unbranded tyres on the fleet of ten taxis. Based on several years of use, the owner-manager found that the unbranded tyres lasted almost as long as the branded tyres, but had the advantage of being obtainable at half the price. The set-up costs of the tyre-fitting business were relatively modest and the owner-manager initially fitted the tyres himself. Demand picked up quickly, however, and he was forced to employ an experienced fitter. A few months later, demand accelerated again and he has just advertised for another fitter but, unfortunately, without success.

The tyre-fitting business has produced additional challenges and the owner-manager is finding it increasingly difficult to manage both the taxi service and the new business where he seems to be spending more and more of his time. He already employs one receptionist/taxi controller, but has realised that he now needs another.

As if this were not enough, he is in the middle of extending his operations still further. Customers who buy tyres frequently request that he check the wheel alignment on their car following the fitting of new tyres. He has started to provide this service, but when done manually it is a slow process, so he has invested heavily in a new piece of electronic equipment. This new technology will speed the alignment operation considerably, but neither he nor his tyre-fitter can operate the equipment. The owner feels that tyre fitters should be able to operate the equipment, and an additional member of staff is not required just to operate the equipment.

To add to all these problems, two of his taxi drivers have resigned unexpectedly. Past patterns suggest that of the ten drivers, normally one or two leave each year, generally in the summer months, though now it is winter.

Given all these staffing difficulties, the owner-manager has made use of a relative who happens to have some HR expertise. She has advised the owner-manager on recruitment and selection, training and development. The relative also suggests that the business needs a well thought out human resource plan.

Requirements

(a) Prepare an outline of human resource plan for the business and explain each aspect of your plan.   **(12 marks)**

(b) Discuss the important human resource activities to which attention should be paid in order to obtain the maximum contribution from the workforce.

> *Important:* *For requirement (b), exclude those areas upon which the relative has already provided advice to the owner-manager (recruitment and selection, training and development).*

(8 marks)
(Total = 20 marks)

Solutions to Revision Questions

4

✓ Solution 1

(a) *Recruitment services*

In a decentralized HR function, these services will have to be provided by each department separately. There will not be a significant difference when preparing job specifications as these would have been done by, or in conjunction with, the department line manager even in a centralised function. However, as regards interviews and preparation for interviews, a significant difference will be noted in a decentralised function. Each line manager would have to sort out applications and CVs. Adverts would have to be prepared and paid for by each manager and duplication of effort will result as well as a failure to achieve economies of scale. Inconsistency in approach between departments would also arise.

(b) *Appraisal procedures*

In both types of structure, it would be the line manager's responsibility to set individual performance targets with the worker's input. The line manager and the worker will also perform a review of the worker's performance together. It is after this stage that differences will be noted between the two structures. In a centralised structure, the HR/personnel department will be the focal point for investigating vacancies throughout the group. It can therefore provide advice and assistance in cases where it has been identified that the worker has outgrown the job or needs personal development in certain areas. With a decentralised structure, the line manager may not be aware of vacancies elsewhere and would have to investigate these him/herself. In addition, there would be the question about the appraisal standards and techniques. If each manager is responsible for appraising as he/she sees fit, how would another manager know that these standards equate with his/her own?

(c) *Job evaluation*

The main purpose of a job evaluation exercise is to achieve a ranking of salaries between jobs. In a centralised personnel function, the personnel staff would be responsible for ensuring that this happens by comparing dissimilar jobs and achieving a standard as far as is possible. They would also collect information from external sources to further this aim. However, where the personnel function is decentralised a consistency problem arises. Each line manager will have a good idea about jobs within his/her area and closely related areas, but little knowledge about other departments. This could result in inconsistency and duplication of effort as each manager attempts to acquire this knowledge.

Once a ranking system has been established by job evaluation, salary scales can be applied to each grade by comparing with competitive rates.

✓ Solution 2

(a) Those seeking work in large corporations like T plc will, in their review of the career literature, look at the kind of company that it portrays itself to be – in other words, at the image of the company. A good public relations effort by the company will sell itself to graduates much more so than one that is not so progressive. In the case of T plc this appears not to be a problem because adequate numbers of candidates have presented themselves for interview. The problem has arisen after job interviews and job offers by the company.

(b) Possible causes and remedies include the following:

1. The public image fostered by the company in its recruitment literature may not have been borne out when candidates visited the company for interview. Perhaps the information presented in the company literature about the nature of the jobs on offer fostered unrealistic expectations on the part of candidates? A first step for the company then might be for it to review its publicity. In doing so, the company might find it useful to consider the ways in which the publicity information is generated within the organisation and, specifically, to enquire whether or not the right kind of information was being gathered from T plc's subsidiaries, and once gathered adequately used to draw up accurate job specifications and attendant recruitment literature. This done, the company would be advised to focus attention on other recruitment procedures including the way the company draws up its plans for recruitment.

2. The subsidiary may have made a bad impression. New graduates are keen and prefer to join an enthusiastic and efficient firm. As the problem applies to the whole group, this must therefore apply to all the sites. If the subsidiaries actually are inefficient or demoralised this problem will have to be solved first.

3. The information given in the question tells us that T plc is a large group in the high-technology field with several subsidiaries. This implies a lengthy chain of command and many specialists. Such conditions inevitably pose a problem for communications. There could, for instance, be a problem in the subsidiaries communicating exactly what their requirements are, especially if the subsidiaries' staff are technical specialists referring vacancies to non-technical personnel staff. Such a communication blockage could well have had knock-on effects when the HR team visited the universities in the sense that non-technical staffs' interpretations of what was required might leave them vague when asked to respond to candidates' queries about specific job details. Possible remedies here include the improvement of communications between technical and personnel staff and perhaps strengthening the HR team who visit the universities by adding a technical representative from the subsidiaries.

4. A problem might arise in the interviewing process itself. This may come about not only due to the problem of communication just discussed but also because of inadequate interview procedures and inappropriate treatment of candidates on visiting the firm. Again, a review by the company of its interview procedures would seem to be called for and comparisons made with the best practice used by competitor companies.

5. Finally, the conditions of employment, promotion prospects and salaries for particular jobs may well look less attractive after a closer inspection by the candidates than

those offered by competitor companies. This could, then, be another area for the company to look at and it might be necessary to bring themselves into line with other companies if indeed employment prospects did fall below those of competitors.

☑ Solution 3

3.1 (D)

3.2 (B)

3.3 (C)

☑ Solution 4

(a) *Draft Human Resource Plan*

The human resource plan should include:

Strategic review

- Maintain taxi service at current level;
- Continue expansion of tyre fitting service by continuing to offer unbranded low price tyres and develop electronic wheel alignment service as an additional optional service.

Audit of Existing HR Staff

- Owner-manager   1
- Taxi drivers   8
- Reception/Taxi Co-ordinator   1
- Tyre Fitter   1

Demand for additional staff due to change in strategy and labour turnover

- Replacement of taxi drivers   2 (possibly 2 more in the summer)
- Appointment of co-ordinator   1
- Appointment of tyre fitter   1

Action plans to reconcile gap between demand and supply

- Recruitment and selection of two taxi drivers;
- Recruitment and selection of a tyre fitter or of a person capable of training to be a tyre fitter;
- Training of taxi drivers;
- Training of tyre fitters in use of electronic wheel alignment equipment;
- Justification of each aspect of the human resource plan.

It is necessary to review the strategy of the organisation because changes in strategic direction usually have implications for human resources. In this case, we have an emergent strategy that is proving very successful in that it is resulting in the rapid expansion of a tyre fitting business. The expansion not only is affecting the tyre fitting side of the operation, but is also impacting on the human resources of the organisation as a whole. The owner-manager can no longer cope with the demands on his time as a manager/operator and so it is necessary for the company to employ additional staff to cope with the co-ordination of the taxi service and reception work.

The audit of the existing staff is necessary to provide a kind of stock-take of what the organisation already has in terms of human resources. In this case, the numbers are small and we can work out mentally what the current human resource situation is.

The demand for additional staff is once again easy to estimate for the company because small numbers are involved and requirements are for a limited range of skills. The principle involved, however, is just the same as if we were looking at the additional demand for workers of many different skills working in a very large and complex organisation. We need to know about any extra numbers demanded because of a change in strategy, or some other reason for extra demand or alternatively for a contraction in demand. It is also necessary to take into account numbers lost through labour turnover during the planning period, so that extra employees with the required skills can be recruited to compensate.

When we have the figures of existing employees, we can use these as a basis to calculate the gap between what we have and what we need by estimating what the expansion is, caused by the change in strategy, entails. This figure plus an adjustment for labour turnover will provide us with the number of employees we need to recruit.

The activities to reconcile demand with supply follow simply from our calculation. It may, as in this case, be difficult to recruit people with specific skills we want and so it may be necessary to recruit unskilled people and provide them with the necessary training (e.g. the use of wheel alignment equipment).

(b) In addition to training and development, and recruitment and selection, the company will need to ensure that other aspects of human resource management are carried out so that the performance of the workforce is maximised.

Two of the most important human resource activities that are necessary in order to ensure good performance of employees are:

1. first, a system of performance appraisal, so that each worker's performance can be evaluated; and
2. second, a system of rewards and benefits that will both compensate workers fairly and motivate them to perform to an appropriate standard.

Performance appraisal is a systematic process of evaluating each employee's contribution, his or her strengths and weaknesses and ways of determining how to improve performance. Such an evaluation may provide the basis for the allocation of merit payments that can be used to motivate workers. The information gained can also be used to move staff either between jobs by way of promotion or even out of the company because of underperformance. It can also be used as a means of identifying training and development needs and it provides an opportunity to provide feedback to employees on their past and present performance and to set targets for future performance.

The reward system is also important; first to compensate workers for their efforts. This is the function of base payments. The company might also make use of incentive payments of various kinds in order to motivate employees to work harder. Taxi drivers, for example, might be rewarded on the basis of their overall takings per week, tyre fitters on the number of extra services they sell, such as number of customers who are persuaded to have wheel alignments carried out.

There are, of course, other important human resource activities that need to be covered such as health and safety provision, which is very important when working with heavy equipment.

5

Operations Management

Operations Management

5

LEARNING OUTCOMES

Operations Management, which includes management of quality, accounts for 20 per cent of the overall syllabus. By completing this chapter, its associated readings and questions you should be able to:

► Evaluate the management of operations

► Analyse problems associated with quality in organisations

► Evaluate contemporary thinking in quality management

► Explain the linkages between functional areas as an important aspect of quality management

► Apply tools and concepts of quality management appropriately in an organisation

► Construct a plan for the implementation of a quality programme

► Recommend ways to negotiate and manage relationships with suppliers

► Evaluate a supply network

► Explain the concept of quality and how the quality of products and services can be assessed, measured and improved.

5.1 Introduction

This chapter introduces the concept of operations management and associated issues including supply networks and quality, in particular the idea of total quality management (TQM).

5.2 A background to the management of operations

As Brown et al. (2001) point out all organisations have an operations function whether it is explicitly called that or not. Put in 'product' terms Galloway (1998: 2) described operations as 'those activities concerned with the acquisition of raw materials, their conversion into finished product and the supply of that finished product to the customer'.

Table 5.1 Examples of operations

Organisation	Operations function	Operation
McDonalds	Kitchen and waiters	Selling fast food
Vauxhall/Opel	Production lines	Making cars
Dell Computers	Production lines, internet	Making and selling computers
Real Madrid	Football coaches, training facilities	Playing football
Schools	Teachers	Teaching children

Most contemporary thinkers would broaden this definition as 'what the company does' so involving service as well as manufacturing organisations. Using this thinking examples of operations are provided in Table 5.1.

Exercise 5.1

Develop a similar analysis for your organisation.

Operations management is concerned with all activities involved in making a product or providing a service: it is responsible for the transformation of various kinds of inputs into useful outputs. This thinking is based on the principle that all organisations can be viewed as transformers of inputs to outputs. This involves taking various inputs (raw materials, money, people, machine time, and so on) and performing operations (manufacturing, assembly, packing, etc.) to produce outputs (goods, services, etc).

Operations management is concerned with the planning, direction and control of the vital operations that link the business of the organisation with the needs and wants of the organisation's customers. It is important to emphasise, that 'products' can be either goods or services, and 'operations' are the processes by which either of these are produced.

> Note: Much of this thinking originated in manufacturing firms but, increasingly it is seen as relevant to all types of organisation. There will be times within this chapter that the word 'product' is used within the context of operations management this signifies services as well as products.

It is clear from this brief introduction that operations and the development of an associated strategy is of vital importance to any organisation. For many enlightened contemporary organisations effective operations is viewed as a strategically critical issue and a vital means of gaining competitive advantage.

5.2.1 Operations: some history

During the eighteenth century the UK experienced dramatic change through what became known as the industrial revolution. It was during this period that the economy was transformed from an agricultural to industrial one and population migrated to towns from the countryside. Key features of the newly formed organisations included:

- the introduction of machines used to mass produce items,
- effective means of warehousing stocks of raw and finished products, and
- effective distribution of finished products.

As reflected earlier, F.W. Taylor and others developed work measurement and applied 'scientific' methods to production from the 1890s onwards. These studies clearly showed that the productivity of organisations depended both on the technology available and how this technology was managed. In essence, the efficiency of an organisation depended on the way it is managed. 'Good' management constituted an application of knowledge and skills of a 'scientific' nature, rather than intuition and guesswork (see Section 3.3.1 earlier). This thinking laid the foundations for the study of an area later referred to as operations management. At its simplest operations management tries to ensure that organisations are run as efficiently as possible.

5.2.2 Operations: contemporary thinking

Two well known management models are presented here in order to illustrate the linkages between functional areas as an important aspect of operational management and quality. They underline the notion that operations are at the heart of an organisation.

'Operations' is a term covering the central core of an organisation. Famously this central core has been used as a springboard for the development of theory by academics such as Henry Mintzberg (1983) who referred to it as 'the operating core' (Figure 5.1 below). Mintzberg put forward a different way of looking at organisations as a whole and suggested that it is useful to view organisations as being made up of five parts (Figure 5.1).

The operating core consists of those people who perform the work of rendering the services or producing products. In a small organisation this operating core may represent nearly all of the organisation, but larger size will require more complex arrangements. There will be a requirement to formulate and implement strategy so that the organisation serves its mission in an effective way; this is the role of the strategic apex which may in some circumstances also be responsible for linking the organisation to the needs of those who own or control it. The middle line represents the hierarchy of

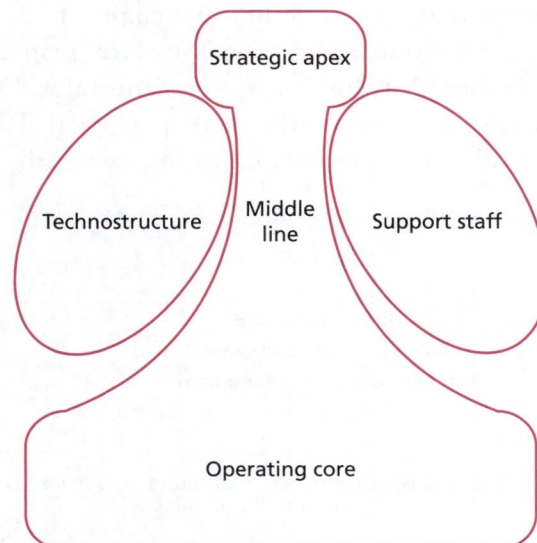

Figure 5.1 Five basic parts of the organisation
From Structures in Fives: Designing Effective Organisations by H. Mintzberg. Reprinted by permission of Pearson Education Inc., Upper Saddle River, NJ.

authority from senior managers to first-line supervisors linking the strategic apex to the operating core. As an organisation continues to grow and develop it is likely to include within its structure specialist staff outside the central line positions (i.e. strategic apex, middle line and operating core). Specialist staff are placed into two categories by Mintzberg:

- The technostructure is concerned with co-coordinating work by standardising work processes, outputs and skills, and will be made up of people such as management accountants, work-study engineers, HR managers, etc.
- Support staff exist to provide assistance to the organisation outside its operating work flow. Examples would be catering services, legal advice and press relations.

Clearly operations management is focused upon the operating core and specialists who form part of the technostrucutre.

✋ Exercise 5.2

Many organisations are now actively seeking flatter hierarchies, better quality and ways of contracting out of non-core activities. What are the implications of these developments for the five basic parts of the organisation identified by Mintzberg?

✔️ Solution

A clearer focus on the core activity and hence further importance attached to operations management.

Economist Michael Porter (1985) first explained the organisation as a business system, which he described as a value chain as it represented a sequence of value-creating activities. Whereas Mintzberg's diagram represents a static description of a vertical organisation the value chain is more of a process (Figure 5.2). Porter saw the 'line' departments linked horizontally together in a chain of sequentially-interdependent activities – from supply sources, to goods-inward inspection, operations (the 'transformation process') then distribution, storage and sales. Organisations structure these activities differently to cope with their particular external environments. Typically departments or divisions are created to interact with specific sectors of the environment.

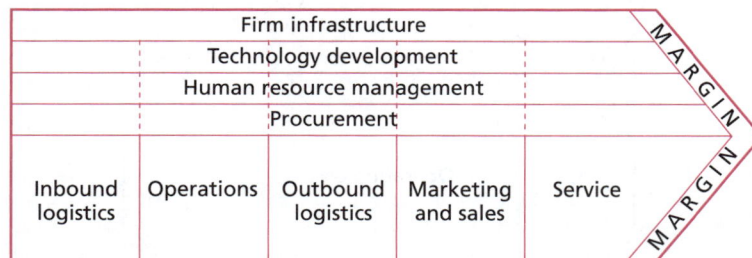

Figure 5.2 Porter's value chain. Reprinted with the permission of The Free Press, a division of Simon & Schuster Adult Publishing Group, from *Competitive Advantage: Creating and Sustaining Superior Performance* by Michael E. Porter. © 1985, 1998 by Michael E. Porter. All rights reserved.

Five primary activities are directly concerned with the creation or delivery of a product:

- Inbound logistics refer to receipt, storage, and distribution. They include material handling, stock control, etc.
- Operations convert these inputs into the final product.
- Outbound logistics involves the distribution to consumers. (For example, in the case of supermarkets it takes place either in the stores, where checkout tills are important, or for on-line computer sales, by assembling and transporting customer orders.)
- Marketing and sales is the mechanism whereby the customer is made aware of the product.
- Service can include installation, training and spares. (Using the example of a supermarket this would refer to customer enquiry/returns/complaints desk and possibly the maintenance of an Internet page.)

Operations management is directly concerned with four of these five primary activities. (Marketing and sales was dealt with earlier in Chapter 2.)

Support activities help to improve the efficiency and effectiveness of all primary activities, specifically:

- Procurement processes at all stages including product purchases.
- Technology development including 'know-how'.
- Human resource management embracing all primary activities and covers recruitment, selection, training, development and reward policies, etc.
- Infrastructure or systems, structures and routines.

Operations management is directly concerned with procurement and elements of technology and infrastructure. (Human resource management was dealt with earlier in Chapter 4.)

Arising from this thinking Table 5.2 illustrates some key issues associated with operations management within a fictional organisation.

This chapter focuses on several of the above dimensions of operations management.

Table 5.2 Example operations management: issues

Purchasing activity capable of buying the raw material, components, tools and equipment necessary for efficient high-quality minimum-cost manufacture.

The provision of economic and efficient storage of consumable goods, raw materials and components for further fabrication. Records capable of ensuring that quantities held in stock are within the predetermined budgets.

Production engineering capability to plan manufacturing methods, use of tools, design of machine tools, assembly, fixtures, etc.

Production control department with the capability of translating customer orders and stockists' requirements into orders in the factory.

The organisation and operation of the manufacturing department and assembly department. Economical and competitive cost of manufacture.

Quality control department with the capability of ensuring adequate quality commensurate with cost, by inspection at various stages of manufacture and assembly and 'bench testing' of final products.

The efficiency of the company's facilities, plant, buildings, tools, etc.

5.3 Purchasing

Recently purchasing has become a strategic issue for firms as techniques such as just-in-time (JIT) operations have taken root in a diversity of industries (initially from successes in motor manufacturing). JIT purchasing involves a system whereby 'material purchases are contracted so that the receipt and usage of material, to the maximum extent possible, coincide' (CIMA 2005). Put simply the stock of raw materials is reduced to near-zero levels. Financial savings are easily apparent as is the requirement to foster an effective working relationship with suppliers.

The purchasing department has always been responsible for a major part of the company's expenditure. Most manufacturing organisations spend more than 60 per cent of total costs in purchasing. Some of the large buyers, for instance, in the automobile companies, have become highly sophisticated materials managers and fully integrate design and purchasing especially as JIT requires exact specifications and materials handling to achieve low inventory levels. Purchasing is also now generally involved with the design and development department with the responsibility of finding suppliers for materials that are to the specifications required by designers.

Chapter 2 underlined the significance of selling as part of the marketing function, and this has been a key emphasis for a number of organisations. Manufacturers, however, are increasingly recognising that buying is as important as selling, and that excellent selling cannot make up for a mediocre buying specification. To implement the firm's buying policies, it must provide much of the information that will enable the firm to establish its policies. Responsibilities include the economic acquisition of raw materials, components, sub-assemblies, consumable stores and capital equipment.

Increasingly, centralisation has enabled savings from scale economies by combining under a procurement 'umbrella' a number of formerly ancillary dispersed activities. These include supplies and capital equipment for offices (e.g. computers, cars, telephone systems, office furniture, paper and other stationery items, etc.). The administrative tasks of purchasing departments involves a tremendous amount of data processing.

Those responsible for purchasing will discuss prices, discounts, delivery lead times and specifications with suppliers, chase late deliveries, and sanction payments for deliveries. They will monitor quality, seek out competitive sources and maximise quantity discount opportunities where several sources are buying from the same supplier.

The tasks include invitations to tender or quote, examinations of tenders/quotations, planning purchase orders, matching purchase orders with goods inwards documentation, progressing orders to ensure good delivery, checking suppliers' invoices and quotations and controlling returned goods and obtaining credit notes.

Gargan (2004) underlines the crucial significance of an organisation's purchasing function, as follows:

- improved purchasing has saved the UK government more than £1.6 billion on an annual spend of £15 billion
- in the manufacturing industry, each 5 per cent reduction of purchasing costs increases profitability by 35 per cent on average.

The following extract from a more complete article makes the financial case for strategic purchasing and sees it as a lever to world class performance:

During the last 20 years, procurement departments around the world have adopted some new and very powerful processes and tools. Done well, advanced procurement and supply management can trigger a compounding positive effect on a company's lifeblood–its return on invested capital.

If you could reduce your product development cycle time by 50 per cent and beat competitors to market, while also reducing costs, would that be meaningful to your business? For most companies, that would be a huge plus. That is why world-class competitors involve their procurement group and other internal functions, plus suppliers, in an aligned effort to increase competitive advantage.

For capital projects, there is a direct correlation between the total costs associated with that project and the stage at which procurement is involved. The message is very simple: involve procurement and suppliers at an early stage to optimise the total costs of any capital project. Getting procurement and suppliers involved early, even at the concept stage, makes it more likely that the best ideas are considered before it is too late, and that the commercial foundation for success is established before too many 'technical details' are locked in . . .

Experience has demonstrated that there are more than 30 critical factors that distinguish truly exceptional supply management performance from the rest of the field. Those common success factors fall into six fundamental categories:

1. procurement strategy
2. objectives
3. leadership
4. optimised organisation
5. best practices
6. innovation and technology.

The exceptional performers in the world of supply management devote their best people to leading this effort.

(*Source:* extracted from 'World-class supply practices boost shareholder value: a focus on both direct and indirect spending, including smaller items, can have a powerful effect on corporate performance. Top companies involve their procurement group and other internal functions, plus suppliers, to boost competitive advantage (procurement)' Robert A. Rudzki, *Financial Executive* 22.3, April 2006, 56(3).

5.4 Managing supply

Having considered the issue of purchasing attention now turns to a related topic of supply and its management. It is perhaps helpful to distinguish the two areas:

- Purchasing deals with day-to-day buying of goods and services, ensuring they conform to the quality demanded, are priced appropriately and delivered to a suitable time scale.
- Supply deals with strategic considerations including planning and implementing a strategy and managing the overall supply process.

Supply, therefore, considers strategic issues such as:

- The suitability, feasibility and acceptability of outsourcing activities
- Strategic partnerships that could be established
- The number of suppliers it should use.

One way of assessing how far supply chain management is being approached as a strategic process is by applying Reck and Long's (1988) strategic positioning tool. This positions the purchasing stage an organisation has reached on a continuum as follows:

- *Passive*. Purchasing acts on requests from other departments, some departments may get involved in the detail.
- *Independent*. A more professional approach to purchasing including enhanced IT and communication.
- *Supportive*. Purchasing is corporately recognized as essential. The function provides timely information about price and availability.
- *Integrative*. Purchasing is integral to competitive strategies and management involved in strategy development.

Cousins' (2000) strategic supply wheel depicts the corporate supply strategy at the hub of a wheel and underlines the need for an integrated approach to supply strategy involving a balancing of all 'spokes' in the wheel, namely:

- Organisational structure
- Relationship portfolio
- Cost/benefit analysis
- Skills and competencies, and
- Performance measures.

From a strategic point of view cohesion between these five elements needs to be achieved, and each factor should be supportive of the other.

- Organisational structure affects interactions with the rest of the organisation and the way in which control is exercised, the three main options are centralised, decentralised or some combination (a hybrid).
- Relationships with suppliers and their nature impact on the strategic success of the organisation. These relationships may be based on driving deals on price and can be quite adversarial. Alternatively, they may be more collaborative where there is a joint quest to reduce costs and a sharing of technology and innovations (known as 'partnership sourcing').
- Cost/benefit analysis is at the heart of rational decisions over the most appropriate strategic approach to follow.
- Appropriate skills and competencies are vital in order to implement a chosen strategy. Long-term relationships with suppliers might (for instance) lead to a need to re-orientate and train key personnel.
- Performance measures, both internal and external aligned with the strategy are necessary for monitoring and control.

✋ Exercise 5.3

What potential performance measures can be used to assess suppliers?

☑ Solution

- Capability
- Delivery performance
- Price competitiveness
- Quality (defect rates)
- Timeliness (which will vary dependent upon the value and volume of the item purchased, e.g. a piece of computer hardware versus nuts and bolts).

Sourcing strategies refer to the way an organisation organises its supply process and clearly these have strategic implications. There are four main sourcing options:

- *Single.* the buyer chooses one source of supply. This may be because of a scarcity of suppliers and under these circumstances the supplier is potentially powerful. One advantage of this option is that it is easier to develop a relationship with a single supplier.
- *Multiple.* the buyer chooses several source of supply. Suppliers are rendered less powerful and prices can be driven down as a result. This is a traditional strategy but may not be conducive to good working relationships, or developing meaningful supplier relationships.
- *Delegated.* the buyer chooses one (first tier) supplier who is responsible for the delivery of for example a complete sub assembly. Using the example of car manufacture, rather than deal with several suppliers to complete a dashboard one first tier supplier would assume this responsibility and deliver a completed dashboard through dealing with a range of other suppliers. This approach allows for a collaboratrive partnership approach to develop including in some cases 'open book' accounting where savings are shared between both parties. One downside is of course that the first tier supplier becomes powerful so must be chosen with great care.
- *Parallel.* a complicated approach that involves mixing all three other approaches in order to maximise the benefits of each.

5.5 Strategic issues

Operations is no different from other functional areas in that it can be approached from a strategic viewpoint. Brown et al. (2001: 39) stress the significance of this thinking as follows:

Operations capabilities are at the heart of the success of companies such as Dell, Nokia and Sony ... Although other areas such as marketing and human resource (HR) management are also important, even with the best marketing or HR plans in the world, without operations capabilities an organisation will flounder because it cannot deliver on its promises to customers. Organisations can no longer compete on a single dimension such as low cost, high quality, or delivery, but must provide all of these (and more!) simultaneously.

The process of strategy formulation reflected in earlier chapters including external and internal scanning and the generation and choice of strategies applies equally to this area. Similarly operations must be central to the development of an overall corporate strategy.

Brown et al. (2001) include six items that as a minimum should be addressed as part of the operations strategy:

- The capability required by the organisation
- The range and location of operations
- Investment in technology, both product and process

- Strategic buyer–supplier relationships
- New products or services
- The organisational structure of operations.

Earlier in the chapter Porter's value chain was explained in the context of operations management (see Figure 5.2). The implications of the value chain and the wider value system has encouraged organisations to consider:

- Business process re-engineering (BPR) whereby activities are reconfigured to bring about a dramatic improvement in performance.
- Supply chain partnerships as part of a wider value system. The value system extends to suppliers, distributors and customers' own value chains. Competitive advantage through linkages between the organisation and its value system components can be achieved by examining supplier specifications, common merchandising, applying total quality management principles or by collaborating with other organisations in the form of strategic alliances or joint ventures.

Porter uses the concept of the value system to describe the position of the firm relative to the firms upstream and downstream of it. Figure 5.3 shows the firm at a point in the value system between suppliers and customers. Relationships between the firms in the value system matter:

- A firm might maximise returns by striking good deals with suppliers (low prices) and customers (high prices) to take as much of the available 'value' (difference between the revenue received and costs) for itself.
- Alternatively, the firm might collaborate with others in the system to increase total value. This would involve increasing the ability of the final product to generate satisfaction (reflected in the price) by working together to reduce the total costs in the value system. Critically, the role of the supply chain and strategic supply networks could be key in gaining competitive advantage, including the development and maintenance of supplier relationships.

5.5.1 Supply chain alliances

Contemporary developments reflect a strategic redefinition of the boundaries of organisations. Interestingly, some organisations are rethinking what should be researched, designed, made or assembled under direct control. This in turn involves long-term alliances in a supply chain. (The increased emphasis on the management of the whole supply chain in the context of promotion was considered in Chapter 2 earlier.)

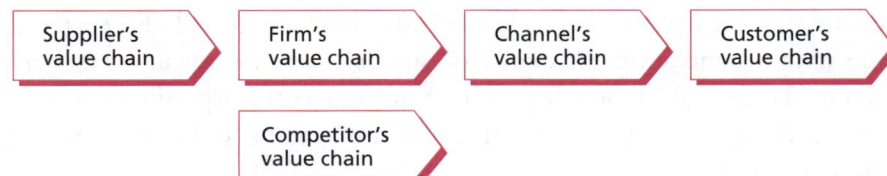

Figure 5.3 Porter's value system. Reprinted with the permission of The Free Press, a division of Simon & Schuster Adult Publishing Group, from *Competitive Advantage: Creating and Sustaining Superior Performance* by Michael E. Porter. © 1985, 1998 by Michael E. Porter. All rights reserved.

Networks have been described as a link between supplier and purchaser in the supply chain but a more accurate and useful division is between different suppliers, and the co-ordination methods employed within the firms. In Italy experiments have been made to introduce networks in technologically similar industries in areas called 'business districts'. In the textile industry, contractors are based in the same region as knitwear firms and often work for several different firms, sometimes in alliances or partnerships with other contractors, sometimes as sole contract-holder. A technology transfer opportunity arises for the major textile firms as contractors learn the businesses of other firms. Savings based on learning and experience become a competitive advantage for all the firms.

Ody (2000) observed:

The supply chain used to be simple, serial and linear, with raw materials moving slowly through manufacturing production and onward via the distribution system to retailers and end-consumers.

Today, talk is of 'supply networks', 'parallel chains', 'enhanced concurrent activities', and 'synchronised supply models', with information technology set to cut both inventory and lead times throughout the pipeline still further.

The new supply chain model demands seamless integration of software and systems and 'visibility' throughout the network so that all trading partners are singing from the same 'available-to-promise' song sheet.

5.6 Managing inventory

Managing inventory is a major contributor to improving material, customer and information flows from the business to satisfy the needs and wants of the customer. All those studying accountancy will readily recognise that inventory can exist in several forms (raw materials, work in progress, finished goods, etc.). They will also know that stock holding has costs attached to it and such costs may ultimately contribute to an organisation becoming uncompetitive.

Brown et al. (2001) point out that different organisations hold inventory in different places. For example, some sandwich shops only sell prepackaged food (finished) while others make on site at a special location, and others still hold a combination of raw materials (salads etc.) and allow customers to customise their basic sandwiches (work in progress). Decisions such as these leads to the concept of 'make-to-order' approaches where inventory is only taken and assembled on receipt of an order or 'make-to-stock' where items are held in anticipation of an order.

Brown et al. (2001) contend that holding inventory can support the performance objectives of quality, reliability, speed, flexibility and cost in a number of ways (Table 5.3).

Table 5.3 Reasons for holding inventory

Protecting against quality problems with either inputs or finished goods
Ensure reliability for the customer
Protect against supply interruptions
Smoothing production flows when demand varies
Meeting unexpected demand
Improving delivery speed
Flexibility built around resource-to-order, make-to-order or make-to-stock
Reducing input costs by negotiating discounts for bulk orders

Source: Based on Brown et al. (2001)

Methods for managing inventory, include:

- *Continuous inventory systems.* Defined as '(a system) where inventory levels are continually monitored, and when inventory levels drop below a predetermined level a fixed amount is ordered to replace it' (Brown et al., 2001: 216). The tinned food in person's home or the cleaning materials held is typically informally replaced in this way. Continuous inventory can be operated using a fixed order quantity replacement system or an Economic Order Quantity system (EOQ), which takes into account variable costs associated with ordering the item and holding the item. As Brown et al. (2001) point out this system encourages buffer stocks and a 'just in case' mentality rather than a 'just in time' approach.
- *Periodic inventory (or bin) systems.* They are commonly used in retail outlets such as supermarkets. They involve a check of stock levels (in this example on the shelves) after a specific time and lead to a variable ordering of new stock.
- *ABC system.* ABC is not an acronym, it refers to a classification conceived out of the Pareto 80/20 rule which suggests that 20 per cent of the items are likely to account for 80 per cent of the annual expenditure on inventory. The goal of the ABC system is to focus on those items that are most important and therefore need careful monitoring and those that are not. A items are all of high value, and close monitoring including managing the supplier/buyer relationship to good effect is strategically important. B are medium items where these issues are less tightly managed and C are low value inventory, for example nails, screws, tacks, etc. requiring little management.

5.7 Operations flows

One important aspect of operations management is to ensure that materials are ready when they are needed. A number of systems are used in improving flows, some through the application of sophisticated IT others through the adoption of Japanese approaches. The specific systems considered here are:

- Manufacturing Resource Planning (MRP)
- Enterprise Resource Planning (ERP)
- Optimised Production Technologies (OPT)
- Just-in-time (JIT).

5.7.1 Manufacturing Resource Planning (MRP)

Manufacturing Resource Planning is a planning and control system designed for organisations that engage in mass production. MRP is a push-based system, pushing work through the system. The computer system MRP II is a form of inventory control matching supply and demand with sophisticated features such as:

- Shop floor control
- Production planning
- Financial analysis
- Capacity planning

- Customer order entry
- Purchasing
- Forecasting.

Brown et al. (2001) cite the benefits as potentially providing:

- Reduced stock holding and stock turnover
- Increased customer service (fewer delays through materials shortage)
- Swift, reliable quotations of delivery times
- Improved facilities utilisation
- Less time spent on hurrying emergency orders
- Better relationships with suppliers by identifying clear lead times.

5.7.2 Enterprise Resource Planning (ERP)

Enterprise Resource Planning integrates internal processes such as MRP II with external processes. ERP is a management system that integrates all aspects of business, including planning, manufacturing, and sales. As ERP has become more popular certain software applications have emerged to help implement activities such as inventory control, order tracking, customer service, finance and human resources. It may be costly and time hungry to implement but it does cohesively link the supply chain.

5.7.3 Optimised Production Technologies (OPT)

Optimised Production Technologies is a production improvement method based on bottleneck improvements. It is built on the idea of constraints and seeks to identify and then remove obstructions that hinder the flow of the system.

5.7.4 Just-in-time (JIT)

There are a number of innovations in organisational systems that are having a significant impact on organisational effectiveness. One of the most noticeable changes has been caused by the adoption of new manufacturing management systems such as total quality management (TQM) and just-in-time (JIT) approaches to stocks and manufacturing.

A JIT system has an objective of producing or procuring products or components as they are required by a customer or for use, rather than for stock (CIMA, 2005).

JIT is a pull-based system of planning and control pulling work through the system in response to customer demand. The obvious advantage of JIT means that goods are produced only when they are needed eliminating large stocks of materials and parts.

JIT approaches are often undertaken in parallel with TQM. TQM facilitates the introduction of JIT because JIT is not feasible with, for example, high reject rates and high wastage in manufacturing, and TQM reduces these. A form of risk assessment in the production department often takes place. The impact of production delays and stock-outs if the JIT system fails has implications. A decision on whether to accept the risk or, perhaps, to carry buffer stocks must be made.

✋ **Exercise 5.4**

What is the main principle difference between MRP and JIT?

✅ **Solution**

JIT is a pull-based system which responds to demand in contrast with MRP which is a push-based system. Push-based systems tend to use stock as buffers between the different elements of the system such as purchasing, production and sales (CIMA, 2005).

5.8 Managing capacity

One important task of operations managers is to balance demand and supply. Supply is inevitably fixed by factors largely internal to the organisation such as facilities, systems, technology, human resources and capability. Demand is an external force. Inevitably there will be fluctuations between these two dimensions. Three main means are used for balancing capacity and demand, namely: level capacity, chase and demand management strategies.

- Level capacity strategies involves the organisation building inventory levels so that these excess stores can be used to deal with increases in demand beyond capacity. Clearly this has cost implications and will not apply to service organisations where excesses of demand over capacity will result in queues (a good example being waiting lists for operations in the UK's National Health Service).
- Chase strategies involve constantly adjusting organisational activity levels to shadow fluctuations in demand.
- Demand management strategies involve attempts to influence demand to smooth variations above or below capacity. Yield management is a variant of this strategy and involves varying pricing to encourage demand. For example a football club that has to attract attendance for an upcoming fixture against 'unattractive' opposition might introduce a two people for one ticket price scheme or a 'kids go free' with an adult initiative. Service organisations as well as manufacturing organisations can apply this strategy. Table 5.4 summarises the main approaches available to service organisations.

Table 5.4 Main approaches for service organisations for matching supply and demand

Managing service capacity through
Managing demand
Complementary services
Reservations
Price incentives
Off-peak demand
Managing supply
Sharing capacity
Cross training employees
Part-time employees

Source: Based on Fitzsimmons and Fitzsimmons (2004)

5.9 Manufacturing

Recently a new form of manufacturing has evolved: the computer-aided design and manufacturing operation (CAD/CAM) which will probably be aligned to new methods of production such as cellular manufacture (small divisions within a factory having responsibility for output quality and costs). CAD and CAM are also the keys to flexible manufacturing as they enable computerised machines to perform a variety of functions. When CAD and CAM are integrated it is possible to achieve computer-integrated manufacturing (CIM) whereby a system directs data flow whilst also directing the processing and movements of material.

These IT developments may be allied to production techniques imported from Japan including JIT. JIT methods of production involves developing 'a production system which is driven by demand for finished products whereby each component on a production line is produced only when needed for the next stage' (CIMA Official Terminology).

The objectives of the manufacturing function are similar to those of operations, except that it is concerned only with that part of the operations function directly related to manufacture. The manufacturing manager will agree with the operations director a plan to make a predetermined quantity of products to predetermined cost and quality and delivery standards.

The departmental measurements will include:

- time taken to acknowledge an order to the customer,
- time taken to process orders into a form acceptable to the factory,
- speed of dispatch to the customer,
- level and value of finished stocks (in cases where manufacture is planned to sustain stock levels at a required amount).

Within the operations system itself recent approaches such as cellular manufacturing have had the effect of altering traditional plant layouts by creating a U-shaped flow of work in which different machines are grouped to make products with similar machining requirements.

The relationship between manufacturing and engineering and maintenance should be acknowledged. Engineering is responsible for providing the methods of manufacture. While they work with design engineers, their task is to provide the most economical way of manufacturing the product, to pre-agreed quality levels, at pre-planned costs, and in respect of forecast quantities. The maintenance department is responsible for the maintenance of the factory buildings, machinery, plant and for power and lighting.

5.10 Maintenance

Total productive maintenance (TPM) is a contemporary idea aimed at increasing the productivity of the organisation's equipment. The fundamental objective of TPM is to prevent quality failures caused by equipment failure or degradation so TPM might usefully contribute a quality management programme. It involves identifying equipment in every division, including planning, manufacturing and maintenance, and then planning and implementing a maintenance programme that covers their entire useful life. Equipment control, both departmentally and at an operator level, is seen as important.

Exercise 5.5

What do you think the major factors that need to be considered in order to implement TPM?

Solution

- training
- equipment maintenance
- planning management
- capital expenditure plans
- maintenance plans
- safety and environment management.

TPM should reduce equipment breakdowns, enhance equipment capability and improve safety and environmental factors.

5.11 Operations in services and manufacturing

Some believe that differences between service and manufacturing organisations may be over played, and there is a potentially universal applicability of operations management concepts. For both types of organisation the operations function provides an agreed volume of products or services within an agreed delivery plan at a pre-planned cost and level of quality. In manufacturing firms it also has to achieve a planned return on assets employed, both capital and stock and work in progress. Some of these measures are now starting to take on relevance for service organisations due to changing technologies. (For instance as banks become less labour-intensive, more capital-intensive, centralised and global, it is possible to complete applications for insurance or credit cards over the Internet.)

Nevertheless there are peculiarities to do with the service offered by each organisational type along a continuum of types of service provider (Table 5.5).

Table 5.5 Overlaps between service organisations and manufacturing organisations

Service		Manufacturing
Simultaneous production and consumption		Goods stored for later consumption
Customised output		Standardised output
Customer participation		Technical core buffered from customer
Intangible output		Tangible output
Labour intensive		Capital intensive
Examples	Overlap	Examples
Airlines	Fast food outlets	Drinks
Hotels	Banks	Steel
Consultancy	Cosmetics	Cars
Teaching/training	Estate agents	Mining
Health	Retailing	

(Note: See also Services Marketing in Chapter 2)

5.12 Quality in organisations

Quality is one of the most important and far-reaching issues in modern organisations. The idea of quality is often difficult to define precisely and may mean different things to different organisations. Quality can be described in terms of fitness for purpose, or the totality of features of a product or service that meets the stated or implied needs of the customer. Notably, the need to satisfy the customer's needs is critical to most definitions of quality. Therefore, it is vital that organisations are able to identify and deliver the needs of its customers.

5.12.1 Quality: manufacturing organisations

Lean production

Lean production and its management involve a consolidation of improvement systems into a single coherent process for continuous improvement. The concept was born from the experience of Western firms competing with Japanese businesses with their emphasis on quality. For some firms this new type of competition proved fatal whilst others realised that if they were to survive they would have to radically change the ways in which they transformed their inputs into outputs. Consequently, 'operations management' has been elevated from being viewed in the West as a largely mundane and unimportant aspect of management to being seen as the key to revitalising organisations. This role was graphically described in the book The Machine that Changed the World (Womack et al., 1990), which traces the impact of new approaches to manufacturing in the automobile industry.

Henry Ford's adoption of assembly line production methods early in the twentieth century transformed the way cars and many other products were made. A 'new way' of making things pioneered by the Japanese is now making mass production obsolete. Lean producers are thought to achieve a 2:1 advantage over non-lean producers. This 'new way' involves bringing together the activities of managers, employees and suppliers into a tightly integrated system that can respond extremely quickly to changing customer demands, the result is what is called a 'lean production' system. Lean production focuses on a removal of all forms of waste from the system, whether parts, people or processes and is explained by Dankbaar (cited in Brown et al.) as:

- Making use of the workforce by giving them more than one task
- Cross-functional management and employee involvement
- Integrating direct and indirect work
- Taking advantage of quality circles.

This leads to the manufacture of a larger variety of products at lower cost and higher quality with less of every input compared to mass production.

From these explanations it is clear that the main characteristics of lean production include:

- flexible workforce practices
- high-commitment human resource policies and
- commitment to continuous improvement.

Lean production is not immune from criticism however, Brown et al. (2001) suggest that it ignores four critical areas of operations;

- manufacturing's contribution to corporate planning
- manufacturing strategy

OPERATIONS MANAGEMENT

- the seniority of operations staff
- potential alliances.

In addition it may not empower employees, indeed it could be seen as a top down approach forcing employees to devise ways of doing more for less resource.

Coote and Gould (2006) evaluate the work of Womak and Jones (2006) and apply it to the latter day finance function as follows:

Womack and Jones set out six simple principles of lean consumption that provide a definition of value for today's consumer:

1. Solve my problem completely.
2. Don't waste my time.
3. Provide exactly what I want.
4. Deliver value where I want it.
5. Deliver value when I want it.
6. Reduce the number of decisions I must make to solve my problems.

Since we are all customers of a wide variety of products and services, we can probably relate all these and have our own views of how different suppliers meet these expectations. They provide a useful structure by which to gauge how well a business delivers value. They can also be used to assess how well its finance function delivers value.

Womack and Jones describe waste as any human activity that absorbs resources but creates no value. They quote the late Toyota executive Taiichi Ohno, who categorised waste (muda) in the following groups:

- Defects (in products).
- Overproduction of goods not needed.
- Inventories of goods awaiting further processing or consumption.
- Unnecessary processing.
- Unnecessary movement of people.
- Unnecessary transport of goods.
- Waiting (by employees for process equipment to finish its work or an upstream activity to be completed).

To these seven they add another, the design of goods and services that do not meet the needs of the customer.

For those of you already working to improve the ability of your finance function to 'deliver customer value without waste', we suggest that you:

- Manage the scope – that is, focus on products where benchmarking shows high costs for relatively little value.
- Understand who the customers of these products are, talk to them and establish their definition of value.
- Assign clear process ownership for the value stream that produces this product. Where it crosses functional boundaries, ensure that this owner has the right sponsorship to make the required changes.

- Establish the clear and frequent measurement of the process's effectiveness and efficiency. The more that this can be integrated into the normal functioning of the process, the easier it will to be maintain.
- Build a culture of continuous improvement – that is, aim for small, regular and highly visible gains that involve many colleagues and are appreciated by the management.
- Use this as a foundation for more transformational change. The stronger the foundation is, the more likely the change will deliver the required results.

World-class manufacturing

Another term often used to describe the fundamental changes required in operations management is 'world-class manufacturing' which is generally concerned with achieving significant improvements in quality, lead times, flexibility and customer satisfaction. By making these improvements, an organisation might realistically become globally competitive. The concept and practice of world-class manufacturing is wide ranging and the term is not always used consistently. However, the core features of most approaches to world-class manufacturing include:

- Strong customer focus which ensures that customer requirements are fully understood and can be satisfied with short lead times.
- Flexibility to respond to changing customer requirements.

CIMA (2005) link 'world-class manufacturing' with international manufacturing excellence, and a supportive organisational culture.

The need for these changes in the United Kingdom was graphically illustrated by a comparative study of Japanese and UK companies in 1993, which suggested that:

- on average the UK firms required twice as many employees as their Japanese counterparts to produce the same number of parts;
- defects averaged 2.5 per 10,000 in the best Japanese plants but averaged 2.5 per 100 components in UK firms.

The reasons for these differences were complex but three key factors contributing to world-class manufacturing in the Japanese organisations seemed to be:

- the organisation of the operations process is highly integrated so that parts travel the minimum distance and the production flow is free of interruptions
- team leaders play a vital role in involving employees, maintaining concern for quality and developing problem-solving skills
- the existence of tightly integrated value chains.

This in turn requires the organisation to develop:

- An emphasis on quality and TQM (see later).
- JIT methods of production and purchasing.
- Cross-functional teamwork.
- Flexible manufacturing.
- CAD and CAM.
- Integration of operations functions and systems with other functions.

Although these features may seem to be 'common sense' when listed in this way, implementing them in practice is far from easy. For instance:

- Cross-functional teamwork involves active project-based communication and problem solving. Inevitably this demands a change of organisational culture in order to overcome damaging inter-departmental rivalry, conflict and politics. Often the only way in this can be facilitated is by organisational restructuring and different specialists working together in the same physical location on common problems (the use of quality circles).
- Flexible manufacturing is only achieved where 'economies of scope' make it economical to produce small batches of a variety of products with the same machines. This represents a stark contrast to the inflexibility of traditional mass production assembly lines with their emphasis on 'economies of scale'.
- Integration of operations functions and systems with other functions means combining operations with functions such as design and marketing.

5.12.2 Quality: service organisations

The new approaches to operations management and quality discussed in this chapter have been most widely applied in manufacturing firms. However, modern advanced economies are now dominated by service organisations and many observers think future economic growth will depend heavily on this sector. The complicated task of running service industries is therefore taking on even more significance. It is becoming apparent to the managers of service organisations that to maintain their competitive advantage they need to embrace the new management philosophy and techniques. However, service industries have certain distinguishing features that may make it difficult to reduce costs and increase quality.

Exercise 5.6

List five distinguishing features of a service as opposed to a good.

Solution

- Services are intangible and it is typically more difficult to measure their quality than it is for a physical product.
- Services are consumed immediately and cannot be stored.
- Customers participate directly in the delivery process in contrast to a manufacturing organisation where production and purchase are usually physically separated.
- The customer when evaluating the quality of the service will take into account the face-to-face contact and the social skills of those providing the service.
- Service organisations tend to be labour intensive.

Despite these difficulties managers of service organisations are now having to come to terms with the requirement 'to do more and better with less' as they face more volatile and competitive markets with more informed and demanding customers. (This dilemma of the need to reduce costs while increasing quality has particular implications for managing human resources in service organisations.) When faced with the need to improve productivity and quality, managers of service organisations have a number of options open to them, including:

- Motivating employees to work harder and more skillfully.
- Automating aspects of the service provision (e.g. in banking the use of automatic teller machines).
- Being innovative and find new services and/or ways of delivery (e.g. telephone-based services).

Over the last 25 years, increasing numbers of service organisations have begun to realise that customer care programmes for their staff could give them competitive advantage. These programmes typically involve training large numbers of staff that come into contact with customers so they might interact with the customers in a more helpful and effective manner. The British Airway's 'Putting People First' programme initially concentrated on the cabin crew and airport terminal staff. Basic customer care skills were stressed, including the importance of always greeting embarking passengers with a smile. More recently the programme has been extended to include pilots and the way in which they handle announcements to passengers so as to establish rapport, and break bad news in an appropriate manner to keep passengers informed about factors such as delays. Many other organisations such as American Express, McDonalds, British Telecom and Barclays Bank have introduced their own customer care programmes for staff.

5.13 Quality: learning from Japanese models

Many managers now see 'quality' as the most important competitive issue for their organisation. Indeed, one could go so far as to suggest that the concept of quality almost destroys the notion of competition based principally on price, which has long held central place in economic models. As indicated earlier, the current interest in quality has its origins in the phenomenal success of Japanese businesses from the 1970s onwards. Strange as it now seems, Japanese products were once seen to be rather cheap and shoddy by consumers in the West. This perception has now fundamentally changed, with almost anything made in Japan having a reputation for quality, which European and American manufacturers find difficult to match.

The growth of international competition has also resulted in dramatic improvements in the quality and efficiency of products and services. Much of this improvement can be attributed to the efforts of Japanese manufacturing companies who developed systems of management that have contributed enormously to higher standards of quality and efficiency. Others have now copied many of these methods and large Western companies are increasingly keen to 'benchmark' themselves against the best in the world.

Glass (1991) concisely idealised the traditional Western and Japanese approaches to quality as summarised in Figure 5.4:

Increasingly traditional Western organisations are adopting Japanese practices in order to compete successfully. Koontz et al. (1986) however focus on two common Japanese practices that few Western organisations have attempted to replicate, namely, lifetime employment and consensus decision-making:

> *Lifetime employment.* Usually employees who work for large Japanese organisations will remain with them for all of their working life. This provides employees with security and a feeling of belonging. Promotion is through merit and seniority. The Japanese believe this approach increases loyalty and a closer identification with the organisation. This approach can add to the organisation's costs as employees are kept on the payroll even though there may be insufficient work.

Quality issues	The West	Japan
Concept of quality	Static	Continuous improvement
Focus of activity	Volume/ profit	Quality/customer satisfaction
Quality responsibility	Quality control department	Mainly workers
Quality training	For QC staff	For all workers
Solving quality problems	QC staff & engineering	Employees, supervisors and managers
Quality targets	Set by QC staff	Set by top managers
Role of QC experts	Inspection	Helping workers

Figure 5.4 Comparison of Western and Japanese approaches to quality
Source: Based on Glass (1991, p. 190)

Decision making. The Japanese believe that all levels of staff should be responsible for generating new ideas or suggesting improved working practices. By encouraging lower-level staff to contribute to the decision-making process it is believed that they will be better prepared for promotion. The supervisor's role is to tactfully question proposals, suggesting amendments or requesting additional information where necessary. Decision-making is by consensus, in which junior staff initiate ideas and then submit them to their supervisors, a process which continues until it reaches senior management. If the suggestion is approved, then it is returned to the originator for implementation. A lot of effort is used in defining the question or problem, and there is a great deal of communication before the decision is reached. Hence decision making can be slow.

The idea of lifetime employment used by large Japanese corporations was also for a time seen as contributing to competitive advantage because it produced a loyal and committed workforce. Mismanagement of the financial system in Japan and low growth in the last decade, however has left many Japanese corporations over-staffed hence lifetime employment is increasingly being seen as a burden rather than an advantage. It is estimated that one-third of the Japanese labour force is covered by this approach.

The difficulties of an unquestioning application of all things Japanese should be apparent. William Ouchi (1982) formulated the concept of Theory Z, which recognised the huge cultural shift required by American organisations (Theory A) to be more like Japanese organisations (Theory Z). In some cases theory Z pragmatically accepts that, for instance, responsibility should continue to be assigned on an individual basis (as with Theory A) rather than under Theory J (a collective approach). In other cases Theory Z requires some movement, best illustrated by approaches to decision making. Under Theory A (the US culture) the individual manager makes the decisions, whilst under Theory J (Japanese) the culture suggests group decision making. Theory Z calls for decisions to be carried with more participation and consensus.

The theory emphasised the following elements:

- interpersonal skills needed for group interaction, and making use of consensus decision-making but retaining individual responsibility.
- informal and democratic relationships built on trust whilst retaining hierarchical authority, rules and control.
- a participative management style, which facilitates the free flow of information, but retaining procedures for planning and setting objectives.

The differences between Theory Z and earlier approaches taken by management includes priority given to 'human' factors, and an erosion of management status in favour of a greater emphasis being placed on team spirit.

5.14   Thinking in quality management

Ironically, much of the success of Japanese businesses has been because of the application of techniques first developed in the West. In particular, W. Edward Deming and Joseph M. Juran spent a good deal of time in Japan in the 1950s and 1960s promoting their thinking, which were largely ignored elsewhere. Initially, many of these ideas were to do with the application of statistical techniques to problems of quality control, but they soon began to cover a much wider philosophy of quality management. Deming, Crosby, Juran and other renowned experts had been pleading the case for quality for decades. The uptake of this advice by the Japanese in the 1950s onwards only began to take root in the West thirty years later. The essence of the argument was indisputable: quality pays. Famously companies like Hewlett-Packard, Xerox, and Motorola, demonstrated that quality could translate into reduced costs that could be reinvested in IT for further improvement.

W Edward Deming

Deming was an experienced statistician who believed that management should concentrate on setting up and then continuously improve the systems in which people work. He emphasised the importance of managers working with other employees, because the best feedback is from those who actually do the jobs. Unlike the scientific management approach, which involves managers setting work standards and methods, Deming stressed the need to train workers in methods of statistical process control and work analysis. This enables the workers to identify what needs changing and how.

Joseph M Juran

Juran worked at the Hawthorne Electricity Plant in Chicago in the 1920s visiting Japan in the early 1950s and teaching based loosely on the Pareto principle, which he explained as the 'vital few and the trivial many'. Juran suggested that, typically (see 5.20.2 later), 85 per cent of quality problems at work are the result of the systems that employees work within and, therefore, there is little point in trying to solve them by seeking to increase worker motivation. His prescription was for managers, with their employees, to identify all the main quality problems, highlight the key ones which if solved will produce the most benefits, and set up projects to deal with them. Juran also believed that anyone affected by the product is considered a customer, so introducing the idea of internal as well as external customers.

Philip P Crosby

Crosby, an engineer, is best known for popularising the Zero Defects concept that originated at a company he once worked for. Eventually, Crosby became Director of Quality and Corporate Vice-President of the ITT Corporation. Crosby's mantra was 'Quality is Free', further that it is not an issue of degree; it is either present or not present. Management must measure quality by continually tracking the cost of doing things wrong: the price of non-conformance. Crosby suggested that conformance to requirements was key.

Crosby (1980) championed a quality improvement process, based on four criteria:

- Quality can be defined as conformance to customer specifications.
- A quality system should focus on prevention, not appraisal and detection.
- The quality standard must be set at zero defects to be considered 'total quality'.
- The measurement of quality is the price of non-conformance, that is the costs incurred from undertaking quality management measures.

This process should be used to ensure that the suppliers, customers and internal staff all understand the quality process.

Exercise 5.7

What suggestions can you give to a car manufacturer firm that wants to begin thinking about how to improve its quality management by moving towards a more Japanese approach?

Solution

The first step for an organisation wishing to move towards the Japanese concept of quality management is to clarify the meaning of 'quality' in its particular sphere of operations. It might be looked at in terms of 'fitness for purpose' from the viewpoint of the customers. The focus of quality is to satisfy customer expectations and anticipate their needs. Looked at from this angle, there can be no automatic assumption that a luxury car, such as a Rolls-Royce, is better than a mass-produced vehicle. The issue of respective quality has to be defined in terms of customer expectations of the product and its price. (It is clearly a mistake to build in features that are not required by customers and then expect them to pay for them).

5.15   Quality as a concept

Although definitions of quality vary (Table 5.6 below), the study of the concepts of marketing (Chapter 2) enhances understanding. It is commonplace to view quality from the perspective of the customer so that the customer's expectations and specific requests are fully met: the need to satisfy the customer's needs at all times is central to most interpretations of quality. Therefore, it is critical that organisations are able to identify these needs at the early stages of the product life cycle. If an organisation can identify the customer's requirements in terms of performance, price, design, features, delivery, safety and other customer activities, this will assist in gaining competitive advantage.

Much of the research into quality in the last half-century has arrived at broadly similar conclusions in terms of what is required, namely:

Table 5.6 Definitions of quality

'The totality of features and characteristics of a product or service that bears on its ability to meet a stated or
    implied need' (ISO 9000)
'Fitness for use' (Juran)
'Quality, meaning getting everyone to do what they have agreed to do and do it right the first time, is the
    skeletal structure of an organisation, finance is the nourishment, and relationships are the soul' (Crosby)

- *Commitment.* Commitment to a quality philosophy within an organisation will be affected by the overall senior management buy-in to quality. If senior management is not fully committed, it is unlikely that customer requirements of quality will be met.
- *Competence.* Quality can only be achieved by competence in the job or activity undertaken. Without competence it is difficult to create quality in a product/service. Competence can only be gained with continual training, development of skills and experience.
- *Communication.* The importance of quality must be communicated throughout all levels of the organisation. Poor communication will lead to lack of clear customer specifications, poor feedback and a lack of understanding. Communication improves the understanding of the purpose and benefits of quality, and ensures that the whole organisation (i.e. from strategic to operational levels) clearly understands the concept of quality and its importance to the organisation and to each individual.
- *Continuous improvement.* The Japanese term, *Kaizen*, signifies continuous improvement in all aspects of an organisation's performance at every level over a period (CIMA, 2005).

There are a number of approaches to ensuring quality and quality management, and these are reflected in the sections that follow.

5.16 Quality control systems

5.16.1 Basic control

The theory of basic control is of some relevance to management accountants because it forms the basis of many of the control mechanisms they will use in their day-to-day work. In addition it goes to the heart of quality control. It consists of analysing a simple input–process–output loop and using of feedback and feedforward controls; a cybernetic control model (Figure 5.5).

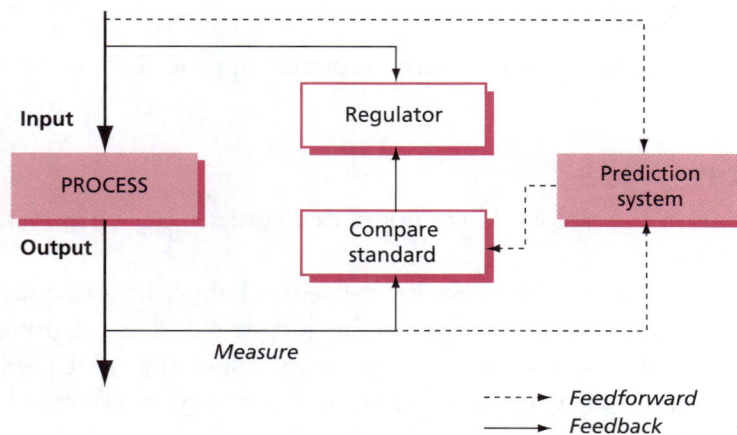

Figure 5.5 A basic cybernetic control model

OPERATIONS MANAGEMENT

Components of basic control systems

Standard	The targets set by the organisation	For example, the budgeted cost of labour
Sensor	The means by which information is collected and measured	For example, the payroll system
Feedback	The measurement of differences between planned outputs and actual outputs achieved, and the modification of subsequent action and/or plans to achieve future required results	*Negative feedback* indicates that a system is deviating from its planned course in a way that is detrimental to the organisation and action is required to move back towards the planned course. *Positive feedback* indicates that a system is deviating from the plan in a way that has a positive impact on the organisation and action may not be required or, if it is, it might be action to increase/encourage this move away from plan, e.g. higher than predicted sales.
Comparator	Means by which actual results are measured against planned	For example, the payroll costs for a particular period compared with budget to give a variance
Effector	Means by which corrective action is taken	For example, investigation of budget variance and instruction to reduce overtime

Definitions based on CIMA's Official Terminology (2005) are as follows:

Feedforward control is the 'forecasting of differences between actual and planned outcomes, and the implementation of action, before the event, to avoid such differences'.

A closed loop system is a control system that includes a provision for corrective action, taken on either a feedforward or a feedback basis. An example of this is the investigation of an aged debt analysis report that allows you to chase debtors (*feedback*) or to revise your credit control procedures (*feedforward*).

An open loop system is a control system that includes no provision for corrective action to be applied to the sequence of activities. An example of this might be where an aged debt analysis report is produced by the debtor system but there is no procedure for it to be investigated.

Double loop feedback (or secondary feedback) is control information that indicates both discrepancies between observed and expected results and the need for adjustments to the plan, for example increased labour costs due to skill shortages would mean that budget was exceeded but that the budget would need to be adjusted to reflect the new situation.

✋ Exercise 5.8

What are the limitations of a simple cybernetic system approach for control?

☑ Solution

- Complex systems in the real world are not closed systems, but open systems interacting with other systems.
- Interaction with other systems leads to unexpected and unpredictable outcomes and questions of probability and risk, giving rise to value judgements and risk preferences.
- The model assumes that control operates on inputs. Especially in the public sector, it can be the case that inputs are fixed and that control can only be effected by changing the process or the goals.

- The model assumes control from outside the system by an external authority, not the self-regulation of most organisations.
- The model ignores time. Measurement, comparison and action all take time. This is a static, not dynamic, model.

5.16.2 Quality control

Quality control is an approach to managing quality very closely allied to the cybernetic control model identified above. It involves (Table 5.7):

- establishing quality standards for a service or product
- designing a process to deliver the service or product to the required quality
- measuring the quality of the service or product
- comparing actual quality with planned quality
- taking remedial action where quality does not meet standard
- reviewing the standard originally set and adjust if necessary.

This is a specific example of a quality control mechanism. Such a mechanism would be used mainly in technical production processes and might be computerised. The mechanism consists of identifying an element of the production process that is critical to the quality of production, then establishing warning limits and tolerances to measure any unacceptable variances. The process is monitored closely to ensure that immediate action is taken to remedy any breach of the tolerance.

The quality control system can be organisation-wide and could include the design process, quality assurance of suppliers of raw materials, production, warehousing, distribution, or after-sales service, etc.

The process of planning and communicating a quality improvement programme based on quality control involves:

- obtaining the commitment of senior management and communicating this commitment to the organisation,
- reviewing the current quality of product/service and administrative processes and using this information as a base for improvement,

Table 5.7 Quality control: a worked example of a roadside breakdown service such as the RAC or AA

Action	Detail
Set standard	98% of breakdowns to be attended to within one hour of the call being received, 75% of breakdowns to be repaired at the roadside.
Organise resources	For example, breakdown vehicles, call centers, trained mechanics, to deliver the service (of the standard) from work records and customer surveys
	The results with the standard;
Measure achievement	
Compare	
Take remedial action	For example, if the target of 98% attended within 1 hour standard is not met it may be necessary to increase the numbers of vehicles and drivers; or if the target of 75% of repairs effected at the roadside is not met it may be necessary to retrain mechanics or improve their equipment.
Review	If the standards are easily met consider revising standards to improve service further.

- communicating the importance of quality and how well it is currently achieved throughout the organisation, using face-to-face communication where possible (e.g. open forum, team briefings),
- setting targets for improvement and identifying methods of achieving the targets in consultation with the people who undertake and manage the activities,
- implementing improvement strategies,
- monitoring achievements of targets, investigating 'missed' targets, identifying lessons to be learned, and disseminating results regularly to all relevant parties.

5.16.3   Quality assurance

Quality assurance (QA) systems are in certain ways superior to quality control systems in that they attempt to *create* quality rather than *control* it. According to Campbell (1997) QA must account for:

- design of products and services
- materials of a consistently appropriate standard
- suppliers who are reliable and consistent in the supply of materials
- plant and machinery that is reliable
- staff that benefit from training development so reducing the potential for human error
- operations procedures and the way in which they are planned, managed and carried out.

The movement from traditional inspection approaches to quality to the setting of quality standards and the encouragement of quality assurance through the use of techniques such as statistical process control might be viewed as a development. Full implementation of a quality management approach usually involves following the path of TQM.

5.17   Quality accreditation

The preceeding sections have considered an organisation's own interpretation of quality. This section deals specifically with external quality standards. The achievement of standards under the BS 5750 or ISO 9000 series relates to responsibilities, procedures and processes required to implement quality management within the organisation, rather than the product itself. Registration under the standards requires the submission and approval of documentation, including a quality manual, procedures manuals and work instructions.

5.17.1   ISO 9000:2000 series

The ISO 9000:2000 series quality award is a form of a quality system standard which *'requires complying organisations to operate in accordance with a structure of written policies and procedures that are designed to ensure consistent delivery of a product or service to meet customer requirements'* (CIMA, 2005). The forerunner of this series of quality standards was the British Standards Institution (BSI) BS 5750 series of quality standards, devised in the 1970s and used extensively throughout the 1980s. This British series of standards was adopted as a full international series in 1987 and revised in 1994.

Table 5.8 Benefits of ISO 9000:2000 implementation

Recognised standard of quality.
Excellent marketing tool.
Better quality will improve customer satisfaction, leading to more sales, competitiveness and profitability.
Customers are less likely to conduct an independent quality audit on the supplier, thus saving costs and time.
Increasingly useful in export markets.

The current series, the ISO 9000:2000 series of quality management and assurance standards has reduced the documentation requirements that were felt to be onerous. It has moved away from a procedurally based approach (stating how organisations control their activities) to a process-based approach (which is more about what organisations do).

To qualify for accreditation an organisation defines for itself a standard for quality and the processes needed to achieve it. It relies heavily on measurement and analysis to monitor the achievement of quality, including customer satisfaction, and to ensure continual improvement of systems. There is an initial external inspection before accreditation is awarded and then regular reappraisal visits. The key feature of the ISO 9000:2000 series is the underlying assurance that customer satisfaction and fulfillment of customer requirements are achieved. Basically, the series of quality standards are designed to:

- provide a clear system of quality management which includes establishing processes, their interactions, the resources required and how to manage and improve the processes
- gain total company involvement and commitment
- obtain a nationally accepted standard of quality
- ensure commitment to quality and customer requirements of quality.

Benefits of implementing ISO 9000:2000 are listed in Table 5.8.

The ISO 9000:2000 requirements can be complementary to a TQM approach (described later), requiring organisations to provide evidence of a comprehensive approach to the quality of processes and documentation of quality standards and performance.

5.17.2 ISO 14001 environmental management systems

The accreditation of ISO 14001 is closely allied to the ISO 9000:2000 series. It specifies a process for controlling and improving a company's environmental performance. It covers:

- environmental policy
- planning
- implementation and operation
- checking and corrective action
- management review.

Environmental management systems focus on the environmental practices in organisations, including:

- use and source of raw materials
- use of energy

- waste
- emissions to air, water and soil
- noise
- aesthetic impact
- use of hazardous substances.

The organisation identifies elements of its business that impact on the environment, sets objectives for improvement and implements a management programme to achieve them. This programme is regularly reviewed for continual improvement.

Exercise 5.9

What are the main benefits of this accreditation?

Solution

Benefits of this accreditation are:

- enhancement of environmental awareness within the organisation
- cost savings and reduction in use of resources
- improved compliance with legislation
- potential competitive advantage over companies without accreditation
- demonstration of environmental commitment to stakeholders.

5.17.3 Criticisms of quality accreditation

To ensure quality throughout the value chain, some organisations insist that their suppliers produce and deliver using a certified quality system.

There are, however, inevitably critics of these types of quality standards, both in management and academic circles. The managers of some small and medium-sized organisations are unhappy at being required to develop what they see as expensive and bureaucratic procedures that are not consistent with their organisation's culture and ways of working. Other critics claim that registration under the standards does not guarantee quality products and services, and that this kind of approach might even make it more difficult to obtain the levels of employee support and involvement required for a Japanese approach to quality management.

5.18 Quality: self-assessment

Self-assessment models for business improvement have become widespread. One of the most common is the European Quality Foundation model. This provides a structured methodology for organisations to measure their own performance in areas that are critical to businesses. It gives a basis for measurement of:

- Enablers, that is, leadership, policy and strategy, people, partnerships and resources, processes.
- Results, that is, customer results, people results, society results, key performance results.

This structure potentially helps drive subjectivity out of the self-assessment. The process of self-assessment focuses attention on quality. The scoring system allows the organisation to monitor its progress in business excellence over time. There are inevitably drawbacks including the 'cost' of time and the need to assessment and implement training. The process is still to a large extent subjective and the reviewers could manipulate the scoring system, intentionally or unintentionally.

Table 5.9 explains one organisations approach

5.19 Total Quality Management

Exercise 5.10

Make a list of some of the quality problems that could be encountered in your own organisation.

Solution

It is likely that you have come up with a number of your own examples. The following list may give you a few more examples (this list is not intended to be exhaustive):

- Billing errors.
- Down-time due to equipment/computer failure.
- Stock shortages.
- Incorrect stock delivered.
- Faulty data entry and calculation.
- Scrap and rework.
- Returned goods.
- Late management reports.
- Contract errors.

Table 5.9 Example of using self assessment models: Thames Valley probation board

The European Foundation for Quality Management (EFQM) Excellence Model® or European Excellence Model is the model chosen by the Government for the public sector.

The model allows strengths and areas for improvement to be identified through self-assessment and thereby contributes significantly to the business planning cycle at a national, regional and local level.

It is a non-prescriptive framework based on nine criteria. The assessment looks at an entire organisation. The nine criteria are divided into Results Criteria (what the organisation achieves) and Enabler Criteria (how results are achieved).

Thames Valley, in common with the National Probation Directorate and the other 41 local areas, undertook its first self-assessment under the model in the summer of 2001 and published the results in the autumn.

Aided by a consultant from TQMI (sponsored by the British Quality Foundation), a cross-grade group of staff gathered evidence throughout the organisation over a period of several weeks. This culminated in a consensus workshop in which the validity and weight of each piece of evidence was analysed. This in turn led to a self-assessment score, and a report to Senior Managers and the Board.

The report contributed significantly to the Area's Business Plan . . . . and also heavily influenced a restructure of the Area's management arrangements and priorities.'

(*Source:* www.thamesvalleyprobation.gov.uk/about/about_eem.html)

Continuous improvement is a philosophy to continually improve the quality of goods/services of an organisation. Kaizen involves the continual analysis of organisational processes to ensure continued improvement in performance and quality. TQM builds on the kaizen concept and can be defined as an all encompassing organisational philosophy that encourages and fosters continuous improvement throughout the whole organisation. The fundamental features of TQM are as follows:

- prevention of errors/defects such as those you have listed in the last exercise before they occur
- importance of total quality in design of products/services and systems.

By breaking TQM down into its constituent elements, the meaning and methodology behind the philosophy can be better understood:

Total	Everyone linked to the organisation (staff, customers and suppliers) is involved in the process. The concept of viewing every business activity as a process that can be improved is shared.
Quality	The requirements of customers are achieved.
Management	Senior managers must be fully committed to continuous improvement if all other parties are to help achieve it.

Importantly, TQM focuses on quality from both an internal and external customer perspective, using a systematic, integrated, organisation-wide approach. TQM encourages the full involvement of all people, at all levels, working within multidisciplinary teams to suggest and implement improvements from within the business. Then the principles of TQM can be implemented throughout the organisation.

There are several approaches to developing a TQM philosophy, however some common features of most approaches include:

- Those departments not directly involved in satisfying the needs of external customers must serve the needs of their internal customers – that is, the departments which use their services within the organisation.
- Open, honest communication is to be encouraged throughout the organisation.
- An investment in employee training and education to equip them with the skills required for TQM and to enable them to realise their potential.
- An emphasis on teamwork and collaboration (some initiatives make use of 'quality circles', in which the employees involved in a process meet at regular intervals to discuss problems and implement improvements).
- Involvement of customers and suppliers as an integral part of the improvement process.

TQM initiatives may be undertaken alongside other Japanese-inspired quality management techniques, including:

- just-in-time production, where goods are produced only when they are needed, eliminating large stocks of materials and parts;
- factory reorganisation to improve work flow and cellular production as part of programmes of continuous improvement (*kaizen*).

The successful implementation of TQM is a long-term process and problems are almost inevitable at some points because of the radical nature of the changes. In some ways managing the introduction of TQM is like any major organisational change, but common reasons for failure in TQM programmes include:

- *Tail-off.* After an initial burst of enthusiasm, top management fails to maintain interest and support.
- *Deflection.* Other initiatives or problems deflect attention from TQM.
- *Lack of buy-in.* Management pays only lip service to the principle of worker involvement and open communication.
- *Rejection.* TQM is not compatible with the organisation's wider culture and ways of doing things, for instance, the systems emphasis does not change from punishing mistakes to encouragement and rewards.

5.19.1   Costs of quality management

Four types of quality cost (Table 5.10) considered in TQM are prevention, appraisal, internal failure and external failure costs.

- *Prevention* costs of activities undertaken to prevent defects occurring in the design and development phase of a product or service.
- *Appraisal* costs incurred while conducting quality tests and inspections in order to determine whether products or services conform to quality requirements.
- *Internal failure* costs associated with the detection and rectification of items that do not conform to quality requirements, but have not yet been passed to the customer.
- *External failure* costs associated with the rectification of items that do not conform to quality requirements and have been passed to the customer.

For any organisation wishing to establish a reputation for quality products these are costs well worth incurring.

5.19.2   Implementing TQM

As TQM focuses on the specific needs of the customer in a competitive marketplace, it follows that in order for organisations to survive they must understand their market, competitors and customers. TQM implementation requires thorough planning and a clear implementation strategy if it is to succeed.

Table 5.10   Examples of quality costs

Prevention costs	Design reviews, drawing and design checks. Supplier evaluation, supplier quality, seminar, specifications review. Operational training, Quality orientation and training. Quality audits, Preventative maintenance
Appraisal costs	Inspection and testing costs. Supplier monitoring. Inspection and testing of receipts. Product acceptance testing. Process control acceptance. Packaging quality inspection. Quality department costs and administration
Internal failure costs	Cost of scrap and material lost. Redesign and rework. Engineering-change orders. Corrective work. Losses due to lower selling prices for substandard goods
External failure costs	Redesign and rework of returned goods. Engineering-change orders. Customer confidence and bad publicity. Poor decisions due to poor information passed to managers. Service and warranty claims. Product liability and damages

OPERATIONS MANAGEMENT

Total quality management should involve embedding shared beliefs and standards permanently. It should not be considered a one-off, quick-fix exercise, as implementation requires thorough planning and a clear implementation strategy if it is to succeed. The decision to implement a TQM progamme is a long-term commitment for an organisation and early TQM pioneers expected it to take up to 20 years before the full benefits were realised. Current thinking suggests that the quest for quality may never be finished but it is still a worthwhile journey. Table 5.11 illustrates a number of useful prerequisites for TQM to be implemented.

One of the first stages of a quality implementation programme is education and training. In order for staff to understand the processes and benefits of a TQM approach, it is important to consult and communicate organisational objectives of introducing TQM. This may involve the following phases:

- *Senior management consultancy.* Senior managers must first be trained at the strategic level, in order to be able to lead and drive the quality programme.
- *Establishment of a quality steering committee/council.* Team members should be drawn from all levels of the organisation, and all disciplines. The quality team/council must also be trained in the TQM philosophy so that they can participate in the training programme as it is cascaded through the organisation.
- *Carry out organisation-wide presentations/training sessions.* This will be general training in the quality philosophy and its long-term benefits, followed by more specific quality-training sessions on an ongoing basis, covering issues such as BPR procedures and benefits; Quality standards and their importance, and Quality Circles membership benefits and activities, etc. Sessions will be led by consultants and members of the quality council. It is critical that clear communication of the quality message is carried out at an early stage and is then reinforced on a regular basis. As already stated, poor communication will lead to lack of understanding of the purpose and benefits, mistrust and poor feedback.

Table 5.11 Prerequisites for TQM

Prerequisite	Feature
Leadership	Senior management commitment
Methodology	Zero-tolerance philosophy
Objective	100 per cent customer satisfaction and competitive advantage
Performance measurement	Quality costs: prevention, appraisal, internal and external failure
	Customer retention and market share
Scope	Total organisation and external stakeholders (suppliers and customers)
Nature	Continuous improvement
Skills	Continuous training
Communication	Quality circles
	Management reporting

- *Establish quality circles.* The next stage of implementation is to get key personnel actively involved in the process. This will involve establishing a number of quality circles and training in problem-solving and quality-related data collection.
- *Documentation.* It is important that the processes, procedures and activities undertaken throughout the implementation of a quality programme is thoroughly and clearly documented and evidenced. This will help to ensure continuity as the programme develops, and it is an important aspect of quality auditing. It is also a further aspect in aiding communication of the quality procedures and successes.
- *Monitor and report back.* Feedback is a crucial aspect of the implementation process. Quality targets need to be set and actual results monitored against these targets and standards on a regular basis. The successes (and failures) of the approach must be reported.

5.19.3 An integrated approach to the management of quality

Lynch (1999) reflecting on organisational difficulties in getting quality initiatives successfully implemented observes that:

Quality is a symptom, an expression of healthy management in an organisation, a reflection of personal responsibility taken by staff. If staff think too much about their delivery of quality, they may ignore the customer – consequently it is not important to 'think quality'. Staff need to 'think customer' and as a result 'be quality'.

Lynch's argument is that generally organisations exist to provide a consistency of goods or services to their customers or clients. Achieving consistency means setting customer expectations at an achievable level, and comprises delivery at the right time, meeting expectations of the customer and differentiating the organisation from competitors.

As already highlighted, TQM focuses on the specific needs of the customer in an increasingly competitive marketplace. For organisations to survive, they must understand their market, competitors and customers, and the drive towards excellence is an important factor. To achieve excellence, organisations must continually achieve high levels of product and service quality. The importance of top-management commitment and leadership cannot be stressed enough in this drive for quality implementation.

In order to fully understand TQM and excellence one can conceive of the organisation as a system. It becomes important how all of the elements of the system work together towards one common goal. Ho's (1999) TQMEX model demonstrated in Figure 5.6 provides an integrated approach of contemporary quality issues to the process of continuous improvement and the management of quality. The TQMEX model is also useful as it indicates the relationship between quality management and other aspects of operations management.

It should be apparent from the above that a firm's functional areas should effectively link together in order to achieve a quality philosophy throughout the organisation.

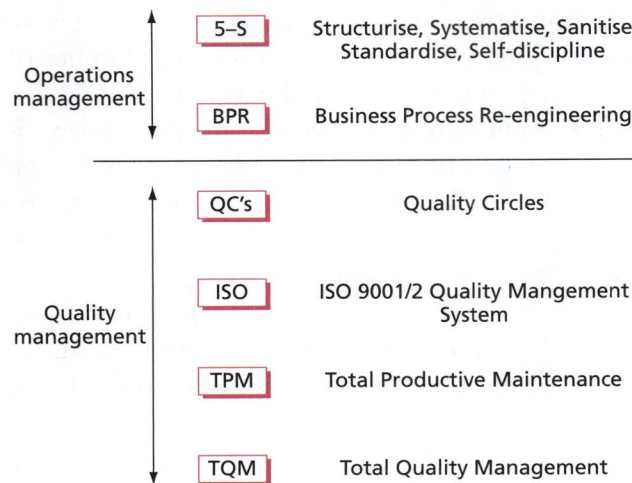

Operations management	5–S	Structurise, Systematise, Sanitise Standardise, Self-discipline
	BPR	Business Process Re-engineering
Quality management	QC's	Quality Circles
	ISO	ISO 9001/2 Quality Mangement System
	TPM	Total Productive Maintenance
	TQM	Total Quality Management

Figure 5.6 The TQMEX model
(*Source:* Ho, 1999, pp. 69–75)

5.20 The tools of quality management

There are many contemporary approaches to the management of quality practices, some of which have already been referred to in passing. It is important to apply these tools and concepts of quality management appropriately in order for an organisation to succeed in its quest for continuous improvement. Some of the main tools are described here including Quality circles, Kaizen, 5S, and 6 Sigma.

5.20.1 Quality circles (QCs)

Prof. Kaoru Ishikawa, pioneered quality management processes in the Kawasaki shipyards following the Second World War. One concept he introduced was that of the Quality circle (QC). QCs are small groups of staff, who meet on a regular basis to identify quality issues and attempt to formulate solutions. QCs are normally multidisciplinary, and are given a brief to work as a team to identify, investigate, analyse and solve work-related problems or tasks. The basic concept is that QCs form part of an organisation-wide quality control activity.

QCs can help the quality process in a number of ways:

- by using interdisciplinary quality teams it helps staff to gain a better perspective of the whole organisation and their part within it
- by strengthening linkages between functional areas
- by devolving authority and responsibility for quality down to the operational level
- by fostering commitment and ownership of problems.

5.20.2 Kaizen

Kaizen involves continuous improvement by small incremental steps over a long period. This Japanese concept emphasises providing the workforce with the tools and techniques for improving operations.

Maurer (2005) stresses Kaizen's impact in setting and achieving higher standards, and the value of Kaizen events in:

- bringing people together to face up to technical and quality challenges
- encouraging stakeholder involvement and interaction
- allowing participants to leave with a plan in hand.

Some of the tools most commonly used include:

- *PDCA*. A cycle that encourages the key stages to continuous improvement, namely plan-do-check-act (PDCA).
- *The fishbone diagram* (again attributed to Ishikawa). This cause and effect diagram is used to analyse all contributory causes (or inputs) that result in a single effect (or output). For example, lost sales because of temporarily stock outs would frustrate quality. The cause, however, might be difficult to pin down and may not be due to a single reason. A map in the form of a fishbone illustrates all the difficulties and so focuses effort. A line is drawn indicating a route to continuous improvement and off this line 'fish bones' will splinter indicating problems that may be encountered. Causes can be arranged into categories (typically systems, technology, people and resources).
- *The Pareto rule*. Italian economist Vilfredo Pareto identified that 80 per cent of the country's wealth was held by 20 per cent of the population. Similar 80/20 classifications occurred regularly in most other areas (e.g. composition of debtors, value of invoices, etc.). The 'rule' encourages a focus of effort on the important 20 per cent in order to be effective.
- *The five why process*. First developed at Toyota; it encourages employees to examine questions by constantly asking 'why' until the real issue is identified.

5.20.3   5-S practice

5-S practice is a technique used to improve both the physical and the thinking environment of the organisation. It encourages standardisation of procedures, and is devised to improve the clarity of management processes. 5-S is based upon five Japanese terms 'seiri, seiton, seiso, seiktsu and shitsuke' or 'organisation, neatness, cleanliness, standardised cleanup and discipline' (interpreted below):

S-word	Meaning	Example
Structurise	Organise	Delete old information, throw away unwanted items
Systematise	Neatness	Clear organisation of documents and filing system
Sanitise	Cleanliness	Individual responsibility for own tidiness and cleaning
Standardise	Standardise	Transparency of storage and filing systems
Self-discipline	Discipline	Do the above daily

5.20.4   Six Sigma

Six Sigma reduces variation in a business by taking customer-focused, data driven decisions. Six Sigma is a methodology interpreted by many organisations as a measure of quality that strives for near perfection. It is a data driven approach for eliminating defects (aiming towards six standard deviations between the mean and the nearest specification limit) in any process. To achieve Six Sigma, a process must not produce more than 3.4 defects (i.e. anything outside of customer specifications) per million opportunities.

The British Quality Foundation (BQF) (2005) observe that 'Successful programmes require tenacity and dedication to the pursuit of perfection'.

Exercise 5.11

What does an organisation need to adopt the Six Sigma philosophy?

- the tools
- the methodology
- training
- metrics
- total commitment from executive level
- significant culture change.

(source: The British Quality Foundation)

5.21 Methods of performance measurement and improvement

Organisations do not remain static; they live and work in an ever-changing environment with rapid technological, competitive and market changes, and increasing demands for (amongst other things) new products, higher quality, improved service and lower costs. An organisation might identify that continuous improvement in itself is insufficient to meet these challenges and that other performance improvement measures are required. Two alternative methods to improving quality and levering change in performance are detailed in this section.

5.21.1 Benchmarking

Benchmarking is the process of systematic comparison of a service, practice or process against one or more similar activities. The process involves the establishment of targets through data gathering and comparison. It is a process of continuous improvement in the levels of service delivery or performance. From benchmarking exercises good or best practice can be identified and detailed analysis allows an understanding of how this has been achieved and then replicated. CIMA (2005) identify four main types of benchmarking that an organisation might engage in:

- *Internal.* The activity is compared with the best that is found elsewhere (usually in the same organisation, for instance unit A against unit B).
- *Competitive or competitor.* The activity is compared with that found elsewhere in the industry, probably a company's direct competitors.
- *Functional.* (*Variously known also as Best practice, generic or operational*) The activity is compared with the practices of an organisation known to excel in that functional area (not necessarily in that industry).
- *Strategic.* Competitive benchmarking with the deliberate intent of bringing about organisational change.
  A number of benefits are associated with benchmarking, including the following:
- It concentrates on organisational performance and value-adding processes. It can potentially increase customer satisfaction, reduce waste, improve quality, reduce

overheads through business simplification and transmit best practice between divisions.

- It improves management's understanding of the value-adding processes of their business. It also allows for a realistic assessment of strengths and weaknesses.
- It can assist in overcoming complacency and driving organisational change. In part this is because it helps shape an organisational culture of mutual betterment and a striving for 'best in class'.
- It provides advance warning of deteriorating performance.
- The organisation engages in learning best practice and also from others' successes and mistakes.
- It can help in identifying and comparing elements of competitors' strategies.

To allow the process of change to be managed efficiently, benchmarking must follow a systematic and planned approach. It is necessary to first understand the current procedures and practices, to obtain information about potentially achievable levels of performance and then to develop an action plan that facilitates the achievement to the desired, improved level of performance. A benchmarking exercise will involve several stages, for example:

- Decide and define what is to be benchmarked.
- Identify suitable and willing benchmarking partners.
- Agree and collect relevant information.
- Analyse and evaluate information.
- Identify best practice and unpack processes and procedures that achieve this.
- Develop action plan for implementation.
- Pilot this in a suitable site within the organisation.
- Evaluate the pilot and refine the model.
- Roll out for full implementation.
- Conduct post-implementation review.

Since benchmarking requires a great deal of co-operation and sharing of sensitive and confidential information, the exercise is frequently carried out through the medium of benchmarking clubs or a benchmarking forum.

Exercise 5.12

What are the drawbacks to benchmarking?

Solution

- Benchmarking generates more systems and paperwork and can be expensive to maintain.
- If comparisons are unfavourable the information could be a source of demotivation and inefficiency in itself.
- Benchmarking can shift the managers' gaze from getting the job done to 'hitting the indicators'. For instance, 'delivery' times could be improved possibly at the expense of accuracy, which would be counterproductive. An unhealthy focus on increasing the efficiency of existing business could be at the expense of innovation and new lines, etc.
- A danger that confidentiality of data will be threatened. Further, a successful benchmarking firm may be swamped with requests for information from non-rival companies, leading to a drain on resources.

5.21.2   Business Process Re-engineering (BPR)

'Business Process Re-engineering' is the popular term for reconfiguring organisational processes and structures to bring about radical process changes in a short time. Business process re-engineering (BPR) is a customer-focused approach that challenges managers and staff to fundamentally rethink the way they do things in order to maximise business effectiveness. It has been described as:

'. . . the fundamental rethinking and radical redesign of business processes to achieve dramatic improvements in critical, contemporary measures of performance, such as cost, quality, service and speed'

(Hammer and Champy, 2001)

and

'. . . areas of business activity in which repeatable and repeated sets of activities are undertaken, and the development of improvement understanding of how they operate and of the scope for radical redesign with a view to creating and delivering better customer value'

(CIMA, 2005)

As the improvement of an organisation's business processes is an integral part of a quality approach, BPR might be used as part of a TQM philosophy. Hammer and Champy identify four themes of BPR:

- Process reorientation, a focus on jobs, tasks, constraints, resources, etc.
- Creative use of IT. (The impetus for doing this might be the introduction of new information technologies.)
- Ambition.
- Rule breaking.

BPR demands five phases: planning, internal learning, external learning, redesign and implentation.

Although hailed as the biggest innovation of the 1990s its effectiveness in bringing about lasting improvement has been questioned more recently. BPR has also been stigmatised because it has been seen as a device to down size organisations and shed jobs.

✋ Exercise 5.13

Compare and contrast benchmarking and BPR.

☑ Solution

Both benchmarking with BPR:

- can bring about radical change
- can utilise IT to bring about improvement
- strive for superior performance
- are involved in learning and improved efficiency.

Whereas benchmarking focuses on other providers, BPR focuses on customers.
Whereas benchmarking concentrates on key measures, BPR looks at entire processes.
Whereas benchmarking is a continuing process, BPR might be a one-off exercise.

5.22   Innovation, IT and IS

Management gurus increasingly regard the role of innovation as the future basis for competitive advantage. Innovation is the introduction of new and improved ways of doing things at work. Innovation involves deliberate attempts to bring about increases in productivity and improvements in the design and quality of products benefits through change. Innovations may include technological changes such as new products, but may also include new production processes, the introduction of advanced manufacturing technology or the introduction of new computer support services within an organisation.

Innovation does not imply completely new solutions. Change can be deemed an innovation if it is new for the person, group or organisation which is introducing it. If an intranet system is introduced into an organisation it can be considered to be an innovation even though others already use it. The intranet could, for instance, be effectively harnessed in meeting customer support needs for that company for the first time.

Innovations vary in their impact and significance, from those that are relatively minor to those that are of great significance. The development of the Internet is obviously of great significance, while the improvement of a bottle opener is of relatively little importance in the order of things. It is also the case that some innovations are produced quickly while others take time. For example it may take only a few months to reorganise the production line in a company but take many years for the same organisation to change its corporate culture to one that places quality at the centre.

Chapter 1 dealt in some detail with the potential offered by information systems across all functional areas and this is particularly so in the area of operations management. Complete organisational restructuring might accompany changes to take full advantage of technology. Examples include:

- Computer aided design (CAD) and computer aided (or automated) manufacturing (CAM) is an integrated solution whereby product design and control of machinery is computer assisted. This allows flexibility and the elimination of waste so contributing to constant improvement. An integrated approach combining both can lead to the use of robots and computerised inventory management.
- The problems of economic machine loading and provision of customer and stockists' requirements is one of the most complex in modern factory management. Today most large companies handle this complicated data processing activity with the help of computers;
- Other examples of IT usage include measures in support of BPR in order to improve inventory management, Electronic data interchange (EDI) to integrate manufacturing with suppliers, and tracking data as part of a benchmarking exercise.

5.23   Quality auditing

It is important that quality implementation is monitored and audited on a regular basis, to continually assess and improve the process. This can apply to a full-blown TQM programme as well as a less comprehensive quality system. A quality audit should be a systematic inspection to appraise whether quality activities achieve the planned objectives, and whether the activities have been carried out effectively. A quality audit can be carried out in a number of ways:

- *Internally.* As the name suggests, an organisation will use its own internal staff, possibly from a specific quality department, to undertake a regular review of quality systems to ensure that quality management is being carried out correctly.
- *Externally.* This is where a certified agency undertakes an external analysis of quality procedures. If the organisation is ISO registered, they will be regularly audited by an externally registered agency, which will carry out a compliance audit to ensure that quality procedures and systems are operating effectively, with a view to renewal of the ISO certification.
- *Supplier.* Organisations may carry out a quality audit on their own suppliers, or may find themselves being audited by their customers, to ensure compliance with the company's (or customer's) quality standards.

5.24 Performance measurement and improvement

Performance measurement of operations straightforwardly involves measuring the inputs and outputs to an operation. Traditionally, financial performance has been a concern, and management accounting is a significant contributor in enabling organisations to perform better in this respect. These of course tend to be historical by nature and include techniques such as activity based costing. Other means of performance measurement include:

- Economy, efficiency and effectiveness. Often this task is conducted by an organisation's audit function as a Value For Money (VFM) audit. The emphasis is placed on calculating and evaluating value for money for activities and systems. In the public sector, the VFM audit offers a useful method of checking for economy, efficiency and effectiveness in the absence of profit measures. The general principles of value for money are also being increasingly applied to profit-seeking organisations, especially in areas where evaluation using accounting information is limited. In this way the operations or quality of an organisation can be measured. The basic approach involves identifying and measuring key aspects of performance: money expended; inputs purchased, outputs achieved. The relationship between money expended and inputs purchased can give a measure of economy. Inputs compared with outputs gives a measure of efficiency and outcomes compared with outputs identifies effectiveness.
- The balanced scorecard, a strategic approach to performance measurement incorporating four areas: financial (such as profitability), customer satisfaction, internal and business efficiency, and innovation and organisational learning. It is evident that the scope of the performance measured includes both financial and non-financial dimensions. CIMA (2005) stress the need for effective management information 'which addresses all relevant areas of performance in an objective and unbiased fashion'.
- Various continuous improvement measures (e.g. benchmarking, PDCA, Five-why, etc.)

Brown et al. (2001) contend that 'enlightened' organisations wishing to measure performance use systems that are:

Table 5.12 Traditional and enlightened (world class) performance measurement systems compared

Dimension	Traditional	Enlightened
Purpose	External reporting	Information for improvement
Emphasis	Financial	Continuous improvement
Cycle times	Long	Short
Production	Batch	Continuous
Volume	High	Just right
Inventory	Buffers	No buffers
Waste	Scrap and rework	No waste
Design	Engineering	Customer value
Employee	Deskilling	Improvement
Environment	Stable	Rapid change

Source: Brown et al. (2001)

- Relevant
- Integrated
- Balanced
- Strategic
- Improvement-orientated
- Dynamic.

In so doing they contrast traditional and enlightened (world class) performance measures. (Table 5.12.)

5.25 Summary

This chapter has described the nature and significance of operations and demonstrated how it supports other aspects of the organisation, both manufacturing and service. It has then considered certain key dimensions of operations and its strategic importance. The influence of Japanese thinking on Western organisations to bring about fundamental changes has been explored and concepts of quality and the accompanying changes required to organisational approaches and systems have also been dealt with. Throughout contemporary thinking and the role of IT have been themes.

Many of the 'new' approaches identified here and the requirement of organisations to become world class or quality orientated often require fundamental changes to be brought about. The way in which change is managed is the subject of the following chapter.

References and further reading

Brown, S., Blackmon, K., Cousins, P. and Maylor, H. (2001) *Operations Management. Policy, Practice and Performance Improvement*, Butterworth-Heinemann.

Campbell, D. J. (1997) *Organizations and the Business Environment*, Butterworth-Heinemann.

CIMA (2005) *CIMA Official Terminology* CIMA publishing, Elsevier.

Coote, P. and Gould, S. (2006) Lean management, *Financial Management*, March, p. 31(3).

Cousins, P. D. (2000) An investigation into supply base restructuring, *European Journal Purchasing Supply Management*, Vol. 5, No. 2, 143–155.

Crosby, P. B. (1979) *Quality is Free: The Art of Quality Certain*. New York: McGraw-Hill.

Galloway, L. (1998) *Principles of Operations Management* (2nd edn), Thompson.

Gargan, J. (2004) Hello, good buys, *Financial Management*, November.

Glass, N. M. (1991) *Pro-active Management*, New York: Continuum International Publishing.

Hammer, M. and Champy, J. (2001) *Reengineering the Corporation: a Manifesto for Business Revolution* (3rd edn), London: Nicholas Brearley.

Ho, S. K. (1999) *Operations and Quality Management*, London: International Thomson Business.

Koontz, H., O'Donnell, C. and Weihrich, H. (1986) *Essentials of Management* (4th edn), New York: McGraw-Hill.

Lynch, D. (1999) Focus on quality, *Management Accounting*, September.

Maurer, R. (2005) Stop me before I Kaizen again, *Journal for Quality & Participation*, Summer, Vol. 28 No. 2, p. 37–37

Mintzberg, H. (1990) *The Structuring of Organisations: A Synthesis of the Research*, Englewood Cliffs, NJ: Prentice Hall International.

Mintzberg, H. (1983) *Structures in Fives: Designing Effective Organizations*, Englewood Cliffs, NJ: Prentice Hall International.

Ody, P. (2000) Working towards a total, visible network, *Financial Times Survey*, October 25, Times Newspapers Limited, London.

Ouchi, W. (1982) *Theory Z: How American Businesses can meet the Japanese Challenge*, Reading, MA: Addison-Wesley Pub Co.

Porter, M. E. (1985) *Competitive Advantage: Creating and Sustaining Superior Performance*, London; New York: Free Press: Collier Macmillan.

Reck, R. F. and Long, B.G. (1988) Purchasing: a competitive weapon, *International Journal Purchasing Materials Manual*, Fall, 2–8.

Rudzki, R. A (2006) World-class supply practices boost shareholder value: a focus on both direct and indirect spending, including smaller items, can have a powerful effect on corporate performance. Top companies involve their procurement group and other internal functions, plus suppliers, to boost competitive advantage (procurement). *Financial Executive* 22.3, April 2006, 56(3)

Womack, J. P., Jones, D. T. and Roos, D. (1990) *The Machine that Changed the World*, New York: Simon & Schuster.

Also

www.thamesvalleyprobation.gov.uk/about/about_eem.html

www.quality-foundation.co.uk/pi_sixsigmaservice.htm (The British Quality Foundation)

Revision Questions

5

? Question 1

P Ltd is a private company, manufacturing and marketing adhesives and other chemical products to industrial customers in a wide range of industries. It employs about 120 workers on a three-shift basis in its factory, using continuous 24-hour process production methods. The cost structure of its finished products is as follows:

Raw materials	78%
Labour	6%
Production overheads	5%
Marketing and administration	6%
Profit	5%

Return on capital employed is satisfactory.

P Ltd's main current problems are minimising wastage of material, financing sufficient material stocks to give good delivery dates, meeting competition from an increasing number of manufacturing subsidiaries of major customers, and realising export potential.

However, the problem that is giving the managing director most anxiety is that to maintain the company's excellent growth record capital expenditure is needed on a scale beyond its means.

One of the company's major suppliers has decided to diversify downstream into the same product range as P Ltd. They have indicated that one option for achieving this objective is to take over P Ltd. The managing director feels that selling out to the supplier would ensure the capital required for growth. He wishes to persuade the directors in charge of production, marketing, and purchasing, that this strategy is good for the company.

Requirement

Explain, for each of these functions, two ways in which they would benefit from being part of a larger organisation, and indicate what dangers there might be that such benefits are not achieved.

(20 marks)

? Question 2

Mintzberg proposed a framework by for any organisation consisting of several parts.

Requirements

(a) Describe the five parts of the framework proposed by Mintzberg
for any organisation. **(5 marks)**
(b) Draw a diagram showing how this framework applies to a product
structure. **(11 marks)**
(Total marks 16)

? Question 3

The divisional managing director of the organisation that you work for has proposed a total quality management (TQM) programme to help change prevailing attitudes and improve results. You have been asked to prepare a report for the next management board meeting as a basis for constructive discussion as to how the TQM programme should be implemented.

Requirements

(a) Explain the critical success factors for the implementation of a programme
of total quality management. **(7 marks)**
(b) Explain the categorisation of quality costs and how such a categorisation
could be of assistance in the establishment of a TQM programme. **(6 marks)**
(Total marks 13)

? Question 4

ABC plc owns 154 stores selling food and drink. Each store is located in a major town, with the stores being spread across a large geographical area in four different countries. A range of 3,500 different products are sold, with prices and layout of each store being determined by the local store manager.

The MD of ABC has recently received a report from the management accountant indicating that the profitability between the stores varies significantly. In an initial attempt to determine why this is happening, the MD has asked you, a newly appointed assistant management accountant, to explain the methods of benchmarking that can be used within ABC.

Requirement

Write a memo to the MD explaining the methods of benchmarking available to ABC plc, providing two specific examples of benchmarking activities that can take place for each of the methods identified. **(Total marks 15)**

? Question 5

5.1 Quality management thinker J. M. Juran once suggested that 85% of the organisation's quality problems are

(A) a result of ineffective control by supervisors and managers.
(B) a result of ineffective systems.

(C) a result of ineffective workers.

(D) a result of ineffective incentive bonus schemes.   **(2 marks)**

5.2 The five S (5-S) practice is a technique aimed at

(A) effective investment of resources in training and recruitment.

(B) standardised procedures to improve the physical and thinking organisational environments.

(C) excellence in strategy, style, skills, staff and structure.

(D) diversity of activity and independence of thought in order to achieve closeness to the customer.   **(2 marks)**

Each of the sub-questions below require a brief written response. This response can be in note form and should not exceed 50 words. Each of these sub-questions are worth 4 marks each.

5.3 Explain the relationship between a JIT system and cash flow management.

(4 marks)

5.4 Explain how computer software can assist in achieving quality in a manufacturing organisation   **(4 marks)**

5.5 Distinguish quality control from quality circles.   **(4 marks)**

Solutions to
Revision Questions

5

✓ Solution 1

The major problems facing the company may be divided into those of the short term and those of the longer term.

In the short term, the key problem is that of controlling raw material costs as these represent almost four-fifths of the company costs and financing sufficient material stocks to achieve delivery dates in the face of fierce competition.

Longer term, the problem is that of maintaining the company's growth record. Assuming the managing director is correct and that a takeover by the major supplier will provide funds for capital growth, then there are certain advantages for the production, marketing and purchasing functions which the managing director can stress in selling the idea to his fellow directors.

P Ltd's production can benefit by use of the funds to upgrade the plant and machinery by introducing the latest computer-controlled technology. The most important concern in this upgrading will be that of improving the utilisation of raw materials, so that wastage can be minimised and yet the quality of the product maintained or improved. A reduction of production costs may also be possible via increased productivity arising either from a speeded-up production process and/or a reduction of labour or combination of measures. Any cost reductions will be helpful to the marketing managers as they seek to win orders from the competition via a strategy of price reductions.

Purchasing can be improved in a number of ways, but the most important benefit of the take-over is that raw material supplies can now be almost guaranteed at cost. This new arrangement also has advantages for the development of Just-in-Time systems which the input of funds could be used to develop with all the advantages which stem from such systems, such as the reduction in the cost of maintaining large inventory stocks.

Marketing, (see Chapter 2) as already noted, can gain a strategic advantage over its competitors as a result of lower costs gained in the other functional areas. In addition, however, the funds maybe used for the employment of additional sales representatives to undertake selling to even more of the wide range of industrial customers to which the company targets its products.

In order that the opportunity of increased funding is not wasted, it is essential that directors take the precaution of reviewing all aspects of the business and that the management functions of organising, directing, coordinating and controlling are carried out with the utmost efficiency. More specifically, it will be necessary to ensure that the additional financial resources are made the best use of by carefully appraising all capital projects. Control of waste will also be critical given the weighting of raw material costs in the overall production process. There will also be the need to ensure that adequate training is provided to sales personnel to help them cope with the wider range of products they will be required to deal with in the larger company. In respect of purchasing, the subsidiary will have to be careful that it does not become the dumping ground for unwanted stock by the group.

✓ Solution 2

(a) The Strategic Apex is the board of directors – executive and non-executive – who decide on the financial structure of R plc and its strategic direction. Typically, it consists of directors who are nominees from major shareholders, appointees from other companies and experts in various fields, plus directors representing operating functions.

The Support Structure consists of staff departments, such as accounting and personnel, planning and marketing, administration, etc., which provide support and back-up for the main core activities. Using the ideas of 'bureaucracy' and 'scientific management', the more they are specialized, the more they can acquire specific knowledge and skills that can also be used to the organisation's advantage.

The Technostructure is similar to Support, but dedicated to the technical side of product and process development and it is, therefore, more directly involved in attaining sustainable competitive advantage. Typically, it consists of the R&D function, which produces and modifies products on the basis of marketing information and, as an ongoing effort, to find new ways of doing things. Internally, the engineering and maintenance departments are those parts of the structure whose main role is to maintain efficient production and, simultaneously, continually improve quality and reduce costs, both of which affect R plc's 'bottom line'. There is a tension, sometimes, between the allocation of departments to these different roles – in some high-tech industries, marketing and sales could be thought of as part of the technostructure, radier than support.

The Operating Core's function is to purchase (though purchasing departments are sometimes located in the support or the technostructure) materials and process them for distribution. As such, it forms a value chain and one could also include the sales force as it may not be simply a support function (sales people taking orders), but more as a management function, for example, the sale people negotiating the sale of aircraft engines or petroleum products. The Midline is the management linkages that form a continuous hierarchy from the apex down to the operating core and is responsible for putting plans into action and co-ordinating efforts across departments.

(b) Divisionalised by product

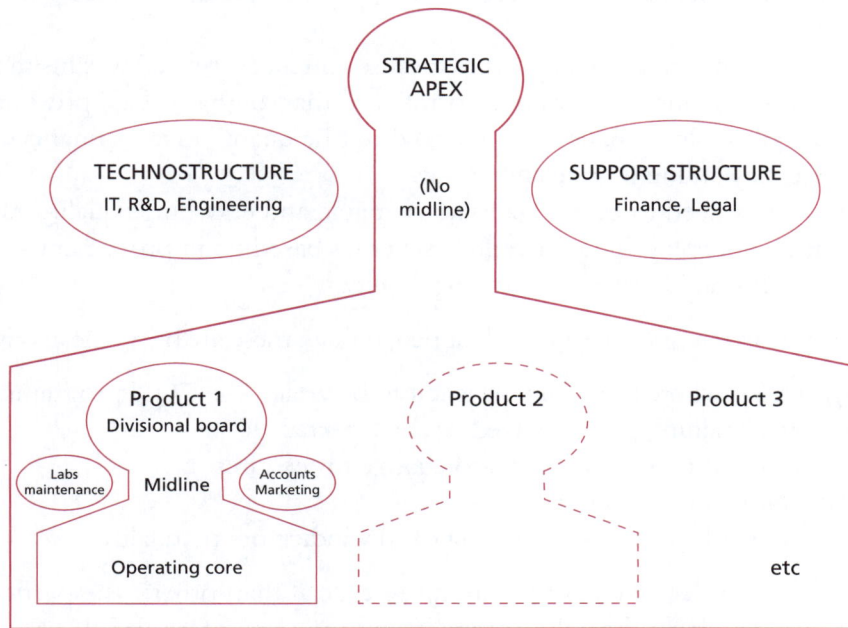

✓ Solution 3

(a) Total quality management (TQM) is defined by CIMA (Official Terminology, 2000):

> An integrated and comprehensive system of planning and controlling all business functions so that products or services are produced which meet or exceed customer expectations. TQM is a philosophy of business behaviour, embracing principles such as employee involvement, continuous improvement at all levels and customer focus, as well as being a collection of related techniques aimed at improving quality such as full documentation of activities, clear goalsetting and performance measurement from the customer perspective.

The key factors in the success of TQM:

- There is a concentration on continuous improvement. This means that small improvements are as important as large leaps in technology. Such improvements may be changes in production flow, product specification or manufacturing methods.
- There needs to be widespread commitment to improvement in quality. All those involved in the company are part of the TQM environment: from board to shop floor.
- TQM should focus on the customer, not on just a single area of a business. This customer focus means the perspective of the company changes from its present obvious production/sales/research one. Within the company, all sections may see themselves as potential customers of other sections and potential suppliers to other sections. This refocusing is vital in this company.
- TQM is about designing quality into the product and the production process. This means there must be a close working relationship between sales, production, distribution and research.
- Concentration on short-term profit needs to be abandoned in favour of long-term quality improvement, which will itself lead to long-term profit improvement. This implies being prepared to invest in changes for the future.

- There is a need for a fundamental culture change. Management, in particular, needs to use feedback and appraisal to find better ways of doing things. Failure to meet targets is probably inevitable, but needs to be met with positive, rather than negative, comment.
- There needs to be a clear willingness to discuss and measure quality. This may involve setting standards and gathering information that perhaps has previously been ignored. Feedback information, which need not be quantitative or financial, must be fed back quickly and in an intelligible way.
- Reward systems need to be reorganised to enable and encourage quality, rather than to prevent it happening. Thus, incentive schemes based on improvement suggestions would be a very rapid way of improving quality.

Other factors that might have been identified, though these are by no means always vital:

- Training in areas where the company is felt to be weak. The TQM programme should identify these. Training possibly needs to be external.
- The establishment of project teams to change procedures.
- The establishment of quality circles.
- The establishment of regular reporting of key indicators of quality.

It is difficult to select factors that are more crucial than others: the particular ones of importance will depend on the company and the areas of shortfall. The most crucial overall area, especially in the company quoted, appears to be the building up of teamwork.

(b) Quality cost is normally defined as the 'cost of ensuring and assuring quality, as well as the loss incurred when quality is not achieved' and may be measured in four ways. These four methods have often been called the 'cost of not achieving quality':

- Prevention cost: The cost of ensuring that poor quality does not happen, e.g. training, planning and administration, checking design is adequate, etc.
- Appraisal cost: The cost of discovering poor-quality items. This would include quality control, inspections, etc.
- Internal failure cost: The cost, internal to the company, caused by poor quality. Costs include rework costs, scrap, re-engineering, retooling, etc.
- External failure cost: The cost of poor quality incurred outside the company: this includes direct costs, such as warranties, repair and after-sales service, and indirect costs such as lost customer goodwill.

These costs are very difficult to isolate and judge. In each area, there is often a need to apportion costs (e.g. training, planning and administration) and there are many areas, especially the external failure cost, where costs cannot be calculated, for example, the opportunity cost of lost sales as a result of poor-quality service.

Nevertheless, striving towards measuring quality costs keeps this issue on the management's agenda. The presence of multiple measures of quality can be helpful in presenting a balanced approach to control and the identification of the key areas for an individual organisation.

Some writers regard the cost of quality as zero, because if TQM is achieved, then none of the costs above will be incurred and so cost is actually reduced. Others see the above costs of quality as being avoidable non-value-adding and therefore costs that might be reduced. This latter view is central to the understanding of how the cost of quality can assist TQM: discovering the cost of wasted resources we have been using to meet current customer standards. It is these costs that need to be reduced and doing so is central to a programme of cost reduction.

✓ Solution 4

Memo

To: MD of ABC plc
From: Assistant management accountant
Subject: Benchmarking activities

There are three main types of benchmarking:

1. Internal benchmarking assumes there are differences in the work processes of an organisation as a result of geographical differences, local organisational history, customs, differences among business units, and relationships among managers and employees. The different locations can then be compared and the best practices or activities identified. They can then be transferred to other locations and performance improvements obtained.

   As ABC plc has stores in many different locations, the processes in each store can be compared to determine whether or not there are any locations that are more efficient or have lower costs than another.

   Sales of different products can be compared and the product mix determined. Although sales of specific items may be affected by the geographical location, trends may be identified. The relationship between store layout and sales performance may be able to be identified and guidance on layout then given to all managers.

2. Competitive benchmarking, where a company such as ABC plc identifies specific information about a competitor's products, processes, and business results, and then makes comparisons with those of its own organisation.

   ABC plc needs a similar company to compare itself with. This maybe difficult to achieve as most companies tend to keep details of profits and processes relatively secret. Staff visiting similar stores and noting prices or accessing competitor's websites and obtaining the information on-line could obtain Price comparisons.

   ABC plc could investigate whether any other stores would be willing to participate in a joint benchmarking scheme.

3. Activity benchmarking involves the identification of state-of-the-art products, services, or processes of an organisation that may or may not be a direct competitor. The objective is to identify best practices in any type of organisation that has established a reputation for excellence in specific business activities.

   Regarding the actual processes, comparisons with a different type of organisation may yield some useful information.

   If we know that detail is needed on a specific area, such as providing quality training, then an orgnisation known for providing good training for its staff can be approached to obtain ideas and comparisons. Some form of joint agreement may have to be signed.

   As an alternative, consultants could be employed to provide a report on best practice and this could be used as a benchmark within ABC plc.

✓ Solution 5

5.1 (B)

5.2 (B)

5.3 JIT system:

- purchase and production of goods only when needed
- aim to eliminate unnecessary stock of material/parts.

As less money is tied up in stock, organisational cash flow should improve.

5.4 Software such as computer-aided design (CAD) and computer-aided manufacturing (CAM):

- Provide flexibility to meet customer requirements more fully
- Eliminate mistakes
- Reduce material wastage.

These advances work towards world class manufacturing performance.

5.5

Quality control	Quality circles
Traditionally western approach to production	Associated with Japanese production
Involves inspection of work by 3rd party	Involves collaborative effort
Rejects defective work that is sampled	Allows idea sharing, problem solving & ongoing quality improvement

6

Change
Management

Change Management

6

This chapter deals with change management, a subject that represents a 10% syllabus weighting. Students should note there are many links to earlier chapters and aspects of the syllabus. This is unsurprising: change is an aspect of management that critically affects all functions of an organisation. You are encouraged to identify these linkages when studying this topic.

LEARNING OUTCOMES

By completing this chapter, including the readings and questions you should be assisted to:

▶ Explain the process of organisational development

▶ Discuss how and why resistance to change develops within organisations

▶ Evaluate various means of introducing change

▶ Evaluate change processes within an organisation.

6.1 Introduction

One quotation often attributed to Albert Einstein of 'there is only one constant in this universe, and that constant is . . . change' establishes the background against which this chapter is set. Certainly we live in a fast changing world and organisational survival is dependant upon the anticipation and management of change.

Accepting that there is an inevitability of change it seems somewhat futile to bemoan what is a fact of life. Change must therefore be recognised as normal, be planned for and form part of the normal processes of management. Sometimes decisions can be made from 'on high' and passed 'down' for others to implement. This can be a mistake as it implies all knowledge falls in the domain of the senior hierarchy. If we are not careful, change management becomes synonymous with project management. This amounts to a 'task then achieve' approach performed as quickly as possible so we can get on with our 'real' work and get back to 'normal'. Real change management provides an organisation with an enduring legacy: much needed competitive advantage. It is a philosophy that permeates an organisational culture; a way of thinking and acting that is endemic and wholly shared.

It is perhaps helpful to reflect on the scale of change. During the 1990s in the UK the Institute of Managers claimed that 70 per cent of their members experienced restructuring every 2 years. More recent research suggests that the pace of organisational change has become even swifter with over 60 per cent of organisations change significantly every year. The focus of this change has been cost reduction; culture change, redundancy de-layering, site closures, temporary or contract staff, redundancies or out sourcing, etc. (Worrall and Campbell, 2000).

It follows that a manager's own ability to manage change has an intrinsic bearing on an organisation's success in achieving its objectives. An ability to accept change as normal and to manage it is a key requirement for all organisations and managers.

Most studies of change management concentrate on the resistance to change, while rather fewer detail the ongoing changes enacted by employees in a continuous fashion (incremental change). Within this literature it is also easy to lose sight of a further dimension to change: positive change. There is a common misperception that change is always resisted, out of motives of protection, fear, uncertainty, etc. (If an organisation were to offer, as IKEA did in October 1999, a distribution of all of its profits on one day to its entire staff in equal amounts surely expect much resistance would not be expected!)

Another aspect of change is its source. Top-down change tends not to be incremental whereas bottom-up change does, and these sources and modes of change affect the possible outcomes. Ideas and theories dealt with earlier in this text are helpful in this context. For instance, McGregor's Theory Y people are innovative maybe even initiators of change (change agents). Under Maslow's hierarchy of need employees get promoted within the organisational hierarchy changing their needs along with cognitive perceptions and emotional feelings over time. People's own agendas for change, including pride, were the basis of the Japanese revolution in quality in manufacturing, and for quality circles and kaizen: the process of ongoing improvement. (These examples illustrate the breadth of thinking that can be applied to the subject of change.)

The questions arising from the challenge of competition and the difference between symptoms, causes and core problems include:

- what to change
- what to change to
- how to change
- how to avoid failure in the change process, (Goldratt, 1992)

This chapter attempts to explore some of these questions but first considers in more detail the 'triggers' to organisational change both externally and internally.

6.2 External change triggers

Change is often necessary because of external developments. It is clear that there are a number of external factors that organisations must come to terms with. These include the implications of a global market place, a wider recognition of environmental issues, health awareness and demographic change (Paton and McCalman 2000). Ultimately these factors become triggers for change.

When considering these external triggers a distinction is drawn between the general (indirect-action) environment and the task (direct-action) environment of organisations;

changes in both sectors need to be monitored and responded to. The 'far' or 'general' environment of an organisation can usually be categorised under a 'PESTLE' framework:

- Political implications of a new government.
- Economic changes such as exchange rates, level of macro-economic activity and global competition.
- Social or demographic changes such as levels of education and changing values/expectations
- Technological changes such as inventions and developments, in both products and processes.
- Legal implications of likely government policies.
- Environment implications of legislation, agreements of widely held values

(See Table 2.4 for more detail.)

Clearly these factors are usually beyond the influence of a single organisation. The organisation however would do well to anticipate and respond to these developments as they translate directly as either a threat that must be overcome or an opportunity to be grasped.

The 'near' or 'task' environment covers all stakeholders who can influence, and be influenced by, the organisation's direct actions. This study system has introduced you to the thinking of economist Michael Porter, a further framework devised by him is helpful in this context, and contains five dimensions:

- *Buyer power*. Single or few customers have more power over the organisation.
- *Supplier power*. Single or few single suppliers have more power over the organisation.
- *Threat of substitutes*. Could the product provided be threatened by buyers choosing to satisfy their need or want by turning to alternative substitute products? (For example, if the postal service is seen as expensive, inefficient or inconvenient the use of e-mail might be seen as a substitute means of conveying messages in writing.)
- *Barriers to entering your market*. If the difficulties and costs are high it is unlikely that new competitors will confront your organisation.
- *The degree of inter-firm rivalry*. How competitive is this rivalry? Does it lead to price wars and the need for expensive advertising?

Changes may be initiated by the organisation in order to influence this 'near' environment or at least respond to it.

✋ Exercise 6.1

Identify one example of a way in which an organisation might influence each of the five factors in this near environment.

✔ Solution

- *Buyer power*. Develop new markets for a product and try to extend the customer base.
- *Supplier power*. Seek out new sources of raw material or 'buy out' your supplier to ensure continuity of supply and price stability.
- *Threat of substitutes*. Develop customer awareness of the benefits of the product not achieved through substitute products. (Based on the postal service example cited earlier an advertising campaign with the strap line 'there is nothing like receiving a real letter', or 'a real letter means you really care', etc.)

- *Barriers to entering your market.* Try to gain economies of scale in production that will mean that cost savings can be passed on to customers. New entrants will not be unlikely as a consequence to compete on cost.
- *The degree of inter-firm rivalry.* Try to get agreement with your major competitors as to the level of advertising both engage in. The more spent on advertising within the industry the greater the drain on total profits, etc.

6.3 Internal change triggers

Internal triggers for change in a rational organisation may be the continuing search for efficiency. Alternatively they might arise as a result of:

- Ratio monitoring as a result of external benchmarking exercises
- Tensions that exist especially at senior levels within the organisation
- Where employee – management conflict is rife.

Within the organisation, the systems approach emphasises the importance of the inter-relationships between the key internal subsystems, namely:

- tasks
- technology
- people
- structure
- management.

It follows that change in response to internal triggers might adjust these subsystems.

Inevitably different thinkers conceptualise change approaches in differently. Ridgeway and Wallace (1996) for instance distinguishes hard and soft issues:

- Hard issues focus on changes to strategy, structures, systems, productivity, performance, etc. The emphasis is more on technical change.
- Soft issues approaches to change by comparison focus on culture, leadership style, behaviour, competencies, attitudes, and motivation. The emphasis here is more people orientated and time scales less definite. Organisational development (OD) is often classified in this way.

6.3.1 Organisational development (OD)

It is difficult to provide a concise explanation of OD as it covers a wide range of activities into the social processes of an organisation. Such approaches are described as 'interventionist' and are focused at developing individuals and groups (Mullins, 2005). Some of the main objectives of OD include:

- Increasing the level of trust among organisational members;
- Allowing problems to be confronted and solved by the people involved rather than being ignored;
- Enhancing openness of communication between and within groups;
- Increasing the level of individual and group responsibility for problem solving and improvement.

Mullins (2005) describes the aim of OD as improved organisational performance, with the major topics associated with organisational development and the management of change being:

- Organisational culture
- Organisational climate
- Employee commitment
- Organisational conflict
- Management Development.

Some of the most well-known and widespread uses of the approach arose in the US aerospace industry. During the space programme many specialists from a wide variety of backgrounds had to work together. Frequently these people found it difficult to collaborate efficiently and OD consultants developed techniques such as T-groups (therapy groups) and confrontation meetings to deal with problems. Essentially, these meetings involved small unstructured groups within which participants are encouraged to explore their own feelings and relationships with others: successful groups will then move on to determine more effective ways of working together.

A key feature of OD is usually the involvement of an independent 'third party' as facilitator for the change. He or she will act as a catalyst by acting as a change agent, helping members of the organisation to diagnose the underlying problems, resolve conflicts, and implement effective change. As part of the initial diagnosis, this third party will often carry out some initial survey of existing attitudes, which will be fed back to all parties involved in the change process.

The types of skills and qualities such an OD consultant would require include the following:

- Sympathy with the underlying OD approach values, which stress openness in communication and interpersonal relations.
- Extensive knowledge of behavioural science theories and practices.
- Data collection and analysis skills.
- The ability to guide and facilitate small groups in general, and particular types of groups such as T-groups and confrontation meetings.
- Team development skills to assist in building effective teams to implement changes.

6.3.2   The change agent

Potentially a change agent could be brought in as an external party (e.g. by appointing from outside a senior member of staff or employing a consultant) or a current member of staff (an internal change agent). Although the change agent is key to the change process, precise roles can vary enormously. Senior and Fleming (2006) identified their usefulness as helping the organisation:

- Define the problem.
- Examine what causes the problem and diagnose how this can be overcome.
- To arrive at alternative solutions.
- Implementation solutions.
- Transmit the learning process that allows the organisation to deal with change on an ongoing basis by itself in the future.

Certain skills and attributes are demanded of a change agent, and Buchanan and Boddy best captured these in their text *The Expertise of the Change Agent: Public Performance and Backstage Activity* (a text presently sadly out of print). These key competences were identified as:

Goals

- Sensitivity to changes in key personnel, top management perceptions and market conditions, and to the way in which these impact the goals of the project in hand.
- Clarity in specifying goals, in defining the achievable.
- Flexibility in responding to changes outside the control of the project manager, perhaps requiring major shifts in project goals and management style, and risk taking.

Roles

- Team building activities to bring together key stakeholders and establish effective working groups, and clearly to define and delegate respective responsibilities.
- Networking skills in establishing and maintaining appropriate contacts within and outside the organisation.
- Tolerance of ambiguity, to be able to function comfortably, patiently and effectively in an uncertain environment.

Communication

- Communication skills to transmit effectively to colleagues and subordinates the need for changes in project goals and in individual tasks and responsibilities.
- Interpersonal skills, across the range, including selection, listening, collection appropriate information, identifying the concerns of others and managing meetings.
- Personal enthusiasm in expressing plans and ideas.
- Stimulating motivation and commitment in others involved.

Negotiation

- Selling plans and ideas to others by creating a desirable and challenging vision of the future.
- Negotiating with key players for resources, or for changes in procedures, and to resolve conflict.

Managing Up

- Political awareness, in identifying potential coalitions, and in balancing conflicting goals and perceptions.
- Influencing skills, to gain commitment to project plans and ideas from potential sceptics and resisters.
- Helicopter perspective, to stand back from the immediate project and take a broader view of priorities.

✋ Exercise 6.2

Based on your own experience of change think about a change agent you have encountered. Do he or she display (or fail to display) these qualities and what were the consequences?

6.4 Parameters for successful change

According to Richard Daft (1998) there are several key parameters that need to be observed if change is to be successful:

Ideas and the need for change. Ideas are generally not seriously considered unless there is a perceived need for change. A perceived need for change occurs when managers see a gap between actual performance and desired performance in the organisation. This can be difficult where the internal culture is strong or where interests are best served by internal stability.

Adoption. Adoption occurs when decision-makers choose to go ahead with a proposed idea. Key managers and employees need to be in agreement to support the change. For a major organisational change, such as an acquisition, the decision might require the signing of a legal document by the board of directors. For a small change, adoption might occur with informal approval by a middle manager.

Resources. Change does not happen on its own, it requires resources not least time in designing, planning and then implementing and reinforcing change. Most innovations go beyond ordinary budget allocations and require special funding. Other changes are very often described as self-funding either directly after implementation (e.g. a staff reduction programme) or after a period of years (such as a change of location of head office to a more rural location).

Implementation. Implementation occurs when an organisation begins to make plans to use a new idea, technique, or system. This can often be done through existing systems such as the capital spending approval system or the departmental or divisional budgeting process. Materials and equipment have to be acquired, and workers may have to be trained to use the idea. Alternatively task teams of interdisciplinary experts are assembled to define the project and drive it forward. Many writers argue for idea champions or change agents. This of course can militate against involvement and participation.

6.5 Types of change

The nature of change can be categorised in various ways. It might for instance be seen as either 'incremental', 'step' or 'transformational'. Alternatively, it could be categorised as either planned or emergent. All these aspects are discussed in this section.

6.5.1 Planned or emergent change

One common categorisation used in describing the nature of change is planned or emergent.

- *Planned.* Organisational change is seen as a process of moving from one fixed state to another through a series of pre-planned steps. As such this approach is entirely consistent with a number of theories and ideas including Daft's key parameters (above). Plans are constructed on the assumption that organisations operate in stable and/or predictable environments (which may not be the case nowadays). The emphasis is upon preplanned, rational and systematic, centrally driven, change. Contemporary criticisms centre on issues of employee commitment and the rigidity of the approach.

- *Emergent.* The popularity of alternative viewpoints including the emergent view arose as the planned approach was challenged as inappropriate given a background of often chaotic environments. The emergent approach is based on a more recent view whereby change is seen as continuous, possibly unpredictable and a process of constant adjustment to the environment. Emergent change approaches coincided with flatter organisational structures, demands for increased participation and an open systems approach. Emergent change emphasises a bottom up approach where managers need to facilitate rather than make the change, making sure employees are receptive to changes and suitably skilled. Emergent approaches assume that organisations operate in unstable and/or unpredictable environments over which they exercise very little control. Change is therefore open ended and on going, and approaches emphasise employee flexibility, cultural adjustment or development, and structural adaptation. Clearly emergent change relies on genuine consultation, good communication, and high levels of co-operation. It also implies a loss of managerial power and more trust in the individual worker which culturally not all organisations might find acceptable.

6.5.2   Incremental change

Incremental change has often comprised changes in response to trends in the environment such as sales growth or more commonly technological improvements. Usually incremental change attempts to match organisational performance with the external environment, and gap analysis feeds back to corrective action. Where the need for change is ignored, organisational decline generally follows.

   IBM perceived a strong need for structural change after the company incurred operating losses for two consecutive years. This was not successful and IBM used several Chief Executive Officers as it struggled to align itself against the new environment of PCs and local area networks, instead of mainframe computers that it had specialised in.

   Although not radical, even 'incremental' change may have its problems. Daft (1998) described several features of this kind of change:

- Continuous progression rather than a 'frame breaking burst'.
- Maintains equilibrium rather than reaching a new equilibrium.
- Affects only one organisational part rather than transforming an entire organisation.
- Effected through the normal structure rather than creating a new structure.
- Involves improved technology rather than breakthrough technology.
- Involves product improvement rather than a new product creating new markets.

6.5.3   Step change

'Step change' involves a situation where the trend line for a particular factor stops becoming smooth and there is a significant and unexpected jump in direction upwards or downwards. The September 11 2001 tragedy in the USA had a longer-term negative influence on world trade, with dented business confidence and prominent sectors such as airlines took many years to adjust. Another contemporary example, this time the natural disaster of the Asian tsunami is still having destabilising effects long after occurring.

There have been other significant step-changes such as political coups and environmental disasters that have changed the environment within which organisations must work in forever. As step change is impossible or at least difficult to spot in advance, strategic planning has moved from trend analysis towards scenario planning.

Johnson, Scholes and Whittingham (2005) describe scenarios as 'detailed and plausible views of how the business environment of an organisation might develop in the future based on groupings of key environmental influences and drivers of change about which there is a high level of uncertainty'. Far from predicting the unpredictable the process offers various logically consistent futures that an organisation might face so that they might not be totally unprepared in the future.

6.5.4 Transformational change

Johnson, Scholes and Whittingham (2005) described a further change type: transformational change. Here radical change is involved and the organisation acts in a way that is currently outside of its existing paradigm (way of thinking). Clearly this involves a huge cultural shift for this change to be successfully brought about.

6.6 Responses to change

6.6.1 Attitudes to change

If change is inevitable then resistance can be predicted. Key questions arise as to how and why resistance to change develops within organisations. Torrington and Weightman (1994) helpfully distinguish four broad types of change experience:

- imposition, initiated by someone else normally from 'on high' or externally
- adaptation, changes in attitude or behaviour at the behest of others
- growth, responses to opportunities normally with favourable consequences, and
- creativity, where individuals are the instigator and are in control.

It follows that imposition meets with resistance, adaptation meets with uncertainty, growth meets with delight and creativity meets with excitement. Management therefore needs skills in:

- Overcoming resistance, or trying alternative change methods.
- Winning over the uncertain.
- Encouraging favourable responses from colleagues and subordinates that will engender an air of expectation and excitement.

There is a spectrum of possible reactions to the objectives of a change programme:

- Enthusiastic co-operation and support, acceptance, or co-operation under pressure from management.
- Passive resignation – indifference, apathy, loss of interest, minimal contribution.
- Passive resistance – regressive behaviour, non-learning behaviour.
- Active resistance – protests, working to rule, minimal work, slowing down, personal withdrawal, committing errors intentionally, sabotage.

Most problems of implementation relate to a failure in identifying and anticipating conflicts between the 'old' and 'new' and subsequent resistance. In particular problems centre on:

- Clashes between traditional hierarchies and structures and the demand for flexibility and change.
- Difficulty in obtaining reliable information in order to monitor and control resistance to change by staff and managers.
- The linkage of reward systems to past achievements rather than current and future performance.

Virtually all attempts to introduce organisational change will encounter some resistance, which, in some cases, may be severe. Resistance is not surprising, since change can be threatening, and if a person's role in the organisation is challenged, defensive reactions are to be expected. The main reasons for resistance can be summarised as including:

- Incomplete understanding of the nature of the change and/or the reasons for it
- Individuals believing the results of the change threaten their own personal interests and ambitions
- Differing assessments of the costs and benefits of the change to the organisation
- Lack of trust in those initiating the change and their motives.

These reasons for resistance can be understood more fully by considering change at the level of the individual, then of the small group within the organisation. Some individuals have a low tolerance for personal change and are, therefore, particularly likely to resist. In part, this low tolerance may be a function of personality. Alternatively, in many cases it is a reflection of the individual's past experiences and socialisation within the organisation, particularly in the case of long-serving employees or managers. It must be remembered that resistance will often be a reflection of genuine and direct conflicts of interest, which are highlighted by the many 'downsizing' decisions being taken by large organisations involving job losses or moves from fulltime to part-time employment status.

Resistance by members of work groups or informal groups, as opposed to isolated individuals, is likely to pose even more problems for the management of change. Group resistance may be generated by the fact that the proposed changes violate important group norms, or indeed the continued existence of the group. A further possibility is that rivalries and conflicts between groups generate resistance to changes because they are perceived to challenge the existing balance of power.

6.6.2 Overcoming resistance to change

The reasons for resistance may simply be due to a lack of understanding, and the solution lies in better communication. However, if there are deeper reasons for resistance, a more complex approach will be required. Managers need to adopt a flexible approach to managing change that recognises the key contingent factors in each situation.

There are numerous sources of resistance, including cultural or belief barriers, group solidarity, rejection of outsiders, conformity to past norms, conflict, the distribution of authority, structural divisions, technology, managerial philosophy and managerial style. Resistance can be frustrating for managers, but moderate resistance to change can be good for an organisation as it provides a barrier to frivolous changes or 'change for the sake of change'.

A frequent cause of resistance is the way the proposed change is introduced. Managers need to recognise the different forms of resistance:

- Ignorance – 'I don't have enough data to decide.'
- Delayed judgement – 'I will wait and see how it goes before I decide.'
- Defensive stances – 'Other solutions are better, I don't think this will work.'
- Deprivation – 'It cannot be allowed to proceed. It will be far too costly for the firm.'
- Anxiety – 'I know I won't be able to operate the new system.'
- Alienation – 'This will mean separating me from my people and my division.'
- Experienced rejection – 'Here we go again. We tried this once before and it failed.'
- Loss of power – 'It means giving up control over budgets.'
- Default – 'I am just not interested in computers.'
- Erroneous logic – 'It didn't work in Kansas, so it won't work in Kandy.'

The list of 'political' games people can play in resisting change is endless. Undermining, circulating malicious rumours, ridiculing the change agent, questioning the motives of managers, and blaming the initiators for any small organisational shortcomings are all familiar tactics.

Resistance might be best met with face-to-face confrontation. Usually it indicates that the objectives or the sources of pressure for change have not been explained. Rumours begin to circulate, and, unless the resistance is seen as constructive and confronted in an open way, the pain and hurt may continue for years. As in all situations of conflict, it is best to hear out the complaints, let the anger surface and then try to build on calmer behaviour.

Kotter and Schlesinger (1979) identified six main methods of dealing with resistance:

- Education and communication.
- Participation and involvement.
- Facilitation and support.
- Negotiation and agreement.
- Manipulation and co-optation.
- Explicit and implicit coercion.

The final two methods raise ethical and legal problems as well as involving considerable risk of making the situation worse. These six approaches are not mutually exclusive and managers may find it effective to use a combination of them. The most appropriate approach in each instance will depend on a variety of factors, including the goals of the change programme and the likely reactions of the people involved. One of the problems of choosing the 'right' approach is that people will not always openly admit the *real* reasons why they oppose changes. In particular, those reasons relating to self-interest are likely to be disguised as technical objections, arguing that the proposed system will not work. Attempts to deal with these technical objections will not get to the root cause of the resistance to change. Only in a climate in which individuals feel free to discuss their objections and fears openly will it be possible for managers to deal with the underlying reasons for resistance.

Exercise 6.3

Review Kotter and Schlesinger's listing and identify the conditions under which each of these methods might 'work'.

✅ **Solution**

There is no right or wrong answer, and your thinking is likely to be as valid so long as it is based on commonsense and your own experience.

- *Education and communication.* This is useful when the basic problem is a lack of information about the need for, or the nature of, the planned change. If people can be persuaded about the change they will be more likely to help with its implementation, but this approach can be very time consuming and will not work by itself if there are other reasons than misunderstanding for resisting the change. One of the principal aspects of successful change management centres on the need to talk. Open management, consultation and participation are fundamental to the effective implementation of change. Owning the problem and being part of the solution are fundamental. No major change will come about unless an organisation's managers plan what needs to be done, when things must be done, by whom and what resources should be acquired and used in order to achieve the objectives. This strategy – and its implications must be spelt out. Also these implications must be communicated to, agreed upon and supported by the organisation's managers. Communication is often described as the lubricant of change. Implementation is about capturing hearts and minds not merely writing a policy statement and pinning it on the office wall.
- *Participation and involvement.* This increases the probability that people will be committed to implementing the change and, if their views are taken into account, this may enhance the effectiveness of the change programme. This method is particularly appropriate when the individuals initiating the change do not have all the necessary information to design a change programme and when the people affected by the change have considerable power to resist it. However, as is the case with education and communication, this approach to dealing with resistance to change can be time consuming, particularly if it results in the design of an inappropriate change programme.
- *Facilitation and support.* This involves the use of techniques such as training, counselling and group discussions designed to reduce fear and anxiety. This is particularly appropriate where the principal reason for resistance is based on insecurity and adjustment problems. Some changes do of course really threaten employee aspirations and job security; in these cases facilitation and support may help but it will not address the fundamental cause of resistance.
- *Negotiation and agreement.* This may be necessary where a group clearly stands to lose out in some way because of the change, particularly if this group has considerable power to resist the change. If applied effectively this method of dealing with resistance to change may help to avoid major problems. The disadvantages are that it can be expensive and also it can encourage other groups to negotiate to 'buy' their compliance.
- *Manipulation and co-optation.* Manipulation is an approach that relies on presenting partial or misleading information to the people resisting the change. Co-optation involves identifying key individuals resisting changes and 'buying them off' by giving them positions of authority to help implement the changes. Although this may be a quick and relatively inexpensive approach, it will probably result in future problems if the people involved realise they have been manipulated.
- *Explicit and implicit coercion.* This involves the use of force, or the threat of force, to enforce the implementation of change. This type of approach may be necessary if the parties involved are operating from fixed positions and there are fundamental disagreements over objectives and/or methods.

Inevitably people feel vulnerable during periods of organisational change. It is part of a manager's job to ensure that people focus on the 'right' issues arising from change. For instance, employees may believe that the most effective way to protect their future employment is to be more conscientious, more loyal, work longer hours, etc. All this may be true but the real goal is to justify ones existence through adding value. To manage change it seems sensible to:

- anticipate where apparent threats are coming from and plan to overcome those problems
- sell the benefits of change through good communication
- consider the resource, staff and training requirements of the change
- consider best/optimum time and method of change
- plan and control the change process.

6.6.3 Managerial barriers

Managers themselves can create barriers to beneficial change by the way the change is conceived, designed and implemented. Management can make mistakes by not thinking through their objectives, the resources available and the options they are competent to undertake. Crucially, the issue of who leads the change is seldom thought through. Daft (1998) described several factors and these are used as framework to discuss this issue.

Excessive focus on costs. Management may possess the mind-set that costs are all-important and may fail to appreciate the importance of a change that is not focused on costs (for example, a change to increase employee motivation or customer satisfaction). In most managerial situations a presentation of an idea that costs more than current practice is unlikely to be accepted unless the future returns are considerable.

Failure to highlight benefits. Any significant change will produce both positive and negative reactions. Education may be needed to help managers perceive more positive than negative aspects of the change.

Lack of co-ordination and co-operation. Organisational fragmentation and conflict often result from the lack of co-ordination for change implementation. Moreover, in the case of new technology, the old and new systems may not be compatible. At the operational level, real progress is painstakingly slow and deliberate as the minute detail of how the present systems work (or do not work) is not known. This is the problem with many business process re-engineering projects, as assumptions about how things currently work are made without proper thought. Taken with uncertainty, managerial actions tend to be about saving face and their own department's reputation is protected at the expense of co-operation with others.

Uncertainty avoidance. At the individual level, managers fear the uncertainty associated with change. Constant communication is needed horizontally so that the team knows what is going on and understand how it impacts on their work. An atmosphere of fear 'we've just got to have this in by . . . 'or 'we've got to get this right first time' leads to a culture of blame and negativity and the excessively defensive process of 'protecting one's own back' and a reluctance to take risks.

Fear of loss. This is of course related to the above. Managers may fear not only the loss of power and status but also even their jobs, especially if implementation is not careful and incremental. Often resistance is assumed to come from below and most effort is related to this rather than focussing on other middle managers.

Some of the above can be reduced or eliminated by a conscious strategic process to manage change through processes found in organisational development.

6.7 Change: approaches and ideas

6.7.1 Change through entrepreneurship

Rosabeth Moss Kanter, a Harvard professor, rose to prominence with the text 'The Change Masters: Corporate Entrepreneurs at Work' where she stressed the need for 'an American renaissance'. She complained about the 'quiet suffocation of the entrepreneurial spirit' in what she called 'segmentalist companies' (functionally-organised firms) particularly the indifference of management to employee innovations. To counteract this trend she produced various cases to show where and how change could be implemented. In common with the 'excellence school' (that included most prominently Peters and Waterman) she emphasised employee involvement and empowerment, together with a discussion of the managerial skills needed to change culture and strategy. In this context she described the 'integrative' approach to problems as 'moving beyond conventional wisdom', using 'ideas from unconnected sources'.

Kanter's offered prescriptions for encouraging organisational creativity as follows:

- Develop an acceptance of change.
- Encourage new ideas at all levels of the organisation.
- Permit more interaction between individuals and groups.
- Tolerate failure, as experimentation requires trying out new ideas, not all of which will work.
- Offer recognition and rewards for creative behaviour.

These prescriptions will be difficult to implement in a traditional, bureaucratic, role culture. Attempts at managing a change in culture may in these circumstances have to go side by side with attempts to improve innovation and creativity. In 'The Change Masters', Kanter neatly summarised some typical managerial behaviours and policies that will effectively stifle innovative efforts (Table 6.1).

✋ Exercise 6.4

Review Kanter's ten rules and try to invert them to provide a checklist of how entrepreneurship can be encouraged.

6.7.2 A staged approach to change

A useful way of looking at successful change was proposed by Kurt Lewin (1975) over half a century ago. He suggested a three-step or stage model of change as follows:

- Unfreezing, which involves finding ways of making the need for change so obvious that most people can readily understand it and accept it.
- Changing behaviour patterns in such a way that the new attitudes, values and behaviour are internalised as part of employees' new ways of thinking.
- Refreezing, whereby supporting mechanisms are introduced to ensure the new behaviour patterns are maintained.

Table 6.1 Rules for stifling innovation

Regard any new idea from below with suspicion – because it is new and because it is from below

Insist that people who need your approval to act first go through several other levels of management to get their signatures

Ask departments or individuals to challenge and criticise each other's proposals (That saves you the job of deciding; you just pick the survivor)

Express your criticisms freely, and withhold your praise (That keeps people on their toes.) Let them know they can be fired at any time

Treat identification of problems as signs of failure, to discourage people from letting you know when something in their area isn't working

Control everything carefully. Make sure that people count anything that can be counted, frequently.

Make decisions to reorganise or change policies in secret, and then spring them on people unexpectedly (That also keeps people on their toes)

Make sure that requests for information are fully justified, and make sure that it is not given out to managers freely (You do not want data to fall into the wrong hands)

Assign to lower-level managers, in the name of delegation and participation, responsibility for figuring how to cut back, lay off, move people around, or otherwise implement threatening decisions you have made. And get them to do it quickly

And above all, never forget that you, the higher ups; already know everything important about this business

Source: Kanter (1983)

In terms of unfreezing, managers often use the threat of external competition to ensure employees are jolted out of complacency with the present, and promises of a more rosy future make change more acceptable. In this environment, change processes can take place, and usually an attempt is made to go for insider solutions (to avoid the 'not invented here' syndrome). These also need to show quick positive results to ensure the change process is not stalled, so that other more difficult items can be scheduled-in. Overcoming resistance is a key feature. Refreezing has its dangers in creating a new status quo.

This process model whereby organisations would attempt to Unfreeze-Change-Refreeze forms the basis of most planned approaches to change.

6.7.3 Identifying forces for and against change

Lewin (1975) also created a concept of the 'force-fields' within a workplace organisation, whereby there are driving forces pushing for change and restraining forces striving to maintain the status quo. By recognising the driving forces and using them to good advantage whilst minimising the restraining forces, bringing about change is possible. Lewin described the process of depicting these as a 'force field analysis' (Figure 6.1). A force field analysis can be constructed by taking a single sheet of paper and following a series of stages:

- Write at the head of the paper on the left hand side 'existing state'.
- Write at the head of the paper on the right hand side 'desired state' (this is the desired change).
- List forces working for the change down the left hand side of the page.
- Put a right facing arrowhead on each force and extend the line dependent upon the relative strength of the force.
- List forces working against the change down the right hand side of the page.

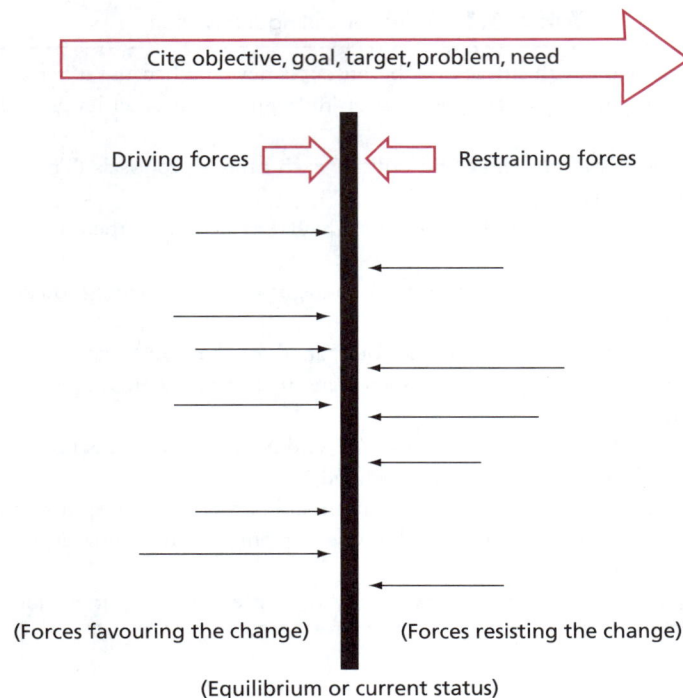

Figure 6.1 Force field analysis

- Put a left facing arrowhead on each force and extend the line dependent upon the relative strength of the force.
- An equilibrium is reach where the forces meet. The challenge for the manager is to bring about movement to the desired state.

6.7.4 Constant change

Tom Peters developed his idea of constant change in his text Thriving on Chaos (1987) in which he declared that the 'modest-sized semi-autonomous, mainly self-managing team should be the basic building-block of organisations'. Peters believed that only organisations that embraced constant change would succeed. This was the best way of improving service and getting close to the customer. (One problem with these 'best practice' approaches advocated by Peters is that a 'one best way' tendency dominates. Samples upon which studies are carried are usually small, and American, and the practical guidance managers need is generally lacking.)

Tom Peters and others regard change as the only constant. Just changing for the sake of it forces people into reviewing and evaluating what they have been doing. In some multinational and global enterprises, executives are rotated every 2 years or so to both prevent them from building up local power bases and to encourage existing cultural recipes for success to challenged.

6.7.5 Change through 'balancing'

Beer and Nohria's (2000) starting point is that a large proportion of all change initiatives fail in the USA. The reason is that the rush to change involves managers immersing themselves in detail and losing focus resulting in mess. Every organisational change conforms to a variant of either:

- *Theory E change strategies.* These are based on measures where shareholder value is the main concern. Change usually involves incentives, layoffs, downsizing, and restructuring.
- *Theory O change strategies.* A 'soft' approach to change, possibly cultural adjustment or enhancing human capability through individual and organisational learning. This involves changing, obtaining feedback, reflecting, and making further changes. Theory O companies have a strong, commitment-based psychological contract with their employees.

The difficulty is that Theory E organisations ignore the feelings and attitudes of their employees, so they lose commitment and the creativity needed for sustained competitive advantage. Alternatively Theory O organisations fail to take 'tough' decisions. Beer and Nohria propose that instead of using only one theory or sequencing both theories, organisations should implement both Theory E and Theory O simultaneously and try to balance the associated tensions.

6.7.6   Change through organisational learning

Peter Senge (1992) has been one of the leading advocates of organisations developing the capacity and culture to become what he terms 'learning organisations'; these are the ones that continually expand their ability to shape their future. This thinking can be related directly to Western economies attempting to implement TQM philosophies (see Chapter 5). He explains this as follows:

The roots of the quality movement lie in assumptions about people, organisations and management that have one unifying theme: to make continual learning a way of organisational life, especially improving the performance of the organisation as a total system. This can only be achieved by breaking with the traditional authoritarian, command and control hierarchy where the top thinks and the local acts, to merge thinking and acting at all levels.

(Senge, 1992, p. 31)

Royal Dutch/Shell is quoted as probably the first global corporation to appreciate and implement the benefits of institutionalising learning as the most effective approach to strategic planning. However, many Japanese firms have long recognised the benefits of institutionalising learning around quality improvement teams and associated issues.

Senge's learning organisation concept demands critical awareness of ones own faults and the necessity of change.

According to Senge, there are five core competencies involved in building learning organisations:

- Building a shared vision to ensure that people are focused around a common sense of purpose. If there is no shared vision of the organisation, its purpose and values, then learning only occurs when there is a crisis that brings everyone temporarily together.
- Personal mastery of learning by individuals who are continually finding out how to create more of what matters to them.
- Working with mental models for people to recognise their unconscious assumptions, and to appreciate how alternative actions at work could create a different reality. For example, Ricardo Semler's book 'Maverick' describes an alternative to the traditional hierarchical model of organisations which may help people to challenge their own assumptions about what is 'inevitable' at work.
- Team learning. A learning organisation requires individuals to come together and act as teams. Therefore, personal mastery of learning has to be accompanied by team learning so that it can be practised when groups of people have to confront controversial issues

and make difficult decisions. Such team learning skills do not come naturally, and this probably explains the poor results of some attempts to use the Japanese practice of quality circles in Western organisations.

- Systems thinking which emphasises the importance of understanding interrelationships, rather than breaking problems down into discrete parts.

A learning organisation is one that learns from its external environment and adapts accordingly. For such an organisation change becomes natural and on going.

6.8 Critical periods of organisational change

It is important to manage critical periods of change throughout the life of an organisation. Organisations are not static over time: they combine both dynamic and stabilising tendencies. Some will adapt to changes but remain essentially the same size, others will decline and perhaps go out of existence or get taken over, while others grow and develop into larger organisations. Those which grow may do so simply because they have found an economical niche that provides opportunities for growth, or because their managers have consciously pursued policies to achieve growth.

Some owners and/or managers of organisations may actively resist growth because of its perceived problems, such as the difficulty of retaining control or the need to borrow capital. However, there are also potential benefits from growth that will be attractive to others: these might include increased equity, higher salaries, greater security, prestige power, and so on.

6.8.1 Growth by acquisition

There are both positive and negative aspects to growth by acquisition. The growth of large UK organisations has been achieved mainly through external growth, acquisitions or mergers, probably more so than any other industrialised economy. The main reasons for growth through acquisition is that it provides:

- A swift means of expansion for organisations currently in mature markets.
- Opportunities for growth without necessarily attracting attention under government competition policy (e.g. investigation by the Competition Commission in the UK).
- More speedy growth than is usually achievable by internal expansion.
- A way of minimising risk of an aggressive takeover bid by another organisation.
- A means of acquiring a more balanced product portfolio for an organisation.
- Opportunities for 'asset stripping' when the shares of the acquired company are believed to be undervalued. This enables parts of the business to be sold off at a profit after the takeover.

Unfortunately, research suggests that external growth through acquisition strategies often fail to achieve the expected benefits. Although mergers and takeovers may appear to be attractive ways to grow and diversify, the benefits of such activities are not always easy to achieve, as Thompson (2005) made clear:

Many acquisitions and mergers lead to disappointing results: profitability is reduced; synergy does not emerge. It is difficult to predict success or failure in advance as issues of both strategy creation and implementation are involved. Changes in corporate strategy are generally more unpredictable and risky than those which concentrate on improving competitive and functional strategies.

The original 'excellence' studies by Tom Peters and Robert Waterman (1982), suggested that successful companies confined themselves to what they are good at ('stick to the knitting'). The difficulties involved in attempting to lever benefits following diversification into unfamiliar areas perhaps reinforce this point.

The fusion of different cultures can be a 'hidden' dimension that is not addressed properly following acquisition.

Peter Drucker (1982) suggested that there are five basic rules or guidelines that must be followed if acquisitions are to be successful:

- *Contribution* the acquiring company must identify exactly what contribution it can make to the acquired company and this must be more than just money.
- *Common core* the companies involved should have some common core of unity in markets, production operations or technology.
- *Value* the company making the acquisition should value the products, services and customers of the other company.
- *Management cover* it is important that there is some top management cover available in case key senior managers in the acquired company choose to, or are required to, leave after the acquisition.
- *Linkage* within a year of the acquisition managers should have been promoted across the boundaries of the two previously separate companies.

External growth need not rely exclusively on acquisitions or mergers as it can also be based on franchising or licensing. The fast food chain McDonalds operates globally and has experienced tremendous growth over a sustained period, in part due to the use of franchised restaurants.

6.8.2 Growth by organic means

If managers do decide to pursue a strategy of internal growth this will typically be achieved organically by reinvesting profits and building on existing strengths. Economists as well as managers are interested in organisational growth, and some have put forward what is known as the 'S-curve hypothesis'. This suggests that firms will typically have short formative periods, followed by periods of rapid growth, before these tail off into greater stability. The thinking behind this approach is that when an owner first sets up a business there will be an initial period when the firm has to establish itself in the market place. It may then be able to demonstrate some competitive market advantage, which permits the owner to plough back substantial profits to exploit the opportunity. The injection of capital from these profits provides a platform for rapid growth, which will eventually tail off because of loss of competitive advantage and/or profit taking by the owner.

The S-curve thinking is interesting to organisation theorists because it suggests that there are a number of different stages of growth, raising different managerial problems. Therefore, a number of writers studying problems of organisation and management have put forward stage models of growth to explain the internal process and problems of growth.

The simplest models of organisational growth take the concept of a 'product life cycle' from marketing (see Chapter 2) and apply it to stages of an organisation's development. Thus there is likely to be an initial stage of establishing the organisation, followed by growth, stability, and eventually decline. This is illustrated in Figure 6.2.

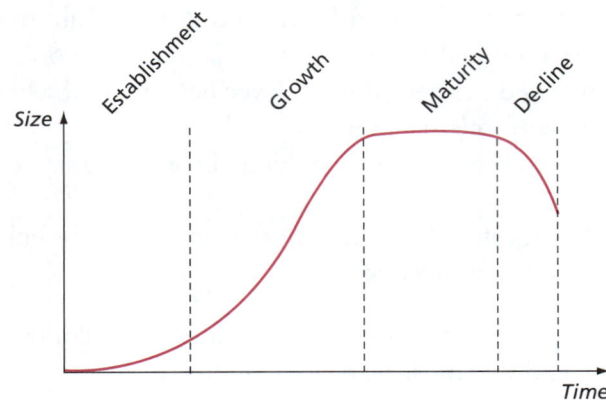

Figure 6.2   The organisational life cycle

Initially, an entrepreneur acts as a catalyst and product champion during the birth and early youth stages of organisational development. As the organisation progresses to early maturity, the entrepreneur will be supplemented or replaced by professional managers. These people are good at running an established business and achieving further growth using their expertise in strategy, organisation and finance.

The danger however is that the successful organisation becomes unwieldy or complacent in the maturity stage and the managers become overly bureaucratic. The departments and divisions within the firm become major barriers to effective communication and problem solving, and the use of fixed rules results in risk aversion and lack of innovation. Stagnation leads to decline, and reversing this decline will require a Herculean effort from managers with very special qualities. Such managers can fit one of two profiles:

- Skilled, seasoned, veterans who see a challenge and know exactly what they are doing (for example famously Lee Iacocca's work in turning around Chrysler automobiles in the USA).
- Those who do not know enough about the business to believe 'it can't work here' and turn it around by ignoring the normal rules (the turnaround of United Airlines by Ed Carlson is quoted to exemplify this).

The organisational life cycle approach is useful but largely descriptive. In order to analyse why these things happen, some explanation is required of the dynamics within the organisation. One such understanding is provided by Larry Greiner (1972), and cited in many texts. Greiner put forward a stage model of growth, arguing that the underlying dynamic in each stage is evolutionary growth that eventually creates a situation of revolutionary crisis, when the organisation's existing ways of doing things are no longer efficient and effective. Thus organisations inevitable experience periods of both evolution and revolution. The implication of this thinking is that change is unavoidable, even predictable and today's solutions become problems in the future. If managers can establish ways of overcoming each crisis there will be a platform for further growth. Failure to deal with a particular crisis will result in decline or demise. Greiner's stages of growth and the crises involved are illustrated in Figure 6.3. A rapidly growing organisation will have a steep line of growth and relatively short periods between crises. Slow growth will produce a flatter line, and consequently longer periods between crises.

The first phase of growth is achieved by some creative idea, product or service that enables the organisation to become established in the market place. This is essentially the first part of both the S-curve hypothesis and the organisational life cycle. Eventually, however, a crisis

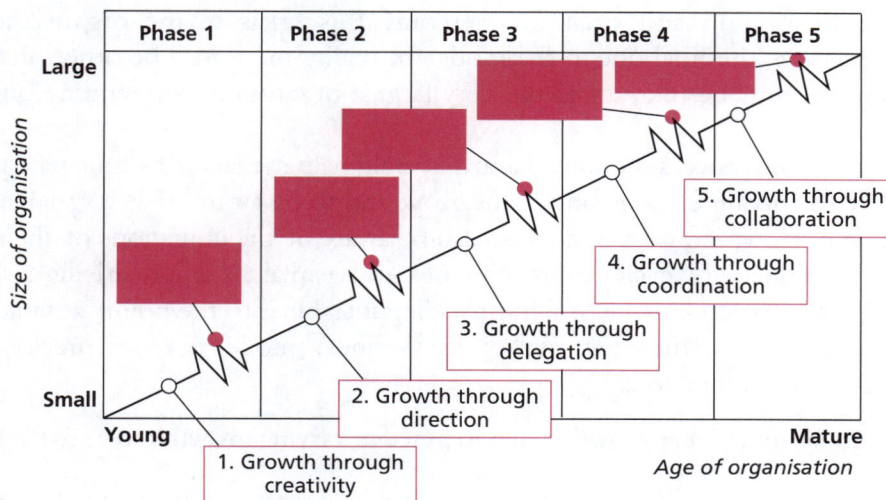

Figure 6.3 The five stages of growth

occurs when the entrepreneur's informal and personal approach to managing the business simply cannot cope with its increased size: this is the crisis of leadership.

If the organisation and the entrepreneur can adopt more formal systems of management, there will be a basis for further growth through direction. This period of growth will last for a considerable period if the organisation is growing slowly, but will be short-lived for the rapidly growing organisation. In both cases a crisis situation will eventually arise, because the organisation has reached a size where the slowness and costs of making decisions in a centralised way through the formal hierarchy are proving to be major stumbling blocks: there is a crisis of autonomy.

Only if ways are found of operating in a more decentralised way will the crisis of autonomy be overcome. Decentralisation will involve the owner and senior managers delegating powers of decision-making to members of the organisation closer to the customers or production processes than they are. There will almost certainly be reluctance to do this, because of the perceived risks involved, but it is essential, if the crisis is to be solved, to permit growth through delegation.

Delegation should permit quicker and more effective decision making. In this way further growth can be achieved, and the organisation is very likely to achieve some of this by diversifying into new areas of business. The next crisis will be when senior managers start to fear that they are losing control over the highly decentralised and diversified organisation. They have to find a solution that does not involve reverting to their earlier directive methods.

The solution to the crisis of control usually involves the implementation of more sophisticated management accounting information systems to permit effective monitoring of decisions without the need to intervene in actually making them all. Other actions may be to introduce product groups and formal planning procedures to improve co-ordination. These actions will facilitate growth through coordination in phase 4.

The final crisis identified by Greiner is one of red tape. This occurs when the procedures and systems introduced in earlier phases of growth start to become obstacles to its continuation. By this time the organisation will be very large, and is likely to be operating on a divisional basis, with some important functions and activities provided by a central headquarters. The tension between divisions and headquarters may eventually result in a mutual lack of trust and harmful internal conflicts. Ways have to be found to encourage collaboration and trust to overcome this crisis if the organisation is to proceed to phase 5, the final one in the model: in reality there may be other phases after this but they will only be relevant to the very largest organisations operating on a global scale.

Knowledge of the processes outlined above should help managers to anticipate problems they are likely to encounter as organisations grow, and to be aware of key variables at each stage of growth. However, managers must also be aware of the limitations of the models.

The organisational life cycle approach does not explain the underlying process of growth, and is not particularly helpful in providing insights into the points at which transitions from one stage to the next take place. Greiner's model is more precise in these respects, but still has limitations:

- It implies consistent, linear growth when in practice varying growth rates are likely at each stage.
- It is vague about how exactly to measure size, and this means it is difficult to predict when crises are likely to happen in particular instances.
- It does not explicitly deal with organisational decline.
- It might give the impression that growth is the normal state of affairs for all organisations, when it clearly is not.

Despite these limitations, models of growth, such as the one put forward by Greiner, do provide managers with some useful general insights into this complex process.

6.8.3 Alternatives to growth

Growth is not inevitable and many organisations may make a deliberate choice not to pursue such a policy. The strategic alternatives to growth include:

- Ignoring growth potential and attempting to maintain existing levels of operation.
- Specialisation of the business, and building a future on distinct organisational competences.
- Innovation of products and markets.
- Divestment strategies whereby parts of the business are closed or sold, usually as part of an attempt to consolidate or re-position the business.
- Reduction in geographical scope/product range.

6.8.4 Unbundling, downsizing and rightsizing

One consequence of many acquisitions and mergers in the 1980s and 1990s was significant programmes of redundancy at all levels in the acquired company. In the USA, Jack Welch of General Electric acquired the nickname 'Neutron Jack' from some commentators because it was alleged he left buildings standing but eliminated the people inside, just as a neutron bomb would! Post-acquisition rationalisations are sometimes referred to as 'rightsizing' while 'downsizing' occurs without company acquisition. Spinning-off operations (unbundling) involves selling parts of an organisation that no longer 'fit' strategically even if they have potential. An example was ICI spinning off its pharmaceutical business as Zeneca (which incidentally soon outperformed ICI financially).

6.8.5 Managing decline

Throughout the early 1990s, because of the depressed state of their national economies, many managers in Europe and the USA were more concerned with the problems of managing decline rather than growth. The problems of managing decline pose particular dilemmas. It places in sharp perspective the ethical dimensions involved in many aspects of management when decisions affecting the workforce, its pay, conditions and employment security are items on the agenda. Slatter (1984) suggested a number of factors that individually, or in various combinations, contribute to organisational decline (Table 6.2 below).

When attempting to manage a situation in which the organisation needs to recover from a depressed situation, the strategic priorities will revolve around:

- reducing costs to improve efficiency and
- improving competitiveness in order to increase revenue.

Initially, when an organisation encounters problems, and revenue and/or profits starts to decline, the typical management reaction is to assume the situation is a temporary one requiring nothing more fundamental than cost cutting. Costs can be reduced anywhere in the supply chain, but the most obvious and usual starting point is to reduce labour costs. At first, this may simply involve altering working patterns to eliminate overtime or, as is increasingly the case, to replace full-time with part-time jobs. If this does not produce sufficient savings, the next step is likely to be voluntary or compulsory redundancies. The danger is that if the cuts are too severe there will be reductions in the quality of the product and services to customers; the impact on employee morale will also make it difficult to achieve the workforce commitment discussed in the previous chapter. Problems of employee morale will be particularly severe if there is a series of cost reduction exercises over a prolonged period. These will result in a loss of trust in management and an escalation in conflicts and levels of political activity.

Table 6.2 Contributors to organisational decline

Inadequate financial control, particularly when the management accounting systems are poorly designed, and/or senior managers do not use management accounting information, and/or methods of overhead allocation distort costs

Poor management, typified by factors such as an overly autocratic chief executive, neglect of the organisation's core business and a weak board of directors

Competitive weaknesses due to products in decline and heavy emphasis on price competition

High cost structures, which may be the result of many factors, such as inability to take advantage of economies of scale or operating inefficiencies

Changes in market demand that the organisation has not anticipated and cannot respond to

Adverse movements in commodity prices can be significant in certain industries

Lack of marketing effort can cause decline; when it is a major contributory factor it is usually related to weaknesses in the senior marketing staff, and associated with other fundamental problems such as price and product competition

Too many big projects involving major capital expenditure

Unwise acquisitions, such as buying organisations which themselves have a weak competitive position, or paying too much for them. However, the most common problem is poor management of the organisation once it has been acquired

Poor financial policies, particularly overtrading and/or inappropriate financial sources

Overtrading, so that sales grow at a faster rate than the organisation is able to finance from its cash flow and borrowings

Source: Slatter (1984)

Exercise 6.5

What other cost-saving measures could be considered by an organisation in such a position?

Solution

- attempting to generate additional revenue through more effective marketing
- improving purchasing policies and procedures
- redesigning the product or service to reduce production costs
- contracting out services that are not considered essential to the core business
- changes to reduce duplication, improving financial control systems and so on.

The difficulty is that certain types of cost-saving measures, such as improving factory layout, might require some initial expenditure, which is not possible if the organisation is already experiencing declining revenues. This exemplifies the problems caused by reactive management.

Managers may then have to consider more fundamental strategic change alternatives in order to face a decline, including:

- Complete retrenchment, doing the same as before but cutting costs drastically.
- Turnaround, whereby the organisation will attempt to reposition itself for competitive advantage. Most commentators believe that replacement of the existing top management

Cause	Strategy
Poor management	New management / Organisational change and decentralisation
Inadequate financial control	New management / Improved financial control / Decentralisation
High cost structure	Cost reduction / Product market
Lack of marketing effort	Improved marketing
Competitive weakness	Product market / Cost reduction / Improved marketing / Asset reduction / Acquisition
Too many big projects / Unwise acquisitions	Asset reduction
Poor financial policy	Asset reduction / New financial strategy

Figure 6.4 Causes of decline and generic strategies

team is a precondition for the successful implementation of such a turnaround strategy. Slatter analysed the principal generic strategies for corporate turnaround and recovery and related them to the initial causes of decline (Figure 6.4).

- Divestment involving the external sale of part of the organisation or the internal closure of units, as part of a rationalisation programme.
- Liquidation of the business by selling it to one or more buyers; this entails an admission of failure by the senior managers, and the fear of loss of face may mean that this alternative is not considered seriously until there are no others available.

All four strategies associated with decline (retrenchment, turnaround, divestment and liquidation) require managers to make difficult decisions, which may have adverse effects on all of the organisation's stakeholders, particularly its employees. These issues are at the heart of business ethics and social responsibility, themes that have been highlighted throughout this study system. Previous chapters have stressed the importance of employee commitment for competitive success and the implementation of approaches such as TQM. Large-scale redundancy programmes harm this process, but managers sometimes have to balance the negative effects on staff against economic realities. This requires them to take into account the relative importance of factors such as effectiveness, effort, loyalty, experience and efficiency.

There are three situations where an employee's post may become 'redundant':

- The overall business may be out of cash and will call in the Receiver to sell the assets at market value or on a going-concern basis. In the latter case there may still be employment opportunities but if the firm ceases to trade, all employees will be redundant.
- If the firm ceases to trade in the area, and transfers work to a new facility, it may be that existing employees will not be needed there (e.g. if demand has fallen) or that they cannot feasibly transfer owing to personal reasons or have to commute daily a long distance. Refusal to undertake a new offer of employment however can be 'unreasonable' and redundancy payments withheld.
- Work that the employee was hired to do may diminish or cease possibly due to changes in demand or technology (e.g. compositors in the print industry using 'hot-metal' technology, human endeavours in a newly automated banking industry, etc.).

Management faces many difficulties when deciding that employee numbers have to be reduced. There is always the claim that with earlier action decline could have been halted so as to avoid redundancy. Additionally, employees and their representatives often claim that such action is merely short-term cost-cutting to show better profits. In the UK, such action on cutting costs has led to complex and network forms of organisation.

6.8.6 Making ethical decisions

Although management has the power to make tough, sometimes unpleasant decisions, the pressure to act honestly, caringly and ethically should be uppermost. An organisation that treats its employees poorly may damage its public image permanently. The importance of managing change carefully is particularly so under conditions of organisational decline. Senior management must exercise their judgement in deciding whether the cause of decline is temporary or more lasting. The conclusions they draw will impact on the way human resourcing is adjusted and potentially how shedding staff is handled.

If the situation is thought to be temporary, management will have to make a judgement on the level of workforce that needs to be reduced. If redundancies are unavoidable then the extent should be carefully gauged:

- if too many core employees are made redundant, continuity of operation may be difficult
- if too few are dismissed then the cost savings may not be enough and a second round of dismissals becomes necessary. Further calls for redundancy affect morale more deeply each time, reflect poorly on management and performance suffers disproportionately.

If there is no way of telling whether the downturn is permanent or not temporary lay-offs and leave of absence may be possible. In one firm, employers were granted two separate leaves of absence. The first was an open leave, the second educational leave. In both cases, employees applied for the leave and were interviewed and selected according to how important their re-employment would be to the firm. Those selected were then paid an allowance and had a contract to return to the firm when given a certain period of notice, which varied with the type of leave given. In this way the psychological contract was not permanently damaged and several employees welcomed in particular the idea of a return to full-time study with a guarantee of re-employment on full wages.

Where the downturn is felt to be permanent, a different approach is needed but this need not imply actions that are uncaring or disrespectful of the individual employees affected. As part of a US government plan to save the Chrysler motor company, Chief Executive Lee Iacocca was faced with the inevitability of shutting plants. Iacocca decided to soften the blow through a series of associated plans designed to get the employees into self-employment or into other forms of work. Some employees reskilled and moved to jobs in other parts of the Chrysler group, but the majority found employment elsewhere locally.

The term 'outplacement' has come to be used to describe the urgent and genuine efforts of management to place redundant employees in other economically active positions. Some consultants have become expert in revising curricula vitae of staff and 'selling' them to a network of contacts. While the term 'redundant' is often tarnished nowadays many organisations go through severe cost-cutting exercises and many excellent staff can become redundant through no fault of their own.

6.9 The context and style of change

There are no simple universal prescriptions for the successful management of change. Each case requires careful analysis and implementation. Sometimes it may be appropriate to force changes through regardless of resistance, but the inherent danger of this approach is that people will return to the old ways of working once the pressure for change is relaxed. In managing change a number of styles are evident, for instance:

- *The participative style.* Extensive delegation of tasks to teams and groups, this requires time, trust and support.
- *The interventionist style.* Limited delegation of some aspects of the change whilst retaining overall direction.
- *The autocratic style.* No delegation direction is centrally driven.
- *The educational style.* Facts are presented to staff and a rationale made for the change before change gets under way (a 'tell and sell' approach).

Exercise 6.6

Under what conditions might the autocratic style be appropriate?

☑ Solution

In periods of extreme crisis where solutions are demanded quickly and decisively. The major difficulty here is potentially a lack of workforce buy-in and potential resistance.

It is difficult to make generalizations but very broadly, successful change usually involves the following:

- Initiation and support by senior management.
- A good understanding of organisational cultures and politics, giving a shared vision of how to manage effectively.
- Some degree of participation to mobilise commitment through the joint analysis of issues.
- Support from formal policies, reward systems and structures.
- Attention to the real sources of resistance to change and means of overcoming them.
- Meaningful communication.

6.10   Change in perspective

Exercise 6.7

Michael Jarrett cited in Stern (2005) identified what he called the 'seven myths of change management'. Based on your own experience and reading you have undertaken try to list arguments both for and against each of the seven items:

Organisational change management creates value	The truth is that organisational change is exceedingly difficult and expected benefits are rarely realised. Academic research suggests that 70% of change management programmes fail.
Resistance can be overcome	Fear and survival are at the roots of resistance. Resistance first needs to be understood and reinterpreted, and cannot be ignored or overcome.
Change is constant	There is a difference between transformational change which is rare and incremental change (or continuous improvement).
Change can be managed	Change agents might stimulate or even steer through change it, but that's not managing it.
The change agent knows best	Ultimately an organisation will find its own ways of responding to change.
Accepted wisdom is to follow the steps	A rational checklist approach is inflexibile, adjustments might be needed in the chaos of rapid change.
Big change require big changes	Small scale changes can build a critical mass, everything does not need to change at once, or on a big scale.

Now refer to the following website and make notes: www.beyondresistance.com

6.11 Summary

The successful management of change is the most crucial issue facing any manager or organisation. This chapter has dealt with certain aspects of this all-embracing and often complex subject. Specific attention has been paid to triggers for change both external and internal, the change process itself and ideas and approaches to change management by exploring the thinking of certain theorists. Finally, the importance of managing critical periods of change through the life cycle of an organisation has been highlighted.

References and further reading

Beer, M. and Nohria, N. (2000) Cracking the code of change, *Harvard Business Review* (May–June): 133–141.

Daft, R. (1998) *Organizational Theory and Design* (6th edn), New York: West Publishing.

Drucker, P. (1982) *The Changing World of the Executive*, London: Heinemann.

Goldratt, E. (1992) 'Introduction to the Theory of Constraints – The Goal Approach' Seminar. Avraham Y Goldratt Institute.

Greiner, L. E. (1972) in Lynch, R. L. (2003) *Corporate Strategy* (3rd edn), Harlow: Financial, Times Prentice Hall.

Jarrett, M. cited in Stern, S. (2005) Forever changing, *Management Today*, February 7, p. 40

Johnson, G., Scholes, K. and Whittington, R. (2005) *Exploring Corporate Strategy* (7th edn), Harlow: Financial Times Prentice Hall.

Kanter, R. M. (1983) *The Change Masters*, New York: Simon and Schuster.

Kotter, J. P. and Schlesinger, L. A. (1979) *Organization: Text, Cases, and Readings on the Management of Organizational Design and Change*, Homewood, Ill: R.D. Irwin.

Lewin, K. (1975) *Field Theory in Social Science: Selected Theoretical Papers*, Westport (Conn.): Greenwood Press A publication of the Research Center for Group Dynamics, University of Michigan Originally published, New York: Harper & Brothers, 1951.

Mullins, L. J. (2005) *Management and Organisational Behaviour* (7th edn), Harlow: Financial Times, Prentice Hall.

Paton, R. A. and McCalman, J. (2000) *Change Management: A Guide to Effective Implementation* (2nd edn), London: Sage.

Peters, T. (1987) *Thriving on Chaos: A Handbook for a Managerial Revolution*, London: Pan.

Peters, T. and Waterman, R. (1982) *In Search of Excellence*, New York: Harper & Row.

Ridgeway, B. and Wallace, B. (1996) *Leadership for Strategic Change*, London: Institute of Personnel and Development.

Semler, R. (2001) *Maverick*, London: Random House Business Books.

Senge, P. (1992) *The Fifth Discipline: The Art and Practice of the Learning Organization*, London: Random House Business Books.

Senior, B. and Fleming, J. (2006) *Organisational Change* (3rd edn), Harlow: Financial Times, Prentice Hall.

Slatter, S. (1984) *Corporate Recovery: A Guide to Turnaround Management*, Penguin: Harmondsworth.

Thompson, J. L. with Martin, F. (2005) *Strategic Management: Awareness and Change* (5th edn), London: Thomson Learning.

Torrington, D. and Weightman, J. (1994) *Effective Management: People and Organisation* (2nd edn), London; New York: Prentice Hall.

Worrall, L. and Campbell, F. (2000) 'Surviving Redundancy: the Perceptions of UK Managers,' *Journal of Managerial Psychology*, Vol. 15, No. 5, pp. 460–447.

Revision Questions

6

? Question 1

Z Ltd is a company created by two young technical specialists – a salesperson and an entrepreneurial financier – who worked long hours for relatively low salaries to build up a successful business. Their stakes in the company have become very valuable. They communicate frequently and freely between themselves and with their staff. They were aware of any successes and failures because they were able to keep in touch with their customers. As the size of the business has grown, a number of issues have arisen:

- larger-scale operations raise the possibility of efficiency gains through economies of scale;
- the informal communication system is proving inadequate for the larger number of employees;
- new managers do not have the same commitment to the company as the founders;
- costs are being incurred of which the managers are not aware;
- the capital required for work-in-progress is soaring.

The founders have decided to appoint a business manager to deal with these symptoms of growth.

Requirement

Recommend, with reasons, the actions the business manager should take to smooth the transition of this small company to the next stage in its development.

(10 marks)

? Question 2

Great Value Foods (GVF) is one of Bigland's leading supermarket chains. Though fierce competitive activity had reduced the major players in the industry to half a dozen large chains in the years since 1970 the competitive pressures and large-scale capital investment required had not prevented all new entrants to the market. A few foreign competitors seeking new markets had managed to secure a foothold by offering unbranded goods at rock bottom prices. These companies kept costs low by displaying a limited range of grocery necessities on pallets in large warehouses and offering only minimal service. This development only served to increase the pressure on GVF since the new entrants nibbled away at what had been part of GVF's traditional customer base.

In the midst of all these difficulties, GVF was suddenly confronted with what seemed to be a golden opportunity. One of its competitors was experiencing trading difficulties and offered GVF the chance to purchase 60 of their stores in the south of the country. The opportunity was too much to resist and GVF borrowed £800 million and thereby doubled its outlets.

As GVF took over the management of their new clutch of southern superstores, however, it realised that considerable time and funds would be required to convert them to their own distinctive format and to the modern standards now expected by consumers. This not only delayed the expected revenue stream from the new outlets, it also required additional borrowing and raised gearing to an uncomfortable level. As if GVF did not have enough problems, the threat of inflation forced government to raise interest rates and so the burdens on GVF increased yet more.

During all this activity, GVF had been seeking to catch up on competitors in a number of ways. It had for instance managed to increase its number of own-label products significantly and had just developed a new central distribution system that experts agreed was among the best in the country. However, there were delays in distribution of supplies to some stores during the run up to the country's most important festive season. This resulted in a considerable loss for the company and three of the directors considered responsible for the problems were sacked.

These problems, together with an accompanying decline in profits, resulted in a fall in the share price GVF had paid too much for its 60 southern stores and that a rights issue would be necessary for the company to reduce its debt burden.

The first weeks of the new CEO were spent reviewing the company and its problems. She found that the company had too many layers of management, narrow functional attitudes and a controlling bureaucratic head office culture. Furthermore, the business was no longer effective and responding to customer needs.

Requirements

(a) Summarise the measures required to turn the company around.   **(5 marks)**
(b) Describe:
  (i) the most likely sources of resistance to change;
  (ii) any model of organisational change and explain how it might be used to implement change in GVF.   **(15 marks)**
                                                                                    (Total marks 20)

? Question 3

Sparks company was until recently the high street market leader of the retail clothiers but last month it reported its worst sales fall in its 120-year history and end-of-year figures are predicted to show that its profits are a quarter of those of the previous year. Analysts have identified a number of problems they believe responsible for Sparks' present situation. These include:

- Lack of anticipation of changing consumer preferences, an over-reliance on the brand image of the company as the primary means of marketing its products, and a relative lack of efficiency in getting its new designs to its stores.
- An unwieldy management structure with many management levels presided over by a large board of directors and an expensive head office in which managers considerably outnumber other members of staff.

- An inefficient distribution system in which goods move via a series of regional warehouses instead of direct from the factory.
- A poor system of purchasing in which Sparks continues to rely on relatively expensive domestic suppliers rather than bring in alternative cheaper supplies that have become available from other countries.

Requirement

As a consultant, advise the board of directors of Sparks to help them to overcome their problems and to turn the company around. **(12 marks)**

? Question 4

R&L is a large manufacturing firm that is well known as a 'good employer'. Over the past few years, R&L has experienced difficult times with reducing sales and mounting losses. In desperation it employed management consultants to analyse its situation. The consultants have concluded that the downturn in sales is permanent and that R&L needs to reduce its workforce by 50% over the next year in order to survive. Reluctantly, R&L's board of directors has accepted these findings, including the need to reduce the number of staff. The directors have also agreed to act as honestly and as fairly as possible, but realise that any changes they propose will be unpopular and may meet with resistance.

Requirement

Discuss the potential strategies available in order to overcome resistance to change, and identify those strategies that would be most suitable for R & L. **(10 marks)**

? Question 5

5.1 Activities associated with Organisational Development:

(A) require agreement that change must take place
(B) require 'interventions' into the social processes of an organisation
(C) naturally occur through a shared sense of purpose and a strong organisational culture
(D) result from the effect of Greiner's life-cycle model.

5.2 The technique of force field analysis depicts:

(A) change as occurring through a series of restraining and driving forces
(B) growth development of organisations through evolution and revolution
(C) an organisation's environment as a series of opportunistic and threatening factors
(D) aggressive management styles used to drive change. **(2 marks)**

5.3 According to Kurt Lewin the final stage of his three stage model of change is called:

(A) unfreezing
(B) refreezing
(C) unbundling
(D) support and facilitation. **(2 marks)**

All the above sub-question are work 2 marks each

Solutions to Revision Questions

6

✓ Solution 1

The founders of Z Ltd should recommend that the new business manager takes the following steps to smooth the development of this growing company:

- To produce efficiency gains through economies of scale, standardisation and specialisation of processes will be necessary. This in turn will require a more formal structuring of the organisation, possibly along functional lines with each founder specialising in their own area of competence.
- The communication system will need to be formalised with established lines of communication between superiors and subordinates within a function, and meetings between heads of departments to ensure co-ordination of functions. Briefing groups of the cascade type may perhaps be introduced so that information can be disseminated and shared. In addition, the use of consultation meetings and quality circles might be used to involve personnel and to aid upward communication.
- The use of incentive schemes and perhaps profit-sharing, together with a management development programme, should help motivation.
- The introduction of adequate control systems in terms of budgets and appropriate accounting systems would aid control of the more complex operations of a growing company. Of particular importance at this stage of growth is the introduction of accounting systems for purchasing and inventory control.
- The focus for efficiency would be the separate functions where streamlined methods of operating could be introduced. The introduction of just-in-time techniques to cut down on the cost of storage for materials and components might usefully be considered as a means of reducing the capital tied up in work-in-progress.

✓ Solution 2

(a) The inefficiency of GVF management appears to be related to the existing structure of the company. According to the CEO analysis there is a need to reduce the number of layers of management, to reduce controls from head office and to change attitudes from a narrow concern with departmental objectives to a broader concern with the demands of the business as a whole. The reduction in levels of management will help to reduce costs and to improve communications within the business. Store managers and others will welcome the reduction in bureaucratic head office controls, as the added autonomy will help motivate them.

2007.1

The CEO's comment that the company 'was no longer effective and responding to customer needs,' confirms what we already know from the case. What GVF needs to know more precisely, however, is exactly what the needs of customers are.

A useful framework for considering the causes of decline and the generic strategies required for turning a company around has been proposed by Slatter.

Reviewing the list of causes and proposed measures for action, it is apparent that many of the causes of decline listed by Slatter occur in the GVF case. Only in the instance of acquisitions is it necessary to note that, in GVF's case, the purchase of the 60 southern stores is probably a sound move. As to the recommendations for action, most of these have been accounted for in the proposals listed earlier.

(b) (i) Resistance to change in organisations can be considered according to whether the resistance comes from individuals, groups or the organisations themselves.

At the individual level the following reasons/causes have been noted as factors involved in resistance: fear of the unknown, well-formed habits, threat to economic interest/status and the threat of inconvenience. Given the present circumstances of GVF, it is likely that all of the above factors will be relevant to employees in the company. The press reports on the present position of the company will lead many of them fear for their job security and whether or not they will be able to continue with their present job or have to learn another one. Some will have few alternatives if they lose their present position and will be faced with the possible prospect of having to move to another part of the country to find another job or face the prospect of a less well-paid position or even to have to exist on state benefit payments. Managers who have heard the new CEO statement about the company having too many levels of management will be the most fearful about the loss of a job. For those with much to lose and little to gain from any impending changes there will be an understandable reluctance to engage in the change process with any enthusiasm. There will of course be those who see the forthcoming changes as long overdue and perhaps as an opportunity to prove themselves and make headway in the organisation under a new regime.

At the group level there will be collections of individuals who see their position threatened and who will combine to resist any threats to their position. This will be particularly the case if the employees are unionised. In some countries it is common for shop workers to be members of a trade union and any changes that affect the union members may be, resisted by threats of some form of industrial action. Even where trade unions do not exist within the organisation, it is possible for groups of employees, including managers, to collude informally to resist changes in an organisation. This may be achieved by such measures as withholding information or not being wholly co-operative with those seeking to implement change. In the GVF case, directors, managers and employees who see their established positions threatened in whatever way are unlikely to give full co-operation unless they can see some long-term advantage for themselves.

At the level of the organisation, a number of factors will operate to make the change process difficult. These include the existing structure and culture of the organisation, the existing investment in resources and past contracts and agreements with various stakeholders within the organisation. The change to a flatter more decentralised structure at GVF, for instance, threatens the jobs and status of some layers of management.

(ii) The new CEO of GVF might use the force-field theory of change proposed by Lewin. Lewin's theory suggests that all behaviour is the result of equilibrium between two sets of opposing forces. One set he refers to as driving forces because they are the forces attempting to bring about change; the other set are referred to as restraining forces because they act in the opposite direction and seek to maintain the status quo.

In the case in question, the driving forces for change in GVF would be those to be implemented by the new CEO and her senior managers. It may be useful to regard the senior management team as an instrument of change because in many ways the team could be regarded as being driven by forces threatening the organisation's survival. Competitors in particular will take more and more of the market share of GVF unless the management team can improve the operational efficiency of the organisation and its effectiveness. As far as efficiency is concerned, better management control is required, especially in the management of the new central distribution system. There is also a need to be more responsive to changes in the market place and this is why the drive to a more decentralised flatter structure is required.

✔ Solution 3

In the case of Sparks, the analysis of the main causes of the company's decline has already been conducted for us and we have the results. It is thus only necessary to examine each of these and to decide on the appropriate action to be taken.

The first set of problems suggests the need for more thorough market research and of increased attention to marketing generally. In particular, Sparks needs to be better able to spot fashion trends and to be ready to cater for a range of customers. The company also needs to be able to get its new designs to its stores as fast or faster than competitors. This will be a difficult task but must be achieved if the company is to compete effectively with the best. Attention to the logistical problems of moving from the design stage to the store shelves will also be required. One way of achieving this, already practised by some competitors, is to have goods delivered directly to stores rather than to regional warehouses.

The expensive head office and tall hierarchical structure needs to be looked at and tackled by a series of linked measures. Sparks needs to look at the possibility of delayering. The removal of layers of management has been common practice by a large number of organisations in recent years as a means of shortening reporting lines and thus enabling companies to be more responsive to competitive and other changes in the environment. This process of delayering will have the added advantage of reducing headcount and thus cutting costs – especially from the management-heavy headquarters.

The purchasing and distribution systems also appear to need a radical overhaul. The fact that Sparks takes so much longer to get its new designs into the stores than its major competitors underlines the need for this. The adoption of some overseas suppliers to replace some existing domestic suppliers could provide a jolt to existing suppliers and encourage them to work with Sparks into improving the efficiency of their supply chain. Care will be necessary in the selection of new suppliers. Though cost is a key consideration in the purchase of items of clothing, both quality and speed of delivery are also major considerations.

✓ Solution 4

Kotter and Schlesinger (1979) identify six main strategies for dealing with resistance. This might usefully serve as a framework for discussion:

- *Education and communication* is particularly useful when the basic problem is a lack of information about the need for, or the nature of, the planned change. The approach can be very time-consuming and will not work by itself if there are reasons other than misunderstanding leading to resistance to change. Such a strategy would seem to be appropriate in this case. As a good employer, R&L is honour bound to present all known facts on the plight of the company and discuss options openly and straightforwardly. A suitable strategy.

- *Participation and involvement* increases the chances of commitment to implementing the change particularly if their views are taken into account. This method is particularly appropriate when the people affected by the change have considerable power to resist it. This approach can be time-consuming. Such a strategy would seem to be appropriate in this case. Whatever positive measure is chosen, participation is vital to ensuring its success. The change is more acceptable if it is done by you rather than to you! A highly suitable strategy.

- *Facilitation and support* involves training, counselling and discussions, designed to reduce anxiety. This is particularly appropriate where the principal reason for resistance is based on insecurity and adjustment problems. Such a strategy would seem to be appropriate in this case; indeed the suggestion of outplacement is an embodiment of this strategy. A highly suitable strategy.

- *Negotiation and agreement* may be necessary to compensate those losing out because of the change. This may help avoid major problems, but it can be expensive in terms of, for example, redundancy packages. If there is little goodwill between the parties it may be protracted and bruising. Such a strategy would seem to be appropriate in this case, as R&L is a good employer there may be genuine goodwill between the management side and trade unions. A suitable strategy.

- *Manipulation and co-optation* involves presenting partial or misleading information to those resisting change and 'buying off' key players. This is a quick and relatively inexpensive approach, but normally results in future problems if the people involved realise they have been manipulated. Such a strategy would be inconsistent with R&L's philosophy of being a 'good employer'. An unsuitable strategy.

- *Explicit/implicit coercion* involves the use of force, or the threat of force, to enforce the implementation of change. It raises ethical (and potentially legal) problems as well as involving considerable risk of making a situation more difficult, especially if trade unions are in a position to provide opposition and protection. Such a strategy would be inconsistent with R&L's philosophy of being a 'good employer'. An unsuitable strategy.

✓ Solution 5

5.1 (B)

5.2 (A)

5.3 (B)

7

Preparing for the Examination

Preparing for the Examination

7

This section is intended for use when you are ready to start revising for your examination. It contains:

- a summary of useful revision techniques;
- details of the format of the examination;
- a bank of examination-standard revision questions and solutions,
- a complete past paper (This should be attempted when you consider yourself to be ready for the examination, and you should emulate examination conditions when you sit it).

Revision technique

Planning

The first thing to say about revision is that it is an addition to your initial studies, not a substitute for them. In other words, do not coast along early in your course in the hope of catching up during the revision phase. On the contrary, you should be studying and revising concurrently from the outset. At the end of each week, and at the end of each month, get into the habit of summarising the material you have covered to refresh your memory of it.

As with your initial studies, planning is important to maximise the value of your revision work. You need to balance the demands for study, professional work, family life and other commitments. To make this work, you will need to think carefully about how to make best use of your time.

Begin as before by comparing the estimated hours you will need to devote to revision with the hours available to you in the weeks leading up to the examination. Prepare a written schedule setting out the areas you intend to cover during particular weeks, and break that down further into topics for each day's revision. To help focus on the key areas try to establish:

- which areas you are weakest on, so that you can concentrate on the topics where effort is particularly needed;
- which areas are especially significant for the examination.

Do not forget the need for relaxation, and for family commitments. Sustained intellectual effort is only possible for limited periods, and must be broken up at intervals by lighter activities. Do not continue your revision timetable right up to the moment when you enter the exam hall: you should aim to stop work a day or even 2 days before the exam. Beyond this point the most you should attempt is an occasional brief look at your notes to refresh your memory.

Getting down to work

By the time you begin your revision you should already have settled into a fixed work pattern: a regular time of day for doing the work, a particular location where you sit, particular equipment that you assemble before you begin and so on. If this is not already a matter of routine for you, think carefully about it now in the last vital weeks before the exam.

You should have notes summarising the main points of each topic you have covered. Begin each session by reading through the relevant notes and trying to commit the important points to memory.

Usually this will be just your starting point. Unless the area is one where you already feel very confident, you will need to track back from your notes to the relevant chapter(s) in the Study System. This will refresh your memory on points not covered by your notes and fill in the detail that inevitably gets lost in the process of summarisation.

When you think you have understood and memorised the main principles and techniques, attempt an exam-standard question. At this stage of your studies you should normally be expecting to complete such questions in something close to the actual time allocation allowed in the exam. After completing your effort, check the solution provided and add to your notes any extra points it reveals.

Tips for the final revision phase

As the exam approaches closer, consider the following list of techniques and make use of those that work for you:

- Summarise your notes into a more concise form, perhaps on index cards that you can carry with you for revision on the way into work (Alternatively consider buying revision cards).
- Go through your notes with a highlighter pen, marking key concepts and definitions.
- Summarise the main points in a key area by producing a wordlist, mind map or other mnemonic device.
- On areas that you find difficult, rework questions that you have already attempted, and compare your answers in detail with those provided in the Study System.
- Rework questions you attempted earlier in your studies with a view to producing more 'polished' answers (better layout and presentation earn marks in the exam) and to completing them within the time limits.
- Stay alert for practical examples, incidents, situations and events that illustrate the material you are studying. If you can refer in the exam to real-life topical illustrations, you will impress the examiner and earn extra marks.

Format of the examination

Organisational Management and Information Systems is a 3-hour paper with two compulsory sections (for 40 and 30 marks, respectively) and one section with a choice of question for 30 marks. The format of this exam paper will be:

- Section A – 40% Compulsory mainly objective test questions
- Section B – 30% Compulsory short answer questions (6 sub-questions at 5 marks each)
- Section C – 30% Short scenario questions (a choice of 1 from 2 questions).

Section A: compulsory objective test questions

Generally, Section A will comprise 20 objective test sub-questions, 10 valued at 2 marks each and 5 valued at 4 marks each.

For the sub-questions worth 2 marks a conventional 'multiple choice' format is likely. The basis upon which these sub-questions are set is that only ONE option represents a correct answer. An example 'multiple choice' sub-question would be:

Local area networking is used for

(A) communication between computers within a limited geographical area;
(B) structuring an organisation within a division or business unit;
(C) exchange of information through a trade association or region;
(D) managing a complex operational issue by global interface with trade associations and professional bodies.

For sub-questions worth 4 marks answers should be in note form, may include bullet points and should not exceed 50 words. The nature of the question may be along the lines of:

'Explain the relationship between a (Just-in-Time) JIT system and cash flow management.'

> **!** Responses for each sub-question are expected to conform to the word limit indicated (in this case 50 words). Responses beyond this limit are not marked.

Section B: compulsory short answer questions

Section B comprises six compulsory short answer sub-questions, each worth 5 marks (in total 30 marks). A short scenario may be given, to which some or all questions relate. As with the 4 mark questions referred to earlier you will be encouraged to answer in a concise fashion. These answers will *not* take the form of either a flowing narrative or a business report, and should be no more than one page in length for each sub-question. This limit was imposed for two reasons:

1. to simulate a real-life scenario in which accuracy, brevity and clarity is called for;
2. to prevent candidates from spending a disproportionate amount of time on 5% of the marks available.

> **!** Responses for each sub-question are expected to conform to the word limit indicated (in this case one page). Responses beyond this limit are not marked.

Section C: a choice of question

You will be required to answer one question, from a choice of two, worth 30 marks. Short scenarios are highly likely to feature.

The Past Paper (see later) is intended to be an indicative guide of the style and type of questions that are likely to appear in future examinations. It does not seek to cover the full range of the syllabus learning outcomes for this subject.

Examination-standard revision questions and solutions

The bank of examination-standard revision questions and solutions is structured, as follows:

Section A style questions
Section A style solutions
Section B style questions
Section B style solutions
Section C style questions
Section C style solutions.

To strengthen your understanding of the subject matter it is strongly recommended that you refer to the appropriate chapter when reviewing your written answers of these as indicated in Table 7.1 below.

Table 7.1 Syllabus weighting and chapter reference

	Information systems	Marketing	Human capital	Operations management	Change
Syllabus Weighting (%)	20	20	30	20	10
Main Chapter Reference	1	2	3 and 4	5	6

Finally, Table 7.2 indicates syllabus coverage of the questions that follow:

2 MARKS	Information systems	Marketing	Human capital	Operations management	Change
A1	✓				
A2				✓	
A3				✓	
A4				✓	
A5			✓		
A6				✓	
A7			✓		
A8			✓		
A9				✓	
A10			✓		
A11			✓		
A12				✓	
A13				✓	
A14	✓				
A15				✓	
A16					✓
A17					✓
A18			✓		
A19			✓		
A20					✓
A21		✓			
A22			✓		
A23			✓		
A24		✓			
A25		✓			
A26	✓				
A27				✓	
A28		✓			
A29			✓		
A30			✓		

4 MARKS	Information systems	Marketing	Human capital	Operations management	Change
A100	✓				
A101	✓				
A102	✓				
A103	✓				
A104				✓	
A105	✓				
A106					✓
A107		✓			
A108				✓	
A109	✓				
A110				✓	
A111				✓	
A112				✓	
A113		✓			
A114			✓		

5 MARKS	Information systems	Marketing	Human capital	Operations management	Change
B1(a)		✓			
B1(b)			✓		
B1(c)		✓			
B1(d)		✓			
B1(e)		✓			
B1(f)		✓	✓		
B2(a)				✓	
B2(b)		✓		✓	
B2(c)				✓	✓
B2(d)				✓	
B2(e)	✓				
B2(f)	✓	✓			
B3(a)					✓
B3(b)	✓				
B3(c)					✓
B3(d)	✓				
B3(e)			✓		
B3(f)	✓				

Marks vary in weighting	Information systems	Marketing	Human capital	Operations management	Change
C1(a)			✓		
C1(b)					✓
C1(c)		✓			
C2(a)			✓		
C2(b)					✓
C2(c)					✓
C3(a)			✓		
C3(b)			✓		
C3(c)				✓	
C4(a)		✓			
C4(b)			✓		
C4(c)			✓		
C5(a)		✓			
C5(b)					✓
C5(c)					✓
C6(a)			✓		
C6(b)			✓		
C6(c)			✓		
C7(a)	✓				
C7(b)	✓				
C7(c)					✓
C8(a)				✓	
C8(b)				✓	
C8(c)				✓	

A Style Revision
Questions

A1 The operating system:

(A) forms part of a system's software
(B) forms part of a system's hardware
(C) is another term for a system's hardware
(D) is a stand-alone end-user (operator) system solution.

A2 Core features of world-class manufacturing involve:

(A) competitor benchmarking and an investment in training and development
(B) an investment in IT and technical skills
(C) global sourcing networks and an awareness of competitor strategies
(D) a strong customer focus and flexibility to meet customer requirements.

A3 An ABC system refers to:

(A) a Japanese style problem-solving device that is particularly helpful in inventory management
(B) an inventory management method that concentrates effort on the most important items
(C) accuracy, brevity and clarity in the quality of system reporting
(D) a mainframe solution to managing inventory.

A4 Corrective work, the cost of scrap and materials lost are:

(A) examples of internal failure costs
(B) examples of external failure costs
(C) examples of appraisal costs
(D) examples of preventative costs.

A5 An assessment centre:

(A) helps selection by assessing job candidates by using a comprehensive and inter-related series of techniques
(B) is the training headquarters where job interviews take place
(C) is a desk-based process of reviewing job application forms for suitability
(D) is a place where job applicants are subjected to psychological testing.

A6 Training workers in methods of statistical process control and work analysis:

(A) overcomes a crisis of control in an organisation's life cycle
(B) is part of a succession planning approach to Human Resources

(C) is part of a quality management approach

(D) is part of a scientific management approach.

A7 The use of standard questions in job interviews helps ensure:

(A) fairness

(B) validity

(C) reliability

(D) completeness.

A8 The so-called 'psychological contract' is a notion that is based on:

(A) segmenting then accessing a market

(B) the buyer–supplier relationship

(C) a distinctive style of testing used in selection procedures

(D) the expectations the organisation and employee have of one another.

A9 Economies of scope refers to:

(A) the economic viability of making alterations to systems

(B) an organisation becoming economically viable through a process of 'rightsizing'

(C) mass production assembly lines achieving economies through volume of output

(D) economically producing small batches of a variety of products with the same machines.

A10 According to Douglas McGregor:

(A) 'Theory X' people dislike work, need direction and avoid responsibility

(B) 'Theory Y' people dislike work, need direction and avoid responsibility

(C) self-actualising people dislike work, need direction and avoid responsibility

(D) hygiene factors determine whether people like work, need direction or take responsibility.

A11 The purpose of a person specification is to provide details of:

(A) organisational size and diversity of activity

(B) the types of responsibilities and duties to be undertaken by the post holder

(C) personal characteristics, experience and qualifications expected of a candidate

(D) individual terms of engagement and period of contract.

A12 Reck and Long's strategic positioning tool identifies an organisation's:

(A) purchasing approach

(B) sales approach

(C) manufacturing approach

(D) warehousing approach.

A13 Inbound logistics is:

(A) a secondary activity that refers to price negotiation of incoming raw materials

(B) a secondary activity that refers to receipt, storage and inward distribution of raw materials

(C) a primary activity that refers to inbound enquiries and customer complaints

(D) a primary activity that refers to receipt, storage and inward distribution of raw materials.

A14   The five elements of a computer system are:

(A) data, communication, flexibility, hardware and data integrity
(B) installation, hardware, maintenance, audit and compliance
(C) hardware, software, procedures, data and people
(D) input, processing, monitoring, control and reporting.

A15   Supply chain partnerships grow out of:

(A) quality accreditation
(B) recognising the supply chain and linkages in a value system
(C) an expansion of trade
(D) adopting a marketing philosophy.

A16   The most radical form of organisational change includes a cultural shift and is described as:

(A) Emergent change
(B) Transformational change
(C) Step change
(D) Incremental change.

A17   Establishing a staff help-line when attempting to cope with resistance to change is an example of:

(A) Facilitation
(B) Manipulation
(C) Coercion
(D) Co-optation.

A18   The processes of job analysis and individual performance appraisal are related in the sense that:

(A) they are different terms for the same process
(B) performance appraisal is based on job analysis
(C) both form part of the selection process
(D) job analysis is based on performance appraisal.

A19   Content theories of motivation tend to focus mainly on:

(A) the needs of the group
(B) feelings of complacency or dissatisfaction
(C) the needs of individuals
(D) the use of 'carrots' and 'sticks' as devices.

A20   Third party consultants, therapy groups and confrontation are normally all associated with:

(A) industrial disputes over terms and conditions
(B) the process of job evaluation
(C) a firm experiencing severe trading difficulties
(D) Organisational Development.

A21 'Market shakeout' involves the weakest producers exiting a particular market and occurs in a period between:

(A) market growth and eventual decline
(B) introduction and market growth
(C) market growth and market maturity
(D) market maturity and decline.

A22 It is the role of 'outplacement consultants' to:

(A) provide help to redundant employees including training and finding jobs
(B) provide help to employees wishing to gain experience in other roles
(C) arrange for placing products in an untested market place
(D) arrange for placing underused assets at the disposal of start-up businesses.

A23 F. W. Taylor's thinking on motivation in the workplace involved a belief that:

(A) social groups and individuals as part of a culture should be key considerations
(B) reward for effort and workplace efficiency should be key considerations
(C) managers had two different sets of assumptions about their subordinates
(D) 'motivators' and 'hygiene factors' should be key considerations.

A24 The choice to buy a fast-moving consumer good (FMCGs) is normally:

(A) a personal choice involving relatively low financial outlays
(B) a personal choice involving relatively high financial outlays
(C) a choice made on behalf of an organisation involving moderate outlays
(D) a personal choice influenced by new features, fashions and old product wear-out.

A25 The twin processes of identifying the target customer group and deciding the best method to reach this market is called:

(A) market research
(B) market development
(C) segmentation
(D) product placement.

A26 A main aim of electronic data interchange (EDI) is:

(A) to improve communication exchanges within an organisation
(B) to replace conventional documentation with structured electronically transmitted data
(C) to allow employees to work at home;
(D) to create a shared data resource within an organisation.

A27 International standard ISO 14001 'Environmental Management Systems' encourages processes for controlling and improving an organisation's:

(A) performance on 'green' issues
(B) performance on quality issues as they relate to the competitive environment
(C) performance on scanning an industry environment
(D) performance on its internal investment in people.

A28 Separate people or groups such as initiators, influencers, buyers and users are all involved in a buying decision in the context of:

(A) fast-moving consumer goods marketing
(B) business-to-business marketing
(C) business-to-consumer marketing
(D) services marketing.

A29 In terms of employment CIM's ethical guidelines requires members to:

(A) act responsibly in way that all other professionals do
(B) act responsibly but in a way that satisfies organisational demands and pressures
(C) act responsibly but in a way that satisfies your own ethical code
(D) act responsibly, honour any legal contract of employment and conform to employment legislation.

A30 360 degree feedback is part of a system that encourages:

(A) organisational appraisal based on feedback from customers and suppliers
(B) organisational appraisal based on relative industry and competitor performance
(C) personal appraisal based on feedback from peers, subordinates, bosses and even external parties
(D) personal appraisal based on feedback from your boss and your self-appraisal documentation.

Answer the following sub-questions using no more than 50 words per sub-question:

A100 Describe the main advantages of an organisation developing and using an 'extranet'. **(4 marks)**

A101 Explain the relationship between open systems and adaptive maintenance. **(4 marks)**

A102 Parallel running and pilot schemes are methods of systems changeover. Explain the reasons why an organisation might instead choose a direct approach to a system changeover. **(4 marks)**

A103 Explain the reasons why a department of an organisation might be continuing to use manual records rather than using a new, recently installed and fully operational computer system. **(4 marks)**

A104 Describe the ways in which Total Productive Maintenance might contribute towards a manufacturing organisation's quality programme. **(4 marks)**

A105 Explain the relationship between 'data independence' and a database approach to flexible data management. **(4 marks)**

A106 Change occurs when there is organisational growth through take over. Certain basic 'rules' for takeovers to succeed have been suggested which need to be considered before the takeover occurs. Identify what these might be. **(4 marks)**

A107 Compare and contrast product orientated organisations and production orientated organisations. **(4 marks)**

A108 Distinguish Quality assurance (QA) systems from quality control systems. **(4 marks)**

A109 Briefly explain the main factors management should take into account when choosing computer hardware. **(4 marks)**

A110 Describe the relationship between operations management and (using Mintzberg's terminology) the organisational technostrucutre. **(4 marks)**

A111 Explain how continuous inventory systems might work against an organisation's JIT philosophy. **(4 marks)**

A112 Identify (with examples) types of external failure costs, and explain the significance for an organisation with a reputation for quality. **(4 marks)**

A113 Distinguish between push and pull marketing policies and their impact on the promotion of goods. **(4 marks)**

A114 Explain the main stages involved in developing human resource plans and programmes following the production of a corporate plan. **(4 marks)**

Solutions to A Style Revision Questions

A1	(A)
A2	(D)
A3	(B)
A4	(A)
A5	(A)
A6	(C)
A7	(A)
A8	(D)
A9	(D)
A10	(A)
A11	(C)
A12	(A)
A13	(D)
A14	(C)
A15	(B)
A16	(B)
A17	(A)
A18	(B)
A19	(C)
A20	(D)
A21	(C)
A22	(A)
A23	(B)
A24	(A)
A25	(D)
A26	(B)
A27	(A)
A28	(B)
A29	(D)
A30	(C)

A100   Extranet: an extended Intranet that links business partners.
Advantages:

- fosters collaboration & information sharing
- adds speed & cohesion
- facility to link & maximise dispersed networks
- enhanced inter-organisational communication

- allows electronic data interchange & e-procurement
- communication strengthens relationships with customers, suppliers, and trade organisations.

A101   An open system interacts with its external environment. This thinking is consistent with adaptive maintenance. Adaptive maintenance is a mid- to long-term process that adjusts Information Systems (IS) applications to reflect changing business operations and environments. In this way it accounts for opportunities or threats.

A102   At a predetermined time old system ceases entirely & new one starts. Why use?

- complete confidence in system
- symbolic act to encourage commitment
- part of unfreezing change process
- reduced system usage: lower risk of disruption at chosen time.

A103

- group resistance to change
- cultural resistance
- lack of confidence in new system
- complexity of new system
- efficiency of manual system
- individuals lack confidence to cope
- individuals jobs feel threatened
- ineffective management, control, communication, training, lack of support, and so on.

A104   Total productive maintenance plans and implements the systematic maintenance of all equipment. This increases productivity and prevents unplanned breakdowns.

- Helps consistent production
- Reduces scrap and rework so lowering cost of quality
- Improves accuracy of forecasting requirements
- Staff morale improved as quality increases.

A105   A database approach involves collecting integrated common data that is then shared throughout the organisation. Data independence is an essential feature of a database approach. It means that data exists independently of the programs that use it. The flexibility this gives includes:

- data or programs can be amended without changing the other.
- multiple users, using different programs can access the same data at the same time.
- data being wholly shared represents an expanded collective resource allowing a greater potential for flexible and enhanced usage

A106   Drucker (1982) feels that there are five basic rules/ guidelines which involve questioning is there:

- Contribution? What contribution can it make (other than money) to the acquired company?
- Common core? Both companies should have common markets, production operations or technology.

- Value? (of the products, services and customers acquired)
- Available management cover – if key managers leave the acquired company?
- Linkage? Within a year there should be promotion of staff across the two previously separate companies.

Note: other alternative thinking on the subject expressed by other authors to that given by Drucker and relevant guidelines published by various bodies also exist. Such relevant alternatives, if quoted by candidates, will receive credit.

A107

	Product orientated	Production orientated
Main focus	Product features	Production efficiency
Quality	May be high	May be low
Cost	May be high	Low
Sales	Not sufficiently considered	Low quality may lead to lower sales

Neither organisation:

- has researched market demand
- is in touch with the customer and their requirements.

Both risk products not selling sufficiently.

Note that an alternative valid interpretation of the organisations could be as follows:

Production-orientated companies have a production department budget (excluding purchasing) representing the largest percentage of company turnover whereas a product-orientated company is one where the design department budget represents the largest proportion of turnover. Examples of the former include a subcontract painter or Rolls Royce, and examples of the latter include an Architects practice or Amstrad with their E phones.

A108 Both have a different philosophy on quality:

- Quality control (QC) systems attempt to *control* quality, whereas
- QA systems attempt to *create* quality.

QC involves managing each stage of production to minimise errors, (a third party, negative intervention process). QC inspects afterwards.

QA check quality in a positive way encouraging worker ownership for quality. QA prevents beforehand.

A109

- Main factors when choosing computer hardware include:
- *Suitability*. Cost, User requirements
- *Acceptability*. Manufacturers reputation, Computer specification, Built in features (e.g. security)
- *Feasibility*. Compatibility with existing systems, Computers used elsewhere within the organisation's industry and so on.

A110 The relationship between operations management and the organisational technostructure.

Operations management:

- Developing outputs (products/services) by transforming inputs (stock, human) through operations (manufacturing, assembly etc).

Technostructure:

- Expert advice, training, research, standardising processes, outputs and skills.
- Involves work-study, HR managers and so on.

Relationship: OM 5 operating core and finances a technostructure that helps make operations effective.

Note to readers: In larger organisations, some parts of the technostructure may devote themselves to operations management issues alone.

A111 Continuous inventory systems working against a JIT philosophy.

Continuous inventory:

- Monitoring to keep above a predetermined level
- Fixed amount ordered.
- Zero demand = buffer stocks ('just in case'); inconsistent with JIT.

JIT philosophy (eliminate all waste; right part at the right place at the right time) better supported with JIT inventory approach.

A112 The type and significance of external failure costs for an organisation with a reputation for quality.

External failure = costs of sub-standard goods sold, for example:

- 'Free' replacement.
- Redesign/rework costs, wastage and so on.
- Warranty claims.
- Product liability and damages.

Significance = Goods with customer, meaning:

- Damaged reputation/staff morale?
- Loss of repeat sales/future custom?
- Reduced customer confidence?
- Bad PR (complaints).

A113 Push and pull marketing policies and their impact on the promotion of goods.

Firms may have:

- Suppliers (downstream)
- Supply others (upstream).

in a value chain that links to ultimate consumer.

	push	pull
Aim	'push' to wholesalers/retailers who sell to customers.	Influence final consumers' attitudes through, for example, advertising. Consumer demand 'pulls' through.
Promotion to consumer	Final firm in value chain.	Shared by manufacturer.

A114   Main stages in developing HR plans and programmes following production of a corporate plan.

Stages:

1. A supply forecast:
   - Analysis of existing resources.
   - Projection of likely changes over period (natural wastage, turnover etc.).
2. Identify demand implied by corporate plan.
3. Articulate both forecasts in HR plan.
4. Develop programmes with target dates to reconcile supply and demand. (Address recruitment, selection, training, management development, transfers, redeployment, redundancies, etc.)

Note: This explanation is based on Mullins (2005). It is not the only way of understanding the stages. Other thinkers may express a need for internal and external data collection and analysis using models such as PESTLE, and so on. Valid alternative approaches to that suggested by Mullins will also receive credit.

NOTE: IT IS IMPORTANT TO CONTAIN YOUR RESPONSES TO THE GIVEN WORD LIMIT

B Style Revision Questions

(Note that all the sub-questions are valued at 5 marks each. Responses for each sub-question should be contained to one page).

B1   Vertigo is an innovative company run on the principles of its entrepreneurial owner. The company operates a package distribution service, a train service, and sells holidays, bridal outfits, clothing, mobile telephones, and soft drinks. Its approach of challenging the norm and 'giving customers quality products and services at affordable prices and doing it all with sense of fun' is well known. Vertigo spends little on advertising but has great brand awareness thanks to the 'visibility' of its inspirational owner.

Vertigo has just announced the launch of 'V-cosmetics' to exploit a gap in the market. The cosmetic range will be competitively priced against high street brands and have the distinctive Vertigo logo.

You work for a market analyst who is about to appear on a radio discussion of Vertigo's business interests. You have been asked to provide a clear, short briefing on the thinking behind 'V-cosmetics'. Your research of the 'V-cosmetics' identifies innovative marketing proposals. V-cosmetics will not be on sale in shops, instead it will use two approaches to promotion and selling, namely:

The use of 'cosmetic associates'. Individuals may apply to become an associate and if accepted are required to buy a basic stock of every V-cosmetic product. The associate will then use these products as samples and 'testers'. After initial training associates organise parties in the homes of friends, and their friends where they take orders for products at a listed price. Associates receive commission based on sales.

The Internet and mobile telephone technology will also be heavily used to offer V-cosmetics to the public.

Requirements

Prepare brief notes containing bullet points and no more than two to three sentences for each of the key points identified below. Use a separate page of your answer book for each key point (meaning that your notes are contained on no more than six pages in total).

(a) Explain how the proposed approach can be understood within the context of the marketing mix.

(b) Outline the human resource implications of using cosmetic associates.

(c)   Explain the concept of direct marketing.

(d)   Explain the advantages of the Internet as a marketing channel.

(e)   Identify how Vertigo might use Internet and mobile telephone technology as part of their marketing approach.

(f)   Identify the main ethical issues associated with the proposal.

B2   You are a researcher employed by a topical business television show 'Round the table'. Next week's discussion is about managing supply to achieve quality and customer satisfaction. Invited guests will be a leading academic, public and private sector senior managers and the chief executive of a car producer.

You have been asked to produce an outline briefing that will give some background information to the show's presenter.

Your research shows that the automobile industry is highly competitive and globally suffers from 'overcapacity'. In certain countries, however, there is unfulfilled demand for specialist makes and models, implying some under capacity 'hot spots'. You understand that for any organisation whether producing goods or services, effective capacity management is vital. It ensures that customers' needs are more fully met, and that there are fewer unfulfilled delivery date promises. There are several ways of dealing with variations in demand and matching production capacity including:

- Concentrating on inventory levels ('Level capacity' strategy).
- Concentrating on demand ('Demand' strategy).
- Adjusting levels of activity ('Chase' strategy).

As part of your investigation you note that distinctive issues exist for service organisations (such as those found in the public sector).

Requirements

As the shows researcher you are required to produce outline notes to support the show's presenter.

These notes should have particular regard to quality, capacity and other organisational issues:

(a)   Discuss why a level capacity strategy might be difficult for a firm wishing to adopt a JIT philosophy   **(5 marks)**

(b)   Discuss the impact of demand strategies on an organisation's marketing practice   **(5 marks)**

(c)   Discuss the relationship between chase strategies and the flexible organisation   **(5 marks)**

(d)   When considering capacity management identify the ways that service organisations differ from manufacturing organisations   **(5 marks)**

These notes should:

(e)   Identify and describe the types of software applications a manufacturing firm might introduce to improve its supply operations

(f)   Describe the types of computerised assistance that could be used by those involved in selling cars and wanting to improve demand.

B3 S & C is a medium-sized firm that is experiencing rapid growth thanks to increased turnover. It has been able to develop a range of new consultancy and specialist business advisory services that it offers to its growing customer base. To cope with these developments several company-wide initiatives have been launched over the past 2 years.

The existing financial systems are struggling to cope with these developments. The replacement of the existing software is due to go ahead within the next 6 months. The new system was justified partly because it could reduce costs (although precise details have not been given). Although the application software does not fit existing business processes exactly it has the clear advantage of giving S & C access to an industry best practice system and is identical to that used by all its main competitors and some of its clients. A three-person project steering group has recommended that a phased approach to introduction will be used and has undertaken most of the project planning. A programme of events for implementing the system has been agreed but is not yet fully operational. This group has not met for a while because the designated project manager has been absent from work with illness.

You are Head of S & C's Central Support Unit. You also serve on the project steering group.

A partners meeting is due to take place soon. The firm's senior partner has asked you to prepare a PowerPoint presentation to other partners on implementation issues. You understand that partners are conscious that system implementation represents a form of further organisational change and are asking questions about the approach that will be taken to the introduction of the new system; likely changes to practices; critical areas for success, system testing, support after implementation and system effectiveness, and so on.

Requirements

You are required to produce *outline notes* that will support your eventual PowerPoint presentation. These notes should:

(a) Explain why a phased approach to introducing the system is, in this case, particularly more suitable than a more direct 'big bang' approach.

(b) Describe the options to overcome the fact that the software does not fit existing business processes exactly.

(c) Discuss the ways in which particular individuals and groups within S & C are important for implementation to succeed.

(d) Explain the aims of a post-implementation review.

(e) Describe the training that should be given in terms of topics, methods and targeted groups within S & C.

(f) Explain how users might be involved in testing the system during the implementation phase.

Solutions to B Style Revision Questions

B1(a)   **The marketing mix**

The marketing mix involves four marketing tools, Product, Price, Promotion and Place, that are 'mixed/blended' in terms of effort, emphasis and integration. Here is V cosmetics' mix:

- *Product*. Good quality and branded products. Likely to be attractive due to brand strength.
- *Price*. Competitive but not cheap (affordable). Price seems inflexible (list price). Are Internet sales also placed at list price? Savings that V made on advertising, shops and expensive distribution networks can be passed on to customers. Also reward associates and invest in IT. Likely to be profitable given saving potential over rivals.
- *Promotion*. Little advertising, focussing instead on Public Relations. Given success in other ventures, this should work with cosmetics. The strength of brand name is significant.
- *Place*. that is getting the right products into the right places at the right time. Approach is through one-level marketing (cosmetic associate) and interactive marketing. Assumes expertise of associates and user acceptance of Internet. As philosophy is based on sense of fun, it may work. Need efficient distribution once order is placed; link to V's distribution services?

Maybe a fifth P is relevant, that is People (see answer to 2 (b)).
Key point: the mix must satisfy customer needs.

B1(b)   **Human resource (HR) implications of cosmetic associates**

The reputation of V is important and must be maintained through effective HR.

- Selection Criteria: Attitude; applicants should (a) display a sense of fun and (b) reflect the image of the company. Trustworthiness important; need for interview and references.
- Training of cosmetic associates in sales techniques and how to arrange parties. Also those servicing the Internet and text queries.
- Remuneration package needs to be right to attract and retain associates. Commission on sales must be sufficient incentive. Appropriate remuneration package for Internet sales needs to be devised.
- Supervision, monitoring and control: A system is needed (maybe customer questionnaires, area supervisors etc.)

B1(c)   **Direct Marketing**

- A business, possibly manufacturer, deals directly with end customer, possibly using the Internet.
- A 'zero level channel', that is, direct between supplier and end customer.
- Shortens supply chain so takes costs out of value system.
- Examples include the web-based company Amazon.com and the direct booking of air travel on line.
- Direct marketing mix implications for place and promotion. 'Place' is not physical, it is cyberspace. Promotion is possible in electronic form through targeting Web users.

B1(d)   **Advantages of the Internet**

- Speed of communication.
- Flexibility of use: promote, answer queries, sell, display products.
- Convenience for user: in own home and can be accessed any time.
- Attractive use of time for user: can compare and contrast prices and so on with rivals 'on line'.
- Potential for lower prices as costs are lower than physical stores with capital and running costs.
- Potential for companies to develop databases of customers, those making enquiries for further sales promotions.

B1(e)   **Internet and mobile telephone: use as part of V's marketing**
         Internet

- Fits sense of fun – not a physical event (browsing, enquiries and purchasing on line):
- Relies on user acceptance of credit cards; this is likely given other V businesses.
- Expectations that prices are cheaper than high street; fits affordable prices philosophy.
- Orders on line (needs efficient distribution once the order is placed, maybe linking to V's distribution services).
- Promotion using, for example, Web banners, affiliation websites, collaboration with other websites and search facilities.

         Mobile telephones ('M-marketing)

- To stimulate product interest, maybe through V mobiles links, text alerts and so on.
- As a sales alternative to the Internet. Novel : fits 'sense of fun'.
- Could be used to arrange a follow up by passing details on to associates.
- To deal with range of customer enquiries. (Need sophisticated IT)

B1(f)   **Ethical issues**
         Ethical stance of an individual business is determined by organisational culture and philosophy.

- What we know about V: entrepreneurial (takes risks?), different, quality products, affordable prices and fun. These factors will be relevant as will legislative frameworks.
- Issue of using associates: are they being fairly treated? (Requirement to buy basic stock, continue to sell products, is remuneration appropriate?)

- Issues of using parties for selling: (Other examples: Tupperware, Virgin Vie, Ann Summers.) Is the public being tricked/pressured into using their home in this way? What is in it for them (gifts, discounts, fees, etc.).
- Issue of selling approach: are associates obliged to adopt impolite or 'pushy' sales techniques, which is unfair on the customer.
- Issue of targeting customers through Internet and mobiles: may be overly intrusive or abuse of databases/relationship (with possible implications for data protection legislation).

B2(a) Level capacity strategy: difficult for a firm wishing to adopt a JIT philosophy.
About level capacity:

- Level capacity involves building inventory levels to deal with increases in demand beyond 'normal'.
- This suggests a building of buffer stocks of (for instance) cars to deal with excess demand.
- The notion of buffer stocks is wholly inconsistent with a firm wishing to adopt a quality-driven just-in-time (JIT) philosophy.

About JIT:
- JIT is considered key to many organisational quality programmes
- JIT production methods involve each component on a production line being produced only when it is needed and not before.
- An outcome of JIT is an elimination of large stocks of materials and parts, not a building of them (as level capacity strategies imply).

Key Points
- Customer satisfaction may be improved short term by adopting a level capacity strategy (making immediate delivery possible). However, these 'buffer' stocks are inconsistent with the JIT quality approach.
- Level capacity increases stockholding costs and may not be the most cost-effective means of capacity management.
- Organisational requirement: more working capital to build stocks.
- A more lasting means of achieving customer satisfaction might be the full adoption of a quality philosophy instead.

B2(b) The impact of demand strategies on an organisation's marketing practice.
About Demand strategies:

- Demand strategies attempt to influence demand to 'smooth' variations so that the organisation is better able to cope.
- This represents a type of manipulation and influence over demand so that it is 'made' to 'fit' supply capability.

About marketing:
The marketing function will want to ensure that the marketing mix (Product /service, Price, Promotion & Place) is appropriate for the individual organisation and may:

- vary price to encourage/slow down demand.
- intensify promotion in 'slack' periods.
- restrict sales outlets (place) when there is excess demand.
  Marketing practice can in ways such as these support demand strategies.

Key Points
- The marketing tactics above represent short-term practices and may not benefit the firm long term. It might, for instance, lead to reduced satisfaction when customers are frustrated by the restrictions of place. They may indeed decide to switch to a competitor's product.
- The use of demand strategies in conjunction with marketing practice suggests that the organisation is not marketing orientated. The main focus is not the customer; it is rather internal production considerations. This philosophy will ultimately hurt quality, which has the customer as central.
- In terms of organisational implications profitability may be affected as a result of financing sales promotions and price reductions.

B2(c)   Relationship between chase strategies and the flexible organisation.
About Chase strategies:

- Chase strategies involve constantly adjusting activity levels to shadow fluctuations in demand. This demonstrates market responsiveness and closeness to the customer demands.

About flexible organisations:
There is something of an organisational trend emerging that has 'non-traditional' organisational structures and a flexible workforce. These measures allow organisations to display maximum flexibility and responsiveness to customer demands.

By using a flexible organisation approach to accommodate 'peaks and troughs', chase strategies will be possible, specifically:

- Organisational structures: may achieve operational flexibility by becoming less rigid in terms of hierarchy.
- Skills flexibility might be achieved by cross training employees to perform different operations. Integration of tasks can occur both horizontally (undertaking a broader range of tasks at the same level as their original task) and vertically (undertaking tasks previously carried out by employees at other levels).
- Atkinson's worker categories involve core and periphery staff (temporary/part-time) to act as a buffer against changes in demand. Numerical flexibility might be achieved by an increased use of temporary, part-time, short-term contract working and outsourcing work at peak times. Such flexibility might be achieved by using both contractors and agency staff.

Key Points
- The two concepts complement one another.
- Such an approach would more easily achieve customer satisfaction.
- It would be consistent with a quality ethos, as flexible manufacturing is at the heart of a quality approach.
- Organisational implications include: structures, HR policies and practice, rewards, recruitment and training. Organisationally there should also be a commitment to continuous improvement, including the use of quality circles.

B2(d) Capacity management: the ways that service organisations differ from manufacturing organisations.
Differences for a service organisation:

- The consumer is a participant in the service process (unlike the purchaser of a manufactured good).
- The characteristics of the workforce determine the effectiveness of the service to a greater degree, as the consumer–worker interaction is central.
- Services are perishable.
- Services are intangible, so communication is more difficult when explaining the benefits of a purchase. This makes marketing more complex.
- Output measurement is less easy to evidence (Outputs for Not for Profit (NFP) organisations are often multiple).
- NFP funding may be government determined and may be insufficient to finance to meet all customer demands immediately, which implies a need for a rationing of service.
- For NFP organisations, consumers may be a different grouping from those paying for the service to be provided. This is confusing when concentrating on customers, as there are multiple customers to satisfy each with different, sometimes contradictory demands.

Key Points

- The level capacity strategy assumes that units of production are durable and can be stored (as is the case with cars). This may not be possible for perishable goods and services more generally (It is impossible to 'stockpile' consultancy advice).
- There may be a lack of customer satisfaction, if (using a medical treatment example) waiting lists appear.
- Quality issues are more overtly of a human kind as the workforce determine the quality of the service.
- Organisational implications include appropriate HR policies to ensure that employees deal with customers appropriately and impact positively on customer satisfaction levels. Good systems to support delivery of the services are also important.

B2(e) This can be understood in the context of Michael Porter's value chain model, as follows:

- Inbound logistics: one of five primary activities directly concerned with the creation or delivery of a product.
- Support activities: help improve the efficiency and effectiveness of primary activities and include technology development (and therefore software applications).

The issue becomes the *types* of software applications that would help with inbound logistics, including receiving, storing and distributing materials, including material handling, stock control, transport and so on. These applications may be developed in-house or purchased as off the shelf.

Types of applications include:

- Software that assists inventory management inventory (whether method used is continuous, periodic inventory or ABC, etc.).
- Warehousing including storage and reordering (Under a Just-in-time system the matching of the receipt of material closely with usage is key to reducing stock-holding levels and costs. Larger organisations would certainly need IT support. Software is capable of producing reports to ensure that quantities held in stock are within the predetermined budgets).
- Software capable of assisting the management of transport including work scheduling.
- Benchmarking database of inbound activities. This allows a convenient and systematic comparison to be made of practice and/or process with suitable comparator organisations and other sections.
- Internet-enabled purchasing software from suppliers possibly using an E-catalogue.
- Software to assist purchasing possibly databases of suppliers where issues of quality and price can be monitored.

One specific example of software:

- Manufacturing Resource Planning (MRP) (e.g. MRP II), a system that assists capacity management through a matching supply & demand. Organisational implications: Reduced stock holding & stock turnover, and improved facilities usage. Customer satisfaction: Fewer delays through materials shortage, certainty over delivery times.

B2(f) Selling cars and wanting to improve demand: the types of computerised assistance that could be used.

Cars are consumer goods and sales and promotion strategies are important to both car manufacturers and dealers. Sales and promotion strategies (along with the others Ps including price) will help 'determine' demand.

Computerised technology might be used in a number of ways in order to communicate with existing, past and potential customers the benefits of the products (car models) and so stimulate demand. Examples include:

Database of potential customers may be good for targeting particular customers and their likely requirements. It enables messages to be personalised. This allows for direct letter mailing of promotional literature. It is also easier to improve customer relationships and hence buyer loyalties by customer follow-up contact after sales are made. In terms of customer satisfaction it might be viewed either positively or negatively as 'junk mail'.

Advertising using the Internet to a less targeted audience. A non-personal presentation using email technology and site 'pop-ups'. In terms of customer satisfaction it might be viewed negatively as 'SPAM' mail and a nuisance, alternatively it might reinforce a positive message.

Engaging in E-Business. A dealer could potentially supplement or replace an existing showroom site by developing electronically based systems and technologies of doing business. Savings made on premises costs could be passed on to customers so enhancing their satisfaction.

Technology-supported market research could help provide in-depth analysis of a single market so enabling informed decisions to be made aimed at improving demand. Technology-supported market research might form a sub-system feeding a more comprehensive marketing database and Management Information System (MIS). MIS might include comparative competitor approaches to stimulating demand.

Vehicle dashboards displays. Cars could be fitted with microchips that indicate when a vehicle is in need of a service (e.g. after 20,000 miles). Alternative examples include a display of dealer contact details when a vehicle is in need of replacement (e.g. after 3 years) and so on.

B3(a)   Options to overcome the software not fitting the existing business process exactly. Change will be required as a result of the mismatch between the software and the existing business process. There appear to be two distinct options:

Option 1, Change the software or
Option 2, Change the business process.

The choice should be made taking account of all relevant costs and benefits and might be made using suitable evaluation criteria such as suitability, acceptability and feasibility (or similar).

The applications software is designed to perform specific financial functions of the business. It is essentially an 'off the shelf' rather than a bespoke solution but could conceivably be adapted. Such an adaptation could be financially costly. There is also a need to identify the necessary expertise to carry out this software development and the company may need to employ outside source for the purpose.

Changing the business process represents yet another change initiative that staff may respond to negatively. As competitors and peers are using the software already it is reasonable to assume that it will encapsulate industry best practice. These organisations apparently operate in that way that is consistent with the software. This implies that S & C may operate in an inconsistent and possibly inefficient fashion.

B3(b)   A phased approach: more suitable than a 'big bang' approach.
The more direct 'big bang' approach generally represents the highest risk, as at a predetermined point in time the old system ceases to operate completely. Using this approach there is no opportunity to validate the new system's output with the old, so management must have complete confidence in the new system. As the software in question appears to be something of an industry standard there is likely to be some general confidence in it. However, there appears to be something of a mismatch between the system and corresponding processes, which could prove a difficulty.

The phased approach involves gradual implementation possibly involving one subsystem at a time. This might involve implementing the system by first converting the customer accounts subsystem, then the reporting sub-system, and so on. This offers distinct advantages in this particular case:

- Staff are likely to be suffering 'change fatigue' from previous initiatives and can only endure so much upheaval while continuing to function effectively.
- The continued support of the partners as project sponsors is important and they are likely to see 'deliverables' sooner with a phased roll-out.

- The phased approach is less risky given that the project manager could be unavailable to oversee the change.
- The project management risk (heightened by the absence of the project manager) will be reduced as issues found in small-scale use of the new system can be remedied in time for wider software roll-out.

B3 (c)   The ways in which particular individuals and groups within S & C are important for implementation to succeed.

- *Partners*. Support from the top is crucial. They must visibly support the implementation.
- *Users*. Successful user acceptance and must buy-in is also key as they are the main recipients of the change. Meaningful communication is necessary, also participation to get commitment through joint analysis of issues to engender feelings of 'ownership'.
- *The users' managers*. These managers will be called upon to help ensure that disruptions are kept to a minimum during and immediately after changeover. Communication and involvement again is necessary (albeit to a different degree to users).
- *Project manager*. Effective project management is crucial which ensures that S & C's corporate performance does not fail. The project manager has been absent with illness and matters cannot be allowed to 'drift'. If the illness is long term, a replacement project manager needs to be appointed swiftly.
- *HR Department*. If system success depends on people behaving in certain ways (e.g. sharing information across departments, taking greater responsibility, etc.) reward systems may need to be adjusted possibly including new incentives, metrics and evaluation criteria. Effective training programmes will also be needed. Formal policies and structures may also need adjustment.
- *Project steering group*. Need to address the real sources of resistance to change and means of overcoming them. Proposals are also needed in order to successfully align financial systems and business processes (It is important that some members of the group are available in the weeks after going live to answer questions and give support to users).

B3(d)   Users involvement in testing the system during the implementation phase.
As mentioned earlier, user acceptance is vital. It is also important to test the system during the implementation phase. It is a good idea to combine these two requirements.
Users might be usefully involved in a number of ways and could be used to:

- Act as guinea pigs for any system developments through testing in association with the new procedures and processes.
- Contribute to quality circles and discussion forums.
- Assess the effectiveness of training programmes, and so on and provide feedback.
- Provide mutual mentoring/assistance 'buddying' to other new users of the system.
- Collect data on the costs and benefits of the overall business change, not just the software application.
- Be involved and act as advocates of change to colleagues.

B3(e)   The training topics to targeted groups within S & C.

The nature and content of training will inevitably need to be tailored to the needs of the relevant groups, for example:

- *Partners*. general overview of the system and its benefits possibly through executive training seminars.
- *Users*. instilling detailed user knowledge on how to operate the new system. Specific detailed applications training (including procedures, commands and data-entry requirements, etc.).
- *Users' managers*. giving an understanding of the elements of the system for which they are responsible, including particular business issues and security and control features related to a particular system. Possibly general training in basic computer literacy and user skills.

The sort of training provision might include:

- Seminars and workshops and so on
- User manuals, 'help lines' and dedicated support teams.
- Online computer-based support.
- On-the-job training while staff are actively using the new system.
- Quality circles and discussion forums for users to address problem areas.
- Short demonstrations and the use of DVD/ Video media support.
- Updates as users become familiar with the system and require further knowledge and skills development or consolidation of existing knowledge and skills.

This can be provided:

- in-house;
- outsourced to specialists; or
- some combination.

B3(f)   Aims of a post-implementation review.

Post-implementation review should be carried out as soon as the system is fully operational, in order to assess the effectiveness of the system, adjustments that may be required and lessons that can be learnt for the future. This should take place possibly between 1 month and no longer than 1 year after changeover is completed. The findings and recommendations from the post-implementation review should be formally reported on.

The specific aims of the review will include:

- Whether the system satisfies user needs.
- How the actual costs and benefit of the system compare with what was anticipated.
- Making recommendations for improvement (if necessary).
- Determining the quality of systems of change and project management.
- Making recommendations that will help shape future management of implementation and change initiatives where necessary.

NOTE: IT IS IMPORTANT TO CONTAIN YOUR RESPONSES TO THE GIVEN PAGE LIMIT

C Style Revision Questions

C1   The country Mythland contains several areas of high unemployment including one where Cardinal Beers was until recently produced. Cardinal was an old, family-owned brewery that supplied licenced outlets including local restaurants with their beer. Cardinal represented one of the last local brewers of any size despite retaining many working practices that were evolved at least a century ago. Situated on a (now) underused dockside site, the company had over the years invested little in plant and machinery and someone jokingly once suggested that much of the brewing equipment should rightfully be in a museum! Despite having an enthusiastic, long-serving, highly skilled workforce and a national reputation for the beer 'Cardinal winter warmer' (thanks to winning several national awards), the company was forced to cease trading last month. The workforce, many of whom have only ever worked for Cardinal Beers, are now facing up to the difficulty of finding alternative work.

In a press statement the owners said that the brewery's closure was sad for the town, the local workforce and traditionally brewed ale in general. The owners blamed the situation on inefficient and expensive brewing methods, fierce competition from large rival brewers and limited geographical sales. They also mentioned a dependence on seasonal sales that made cash flow difficult (35% over Christmas and the New year period). They concluded that they would like the Cardinal tradition to continue and sell the company as a going concern, however unlikely this was. It is speculated that property developers may be interested in the site as the dockland area is showing signs of regeneration as a leisure and tourism attraction (thanks to the efforts of government). However, two of Cardinal's managers would like to save the business and are drawing up a business plan for a management buy-out. They have three main initiatives that they feel could in combination save the enterprise:

- Use the site as a basis for a living museum of traditionally brewed ale (with the dated brewing equipment and methods of working as an attraction).
- Produce bottled beer for sales in supermarkets.
- Employ a more flexible but suitably experienced workforce.

One of the managers (your former boss) has asked for your help in advising him how to draft a detailed human resource plan to inform the business plan.

Requirements

(a) Describe the main issues and stages involved in developing a human resource (HR) plan for the Cardinal buy-out idea. **(12 marks)**

(b) Explain how the buy-out team can achieve workforce flexibility. **(8 marks)**

(c) Explain the concept of market segmentation and how it might apply to the to initiatives to save Cardinal Beers. **(10 marks)**

(Total = 30 marks)

C2 R & L is a large manufacturing firm that is well known as a 'good employer'. Over the past few years R&L has experienced difficult times with reducing sales and mounting losses. In desperation it employed management consultants to analyse their situation. The consultants have concluded that the down turn in sales is permanent and that R&L needs to reduce its workforce by 50% over the next year in order to survive. Reluctantly, R&L's board of directors have accepted these findings, including the need to shed staff. They have also agreed to act as honestly and fairly as possible but realised that any changes they propose will be unpopular and may meet with resistance.

Requirements

(a) Identify what positive initiatives R&L can take to achieve job losses needed.

(8 marks)

(b) Discuss the potential strategies available in order to overcome resistance to change, and identify those strategies that would be most suitable for R&L.

(15 marks)

(c) Delayering, downsizing and outsourcing all normally have the effect of reducing staff numbers. Distinguish each of these terms, providing examples drawn from the scenario. **(7 marks)**

(Total = 30 marks)

C3 National Secure is a large insurance company. The company is structured into four Divisions and supported by a small headquarters that includes the personnel function (recently renamed the Human Resourcing (HR) Division). The post of Head of HR is vacant following the retirement of the long-serving post-holder, and the HR strategy is in urgent need of review and revision.

National Secure has recently announced a new corporate initiative of continuous improvement through the empowerment of its workforce. The Chief Executive explained: 'We value our people as our most prized asset. We will encourage them to think, challenge and innovate. Only through empowering them in this way can we achieve continuous improvement. Staff will no longer be expected just to obey orders; from now on they will make and implement decisions to bring about continuous improvement. We want to develop clear performance objectives and be more customer focused.'

Your line manager is one of the four Divisional directors and will soon form part of a panel that will interview candidates for the vacant role of HR director. She is particularly keen to ensure that the successful candidate would be able to shape the HR Division to the needs of the organisation. She is aware of your CIMA studies and has asked for your help in preparing for the interview.

Requirements

Produce outline notes for your Divisional director which discuss the main points you would expect candidates to highlight in response to the following two areas she intends to explore with candidates at the interview, specifically:

(a) The likely role that the HR function will perform in the light of the changing nature of the organisation. **(10 marks)**

(b) The aspects of a revised HR strategy that will show significant change given the nature of recent organisational developments. **(10 marks)**

(c) Explain the concept of continuous improvement and its relationship to empowerment. **(10 marks)**

(Total = 30 marks)

C4 'Supreme Snax' is a growing company that has successfully used local radio advertising for the past few years to raise awareness of its products. It supplies fresh 'quality' sandwiches, home-baked snacks, the finest coffee and freshly squeezed fruit juices for sale at premium prices in petrol filling stations. Products are produced by traditional methods from very early morning by a team of employees at a central depot and are delivered throughout the day by a few casual workers in a fleet of vehicles.

'Supreme Snax' has for the first time undertaken a full strategic marketing planning process. One weakness identified was that the number of deliveries required was increasing, while some of the drivers were becoming increasingly unreliable. The owner is worried that this may create an unfavourable image with customers and lead to delays in delivery.

In terms of opportunities, the owner of 'Supreme Snax' is now aware that by using technology to a greater degree and identifying customer needs more fully, the firm can grow at an even greater rate. To this end it is proposed that that time-saving food preparation and packaging equipment be purchased. This will mean considerably less people involved in food preparation but the owner feels that some employees could be redeployed as drivers on a permanent basis. The role of the driver would be redefined, and in addition to making deliveries, he or she would be expected to:

- get direct feedback from customers
- persuade petrol stations to take new product lines
- provide intelligence on competitor's products and likely future demand
- hopefully persuade other petrol stations and outlets (such as railway stations and newspaper shops) to stock 'Supreme Snax' products.

The owner is keen to progress change, consequently:

- The Head of delivery and customer relationships has been tasked with developing new job description for the driver posts. This will then be discussed with existing food preparation staff.
- A marketing action plan will soon be prepared based on the strategic marketing plan, which will contain immediate marketing issues and actions required.

Requirements

(a) Based on your understanding of the changes proposed by 'Supreme Snax', identify the main issues that will be included in the marketing action plan and discuss the implications of these. **(10 marks)**

(b)   Based upon the information given to you concerning 'Supreme Snax', and your own study and experience, produce a draft job description for the redefined post of driver.   **(10 marks)**

(c)   Based upon the information given to you concerning 'Supreme Snax', and your own study and experience, produce a draft person specification for the redefined post of driver.   **(10 marks)**

(Total marks = 30)

C5   Banking services within Everland are provided exclusively by a few, well-established banks, all offering broadly similar 'traditional' banking services. Overall, the industry performance is viewed from within as satisfactory and over the decades all banks have maintained stable profits and employment levels. Marketeers would describe the industry as being classically 'product oriented'. The profile of senior Everland bank officials and managers is of well-qualified professionals, possessing long banking industry experience and considerable financial skills. Within the combined workforce other business skills (in for instance HR or marketing) are noticeably lacking.

In the external environment the government will soon pass new legislation that will effectively break the oligopoly-type position of banks and open the market up to other providers. Senior bank officials, however, are unconcerned feeling that banks are in 'reasonable shape' to face any new challenge. The economy is buoyant and the banking officials remain confident.

You work for the independent body of the Everland Banking Advisory Group (EBAG) and have been asked to analyse the banking industry in the country of Utopia to identifying lessons that might be learnt. Your investigation reveals that since the sector opened up to more competition a much wider range of financial institutions offer banking services. There has also been a recent growth in on-line banking as an option. Despite this Utopia banks have all prospered over the past few years. This is thanks to wide-ranging changes in how they operate, the products and services they offer and their organisational structures. You identify some significant trends within the Utopia banking industry, including:

- the use of marketing techniques
- a clearer focus on customers (who have become increasingly more demanding)
- a new generation of bank employees, many with commercial backgrounds
- banks now exhibiting a strong sense of ethical and social responsibilities towards customers.

The EBAG chief executive has asked for an interim report that addresses the following points:

Requirements
You are required to draft an interim report that:

(a)   Discuss the danger to Everland banks if they continue with their existing product orientation and associated practices.   **(8 marks)**

(b)   Discuss the types of changes that banks should be making in order to survive and prosper in Everland.   **(15 marks)**

(c)   Based on the information contained in the question, produce an analysis of Everland's macro-environment and comment on the most significant features as far as banks are concerned.   **(7 marks)**

(Total = 30 marks)

C6 CQ4 is a leading European industrial gas production company. CQ4's directors are each responsible for a geographical region comprised of several small strategic business units (SBUs). SBU managers report in monthly review meetings in great detail to their directors. CQ4 is showing signs of declining profitability and a new chief executive has been appointed and wishes to address the situation. She has complete freedom to identify organisational problems, solutions and strategies.

She announces two new initiatives 'to address the lost years when managers were prevented from delivering truly excellent CQ4 performance':

- Revision of the existing performance appraisal system. Bonuses paid on sales will be replaced by performance-related pay for achievement of individual 'performance target contracts'. Individual SBU managers will sign contracts to deliver these targets. Performance will now be reviewed at yearly rather than monthly meetings with directors. The remuneration package will be adjusted appropriately with the current emphasis on increasing turnover shifting to profitability and innovation. At their annual conference she tells SBU managers that they hold the key to improved company performance. She has a vision of CQ4 achieving longer-term strategic goals of increased profitability, risk taking and innovation. Under the slogan 'support not report' directors will in future support and provide assistance to their managers to a greater degree, and the frequency and detail of reporting by managers will be reduced.
- A structural review to focus resources and efforts of SBUs on improving net profit. Part of the restructuring will involve SBUs no longer providing their own 'enabling' services such as finance, information technology and health and safety. These 'distractions from doing the real job' will in future be organised centrally. SBUs will, however, receive far greater responsibility, autonomy and influence over their own profitability.

She tells managers that she is stripping away the things that stop them doing their job properly. In return they must manage their SBU in the way they see most appropriate. They will be better rewarded and 'star achievers' will be fast tracked to senior positions. SBU managers are informed that already the HR department has been tasked with redesigning the remuneration and reward package.

Informal discussions amongst managers afterwards confirm that the new chief executive's message has been well received. Comments such as 'work might be more enjoyable without central interference' and 'for the first time I can do my job properly' were overheard.

Requirements

(a) Explain the thinking behind the two initiatives announced by the new chief executive using Herzberg's motivation-hygiene (dual factor) theory as a framework.

(10 marks)

(b) Discuss the factors that should be taken into account by HR department when redesigning the remuneration and reward package for SBU managers.

(10 marks)

(c) Explain the relevance of what Schein and others have called the 'rational economic man theory' in the context of CQ4.   **(10 marks)**

(Total = 30 marks)

C7 ABC Company distributes household appliances and spare parts. ABC has moved swiftly and within a short period has managed to takeover two small rivals and a major competitor. All three companies were previously trading successfully and ABC feels it now has the potential to access new markets and an expanded customer base.

Although none of the takeovers were 'hostile' there has been some staff turnover and there is a need to rationalise ABC completely. It now has four branches that were previously independent companies. The branches currently organise their own purchasing and sales functions, and maintain their own stock records. The two larger branches have incompatible computer systems, while the smaller branches have manual records. After a feasibility study, management has decided to introduce a new central computerised database system that will include the 3,500 stock items currently held at the various locations.

Following the first years trading as a four branch operation disappointing financial results have emerged.

Requirement

(a) Discuss alternative methods of changeover from the systems used at the branches to the new centralised stock control system, and recommend, with reasons, the method you prefer. **(10 marks)**

(b) Describe the most important properties that a database system should have in order for it to provide maximum benefit to ABC. **(10 marks)**

(c) Explain the degree to which ABC has followed accepted management 'rules' for takeover and why it should not be surprised that disappointing financial results have emerged. **(10 marks)**

(Total = 30 marks)

C8 XYZ Bank has over 2 million customers and nearly 700,000 credit card holders. The bank employs 4,000 staff in 22 locations throughout the country and each week handles over 5 million transactions. New services are developed by project teams before being offered to customers.

Last year a new chief executive set an agenda some years ago to focus on the features, benefits and drawbacks of contemporary approaches to the management of quality. Since this time XYZ has been involved in implementing a TQM programme and a Quality Assurance section and Customer Complaints section have been established at the corporate headquarters.

Requirements

(a) Explain the critical elements of XYZ's TQM approach to Quality improvement, Customer care and Quality Assurance. **(10 marks)**

(b) Outline a plan so that a new branch needing to introduce TQM could communicate the quality approach to its staff and help overcome resistance to the initiative. **(10 marks)**

(c) Explain with examples the types of costs associated with operation of a quality programme within XYZ. **(10 marks)**

(Total marks 30)

Solutions to C Style Revision Questions

> *Important note:* The solutions suggested here (and elsewhere in earlier sections) use specific models, frameworks and theories in order to address the question in hand. The identification of alternative valid approaches by candidates will in the examination also receive appropriate credit.

C1(a)   Considerations/Issues:

Human resource planning involves developing a plan for the acquisition, utilisation, improvement and retention of an organisation's human resources. Such a plan needs to be integrated into the broader process of business planning if it is to be useful. In this case the Cardinal's managers business plan for a management buy-out.

The HR plan will need to take account and support the three main initiatives identified as part of the buy-out:

- Heritage 'real ale' tours using the dated brewing equipment and methods of working as an attraction.
- Bottling beer for sales in supermarkets.
- Employing a more flexible but suitably experienced workforce.

The plan will need to reflect:

- how HR flexibility will be achieved
- retraining in new skills
- budgets, targets and standards
- reward systems
- responsibilities for implementation and control (including the appraisal process);
- reporting procedures that will enable achievements to be monitored against the plan.

Consideration will need to be taken of what Cardinal represents: tradition, national reputation and 'real ale' production.

The plan itself will need to meet certain key criteria: it will need to be realistic, accurate, suitable, consistent and so on.

Stages:

The HR planning process normally consisting of four main phases:

1. Conducting an audit of the existing human resources in the light of any corporate or business changes.
2. Forecasting future demand for labour.
3. Assessing the external labour market and forecasting supply.
4. Establishing a plan reconciling demand and supply.

Applying this thinking to the scenario:

- *Audit of the existing human resources.* Clearly there have been big changes and technically no existing human resources exist! However, as the shut down only happened last month and as the workforce has specialist skills that are likely to be unused in an area of high unemployment, most will be available for reemployment. HR records can be accessed to determine key pieces of information. The selection process will be important to ensure that Cardinal obtains people with the right skills and/or the potential to develop such skills.
- *Forecasting future demand for labour.* Based on past experience a good estimate of minimum and maximum numbers required will be possible. In addition to numbers the skill requirements of people is also important. Again based on past experience projections can be made. As there appear to be no proposals for new technology/automation/reequipping skills, numbers can be confidently predicted. However, a number of important factors need to be taken into account when forecasting demand:

  - the introduction of anew products: bottled beer which will have new skill implications
  - the development of brewery tours which will have new skill implications the seasonal nature of sales
  - financial limits on manpower costs as part of the business plan (i.e. What can be afforded)

- *Assess the external labour market and forecasting supply.* Supply is likely to be plentiful, due to unemployment and unique skills. It is possible to use personnel (HR) records as the database for analysis of the past Cardinal workforce. From these records it is possible to derive a wide range of information about the numbers, current skill, age, training undertaken, performance levels and so on. This information can provide knowledge of the supply of labour available locally.
- *Establish a plan reconciling demand and supply.* Having made an estimate of the labour required to staff the organisation and considered the supply of labour available, the next step is to put together action plans for the recruitment, and where necessary retraining in new skills of the workforce so that the demand and supply of labour can be reconciled. Considerations of motivation are normally relevant as part of this stage. As the workforce was previously highly motivated, the opportunity to be part of a relaunch of Cardinal that offers them employment means that this is less of a consideration.

It must be acknowledged that in reality the process is rarely as linear and sequential as these phases suggest and many aspects progress together.

C1(b) Work at present is very seasonal (the winter months being heaviest) and although brewery tours and bottled beers may help smooth fluctuations in work, more flexibility in the workforce is demanded for the new company to survive. Change in practices is clearly requited and the new Cardinal organisation may take on a different form to the old one.

To provide for flexibility other firms including have adopted various approaches:

New forms of employment terms (e.g. fixed-term contracts, part-time contracts or systems of 'annual hours') to smooth the use of staff over critical periods such as seasonal shortages. The annual hours approach could work well at Cardinal brewery.

Outsourcing certain functions to outside contractors rather than addressing these directly. For Cardinal this might mean all administrative, payroll and marketing functions for instance.

Handy's 'shamrock' organisation with an employed core of professional workers, a contractual fringe providing specialist and non-essential services and flexible part time and temporary workers might be one model for Cardinal (This is consistent with Atkinson's (1984), ideas for core employees and periphery workers on temporary or part-time staff to buffer against changes in demand).

For Cardinal flexibility may take one or several of number of forms:

Numerical flexibility

The development of a numerically flexible workforce involves flexing the labour employed.

Temporary, part-time, short-term contract working and sub-contracting is used in additional to full-time employment. This might be achieved by only bringing in employees when they are needed (during the seasonal rush in the run up to Christmas and new year). This is often referred to as a flexible firm approach.

- *Task or Functional flexibility*. This involves recruiting and developing staff with a wide range of skills, so that such an employee can carry out a range of tasks. This saves the company from having to employ as many specialist workers as it might otherwise have to and also means those employees can cover for each other in case of absence. A Cardinal employee of the future might, for instance, be required to brew on one day, carry out vital maintenance on another, and conduct a brewery tour on a third.

- *Financial flexibility*. This is often used achieved through some form of performance-related payment. This might be related to bottles produced, sales figures, numbers on brewery tours, achieving financial targets identified in the business plan and so on.

C1(c) 'Market segmentation' is a technique based on the recognition that every market consists of potential buyers with different needs, and different buying behaviour. These different customer characteristics may be subgrouped (or segmented) and a different marketing mix applied by an organisation to each target market segment.

Market segmentation may therefore involve the subdividing of a market into distinct subgroups of customers, where any subgroup can be selected as a target market to be met with a distinct marketing mix.

The important point of market segmentation is that although the total market consists of widely different groups of consumers, each group consists of people with common needs and preferences, who perhaps react to market stimuli in much the same way. Recognition of segmentation will enable a company to adopt a more refined approach to selling to a given group of potential customers.

Segmentation:

- accounts for the fact that the same product cannot satisfy everyone completely
- allows differentiation to take place
- can improve a company's competitive position
- offers an opportunity for an organisation to select the most appropriate target group.

Two of Cardinal's managers would like to save the business and are drawing up a business plan for a management buy-out. Apart from employing a more flexible but suitably experienced workforce, they identify two initiatives that they feel could in combination save the enterprise:

1. Using the site as a basis for a living museum of traditionally brewed ale (with the dated brewing equipment and methods of working as an attraction).
2. Producing bottled beer for sales in supermarkets.

Through market segmentation the managers might determine whether or not the target segment is significant enough to save the enterprise. Segmentation might produce profiles as follows:

Segmentation variable	Living museum	Bottled beer
Benefit sought	Those who like trips out	Those who drink at home
Occasion & usage	Holiday periods, one off outing	Weekly consumption, repeat purchases
Perception, beliefs	Like a day out with a difference	Prefer real ale
Lifestyle	Families, couples used to trips out	Prefer beer to wine with a meal at home
Gender	Whole family	Mainly male
Socio-economic	Employed (it is a luxury)	Employed (it is a luxury)
Geographic	Near enough to travel	Local: depends which supermarkets stock it

C2(a) Positive initiatives

A number of positive initiatives could be adopted by R&L. In the first instance, R&L should review staff turnover rates that presently exist and determine how much of the 50% can be achieved through natural wastage. They should also be able to project from HR records those who will reach retirement age within the next year.

   As a next step R&L should then put an embargo on further employment and seek to fill vital posts short term through inter-company transfers of staff. They should also stop any overtime and seek to spread excess work to other under-utilised employees.

R&L will need to consider and discuss possible alternatives with the relevant trade unions or staff representatives such as:

- Contracting out non-core functions (e.g. IT) and try to negotiate a transfer of staff to the outsourcing firm.
- Encouraging those over retirement age to leave.
- Job-sharing (between two or more people?).
- A shorter working week.

The important thing is that any initiative is adopted in conjunction with employee groups (e.g. trade unions) rather than being imposed.

C2(b)   Kotter and Schlesinger (1979) identify six main strategies for dealing with resistance. This might usefully serve as a framework for discussion:

1. Education and communication is particularly useful when the basic problem is lack of information about the need for, or the nature of, the planned change. The approach can be very time-consuming and will not work by itself if there are other reasons than misunderstanding leading to resistance to change. Such a strategy would seem to be appropriate in this case. As a good employer R&L is honour bound to present all known facts on the plight of the company and discuss options openly and straightforwardly. A suitable strategy.

2. Participation and involvement increases the chances of commitment to implementing the change particularly if their views are taken into account. This method is particularly appropriate when the people affected by the change have considerable power to resist it. This approach can be time-consuming, but such a strategy would seem to be appropriate in this case. Whatever positive measure is chosen, participation is vital to ensuring its success. The change is more acceptable if it is done by you rather than to you! A highly suitable strategy.

3. Facilitation and support involves training, counselling and discussions, designed to reduce anxiety. This is particularly appropriate where the principal reason for resistance is based on insecurity and adjustment problems. Such a strategy would seem to be appropriate in this case; indeed the suggestion of outplacement is an embodiment of this strategy. A highly suitable strategy.

4. Negotiation and agreement may be necessary to compensate those losing out because of the change. This may help avoid major problems, but it can be expensive in terms of, for example, redundancy packages. If there is little goodwill between the parties it may be protracted and bruising. Such a strategy would seem to be appropriate in this case, as R&L is a good employer there may be genuine goodwill between the management side and the trade unions. A suitable strategy.

5. Manipulation and co-optation involves presenting partial or misleading information to those resisting change and 'buying off' key players. This is a quick and relatively inexpensive approach, but normally results in future problems if the people involved realise they have been manipulated. Such a strategy would be inconsistent with R & L's philosophy of being a 'good employer'. An unsuitable strategy.

6. Explicit/implicit coercion involves the use of force, or the threat of force, to enforce the implementation of change. It raises ethical (and potentially legal) problems as well as involving considerable risk of making a situation more difficult, especially if trade unions are in a position to provide opposition and protection. Such a strategy would be inconsistent with R & L's philosophy of being a 'good employer'. An unsuitable strategy.

C2(c) Delayering, downsizing and outsourcing all normally have the effect of reducing staff numbers:

'Delayering' is a term used when an organisation removes layers of the workforce from the structure. If an organisation has a hierarchical way of operating with lots of management layers, then there is ample scope to reduce staff numbers in this way. The effect would probably be to get rid of middle management posts, which would leave the structure flatter and significantly closer in touch with customers and their needs.

Downsizing normally occurs when an organisation decides that it can operate with fewer staff numbers overall. This might be a decision unforced by a takeover and unlike delaying may not have the effect of flattening the organisational hierarchy.

Outsourcing by comparison occurs when an organisation decides that instead of providing central ancillary or central services for themselves it is cheaper or makes more sense to get outside contractors to perform that service for them. It follows therefore that outsourcing might contribute to downsizing.

R & L is well known as a 'good employer' but is faced with the dilemma that the down turn in sales is permanent and that it needs to reduce its workforce by 50 per cent over the next year in order to survive. It is likely that each of the three alternative staff reduction strategies might be considered.

1. *Delayering.* R&L might decide the structure and staff mix that it needs in the future and this may involve removal of surplus layers of workers, possibly middle managers.
2. *Outsourcing.* Contracting out non-manufacturing activities (e.g. finance, information management facilities, catering, cleaning, etc.) will certainly reduce its workforce nearer the target of 50%. The effects, however, may not be to reduce cost by the same proportion, and replacement consultant provided services will still have costs attached. In practice, outsourcing might be transfer costs from R&L's payroll to consultancy fees.
3. *Downsizing.* This will be the dominant action with a likely shedding of staff in all areas: including production. The reason is that the downturn is permanent and R&L now have overcapacity for the potential demand.

C3(a) Likely role HR will perform in the light of the changing nature of the organisation.

- *Company background.* The company appears to be 'traditionally' structured with four divisions and a small HQ staff. The signals for change include a re-branding of personnel to Human Resources. The retirement of the long-serving head of this function is also of significance. This implies that a traditional well-established way of operating in the past is not required in the future. The fact the HR strategy is in 'urgent need' of review and revision underlines this point.
- *An HR rather than Personnel role.* Personnel Management is seen as focusing on day-to-day 'people-related' issues. In the past, NS's small specialist personnel support function would undoubtedly have attempted to ensure consistency and fairness of treatment throughout the organisation. Personnel Management is seen as ensuring compliance with organisational procedures as well as reacting and responding to external environmental changes (including employment legislation and labour market conditions). The changes taking place at NS mean that the function will have different objectives more easily identified as human resource management (HRM).

- *A strategic role.* The new function would be expected to view employees in a different, more strategic way. A reasonable revised focus would be upon the long-term development of human resources in such a way as to deliver the strategic aspirations of the company (i.e. to achieve continuous improvement). The specialist HR Division should provide support to Divisional Directors and other managers in order to meet detailed organisational objectives.

    The new HR function would be expected to have key inputs into the strategic deliberations that are apparently underway including the setting of clear objectives. The HR Division will now be expected to shape and deliver strategies.

- *A training needs role.* NS's new corporate initiative of continuous improvement through empowerment is of major significance for the HR Division. Under the initiative people are seen as crucial, exercising skills of thinking, challenging, innovating and implementing. The function will need to ensure that the workforce have these skills.

    Empowerment involves passing power downwards for staff 'closer to the action' to be responsible for making decisions and initiating actions. This involves a high degree of trust in the workforce and less directive, authoritarian control from management. This new management style means that Departmental Directors and managers will need to be encouraged by the function to make this change

- *A role in cultural shaping.* NS's initiative of an empowered workforce normally involves a major organisational cultural change. There is no evidence from the scenario as to how this is to be brought about other than an apparent rethink of the role of specialist personnel function. The HR function will be crucial in affecting the necessary cultural change and the new Head might be expected to perform a change agent's role.

- *A role in championing corporate initiatives.* In an empowered organisation, people are active in solving problems, looking for better ways of working, and co-operating freely with others in and across teams. Continuous improvement is a collective approach towards improving performance throughout the organisation. Clearly the HR function will need to champion and support these developments.

C3(b)   Aspects of HR strategy showing significant change given the nature of recent developments.

Given the changing nature of the organisation and the initiatives being progressed, attention should be given to the following aspects of the HR strategy:

- *Structure and job roles.* The overall structure should be configured in order that individuals are developed to their full potential and encouraged to do 'things right' (what needs to be done in organisational terms), not merely 'the right things' (what job descriptions require of them). The strategy will need to articulate the structure, control and functioning of the organisation. Layers of management that add no value or that damage empowerment should be eliminated as part of a systematic review.

- *Job content.* Job content will also need to be reviewed and then be articulated in overall terms in the strategy. This review could conveniently follow on from the structural review identified earlier and might feature broader spans of managerial control. This should in turn encourage managers to delegate and trust subordinates to exercise their increased autonomy and power effectively.

- *Education and Training*. Education and Training in empowerment and continuous improvement will be vital components of the strategy. This might be achieved by facilitating workshops and ongoing support mechanisms such as mentors, buddying systems and/or counsellors. Changes to role requires training at all levels, particularly senior management, where individuals will need to be persuaded to relinquish power. For 'front line' staff, mechanisms for training and building self-confidence are vital. This will undoubtedly involve enhancing existing skills and the identification of new skill requirements.

  It is good practice to undertake a training needs analysis of the workforce and shape the strategy accordingly. Specific likely skills will include problem-solving, data-gathering techniques, teambuilding, listening and customer care. Teams of people will need to be built that co-operate and support one another in continuously improving customer service and improving efficiency.

  Senior managers may need training in facilitation and leadership skills. It is vital that senior managers (whose role should include setting the 'right' examples) provide consistent messages and behaviour.

  The strategy will need to articulate how this is delivered (whether in-house by trainers, externally, or by the use of existing managers). Systems for monitoring the effectiveness of these 'interventions' will also need to be articulated in the strategy.

- *Reward systems*. These systems represent the ways in which staff are recognised and rewarded for their endeavours. A revised strategy must ensure that such systems are consistent with, and encourage, the identified concepts of empowerment and continuous improvement. The HR function in conjunction with senior managers will need to agree behaviour patterns required in the future and ways of measuring outcomes. Those who actively support and embrace the twin concepts identified (of empowerment and continuous improvement) should be rewarded appropriately. Typical organisational rewards usually include pay, promotion and other rewards. Other rewards need not have financial implications and might, for instance, include still greater empowerment. It is a good idea to communicate these points widely and reward publicly, making role models and heroes of those who achieve. In this way positive performance standards might be signaled.

This thinking should be embodied in the HR strategy.

- *Target setting and appraisals*. A mechanism for review and target setting will need to be considered in the strategy. Although this might already exist, major revisions to these targets will be needed in the light of organisational initiatives. New personal plans/targets/key performance indicators (KPIs) will need to be created for every manager and then cascaded down through subordinates and work groups so that the whole organisation's performance is assessed having regards to the twin initiatives. Reviews of performance after a few months by using small groups should highlight progress, problems and areas for adjustment. Once overall review mechanisms are established, annual appraisal and monthly target setting might reasonably be employed. Upward and 360 degree appraisal schemes might be considered in order to strengthen reflective practice.

- *Review mechanisms*. Revised review mechanisms should concentrate on monitoring progress on the initiatives and taking corrective action where necessary. This should be at the expense of previous forms of control, direction and reporting in order to drive decision-making down to the lowest level.
- *Communication systems*. Channels of official communication should be articulated in the strategy. The existing strategy may already do this but the focus may need to be reorientated in the light of new corporate initiatives. A new emphasis should be placed upon encouraging open communication, sharing of information and honesty.

C3(c) Empowerment is a management technique whereby power and authority is delegated downwards within an organisation. The effect is that subordinates are trusted to work towards their managers' goals. This is obviously an enlightened and wholly sensible strategy to pursue so long as there is mutual trust, sufficient training and a supportive culture.

The fact that National Secure has recently announced a new corporate initiative based on empowerment underlines their commitment to it. There is clear evidence that the Chief Executive trusts the workforce and provides sufficient encouragement, specifically:

- People are apparently valued and regarded as National Secure's most prized asset.
- Staff are encouraged for them to think, challenge and innovate.
- Clear individual performance objectives are to be determined
- Staff are no longer expected just to obey orders instead they will make and implement decisions.

The fact that the Chief Executive sees this as bringing about continuous improvement is of relevance. He/She states quite clearly: 'Only through empowering them in this way can we achieve continuous improvement.' The process is meant to enable National Secure to become more customer focused.

Continuous improvement is closely linked with the process of TQM: Total Quality management. It is a philosophy to continually improve the quality of goods or services (in this case services), and hence performance and quality. TQM as a philosophy encourages and fosters continuous improvement throughout the whole organisation:

Total	Everyone linked to the organisation (staff, customers and suppliers) is involved in the process. The concept of viewing every business activity as process that can be improved is shared.
Quality	The requirements of customers are achieved.
Management	Senior managers must be fully committed to continuous improvement if all other parties are to help achieve it.

This all-inclusive approach including the consideration of quality from a customer perspective is entirely consistent with empowerment. (Some would go further and argue it is dependent upon it.) TQM encourages the full involvement of all people, at all levels, working within multidisciplinary teams to suggest and implement improvements from within the business. This corresponds with National Secure's philosophy on its workforce and their value.

The Chief Executive's standpoint that empowerment is the only route to continuous improvement appears well founded.

C4(a)   One structure for identifying main immediate marketing issues is the 'Ps' framework. These issues will need to be addressed in the marketing action plan. Students are advised to consider only product, place and promotion.

- *Product.* There do not appear to be any plans to expand the product range (currently fresh 'gourmet' sandwiches, home-baked snacks, 'real' coffee and freshly squeezed fruit juices). One key issue is the maintenance of quality, which is vital to the company's reputation. The new technology proposed in preparing and packaging should be a timesaver and should help achieve consistency of standard. It might be helpful in the marketing action plan to identify the need to articulate product standards and procedures.

- *Place.* Petrol filling stations apparently currently represent the organisation's sole distribution outlets. The proposal that there is potential for stocking their products in newspaper shops and railway stations represents a form of market development. However, the method proposed of extending 'place' in this way is rather more questionable. Much depends on the effectiveness of drivers, and a reliance on them to perform this task is perhaps ambitious. Nevertheless, the marketing action plan will need to identify precise targets and commit training resources towards this aim. Additional time will need to be allocated to drivers rounds in order to perform their expanded duties and projected additional new locations will need to be factored into revised driving rounds. This may necessitate the use of extra vehicles and this should also be articulated in the plan.

- *Promotion.* Local radio advertising appears to be successful in expanding operations so far. The growth strategy up until now has been based on 'more of the same' and repeat purchases. The use of drivers to cement existing sales relationships is a sensible policy but the effectiveness of using 'cold call' selling is (according to conventional wisdom) questionable. The action plan will need to attach SMART targets to these aspirations (specific, measurable, realistic, time bound) and quantify the amounts that will be spent on radio adverting as well as the time to be allocated to 'cold calling' by drivers.

- *People.* Those employees used in preparation could according to the owner be redeployed as drivers. These drivers will be expected to get direct feedback from customers, provide intelligence on competition, future demand, and hopefully persuade other petrol outlets to take new product lines. There are clear training implications that will need to be costed. The action plan will need to project the number of drivers required and if there are insufficient through redeployment a programme for recruitment and selection will be necessary.

- *Price.* If charging premium prices is to be a sustainable pricing strategy, price will need to be commensurate with quality in the opinion of the customer. The marketing action plan will need to articulate how quality assurance systems support this strategy in order that quality is maintained and hopefully improved upon. Sales trends and periodic customer surveys might be good ways of determining whether pricing is appropriate.

C4(b)   *The job description*

The job description defines the job: its overall purpose and the main tasks to be carried out. These aspects are reflected in the following draft:

Draft Job description

Company Delivery and customer interface department

Job title: Permanent driver

Responsible to: Head of delivery and customer relations

Posts responsible to the jobholder: none

Brief description and overall purpose

The purpose of the job is to load a delivery vehicle at the depot and make timely deliveries of company products to the locations listed on the delivery round throughout the day.

The post requires finding the customer's location, dealing with relevant paperwork, talking to customers' employees, and reporting back.

The post holder will be required to get direct feedback from customers, and liaise with outlet personnel to:

Ascertain customer perceptions

Discuss possibilities for taking new product lines and likely future demand

Gain information on competitor's products.

The post holder will also be required to discuss the possibility of stocking company products at other outlets that are located on or near the delivery round.

The post holder will be required to complete simple computerised daily returns to Head of delivery and customer relations based on interactions with customers, outlets and potential outlets.

Technical procedures/tools/machinery/equipment used:

The post holder will be required to drive a delivery vehicle.

The post holder will be required to use a laptop computer (provided) to complete daily reports.

Special requirements to deal with outside contacts

The post holder will be required to maintain a good working relationship with existing outlet staff and agree delivery quantities.

The post holder will be required to liaise with customers, existing outlet staff and potential outlet staff.

Physical location of job and travelling required.

The post holder will be based at company depot but required to complete delivery rounds specified on a daily basis

Special circumstances

Products are delivered throughout the day. The post holder will be required to complete an 8-hour shift. The post holder may be required to work overtime/or weekends dependent upon the overall requirements of the department.

The post holder will be required to lift and carry relatively lightweight loads as part of the delivery pattern.

Other Responsibilities
The post holder will be required to complete basic paperwork
   There will be no budgetary responsibility
Miscellaneous
Terms and conditions of employment including salary, details of shifts and holiday entitlement are embodied separately in the post holder's letter of appointment

C4(c) **Person specification**

The person specification defines the personal requirements of the post holder including characteristics, qualifications and experience. These aspects are reflected in the following draft. (There is more than layout for achieving this. The draft below reflects the Seven-Point Plan format.)

Draft person specification: Permanent driver

	Essential (unless stated as desirable)
Physical make-up:	Good health record. Able to handle goods
	Smart appearance.
Attainments:	Evidence of basic English, Maths and IT skills
	Desirable: Recognised English, Maths and IT to secondary school level
General intelligence:	Above average. The ability to handle paperwork such as delivery notes, simple receipts and use computerised reporting equipment.
Special aptitudes:	Ability to drive and a full 'clean' driving licence
	Skill in handling and lifting of goods.
	Experience of working unsupervised
	Some familiarity with the concepts and techniques of selling, customer care
	Good listening skills and the ability to interpret and analyse information.
	Desirable: experience either in delivery or sales
Interests:	Meeting people
Disposition:	Prompt, reliable, able to project favourable image with customers
Circumstances:	Living relatively close to central depot or have easy access to it through vehicle ownership

C5(a) Dangers to Everland banks if they do not change.

Position Statement

Product-orientated organisations, like Everland banks, have a main focus of product (or service) features. This does not necessarily imply that Everland banks are offering shoddy services – indeed they concentrate their attention on the services they offer. The danger is more that such offerings are unsupported by research of the markets needs or by deep understanding of what customers want and in what quantity. Services are therefore a result of intuition, trial and error and may not match demand. This is an inefficient method of operating.

Dangers to Everland

The biggest danger to Everland banks is the complacency it exhibits in the light of an external environment that is about to change radically.

If banks within Everland do not become marketing orientated there are clear dangers, mainly that they will loose out to much more effective new competitors.

There are presently only a few banks operating in Everland, and these enjoy an oligopoly-type position. The difficulty is that this protection has apparently led banks to be complacent and failing to innovate their portfolio of services. As a consequence customers may well be frustrated by the limitations of these services. The anticipated increased competition may be too hard to handle now that new legislation has opened up the market to competition by international players and other financial institutions. These institutions are likely to have a broader experience of customer orientation and diversity of management skills than that currently exhibited by Everland's banking industry.

Unless Everland banks reform quickly and change their philosophy away from the present product orientation more customer-focussed rivals may be driving them out of business. (The emerging use of cross-national online banking and the experience of Utopia banks may ideally suit them to competing for market share in Everland, for instance.)

Lessons from Utopia

A marketing philosophy similar to that being pursued in Utopia places customers at the heart of all organisational activities and focuses on satisfying customers needs and wants. These 'market-orientated' banks put customer needs first and provide services that meet their needs. Marketing-orientated organisations have a main focus of the customer and their demands. The benefit is that the services offered are determined by consumer demands.

Emerging trends

The evidence of Utopia is that customers are becoming more demanding and that vital marketing thinking and techniques are needed to meet these demands. If customers in Utopia feel this way, then this is also a likely trend in Everland. The danger of Everland banks not changing is that they will not fulfil customer demands in the same way that new competitors may be able to.

C5(b) Types of change that banks should be making in order to survive and prosper. Some of the change which the adoption of marketing concepts and techniques in the banking sector could give rise to are included in the listing below:

Techniques:

- Greater market research and analysis in order to keep abreast of customer needs.
- More sophisticated monitoring of levels of customers' satisfaction.
- More effective marketing planning emphasising techniques such as market segmentation.

Structure:

- Marketing expertise elevated to the position of providing a strategic co-ordinating role for the resources and activities of the business.

- Organisational restructuring based around customer and market requirements. This might, for example, involve a structure based on products and market segments.
- New marketing style positions at the expense of traditional banking roles.

Skills:

- New specialist skills such as 'brand managers' and 'market analysts' may be seen as vital. These may be fundamental to a revised organisational structure.

Systems:

- More effective marketing control and feedback systems.
- An increased emphasis on quality, service and customer care.
- Maximising use of some of technology in marketing in order to (for example) support relationship marketing with customers.
- Systems that provide awareness of wider environmental forces and enhanced recognition of ethical and social responsibilities towards customers.

HR policies:

- Effective HR policies such as recruitment and training are necessary in order to equip the workforce with the necessary skill mix. This is to remedy the position of senior management of commercial banks coming from a banking back-ground and possessing few, if any, marketing and HR skills.

C5(c) Based on the information contained in the question produce an analysis of Everland's macro-environment and comment on the most significant features as far as banks are concerned.

Within the external business environment, Johnson, Scholes and Whittington (2005) identify three layers of influence:

1. Competitors and markets
2. Industry (or sector)
3. Macro-environment.

One framework for understanding the macro-environment is through an analysis of the political, economic, sociocultural, technological, legal and environmental factors (PESTLE).

Based on the information contained in the question an analysis could reasonably contain the following main features:

Political

The fact that Everland's Government will soon 'pass new legislation' suggests that the country enjoys a mature democracy, and hence a degree of stability. This is important for the banks as they know that their profits or assets are unlikely to be unfairly appro-priated and that taxation policies are likely to be transparent and potentially just.

Economic

The economy of Everland is said to be 'buoyant' which is likely to involve low levels of inflation, unemployment and interest rates. Levels of disposable income tend to be higher under such conditions. The fact that the banking industry performance has been viewed as consistently satisfactory with stable profits and employment levels hints as much: normally banking is one barometer for the economy. The economic conditions provide a favourable trading and hence banking environment.

Sociocultural

There has also been a recent growth in online banking suggesting a preference for personal computing and instant access to banking within society. In the comparator country of Utopia, banks have responded to consumer demands for a greater choice of products and services, and customers have become increasingly more demanding. The fact that Utopia banks are now exhibiting a strong sense of ethical and social responsibility undoubtedly reflects society's attitudes. A similar trend within Everland could reasonably be speculated upon. This will present both opportunities and challenges to the banking sector.

Technological

The only hint on technological issues is the recent growth in online banking suggesting that companies are taking advantages of technological developments through e-commerce. Everland is likely to be representative of other countries, which experience continual technological developments with increased user speed, power and lowering costs. Conversely rates of obsolescence are likely to be high. The potential offered by this will be a significant feature for Everland's banks to consider.

Legal

The most significant feature will be new competition laws that will effectively break the oligopoly-type position of banks and open the market up to other providers. Clearly this represents a threat to current operations and a stimulus to change.

Environmental

As Utopia banks are now exhibiting a strong sense of ethical and social responsibility, this is a trend that Everland banks would do well to note and respond accordingly.

C6(a) The initiatives identified using Herzberg's motivation-hygiene (dual factor) theory as a framework.

The first initiative involves a revision of the system that measures managerial accountability (now on net profit rather than increasing turnover). The second involves a restructure and reallocation of duties giving SBUs greater control over their own performance.

This thinking can be explained within the context of Frederick Herzberg's motivation-hygiene, or dual factor, theory. Herzberg's contention was that the opposite of job satisfaction is the absence of job satisfaction and not job dissatisfaction. By extension, the opposite of job dissatisfaction is an absence of dissatisfaction. Herzberg's research indicated that satisfaction and dissatisfaction are influenced and created by different variables. His theory has been very influential across a wide range of jobs, organisations and countries.

His initial study in the 1950s of 203 Pittsburgh accountants and engineers focussed on when they felt either exceptionally good or exceptionally bad about their job. This ultimately led to a two-factor theory of motivation:

- Motivators (or satisfiers) are factors that if present within a job encourage individuals to greater effort and performance through higher levels of job satisfaction (but not dissatisfaction). These factors relate to what people are allowed to do and the quality of human experience at work. These are the variables that motivate people. Examples include job role, organisational recognition, personal growth and a sense of achievement, advancement and responsibility. These factors are said to relate to job content.

- Hygiene factors (or dissatisfiers) are factors including status, pay, interpersonal relations, supervision, organisational policy and administration, job security and working conditions. These factors relate to job context.

In this case both motivators and hygiene factors have been addressed as follows:

Motivators:

- Achievement of individual 'performance contracts'.
- Recognition by the chief executive of the vital role played by SBU managers.
- Promises of advancement by fast tracking to senior positions.
- Greater responsibility to get on with the real job.
- Greater autonomy and influence over the SBU managers' own 'bottom-line' performance.

Hygiene factors:

- New remuneration package reflecting bonuses for increased profitability.
- Organisational policy and administration adjusted with SBU managers in mind.
- Potential to improve working conditions as managers are given greater freedom to run their SBU in the way they see most appropriate.

Both of the initiatives therefore go to the heart of motivation and performance. Measurements of performance within someone's control against corporate objectives such as with CQ4 can in themselves be powerful means of positively influencing individuals. There is also a well-researched connection between reward and performance. The way in which the remuneration package is adjusted therefore is crucial in this respect.

C6(b)   Factors that should be taken into account by HR department when redesigning the remuneration and reward package for SBU managers:

- *Control of total payroll costs.* CQ4 needs to decide how much overall it can afford in payroll costs. Once the costs associated with other groups are calculated, the overall base salary costs and bonus payments for managers can be determined.
- *Appropriateness of overall package.* The remuneration strategy needs to appropriately balance base and performance-related pay. The base pay element should recognise factors such as size of SBU, relative contribution to the company as a whole, and specific skills and competences demanded of the individual manager and so on. The reward package will need to address not only internal targets but also market place levels of reward for similar work in order that there are not problems associated with retention of staff. As CQ4 is a European operation it is likely that local pay rates will vary enormously between countries in which SBUs are situated.
- *Money available for performance-related pay.* Performance-related pay represents an attempt to establish closer links between results and rewards. The success of the chief executive's new initiatives is dependent on people, primarily managers, behaving in certain ways. Rewards should be directed towards those who adopt the behaviours required. The incentive of performance-related pay should be seen as no less generous than the previous bonus scheme, and sufficient to make managers innovate, take risk and improve bottom-line performance. HR professionals

need to know the total amount available to finance the new scheme. Based on this, decisions can be made as to how the scheme can be implemented (whether as a per cent of basic pay, a per cent of net profit, or incremental flat rate payments, etc.).

- *Rewards encouraging risk taking and innovation.* The new chief executive's vision of risk taking and innovation when translated into reward systems can be problematic. Whilst precise quantitative measures are readily available to measure net profit, the other factors suggest difficulties in identification and measurement. Judgements on, for instance, the number and quality of initiatives taken may lead to feelings of unfairness. In addition there needs to be a shared understanding of the relative weighting given to profitability, risk taking and innovation. Appropriate metrics and evaluation criteria need to be agreed upon and put in place.

- *Impact of adjusted HR policies on other groups.* SBU managers are the main focus of remuneration and reward systems. This can present some difficulties, as it is probable that others (e.g. directors, SBU workforce, etc.) will also be involved in achieving the level of SBU performance. If the manager is perceived to be receiving unfair reward and recognition, this might have a negative impact on these other groups and may lead to workplace disharmony and endanger improved performance. The positive impact of work groups on individual motivation has long been recognised and was famously illustrated by the Hawthorne Studies. The new reward system should not therefore be seen as a cause of undermining teamwork within SBUs. It is likely that HR policies will also need to be reviewed for all other groups to prevent this happening.

- *Accounting for non-controllable factors that influence managerial performance.* An underlying philosophy of performance-related pay should be to provide a fair and consistent basis for rewarding managerial performance. However, other organisational factors, such as the availability of technology, raw materials and financial resources will also have an important effect on SBU performance. Consideration needs to be given as to how to account for these factors.

- *Translating longer-term objectives into short-term targets and rewards.* Strategic objectives such as those expressed by the chief executive are longer term but managers need shorter-term targets and rewards. Careful development of individual 'performance contracts' will need to take place in order to translate these longer-term objectives into shorter-term personal targets split into agreed milestones.

- *Non-financial incentives.* A belief that money alone can encourage the enhancement of individual management performance is inaccurate. Other forms of incentive can also include promotion and career development opportunities. The reward system should therefore involve adjustment to issues such as succession planning and career progression or promotion using developmental pathways and career ladders and so on. The chief executive has promised as much for 'star performers'. This may necessitate a review of the existing structure above SBU level in order to ensure that such positions exist.

- *Consultation with SBU managers, trade union and other relevant groups.* If the revised scheme is to be accepted by SBU managers as appropriate, there needs to be a wide consultation in order that there is universal 'buy in'.

C6(c) The initiatives to encourage managers to deliver 'truly excellent CQ4 performance' includes an adjustment to the current performance appraisal system. Existing sales bonuses will be replaced by annual performance-related pay for achievement of individual 'performance target contracts' (focussed on SBU profitability and innovation).

Managers will potentially be 'better rewarded' suggesting potential for increased earnings from performance-related pay (although the HR department has yet to redesign the remuneration and reward package). The proposal has apparently been well received by managers.

One theory of motivation often used to explain the adoption of financial incentive schemes like that operated by CQ4 is what Schein and others have called the 'rational economic man theory'. This theory assumes that people are motivated by self-interest and that the opportunity to accumulate significant sums of money. This will stimulate individuals into making extra effort that the organisation can benefit from.

In this case it would be the manager meeting his or her performance target contract with targets undoubtedly including increased innovation and improved SBU 'bottom line' financial performance. The fact that the new system offers greater potential for earning means that under this theory all managers would be motivated to achieve the new demands upon them.

The 'rational economic man theory' is simply to understand and easy to apply. The main limitation of the theory, however, is that it is perhaps too straightforward and only recognises the most obvious dimensions of the complex subject of motivation.

It is inescapable that most people are motivated by factors other than money: but this theory takes no account of this. The more complex psychological theories of Maslow and Herzberg, for instance, indicate that although it can role in motivating people, it is not the only incentive (see part (a)). Maslow emphasises that once basic needs are satisfied, people are motivated by things like opportunities to gain status, recognition, a sense of achievement, a feeling of power and self-actualisation. Money and wealth can, of course, act as a measure and a source of some of these rewards for effort, but the point is that many of these things that satisfy deeply felt psychological and social needs can be attained without money as an incentive.

C7(a) There are four main distinct changeover methods that ABC may wish to consider. These are:

1. Direct changeover whereby the old system is completely replaced by the new one in one move.
2. Parallel running is a form of changeover where the old and the new systems are run side by side for a period of time.
3. Pilot operation, where a part of the system is operated as a pilot scheme; if it works the rest will be changed.
4. Phased approach where introduction takes place in a phases fashion.

For ABC direct changeover may be unavoidable where systems are substantially different from one another. This method is relatively cheap but is risky, and ABC management must have complete confidence in the system as it must work first time. Clearly the chosen system can be directly introduced into the branches with manual records.

Under parallel running both computerised systems process the current data and provide output. The output of each system should be reconciled. This method is relatively safe; if the new system does not function correctly it can be discontinued and be corrected before being implemented. There is however some cost attached to the safety comfort offered to ABC managers (parallel running doubles the work-load and increases costs in the short term).

Pilot changeover would be a cheaper option than a full parallel run for ABC and safer than a full direct changeover.

The phased approach involving a pilot scheme would be recommended as it limits risk and is only moderately expensive compared with a full parallel run at each site. With a number of sites to change over, a phased approach may be appropriate. It could operate as follows:

- One site could be selected as a pilot site.
- The system at this site could be run in parallel and would be closely monitored.
- After it had been checked and proved satisfactory the other sites could be changed as a direct changeover.

- There would need to be different methods applied to the computerised branches and the manual branches, so there may be a need for a second pilot to be run to check the changeover arrangements for the manual systems.

C7(b) The essential feature of a database approach is that data is regarded as a central resource of ABC. Data, like other assets, should be owned and maintained for the use and benefit of the business as a whole.

For a centralised database system to be successful, it must have the following properties:

- Data independence. The data must be defined and exist independently of the programs that use it. The logical definition of data in the database is different from the physical organisation and storage on the disks (so-called 'physical independence'). The logical data in an application is viewed from the perspective of that application; this is different from the logical definition of data in the database (known as 'logical independence'). As the data and programs are independent of each other, either can be amended without changing the other.

- The database must be capable of being shared across and within branches. Different users, using different application programs, must be able to access the same data, often at the same time.
- Duplication of data and data redundancy can be reduced as only one entry per record or transaction is needed in the database. Data inputs may also be reduced as data is only required to be input once to update all files. There is potential therefore for some cost saving within ABC.
- Integrity of the data in the database must be maintained. Controls need to be implemented to ensure that the data remains accurate at all times.

- The database should be flexible and be capable of evolving with the needs of ABC. The database will need to change and develop as ABC consolidates its trading position and seeks either new markets or customers.
- The database should be able to connect to Web server to support dynamic e-commerce transaction: a development that ABC may wish to consider in the future as they seek to access new markets or customers.

C7(c)   The main reasons that ABC decided to acquire two smaller rivals and a major competitor seems to be that apart from reducing competition, it has allowed for a swift means of expansion and opportunities for growth potential. External growth by acquisition, as in the case of ABC, offers a number of benefits but also some downsides.

Perhaps ABC should not be too surprised by initial adverse financial results for two reasons:

- A takeover of one company at a time presents a challenge, the takeover of three within a short period, more so.
- One year's trading figures represent a very short-term perspective. It may be that results improve once systems, structures and staff have been more properly integrated.

ABC should be aware, however, that research suggests that external growth strategies often produce disappointing longer-term results. Thompson (2005) cites reduced profitability and a lack of synergy as often occurring. In the case of ABC the need to adapt four different organisational cultures to create a new one is always going to be a challenge.

Peter Drucker (1982) suggested that there are five basic 'rules' or guidelines that must be followed if acquisitions are to be successful:

1. *Contribution*. The acquiring company must identify exactly what contribution it can make to the acquired company beyond finance. In this case what benefit can ABC's headquarters offer their new branches?
2. *Common core*. The companies involved should have some common core of unity in markets, production operations or technology. In this case ABC has a common core based on the products it offers (household appliances and spare parts).
3. *Value*. The company making the acquisition should value the products, services and customers of the other company. It may be that ABC has paid too expensively for the companies it has acquired.
4. *Management cover*. It is important that there is some top management cover available in case key senior managers in the acquired company choose to, or are required to, leave after the acquisition. The scenario indicates that there has been high staff turnover following acquisition. If this has included vital management posts, then ABC may be far less effective than it should.
5. *Linkage*. Within a year of the acquisition, managers should have been promoted across the boundaries of the previously separate companies. There is no indication from the scenario that this has taken place.

C8(a)   Often quality programmes are undertaken for the wrong reasons. It is important that organisations ensure that both internal and external quality needs are assessed and addressed.

The critical elements of XYZ's TQM approach can be summarised as:

Quality improvement programme

- Identification, elimination and prevention of processing errors, rework and wastage via systematic audit processes.
- Design control of all processes, products and services.
- The development of beneficial partnerships with all external suppliers.
- A shift in culture so that the whole workforce becomes active in the quality process.

Customer care programme
(Focusing on the needs of the external customer and internal customer relationships)

- Market research to understand customer needs and current customer perceptions of products and service quality.
- Staff perception: research to ascertain staff attitude to quality and their interactions with external customers. (Staff interaction with customers will determine the customer perception of the service.)
- A complaints-handling service designed to be highly and speedily responsive to customer issues.
- Effective and regular customer care training for all staff.
- Effective customer communication and reporting procedures to keep customers informed on organisational issues.

Quality assurance programme
This should lay down the standards for performance and implement and manage a quality management system, ensuring compliance to standards (ISO 9000).

- Ensure XYZ is an ISO-registered firm.
- Benchmark against other banks and service providers to monitor performance and to ensure constant awareness of external quality assurance programmes.

C8(b)   Plan to communicate quality

Overview
The plan should have a clear objective, timescale and resource implication. It may be that for certain stages there will be the need to employ an external consultant or facilitator who has particular expertise in this area.

Stage 1   Present TQM philosophy to the senior management team to instill TQM at the top level. Provide information and be prepared to answer questions. The presence of the chief executive to personally outline the agenda to focus on the features, benefits and drawbacks of contemporary approaches to the management of quality would provide a great impetus.

Stage 2   Set up quality groups/circles within the branch to tackle specific quality issues.
Provide support, encouragement and incentives for participation.

Stage 3   Run TQM workshops and training sessions for circle co-ordinators to ensure the quality message is received and reinforced.

Stage 4   Establish departmental/group quality standards. Possibly implement reward systems for quality improvements.

Stage 5   Agree quality performance data/standards for the branch to monitor quality achievements. (This process should be led by the Quality Assurance section.)

Comparative data from other branches could be used in a form of internal benchmarking exercise.

Kotter and Schlesinger (1979) identify six main strategies for dealing with resistance to change initiatives, one of which is education and communication. This strategy is particularly useful when the basic problem is a lack of information about the need for, or the nature of, the planned change. This is exactly the case with the establishment of the TQM philosophy within the new branch. The approach can be very time-consuming but is generally welcomed by staff and regarded as an ethical management strategy.

C8(c)   The TQM philosophy is equally applicable to both the service and the manufacturing sector. Various types of costs are associated with the operation of a quality programme, and although these may be more visible in a manufacturing organisation (e.g. reworking, costs of scrap, etc.) they still remain for a service organisation such as the XYZ Bank.

Prevention costs. These are the cost of activities undertaken to prevent defects occurring in the design and development phase of a product or service. XYZ presumably offers a range of financial services to its customers. Costs associated with engineering quality into the design of its services might include careful supplier evaluation (e.g. if ABC offers insurance services on behalf of a partner) or operational training for its 4,000 staff staff and in particular project team members who will need additional training. Performance indicators should be identified, agreed upon and established for service quality against which measures might be taken.

Appraisal costs. These are the costs incurred while conducting quality tests and inspections in order to determine whether services conform to quality requirements. These may include quality audits and the operation of a Quality Assurance section. Service testing might be performed by, for instance, recording telephone conversations with customers to ensure that staff makes appropriate responses. Statistics will need to be collected in order to determine whether performance indicators are being achieved or not.

Internal failure costs. These are costs associated with the detection and rectification of items that do not conform to quality requirements, but have not yet been passed to the customer. This might include the rejection of proposals to launch a new product requiring a redesign of that product by the project team. Costs will also be associated with the trialling of new services to a controlled group of customers.

External failure costs. These are costs associated with the detection and rectification of items that do not conform to quality requirements and have been passed to the customer. They might include the operation of the Customer Complaints Section and their associated procedure and 'goodwill' incentives for any of the 2 million customers or 700,000 credit card holders who have legitimate grievances.

November 2006
Examination

November 2006 Examination

Managerial Level

Organisational Management and Information Systems

The answers published here have been written by the Examiner and should provide a helpful guide for both tutors and students.

Published separately on the CIMA website (www.cimaglobal.com/students) from mid-February 2007 is a Post Examination Guide for this paper, which provides much valuable and complementary material including indicative mark information.

Important Note

This examination paper reflects an earlier weighting of sections. Please note that the advice given earlier on pages 279 and 280 is correct.

CIMA

Business Management Pillar

Managerial Level Paper

P4 – Organisational Management and Information Systems

22 November 2006 – Wednesday Afternoon Session

Instructions to candidates

You are allowed three hours to answer this question paper.
You will be allowed 20 minutes reading time **before the examination begins** during which you should read the question paper and, if you wish, make annotations on the question paper. However, you will **not** be allowed, **under any circumstances**, to open the answer book and start writing or use your calculator during this reading time.
You are strongly advised to carefully read ALL the question requirements before attempting the question concerned (that is, all parts and sub-questions). The question requirements for Sections B and C are contained in a dotted box.
Answer the ONE compulsory question in Section A. This has twenty sub-questions and is on pages 339 to 341.
Answer ALL six compulsory sub-questions in Section B which is on pages 342 to 343.
Answer ONE of the two questions in Section C on pages 344 to 345.
Write your full examination number, paper number and the examination subject title in the spaces provided on the front of the examination answer book. Also write your contact ID and name in the space provided in the right hand margin and seal to close.
Tick the appropriate boxes on the front of the answer book to indicate which questions you have answered.

SECTION A – 50 MARKS

[the indicative time for answering this section is 90 minutes]

ANSWER *ALL* TWENTY SUB-QUESTIONS

Instructions for answering Section A

The answers to the twenty sub-questions in Section A should ALL be written in your answer book.

Your answers should be clearly numbered with the sub-question number and ruled off so the markers know which sub-question you are answering. For multiple choice questions you need only write the sub-question number and the answer option you have chosen. You do not need to start a new page for each sub-question.

Each of the sub-questions numbered from **1.1** to **1.15** inclusive, given below, has only ONE correct answer. Each is worth two marks.

Question One

1.1   Frederick Herzberg's study of work and people is of significance to managers because it identifies

   (A)   a framework for HRM involving appraisal, training and motivation.
   (B)   the need to assess the personality of job applicants.
   (C)   factors associated with job satisfaction called motivators.
   (D)   satisfaction from a participative, problem solving environment.   **(2 marks)**

1.2   Data redundancy arises as a result of

   (A)   viruses and computer misuse.
   (B)   downsizing the organisation.
   (C)   a lack of password controls.
   (D)   duplication of data held.   **(2 marks)**

1.3   Kurt Lewin's ideas on change are based on the view that change is

   (A)   capable of being planned.
   (B)   emergent.
   (C)   inevitable and uncontrollable.
   (D)   transformational.   **(2 marks)**

1.4   A network topology refers to

   (A)   the physical arrangement of a computer network.
   (B)   the type of hardware used.
   (C)   the hierarchy of access.
   (D)   the range of software operated.   **(2 marks)**

1.5 Adding new tasks to a person's job, so increasing their responsibility, is called

    (A) process re-engineering.
    (B) job enrichment.
    (C) HR development.
    (D) career scoping. **(2 marks)**

1.6 Data integrity refers to its

    (A) accuracy.
    (B) security of storage.
    (C) adaptability for multiple use.
    (D) ethical use of personal details. **(2 marks)**

1.7 Entity relationship modelling is a technique used within

    (A) an assessment centre test used in staff selection.
    (B) market research and product testing.
    (C) database analysis and design.
    (D) business process re-engineering. **(2 marks)**

1.8 The intervention of a consultant or change agent is a common feature of

    (A) co-operation and negotiation strategies for change.
    (B) an inclusive culture.
    (C) high levels of management visibility.
    (D) a programme of Organisational Development (OD). **(2 marks)**

1.9 A local area network (LAN) normally contains

    (A) a file, print and communications server(s).
    (B) distributed processing and local solutions.
    (C) e-trading and e-marketing.
    (D) internet access and firewall protection. **(2 marks)**

1.10 Public relations activity can be used within marketing as part of

    (A) marketing decision support activities.
    (B) a promotional mix.
    (C) customer feedback processes.
    (D) segmentation practices. **(2 marks)**

1.11 Remuneration is an example of

    (A) self-actualisation reward.
    (B) an intrinsic reward.
    (C) an extrinsic reward.
    (D) an individual's work/life balance. **(2 marks)**

1.12 'Spot rates' normally refer to a specific pay rate determined by reference to

    (A) the market place.
    (B) incremental progression.
    (C) a negotiated point on a pay spine.
    (D) experience and qualifications of a newly recruited person. **(2 marks)**

1.13 Charging a very low price on one item in order to generate customer loyalty and increased sales of other items is called

(A) market penetration.
(B) loss leader pricing.
(C) product penetration.
(D) skim pricing. **(2 marks)**

1.14 'Corrective', 'perfective' and 'adaptive' are terms associated with

(A) system maintenance.
(B) change management approaches.
(C) quality assurance.
(D) HR disciplinary processes. **(2 marks)**

1.15 In the expectancy theory of motivation 'valence' refers to

(A) a belief that an outcome will satisfy organisational tasks.
(B) a person's own preference for achieving a particular outcome.
(C) a belief that the outcome will be shared by others equally.
(D) an understanding of the probability of an event happening. **(2 marks)**

(Total for sub-questions 1.1 to 1.15 = 30 marks)

Requirement

Each of the sub-questions numbered **1.16** to **1.20** below requires a brief written response.

Each sub-question is worth 4 marks.

This response should be in note form and should not exceed 50 words per sub-question.

1.16 Explain the concept of physical evidence when applied to the marketing mix.
(4 marks)

1.17 Identify the potential benefits of a marketing database and the source data from which it might be constructed. **(4 marks)**

1.18 In HR planning how might an organisation match the projected 'supply' of human resources to future demand. **(4 marks)**

1.19 Identify the advantages and disadvantages of a policy of succession planning for a large organisation. **(4 marks)**

1.20 Identify both the advantages and the disadvantages of a decentralised Human Resource provision for an organisation that has many business units and sites.
(4 marks)
(Total for sub-questions 1.16 to 1.20 = 20 marks)
(Total for Section A = 50 marks)

SECTION B – 30 MARKS

[the indicative time for answering this section is 54 minutes]

ANSWER *ALL* SIX SUB-QUESTIONS. EACH SUB-QUESTION IS WORTH 5 MARKS.

Question Two

The country of Chapterland has a principle that healthcare should be free to its citizens at the point of access. Healthcare is funded from national taxation and organised through a series of large health units, one of which is known as 'Q2'. Q2 operates a huge, single site hospital and offers a variety of community services (such as health visiting) that are taken to the local population. Q2 has a management structure consisting of eight clinical and administrative directors who report to Q2's Chief Executive Officer (CEO). The Q2 CEO is directly accountable to the national government through regular returns of information and year-end reporting.

Published 'quality league tables' of hospital performance against government targets suggest that Q2 has one of the worst records in the country. (Targets are for cleanliness of hospital wards, treatment waiting times and staff employed per patient cases dealt with.) In addition, Q2 has in recent years been operating to a budget in excess of its funding, which is against government regulations. The current year budget again exceeds projected funding.

Last year, Q2's previous CEO decided that certain changes were necessary including:

- better cost control;
- improved performance measurement; and
- benchmarking.

He revealed this thinking for the first time in a global email he sent to Q2's staff. Later, when conducting the annual performance appraisal of the Director of Human Resources (HR), he tasked her with implementing 'each and every form of benchmarking' within the next four months so that 'true' performance deficiencies could be addressed. However, the Director of HR left for a new job elsewhere within that period. The CEO then undertook to manage the changes himself but was surprised to find directors unenthusiastic and even uncooperative. Under pressure from the government the CEO resigned 'for personal reasons' and no progress was made with his initiatives.

A new CEO has just been appointed. Her immediate concern is to reduce expenditure and improve performance. On her first day as CEO she spoke of a need to re-establish a culture of 'care through quality' within Q2. She wishes to discuss a number of ideas and issues with her clinical and administrative directors at a special 'away day' meeting to be arranged soon. You work in the CEO's central policy team and she has informed you that some ideas for initiatives include outsourcing, improved supply management and new performance management measures.

Requirements

You have been asked to provide the new CEO with briefing notes on a number of issues that will help prepare her for the 'away day' meeting. These notes should:

(a) Explain why the changes attempted by the previous CEO were unsuccessful;

(5 marks)

(b) Explain the role Human Resources could perform in supporting any new initiatives for change; **(5 marks)**

(C) Analyse the potential of outsourcing as a means of overcoming some of the problems facing Q2. (The CEO has identified two services initially; IT/IS and cleaning.); **(5 marks)**

(d) Discuss which forms of benchmarking Q2 should use in order to contribute to better performance management; **(5 marks)**

(e) Discuss how a culture of 'care through quality' might be established within Q2;

(5 marks)

(f) Describe the performance measures that will be needed in order to satisfy future management and strategic reporting requirements of Q2. **(5 marks)**

(Total for Question Two = 30 marks)

Important note: Use a separate page of your answer book for each sub-question. You should limit your answer for each sub-question to no more than one page.

(Total for Section B = 30 marks)

SECTION C – 20 MARKS

[Indicative time for answering this question is 36 minutes]

ANSWER ONE QUESTION ONLY

❓ Question Three

B3 is a family run personnel agency. It offers a range of services to both individuals and corporate clients (mainly local medium-sized organisations). The son of the managing director (MD) is currently studying for a specialist university business degree. His course includes a 'management consultancy' module where students are required to analyse an organisation and identify a range of development options for the business. The MD's son's investigations of B3 have led to a consultancy report being produced, extracts of which include:

'B3 should maximise the opportunities offered by information technology to a greater extent. In particular:

- *Opportunity 1*. B3 could develop its recent successful experiment in e-cruitment (the identification of employment opportunities through the World Wide Web and the emailing of clients). Currently details of vacancies are collected and matched to individual client's search criteria. When a match is identified clients are emailed and, if they are interested, interviews arranged. This service is not offered by any of B3's main competitors. There is a difficulty, however, in that many companies have barred access to personal emails at work and web access to recruitment sites such as B3's site from their offices. Market research suggests that significant opportunities for m-cruitment (jobs by mobile telephones) also exist. Making use of recent software developments, a text message containing a job title and some contact details could be sent out to individual clients instead of an email, so providing a more convenient and speedy service.
- *Opportunity 2*. Virtually all CVs are currently received in electronic form and a policy decision should be made to develop a paperless operating environment through the development of databases, so upgrading existing office technology.

Analysis of profit indicates that executive searches, corporate 'headhunting' and vacancy identification for individuals (traditional and especially e-cruitment) are all profitable activities.

Involvement in selection processes with corporate clients is unprofitable and should be discontinued. Instead B3 should identify clear guidelines for corporate clients to follow once the short-listing of candidates has occurred'.

Requirements

(a) Evaluate the opportunities for B3 identified in the consultancy report.

(12 marks)

(b) Produce guidelines for the selection process that should be adopted by an organisation presented with a short-list of candidates. **(8 marks)**

(Total for Question Three = 20 marks)

? **Question Four**

CM's founder first began producing breakfast food from a start-up unit on a small industrial estate. Now CM is the market leader in Europe and Oceania. Once established in Europe, the company made the breakthrough into Oceania thanks to demand from ex-pats and contacts with a family member who happened to be a director of a supermarket chain in Australia. The company's founder is very 'hands on' and has made all the major strategic decisions to date based on intuition.

CM spends heavily on promoting most of its 20 products on television, normally before and after childrens' programmes with high viewing figures. Research conducted ten years ago shows that children love small gifts contained within packs and the association of certain of the products to cartoon characters. CM also manufactures its most popular lines and packages them as 'own brand' alternatives for some large supermarket chains. These sell more cheaply than CM branded products, are less costly to produce (they contain inexpensive packaging and no gifts) but sales remain low.

CM is now facing a more uncertain environment with increasing competition (from a North American firm), sales levels that seem to have peaked and the prospect of the founder retiring very soon. Management consultants advising CM have identified a need to develop a structured marketing strategic plan for the organisation and for greater involvement of other staff in future strategic decisions. As a further complication, CM has recently received some adverse publicity from an international health 'watchdog' body that claims that CM's products contain potentially harmful levels of both sugar and salt.

Requirements

(a) Evaluate CM's situation making specific mention of marketing and ethical issues.

(10 marks)

(b) Explain how CM might develop a marketing strategic plan. **(10 marks)**

(Total for Question Four = 20 marks)

(Total marks for Section C = 20 marks)

> *Important Note*
>
> This examination paper reflects an earlier weighting of sections. Please note that the advice given earlier on pages 279 and 280 is correct.

The Examiner for Organisational Management and Information Systems offers to future candidates and to lecturers using this booklet for study purposes, the following background and guidance on the questions included in this examination paper.

Section A – compulsory

Question one in total accounts for 50% of the paper and in so doing tests the topics in all sections of the syllabus apart from Operations Management (which is tested in question two).

Question one, parts 1.1–1.15 test candidates' knowledge of a wide variety of topics within the syllabus through the use of objective test questions in a conventional 'multiple choice' format.

Question one, parts 1.16–1.20 provide further objective testing through limited word responses. These sub-questions (valued at 4 marks each) test knowledge and understanding.

Sub-questions 1.16 and 1.17 test aspects of Marketing (learning outcomes D(iii) and D(v)), while **1.18–1.20** test learning outcomes E(i), E(ii) and E(v) of Managing Human Capital. Responses for each sub-question are expected to conform to the word limit indicated.

Responses beyond this limit are not marked.

Section B – compulsory

Question two represents 30% of the paper and tests topics from Operations Management, as well as part testing Change Management and Managing Human Capital. As with previous papers a common workplace related scenario is used from which all sub-questions are drawn. Question two parts (c), (d), (e) *and* (f) test candidates' knowledge and understanding through the application of thinking from Operations Management (learning outcomes C(ii), (vi) and (ix)). Part (a) involves an examination of why a change attempt was unsuccessful (learning outcome B(iv)), and Part (b) explores the potential role HR might perform (learning outcome E(i)). Responses for each sub-question are expected on a single side of A4 in a form that might include a few sentences and bullet points. This limit simulates a real-life scenario in which accuracy, brevity and clarity is called for and also hopefully prevents candidates from spending a disproportionate amount of time on each sub-question. Responses beyond the limit indicated are not marked.

All sub-questions require application of knowledge to the scenario.

Section C – one question from two

Section C accounts for 20% of the paper and in so doing part tests aspects of the syllabus topics of Information Systems, Managing Human Capital and Marketing. Both questions involve the use of business scenarios as contexts. All sub-questions require the application of knowledge and understanding to the scenario.

Question three tests candidates' understanding of issues associated with Information Systems and Managing Human Capital. The question requires an application of knowledge and understanding to the scenario of a family run personnel agency facing up to the opportunities offered by information technology. Question three Part (a) requires the candidates to evaluate these opportunities (learning outcome A(iii) is tested). This is worth 12 marks. Question three Part (b) requires the production of guidelines for selection of job candidates (learning outcome E(iii) is tested). This is worth 8 marks.

Question four tests candidates' understanding of issues associated with Marketing and is set within the context of a breakfast food producing company at something of an organisational cross roads. Part (a) requires an evaluation of the organisation's position having regard to both marketing and ethical issues (learning outcome D(ii)) and Part (b) requires the candidate to explain how a marketing strategic plan might be developed (learning outcome D(vi)). Both parts of the question are equally weighted.

The Examiner's Answers for Organisational Management and Information Systems

SECTION A

Question One

1.1 **(C)**

1.2 **(D)**

1.3 **(A)**

1.4 **(A)**

1.5 **(B)**

1.6 **(A)**

1.7 **(C)**

1.8 **(D)**

1.9 **(A)**

1.10 **(B)**

1.11 **(C)**

1.12 **(A)**

1.13 **(B)**

1.14 **(A)**

1.15 **(B)**

1.16 Marketing mix = a manufacturing firm's 'blend' of price, product, promotion, place.
  For Service organisations other relevant factors include a lack of 'physical evidence' because:

- Services are intangible
- Potential customers may therefore feel greater risk.

  Reassurance is therefore needed, for example testimonials/references from past customers.
  Note: Other examples apart from testimonials/references might be given such as internet pages, paperwork, brochures, uniforms, the corporate logo, buildings, furnishings and signage and so on.

1.17

Sources	*Benefits*
One-off market research data already available	Improves problem solving capacity
Other marketing intelligence	Method of structuring decisions
Internal information on products, trends, markets and competitors, etc.	Integrates all types of knowledge
	Maximises IT potential
	Total system of marketing information to support decisions

1.18 HR planning: satisfying projected demand by adjusting projected 'supply'.

Increasing	*Reducing*
Re-training / re-skilling / multi-skilling for potential 'gaps'	Early retirements
Development for internal promotions (succession planning)	Redundancy
Overtime	Short-time working
Increased use of IT	Job-sharing
Outsourcing	
Recruitment and selection (new employees)	

Internal transfers / re-deployment to balance requirements

1.19

Advantages	*Disadvantages*
Career structures, rewards visible	Lack of exposure to other influences
Positive motivation	Ignores possible better candidate from outside
Reinforces existing culture	Trend for movement between companies strong
Rational approach	Vacancies may arise at inconvenient times
	Expensive (?)
	Needs managing
	Only possible within a very large organisation
	Outdated concept?

1.20

Advantages	*Disadvantages*
Empowerment/delegation strengthened	Lack of central control
In touch with detained unit/site issues	Lack of specialist knowledge
Greater local knowledge	May lead to 'maverick' actions/policies
Visible	HR function may be diluted
	Uneven provision within organisation

SECTION B

Question Two

(a) Why the changes attempted by the previous CEO were unsuccessful.
A number of mistakes were evident in the management of the changes:

Lack of consultation

The CEO rightly decided that certain key changes were necessary. Although he may have been correct in identifying the areas he did, there is no suggestion that he consulted on the required key changes. As a result, there is no certainty that these initiatives alone would bring about the desired changes. The changes needed may have involved a need for cultural change, which appears to have been ignored.

Lack of two-way communication and ownership

The CEO revealed his thinking for the first time in a global email sent to Q2's staff. It may have been advisable to use these thoughts as a basis for discussion and involve staff in order to:

* raise awareness of the issues
* generate new thinking and ideas
* take ownership of the change initiatives.

Not taking responsibility for the change

The use of the annual performance appraisal process to delegate responsibility for the changes was not advisable. Further, it is debateable whether the Director of HR should have been made responsible for it. It could be seen that the CEO abdicated responsibility rather than assuming a role of a visible driving force in the early stages. For such important developments, the CEO or perhaps some management consultant may have been more appropriate to lead the change programme. When the Director of Human Resources left for a new job elsewhere, the CEO became the change agent himself. This meant that the impetus for change had been lost. The Chief Executive Officer's subsequent resignation meant that two change agents had been unsuccessfully used.

Lack of involvement of clinical and administrative directors

Directors other than the Director of HR may have felt excluded from the process (hence their apparent lack of enthusiasm and cooperation). It would have been advisable to discuss matters with them initially before all staff were communicated with. They may have felt undervalued and also felt that their authority had been undermined.

Inappropriate communication method

Using email to inform staff of such important changes is inappropriate for communicating a change of this magnitude. Email is impersonal and it is unlikely that every member of staff would be able to access this medium. Email is in any case best for quick factual information sharing only.

Faulty planning

There is no evidence of

- how cost control might be improved
- specific plans for how changes were to be implemented
- allocations of extra time and resources
- sensitivity as to how the changes would affect staff.

(b) The role Human Resources could perform in supporting any new initiatives for change. The role identified by the previous CEO for the Director of HR took insufficient account of the potential contribution that the HR function can make to organisational change. (See *(a)* earlier). Human Resource Management (HRM) involves the following:

- A strategic approach.
- Acquisition, motivation, development and management of the organisation's human resources.
- Helping achieve corporate performance through people.
- An alignment of HR practices to corporate strategies.
- The use of HR specialists to help organisational controllers (in this case directors and managers within directorates) to meet management objectives.

Within this context HR could properly help support the new initiatives for change through:

- Discussion of the proposed initiatives and a contribution to their formulation in conjunction with other professional and clinical groups.
- Obtaining intelligence on HR practices used in other health units that appear to be performing better than Q2.
- Developing HR practices that will support the agreed initiatives (for example identifying expertise necessary to make the changes, new skill requirements, the appropriateness of reward packages that will support implementation of changes, liaison with staff and trade unions groups and so on).
- Identifying, then arranging for, HR actions to support the initiatives specifically staff training, a different emphasis when recruiting, and performance measures and bonuses to encourage quality and cost control.
- Considering the changes required to the Q2 culture and ways of achieving these.
- Constant support, counselling, coaching and communication with those individuals identified as key in bringing about the necessary changes.
- Developing appropriate HR monitoring and control mechanisms that will support the initiatives.

(c) Outsourcing as a means of overcoming some of the problems facing Q2. (Initially: IT/IS and cleaning.)

Problems facing Q2

- Expenditure in excess of funding.
- A relative failing in terms of government targets on cleanliness, waiting times and staffing levels. Government and the new CEO apparently interpret this as indicating 'poor quality'.

About Outsourcing

Involves contracting out non-core services to specialist providers rather than attempting to provide them in-house. Consistent with a 'stick-to-your-knitting' concept, in this case providing health care not those things that support it.

Some issues

All organisations view outsourcing differently (for example hostile, apathetic, a necessary evil, a positive development and so on). If outsourcing is not viewed favourably there is likely to be strong resistance to the proposal. There is no indication how Q2 feels but it may be counter productive if there is likely to be strong staff and union resistance.

- Unclear why information services and cleaning have been chosen as pilots: possible staffing/resourcing difficulties?
- What is the experience of other health units?

Advantages of Outsourcing

- Helps numerical flexibility and should improve performance against government target on staff employed per patient cases.
- May reduce costs initially (but debatable if it will improve quality performance).

Disadvantages of Outsourcing

- Potential lack of understanding of health service ethos by contractors of the outsourced service.
- May not contribute positively to culture of 'care through quality'.
- Additional cost associated with determining service specifications, and ultimately monitoring performance.
- Q2 is already under performing in cleaning: will outsourcing make it worse?
- Possible resistance from unions representing in-house service workers who will lose their jobs within Q2.

Summary

It is unclear how the outsourcing of these services (particularly IT) can directly contribute to solving Q2's problems.

If there is likely to be low resistance to the initiative it could be seen as a good idea for the following reasons:

- It indicates to government that something is being done.
- Short-term 'hit' against government targets of staff employed per patient cases dealt with.

The initiative's contribution to the more enduring goal of 'care through quality' is more uncertain.

(d) Benchmarking Q2 should use in order to contribute to better performance management. Benchmarking is:

- a process of systematic comparison of a service, practice or process against one or more similar activities.
- a contributor to continuous improvement in the levels of performance.

- a means of identifying good/best practice which could lead to an understanding of how this has been achieved and therefore how Q2 might improve.
- a means of overcoming inertia and driving organisational change.

Relationship to performance management:

- concentrates on performance and value-adding processes.
- improves management's understanding of Q2's relative strengths and weaknesses.
- helps shape a culture of striving for 'best in class'.
- provides advance warning of deteriorating performance.
- establishes key information that management can use to exercise control and make effective decisions.

Main types of benchmarking:

Internal benchmarking: based on the notion that there are performance differences *within* the organisation itself (these may be as a result of geographical differences, history, customs, working relationships and so on). As Q2 is a single site hospital, it is unlikely that internal benchmarking will be of much value.

Competitive benchmarking: comparison of various activities with those of competitors. Q2 needs to identify a similar hospital to compare itself with. This may be rather easier within the public sector than in the private sector where details of profits and processes are kept as secret as possible. Published 'league tables' of hospital performance are an existing form of competitive benchmarking but are restricted to cleanliness, treatment waiting times and staff employed per patient cases. The government may have other comparator ratios readily available (based on annual returns) and is likely to be sympathetic to letting Q2 use them in this way.

Best practice activity benchmarking: the identification of state-of-the-art products, services or processes of any relevant organisation (not necessarily in healthcare). The objective is to identify best practice in any type of organisation that has established a reputation for excellence in specific business activities. (This might be in catering, telephone response times, IT or other support services.)

In summary aspects of benchmarking for Q2 to progress:

Priority 1: Competitive benchmarking against performance of other health units.
Priority 2: Best practice where relevant comparator established.

(e) How a culture of 'care through quality' might be established within Q2.
On her first day the new CEO spoke of a need to re-establish a culture of 'care through quality'.

The implications of this are as follows:

- To improve healthcare, Q2 needs to improve quality in everything it does.
- This implies a shared philosophy (as part of a cultural understanding) rather than an accreditation process, namely a total quality management (TQM) approach to quality.
- The use of the phrase 're-establish' suggests that this was once present in Q2 staff but will mean a return to past core values. This suggests that there will be little cultural resistance.

TQM as a way of achieving 'care through quality' means:

- An integrated, comprehensive system of planning and controlling all business functions.
- A philosophy of business behaviour embracing principles such as employee involvement, continuous improvement at all levels and customer focus, as well as being a collection of related techniques aimed at improving quality such as full documentation of activities, clear goal setting and performance measurement from the customer perspective.

How this might be established within Q2:

Developing a commitment to quality at all levels in Q2 and a focus on continuous improvement (Kaizen) of everything however small. (Kaizen involves the continual analysis of organisational processes to ensure continued improvement in performance and quality.)

- Re-establishing a widespread commitment to quality improvement amongst staff and those contracted to work on behalf of Q2 through improved communication.
- Focusing on patients, local citizens and government as Q2's customers.
- Strengthening working relationships between all clinical and administrative directorates and the building of multi-functional teams.
- Involvement of all in discussing and measuring quality, including setting of standards and gathering information.
- Establishing relevant review, feedback and appraisal processes to find ways of doing things better.
- Investing in systems that will provide relevant timely information and the establishment of regular reporting of key indicators of quality.
- A realignment of reward and incentive systems to positively encourage quality.
- Training in areas where Q2 is felt to be weak. Quality can only be achieved by competence in whatever job or activity is undertaken.
- The establishment of quality circles and project teams to bring about positive change.

(f) Performance measures needed in order to satisfy future management and strategic reporting requirements of Q2.

Q2 needs to develop an integrated package of performance measures that will support future performance management. These will need to incorporate:

Management

- Data required by government in the compilation of its league tables. Targets are currently for cleanliness of hospital wards, treatment waiting times and staff employed per patient cases dealt with. More information may be needed in the future as a result of government decisions. Good practice suggests that this data converted into ratios and so on would also be useful to management in interpreting, monitoring and controlling performance.
- Year-end returns including budgetary performance. This also is a requirement when reporting to government
- Data required as a result of decisions on benchmarking.

- Data required in support of TQM initiatives and other continuous improvement measures will need to be established and gathered. Historical trends can then be produced that should identify improvement over time.
- Information on financial aspects of the operation including costs, performance against budgets, activity-based costing and so on. Overall financial performance is a concern, and management accounting has a significant role to play in developing relevant measures. Appropriate management accounting information (such as costs per medical procedure) might usefully be progressed.

Strategic

In addition Q2 may wish to develop further measures of performance that will require data of a quantitative and qualitative nature for instance:

- A balanced scorecard, a strategic approach to performance measurement incorporating measures within four dimensions: financial, customer, internal and business and innovation and learning.
- Value For Money (VFM) measures aimed at gauging overall economy, efficiency and effectiveness in the use of resources in the absence of a profit measure.

SECTION C

Question Three

(a)   Evaluation of the opportunities for B3

Opportunity 1

The opportunities are those offered by information technology (IT). In the case of Opportunity 1 this relates to the potential offered by the advances in technology.

The proposal is that B3 could extend e-cruitment to m-cruitment. When e-cruitment was introduced it was apparently 'recent', 'experimental' and not offered by competitors. Evidently it was introduced alongside 'traditional' services, presumably the use of older technologies such as post and telephone. The proposal could be viewed as being worthy for a number of reasons:

Extended service offering

e-Cruitment has proven to be both popular and profitable. The proposal involves extending this experiment using text messaging. To introduce m-cruitment **instead** of other methods would be unwise. Instead, a more sensible approach would be to offer clients an option of either:

* 'traditional' services;
* e-cruitment; or
* m-cruitment.

This would expand the company's expertise and range of service offering.

Positive image projection
Potential clients undoubtedly would view this as a positive attempt by the company to tailor its services to the individual's own needs and preferences.

Enhance competitive strategy

e-Cruitment has involved B3 in successfully differentiating its service from other competitors. Competitors are likely to copy this approach soon. A differentiation strategy such as this suggests that B3 needs to stay one step ahead, hence m-cruitment could be seen as a natural and desirable development.

The problems with this proposal include:

IT, IS costs and expertise

As long as B3 has the expertise and technology available to provide the service there will be no difficulty. (The experiment with e-cruitment suggests that there is no cultural resistance to the use of new technology.) If, however, additional costs are involved in time, training and software, m-cruitment might be an expensive distraction.

Ethical implications

Many companies have barred access to personal emails at work and web access to recruitment sites such as B3's site from their offices. m-cruitment is portrayed as a means of overcoming this. Although B3 would be meeting its individual clients needs, it would be frustrating companies who do not want their employees to search out new jobs in works time. This could be viewed as unethical.

Damaged reputation amongst corporate clients

B3 has corporate clients, mainly local medium sized organisations. It could adversely affect future business opportunities if employers realise that B3 is acting unethically.

Image of the company

Text is impersonal and lacks human interaction (even more so than emails). This could project an image to potential customers of being distant, impersonal and uncaring.

On balance, it might seem sensible to trial m-cruitment for a period of time (say 6 months) and assess the outcomes.

Opportunity 2

The opportunities are those offered by information technology (IT). In the case of Opportunity 2, it is the potential to use IT to run information systems (IS). The proposal is that a paperless operating environment should be developed.

In support of the proposal:

Potential

At the moment there appears to be a high degree of technology uptake and B3 makes use of web-based technology including email. In addition, 'virtually all' client CVs are in electronic form.

Image

A paperless environment could project a favourable image to potential clients. It could also be a springboard for the company to expand beyond its regional base.

However, it might sound modern and exciting but experience of other organisations has proved that it is an elusive concept in practice. There are several difficulties associated with this proposal, including:

Cost

The report suggests that it will involve upgrading existing office technology. The benefits of a paperless office would have to be persuasive to justify this and other costs.

Implications

The report suggests a need to 'develop databases'. This may in itself be insufficient to achieve a paperless office.

Resistance by clients

Some individuals and organisations are reticent to trade over the Web. These clients may be 'lost' to competitors using more traditional trading methods.

Security and backup

The development of secure sites especially for the transfer of personal details and payment transfers would need to be carefully planned and installed. As sensitive data such as CVs are to be stored, there needs to be high levels of security and practices such as disaster recovery planning and risk assessment to consider.

On balance, paperless trading might more sensibly be viewed as an ultimate goal that the company works towards rather than a short-term strategy involving replacement of all existing practices.

NOVEMBER 2006 EXAMINATION

(b)   *Guidelines for selection processes for adoption*
(Following advertisement of vacancy, preliminary contact with potential candidates, initial screening and final shortlist of agreed candidates.)

Agreement of selection criteria and testing method
Use of person specification and job description and so on to determine criteria.
Develop scorecards based on agreed criteria.
Agree common questions to be asked of all candidates.
Agree range, nature and complexity of selection processes to be used to test against criteria. (Processes must be cost-effective, that is justified in terms of the benefits of selecting good applicants for the particular job in question.) Processes will include formal structured interviews (decide whether 'one to one', tandem, panel, sequential and so on)

Testing against selection criteria
Review of formal application forms to determine areas of experience and so on that need to be explored through interview and so on.
Make arrangements for formal interviews and other candidate testing.
Administer formal interviews and candidate testing.

Processes should be:

- Reliable: give consistent results
- Valid: accurately predict performance
- Fair: candidates should be treated in a non-discriminatory way (for example in terms of race, gender, age and so on).

Choosing the most suitable candidate
Final analysis and choice based on criteria.
Approach successful candidate and make offer subject to reference and medical checks.
Send official job 'offer' letter on the same basis.
Feedback to unsuccessful candidates.

Administration
Conduct reference checks being mindful of accuracy of factual data presented by the candidate.
Arrange for medical examination.
Issue letter confirming terms and conditions of service including pay rate and start date.
Tidy relevant paperwork and file to evidence the process.

Review
Conduct a critical review of the process including successful and unsuccessful aspects and lessons learnt. Disseminate this information and revise future practices accordingly.

Question Four

(a)   Situation evaluation.

Major challenges
CM is said to be facing three major challenges:

- Increasing competition
- Sales levels that seem to have 'peaked'
- The prospect of the retirement of the key decision maker.

Competition
CM is the market leader in breakfast food manufacture in Europe and Oceania but is facing increasing competition (from N. America). CM appears to have no presence on the other continents, making it an international rather than global player. Although diets vary across continents it is likely that the North American diet is (at least) similar. This means that potentially other firms are supplying the American market and these competitors could be powerful and have the ability to challenge CM's leadership in its own markets. CM needs to decide how it responds to this threat from international competition. There is no information on the basis upon which CM's competitor's marketing mix varies from its own. If an alternative mix to CM is apparently proving more successful then CM should re-examine its own mix accordingly. (See later.)

More positively CM should recognise that potential markets on other continents exist and these represent opportunities for development.

Sales
Sales levels seem to have 'peaked'. One interpretation can be drawn from an understanding of the concept of the market life cycle. When the life cycle of a market reaches the so-called 'maturity' stage, demand will have reached its limit. If this is the case, CM should consider new products or new markets before the market life moves into the 'decline' stage. In terms of product range CM has a portfolio of twenty product items, but it is unclear how often this range is 'refreshed'. Reference to potential new markets, maybe outside Europe and Oceania, has been made to earlier.

Decision making (and Strategic Marketing approach)
CM's founder, as the key decision maker, is retiring soon. He/she is credited with growing CM to its present size from a business 'start-up' operation. He/she is very 'hands on' and has made all the major strategic decisions to date based on intuition. (It is apparent that there is no structured strategic marketing plan.) The development into another geographical market typically seems to have resulted through good fortune and market demand rather than rational decision making and promotional efforts. (CM made the breakthrough into Oceania thanks to demand from expats and contacts with a family member who happened to be a director of a supermarket chain in Australia.) Organisationally, it is difficult to continue operating in this way, particularly with the retirement of the founder. Although the organisational culture could properly be described as entrepreneurial, CM's sheer size may mean that some of the spirit is in any case diminishing.

This can in part be explained by reference to Greiner's organisational growth model (1972). Under this model, firms can experience evolutionary growth which eventually leads to a situation of revolutionary crisis, when the organisation's ways of doing

NOVEMBER 2006 EXAMINATION

things become less effective. The implication of this thinking is that change is unavoidable and ways of overcoming each crisis need to be determined for the organisation to continue growing. Under the model, the first phase of growth is achieved by some creative idea, product or service that enables the organisation to become established in the market place. A crisis occurs when the entrepreneur's informal and personal approach to managing the business simply cannot cope with its increased size. This crisis of leadership appears to have been reached within CM. If the organisation can adopt more formal systems of management (in CM's case strategic marketing), there will be a basis for further growth through 'direction'.

Other issues

Ethical issues

The adverse publicity from an international health 'watchdog' body that claims that CM's products contain potentially harmful levels of both sugar and salt raises ethical concerns. CM spends 'heavily' on TV advertising and undoubtedly the target audience for CM's promotional effort is children as it advertises before and after childrens' programmes. The inclusion of small gifts contained within packs and the association of certain of the products to cartoon characters and expensive packaging confirms as much. Children influence their parents to purchase the product. The ethical issues are as follows:

- Is it 'right' that promotion is based upon children placing demands on their parents, particularly if their parents cannot afford to buy the product?
- The sugar and salt content are apparently important in achieving a taste that children like. Is it ethical to manufacture and sell products that might be unhealthy to vulnerable children.
- The adverse publicity may impact upon sales. CM will need to decide how it responds to these claims, for instance:
- Conduct its own research and possibly challenge the watchdog claims.
- Discredit the findings and the body making the claims.
- Modify its product content so there is less salt and sugar present.
- Increase promotion to compensate any fall off in sales as a result of adverse publicity.

Product nature

There is good reason for believing that the associated features and packaging is the most significant product feature, specifically:

- Past research confirms that children love small gifts contained within packs and the association of certain of the products to cartoon characters.
- Some products are sold as 'own brand' alternatives for some large supermarket chains.

Although these sell more cheaply than CM branded products they are less costly to produce as they contain inexpensive packaging and no free gifts. The minimal sales underline the point that packaging and advertising are crucial.

Marketing mix

CM's current marketing mix has evidently developed over time and seems to be the product of decisions made by the company's founder. CM can properly be described as a 'marketing oriented' organisation as it has a main focus of the customer (children) and their demands. The mix exhibits in particular **product** features and packaging, **promotion** through expensive advertising, and (using the fifth P of the marketing mix) the founder as the key **person**. In terms of **place**, sales are through supermarkets and based on two continents. The **price** reflects high promotional costs and expensive packaging.

(b) Developing a marketing strategic plan for CM.

An important point, particularly given CM's own position of a lack of formal strategy and the past influence of a single person (the founder), is that a range of people from within the organisation should be involved. Although marketing specialists might lead processes, all functional areas should participate in developing the strategy. This is important so that there is ownership, realism and co-ordination.

In order for CM to develop a Marketing Strategic Plan, a number of key processes will need to be undertaken concurrently, and are identified below.

Identify and articulate CM's corporate objectives and the role that marketing can play in achieving them.

Conduct an audit of the external environment

This will involve a detailed investigation of the following:

- The market for manufactured breakfast food.
- The market segments which CM is interested in (e.g. European childrens' eating habits and preferences).
- The trends influencing the market, typically using a PEST (political, economic, sociocultural and technological) framework for analysis*. A consideration of CM's position relative to the most significant factors (including potential realistic ways in which the organisation might influence such factors) should be undertaken.
- The activities, strategic capability and strengths and weaknesses of competitors.
- Future potential scenarios and trends, possibly using industry and other experts.

Conduct and internal analysis

This will clarify what CM wants to achieve over the planning period and its capability, specifically:

- The identification of the factors that contribute towards CM's strengths and weaknesses. These internal factors are controllable and may lead to the development of targets.
- The agreement of corporate aspirations including specific marketing objectives and SMART (specific, measurable, achievable, realistic and time bound) targets.

Synthesis and discussion

Some of the main factors arising from the above processes might be synthesised into a SWOT (strengths, weaknesses, opportunities and threats) analysis. (SW are internal and OT external factors.)

Discussions should focus on developing an appropriate mix of marketing factors to achieve CM's objectives in the light of earlier analysis; this will include any actions necessary to bridge gaps between expectations and capability. Specifically, the mix will address future actions relating to pricing issues, promotional activity, place and product features.

Communication and co-ordination

A strategy can ultimately be developed. It will, however, need to be carefully co-ordinated with other functional strategies including Finance, IT and HR.

The strategy should be written, approved by CM's decision makers and clearly communicated to the workforce. The strategy will include:

- Clear marketing goals and objectives.
- Targets, measures and performance indicators.
- The costing of the plan and the development of a revenue budget.
- An identification and costing of any capital requirements.
- Identification of strategic alternatives.
- A detailed action plan.

Other alternative frameworks might be used including PESTEL which also recognises environmental and legal factors and so on.

Index

ORGANISATIONAL MANAGEMENT AND INFORMATION SYSTEMS

ORGANISATIONAL MANAGEMENT AND INFORMATION SYSTEMS

Get **10% Discount** and **Free P&P**
off your next order

Quote APP6 when ordering or
add it to the offer code box online.

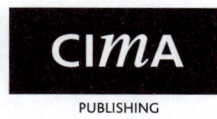

ELSEVIER

CIMA PUBLISHING

Order Form
For CIMA Official Study Materials for 2008 Exams

QTY	PAPER	TITLE	ISBN-13	PRICE	TOTAL
		CIMA Official *Learning Systems*			
	P1	Performance Evaluation	978 0 7506 8430 9	£35.00	
	P2	Decision Management	978 0 7506 8535 1	£35.00	
	P3	Risk and Control Strategy	978 0 7506 8497 2	£35.00	
	P4	Organisational Management & Information Systems	978 0 7506 8428 6	£35.00	
	P5	Integrated Management	978 0 7506 8540 5	£35.00	
	P6	Business Strategy	978 0 7506 8467 5	£35.00	
	P7	Financial Accounting and Tax Principles	978 0 7506 8541 2	£35.00	
	P8	Financial Analysis	978 0 7506 8429 3	£35.00	
	P9	Financial Strategy	978 0 7506 8538 2	£35.00	
	P10	TOPCIMA	978 0 7506 8445 3	£35.00	
		CIMA Official *Exam Practice Kits*			
	P1	Performance Evaluation	978 0 7506 8401 9	£14.99	
	P2	Decision Management	978 0 7506 8403 3	£14.99	
	P3	Risk and Control Strategy	978 0 7506 8410 1	£14.99	
	P4	Organisational Management & Information Systems	978 0 7506 8332 6	£14.99	
	P5	Integrated Management	978 0 7506 8376 0	£14.99	
	P6	Business Strategy	978 0 7506 8400 2	£14.99	
	P7	Financial Accounting and Tax Principles	978 0 7506 8394 4	£14.99	
	P8	Financial Analysis	978 0 7506 8373 9	£14.99	
	P9	Financial Strategy	978 0 7506 8390 6	£14.99	
	P10	TOPCIMA	978 0 7506 8329 6	£14.99	
		CIMA Official *Revision Cards*			
	P1	Performance Evaluation	978 0 7506 8123 0	£8.99	
	P2	Decision Management	978 0 7506 8124 7	£8.99	
	P3	Risk and Control Strategy	978 0 7506 8120 9	£8.99	
	P4	Organisational Management & Information Systems	978 0 7506 8121 6	£8.99	
	P5	Integrated Management	978 0 7506 8122 3	£8.99	
	P6	Business Strategy	978 0 7506 8119 3	£8.99	
	P7	Financial Accounting and Tax Principles	978 0 7506 8126 1	£8.99	
	P8	Financial Analysis	978 0 7506 8125 4	£8.99	
	P9	Financial Strategy	978 0 7506 8118 6	£8.99	
		Books			
		Principles of Business Taxation	978 0 7506 8457 6	£49.99	
		CIMA: Pass First Time!	978 0 7506 8396 8	£12.99	
		Better Exam Results	978 0 7506 6357 1	£12.99	
			Postage and packing		£2.95
			TOTAL		

Elsevier Ltd, Science & Technology Books, retains certain personal information about you in hard copy and on computer. It will be used to inform you about goods and services available from Elsevier Ltd and its offices worldwide in which you may be interested.

Please tick the box if you do NOT wish to receive this information. ☐

Post this form to:

CIMA Publishing Customer Services
Elsevier
FREEPOST (OF 1639)
Linacre House, Jordan Hill
OXFORD, OX2 8DP, UK

Or **FAX**   +44 (0)1865 314 572
Or **PHONE**   +44 (0)1865 474 014
Email: cimaorders@elsevier.com
                        www.cimapublishing.com

Name:

Organisation:

Invoice Address:

Postcode:

Phone number:

Email:

Delivery Address if different:

FAO

Address

Postcode

Please note that all deliveries must be signed for

1. Cheques payable to Elsevier.

2. Please charge my:

☐ Visa/Barclaycard   ☐ Access/Mastercard

☐ American Express   ☐ Diners Card

☐ Switch   Issue No._____

Card No.

Expiry Date

Cardholder Name:

Signature:

Date:

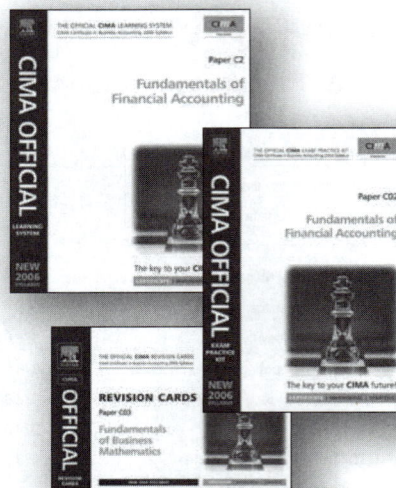

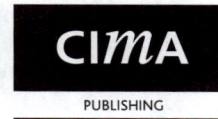

Give CIMA Publishing Your Feedback and Win a Prize

Win your choice of 3 further *Learning Systems* or an iPod

Help us to improve our product for next year by telling us of your experience using this product. All feedback forms returned will be entered into a prize draw. The first three forms drawn on 30 November 2007 will receive either three *Learning Systems* of their choice or an 2Gb iPod Nano. The winners will be notified by email.

Feedback form:

CIMA Official *Learning Systems* 2008 Editions

Name:

Address:

Email:

■ **How did you use your CIMA Official** *Learning System*?

☐ Self-study (book only)

☐ On a full course?
How long was the course?
Which college did you attend?

☐ On a revision course?
Which college did you attend?

☐ Other

Additional comments:

■ **How did you order your CIMA Official** *Learning System*?

☐ Carrier sheet from CIMA Financial Management magazine

☐ CIMA Publishing catalogue found in Financial Management magazine

☐ Order form from the back of a previous *Learning System*

☐ www.cimapublishing.com website

☐ Bookshop
Name
Branch

☐ Other

Additional comments:

Your ratings and comments would be appreciated on the following aspects. Please circle your response, where one indicates an excellent rating and four a poor rating.

	Excellent			Poor
☐ Topic coverage	1	2	3	4
☐ Accuracy	1	2	3	4
☐ Readings	1	2	3	4
☐ End of chapter questions and solutions	1	2	3	4
☐ Revision section	1	2	3	4
☐ Layout/Presentation	1	2	3	4
☐ Overall opinion of this study system	1	2	3	4

Additional comments:

_____

_____

_____

_____

■ Would you recommend CIMA Official *Learning Systems* to other students?

Please circle: Yes   No

Additional comments:

_____

_____

_____

■ Which CIMA Publishing products have you used?
☐ CIMA Official *Learning Systems*
☐ Q&As
☐ CIMA eSuccess CDs
☐ CIMA Revision Cards
☐ CIMA Exam Practice Kits

Additional comments:

_____

_____

_____

■ Are there any related products you would like to see from CIMA Publishing? If so, please elaborate below.

_____

_____

_____

_____

_____

_____

■ Please note any further comments or errors found in the space below.

_____

_____

_____

_____

_____

_____

_____

_____

_____

Thank you for your time in completing this questionnaire. We wish you good luck in your exam.

Please return to:
Claire Lawlor
CIMA Publishing
FREEPOST – SCE 5435
Linacre House
Jordan Hill
Oxford, OX2 8DP, UK

Or Fax: FAO C. Lawlor to: +44 (0) 1865 314572

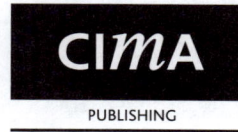

MAY 07 Q&A

To access the May 07 Q&A for the book you have bought please follow these instructions:

Go to
http://cimapublishing.com/QandA

▊ Enter in the passcode found on the back cover of the book

▊ Fill in the registration form

▊ Download the PDF for immediate access to Q&A